Praise for *The Hundred Years' War on Palestine*

"For those who want to learn about the course of the Israel-Palestine conflict up till now, and are open-minded: read this book. It comes over as a brilliant synthesis of high scholarship and experience, fair-minded despite its overtly Palestinian leanings, and highly readable. Americans and Israelis especially should read it, including the younger, more liberal ones, into whose hands the fates of both of the legitimate nations in this region must now pass. Please don't let this go on for another hundred years."
—Bernard Porter, *Jacobin*

"After decades of scrupulous objectivity, Khalidi has now written a very personal book . . . [*The Hundred Years' War on Palestine*] is a roller-coaster ride through Palestinian history, one hundred years without a moment of solitude."
—Bruce Robbins, *The Baffler*

"This book is a masterful work of scholarship and personal history excavating unlike any I've seen before; this will become a major force in the Palestinian historical canon in the years to come."
—George Abraham, *Literary Hub*

"A richly informed, personalized account of a century of repression of a peoples' national aspirations . . . Original and distinctive . . . A remarkable testament to the stubborn resistance that characterizes the Palestinians."
—Walter L. Hixson, *Washington Report on Middle East Affairs*

"Masterful . . . Brilliant . . . This major work will occupy a central position in the literature of Palestinian history."
—*Al-Quds Al-Arabi*

"Riveting and original . . . [Khalidi] skilfully balances his professional analysis of historical and diplomatic documents with insights of his own and his relatives who had leadership roles throughout the twentieth century . . . A profoundly moving account."
—Lahoucine Aammari, *Hespéris-Tamuda*

"Meticulously documented . . . [Rashid Khalidi's] exhaustive research . . . leaves no doubt that the Jewish colonizers were acutely aware from the start that the Palestinian people had to be subjugated and removed to create the Jewish state."
—Chris Hedges, *Truthdig*

"Heart-wrenching . . . Powerful and brave . . . As part of their professional training, historians are warned against injecting their personal narrative into their account

of events. [*The Hundred Years' War on Palestine*] is a valuable violation of this taboo."
—Moshé Machover, *Weekly Worker*

"A timely, cogent, patient history of a seemingly intractable conflict told from a learned Palestinian perspective."
—*Kirkus Reviews*

"[Khalidi] skillfully balances his professional analysis of historical and diplomatic documents with insights of his own and his relatives who had leadership roles throughout the twentieth century . . . Highly recommended."
—Elizabeth Hayford, *Library Journal* (starred review)

"*The Hundred Years' War on Palestine* presents a vital perspective on one of the planet's most intractable geopolitical and humanitarian crises."
—Tobias Mutter, *Shelf Awareness* (starred review)

"Rashid Khalidi enjoys a well-deserved reputation as one of the greatest living historians of the Palestinian people . . . Khalidi is a sophisticated and unapologetic exponent of . . . [an] increasingly widely held view of the Israel–Palestine conflict."
—Ian Black, *Literary Review*

"Superb . . . [A] no-holds-barred history of the Palestinian struggle for liberation . . . Rashid Khalidi pulls no punches in criticising the abject failings of both global and domestic politicians who have helped perpetuate the continued misery in Palestine."
—*Morning Star*

"Focused on the Palestinians' lived experience of a century of war, never losing sight of the geopolitical forces that fostered it, Rashid Khalidi has written a book of comprehensive scholarship with the delicacy and intensity of a novel."
—Ahdaf Soueif, author of *The Map of Love*

"With wisdom and insight, Rashid Khalidi lays to rest the illusions of Israelis and Palestinians alike. He combines brilliant scholarship with extensive first-hand experience of war and diplomacy in a call for mutual acceptance and equality of rights as the only way to end a century of conflict. An outstanding book."
—Eugene Rogan, author of *The Arabs: A History*

"A riveting and original work, the first to explore the war against the Palestinians on the basis of deep immersion in their struggle—a work enriched by solid scholarship, vivid personal experience, and acute appreciation of the concerns and aspirations of the contending parties in this deeply unequal conflict."
—Noam Chomsky, author of *Failed States: The Abuse of Power and the Assault on Democracy*

"Brave, brilliant, and magisterial, this outstanding work of historical scholarship is also full of high drama and fascinating narrative. Rashid Khalidi presents compelling evidence for a reevaluation of the conventional Western view of the subject in a book that is a milestone in the study of the Arab-Israeli conflict."

—Avi Shlaim, author of *The Iron Wall: Israel and the Arab World*

"This is the first true people's history of the hundred-year struggle of the Palestinian people, a beautifully written text and a call for justice and self-determination."

—Roxanne Dunbar-Ortiz, author of
An Indigenous Peoples' History of the United States

"A meticulous account of Palestinian history that provides a brilliant framework for the study of settler colonialism on a global scale. You can disagree with Khalidi, but you cannot afford to miss the opportunity of arguing with him."

—Homi K. Bhabha, author of *The Location of Culture*

"Through a scholarly narrative rooted in his own family history, Rashid Khalidi offers a fresh interpretation that shows Palestine as a violent, grinding fault in the shifting tectonic plates of Great Power politics. This book is sure to become a classic account."   —Elizabeth F. Thompson, author of *Justice Interrupted: The Struggle for Constitutional Government in the Middle East*

"This book is a remarkable interweaving of three distinctive strands: a deeply researched history of the struggle between Zionist aspirations and Palestinian resistance, an analytical framework that places the conflict within the context of settler colonialism, and a personal family history that brings the narrative alive. Newcomers and specialists alike will learn much from reading this sweeping account."   —William B. Quandt, author of *Peace Process: American Diplomacy and the Arab-Israeli Conflict Since 1967*

"Learned and clear-eyed, this compelling history of the long war to deny Palestinian rights exposes a century of blunders, misjudgments, and willful deceptions. Highly recommended."   —Stephen M. Walt, coauthor of
The Israel Lobby and U.S. Foreign Policy

"Beautifully written and accessible, this book is an invaluable examination of the Palestinian-Zionist encounter as a struggle against settler-colonial domination, not as an issue of conflict resolution—a vital difference, necessary for a deeper understanding of the war and for its meaningful resolution."

—Sara Roy, author of *Hamas and Civil Society in Gaza: Engaging the Islamist Social Sector*

"As in any book by Rashid Khalidi, there is history, erudition, politics, and passion aplenty. There is also his tenacious conviction that 'there are now two peoples in Palestine, irrespective of how they came into being, and the conflict between them cannot be resolved as long as the national existence of each is denied by the other.'"
—Rob Malley, International Crisis Group CEO and White House coordinator for the Middle East under President Barack Obama

"Rashid Khalidi makes clear that the Zionists could not have created modern-day Israel without abundant help from Britain and the United States. A must-read for the growing number of people who are interested in understanding the real roots of the Israeli-Palestinian conflict."
—John J. Mearsheimer, coauthor of The Israel Lobby and U.S. Foreign Policy

"With moral passion and analytical rigor, Rashid Khalidi skillfully unearths the narrative of a long and bitter national conflict, providing a multitude of timely, acute, and original insights. This compelling book is a must-read."
—Zeev Sternhell, author of The Anti-Enlightenment Tradition

"In a painfully sober analysis of what made Zionism, an anachronistic colonialist enterprise, so successful, Rashid Khalidi also shows how Palestinians defy fatalism and refuse to vanish. His book is a tribute and contribution to his people's perseverance."
—Amira Hass, author of Drinking the Sea at Gaza: Days and Nights in a Land Under Siege

"This fascinating and instructive blend of autobiography and history should be read by anybody who wants to understand the tragedy of Palestine and the Palestinians."
—Patrick Cockburn, author of The Rise of the Islamic State: ISIS and the New Sunni Revolution

"This searing account makes clearer than ever the often deliberately understated colonial nature of the Palestinian experience—and it reminds us of the Palestinians' extraordinary capacity to remain steadfast despite the local and global forces arrayed against them."
—Saree Makdisi, author of Palestine Inside Out: An Everyday Occupation

RASHID KHALIDI

The Hundred Years' War on Palestine

Rashid Khalidi is the author of eight books, among them *Palestinian Identity*, *Brokers of Deceit*, and *The Iron Cage*. His writing has appeared in *The New York Times* and *The New York Review of Books*, among many other publications. He is the Edward Said Professor of Modern Arab Studies at Columbia University in New York and coeditor of the *Journal of Palestine Studies*.

ALSO BY RASHID KHALIDI

Brokers of Deceit: How the U.S. Has Undermined Peace in the Middle East

Sowing Crisis: American Dominance and the Cold War in the Middle East

The Iron Cage: The Story of the Palestinian Struggle for Statehood

*Resurrecting Empire: Western Footprints and America's
Perilous Path in the Middle East*

Palestinian Identity: The Construction of Modern National Consciousness

Under Siege: PLO Decisionmaking During the 1982 War

British Policy Towards Syria and Palestine, 1906–1914

The Hundred Years' War on
PALESTINE

A HISTORY OF SETTLER COLONIALISM
AND RESISTANCE, 1917–2017

Rashid Khalidi

Picador

Metropolitan Books

Henry Holt and Company   New York

Picador
120 Broadway, New York 10271

Originally published in 2020 by Metropolitan Books / Henry Holt and Company
First Picador paperback edition, 2021

The Library of Congress has cataloged the Metropolitan Books hardcover edition as follows:
Names: Khalidi, Rashid, author.
Title: The hundred years' war on Palestine ; a history of settler colonialism and resistance,
    1917–2017 / Rashid Khalidi.
Description: New York : Metropolitan Books, Henry Holt and Company, 2020. | Includes
    bibliographical references and index.
Identifiers: LCCN 2019008933 | ISBN 9781627798556 (hardcover) Subjects:
LCSH: Palestine—History—20th century. | Palestine—History—21st century. |
    Palestinian Arabs—Politics and government—20th century. | Palestinian Arabs—
    Politics and government—21st century.
Classification: LCC DS119.7 .K4279 2019 | DDC 956.9405— dc23
LC record available at https://lccn.loc.gov/2019008933

Picador Paperback ISBN: 978-1-250-78765-1

All maps created by A. E. Hocherman
Designed by Kelly S. Too

The ruins that appear on the cover are what remains of the Tal al-Rish home of Hajj Raghib al-Khalidi, the author's grandfather. The structure was left standing after 1948, unlike most Arab houses on the outskirts of Jaffa, as a protected artifact of Israeli history: a group of early Zionist settlers known as the Bilu'im had lived there briefly before moving on to found one of the first Zionist agricultural colonies in Palestine. The Bilu'im House, as it is now called, is preserved as an Israeli heritage site.

I dedicate this book to my grandchildren, Tariq, Idris, and Nur, all born in the twenty-first century, who will hopefully see the end of this hundred years' war

We are a nation threatened by disappearance.

—'Isa and Yusuf al-'Isa, *Filastin*, May 7, 1914

CONTENTS

The Hundred Years' War on Palestine

Introduction

For a few years during the early 1990s, I lived in Jerusalem for several months at a time, doing research in the private libraries of some of the city's oldest families, including my own. With my wife and children, I stayed in an apartment belonging to a Khalidi family *waqf*, or religious endowment, in the heart of the cramped, noisy Old City. From the roof of this building, there was a view of two of the greatest masterpieces of early Islamic architecture: The shining golden Dome of the Rock was just over three hundred feet away on the Haram al-Sharif. Beyond it lay the smaller silver-gray cupola of the al-Aqsa Mosque, with the Mount of Olives in the background.[1] In other directions one could see the Old City's churches and synagogues.

Just down Bab al-Silsila Street was the main building of the Khalidi Library, which was founded in 1899 by my grandfather, Hajj Raghib al-Khalidi, with a bequest from his mother, Khadija al-Khalidi.[2] The library houses more than twelve hundred manuscripts, mainly in Arabic (some in Persian and Ottoman Turkish), the oldest dating back to the early eleventh century.[3] Including some two thousand nineteenth-century Arabic books and miscellaneous family papers, the collection is one of the most extensive in all of Palestine that is still in the hands of its original owners.[4]

At the time of my stay, the main library structure, which dates from around the thirteenth century, was undergoing restoration, so the contents were being stored temporarily in large cardboard boxes in a Mameluke-era building connected to our apartment by a narrow stairway. I spent over a year among those boxes, going through dusty, worm-eaten books, documents, and letters belonging to generations of Khalidis, among them my great-great-great uncle, Yusuf Diya al-Din Pasha al-Khalidi.[5]* Through his papers, I discovered a worldly man with a broad education acquired in Jerusalem, Malta, Istanbul, and Vienna, a man who was deeply interested in comparative religion, especially in Judaism, and who owned a number of books in European languages on this and other subjects.

Yusuf Diya was heir to a long line of Jerusalemite Islamic scholars and legal functionaries; his father, al-Sayyid Muhammad 'Ali al-Khalidi, had served for some fifty years as deputy *qadi* and chief of the Jerusalem Shari'a court secretariat. But at a young age Yusuf Diya sought a different path for himself. After absorbing the fundamentals of a traditional Islamic education, he left Palestine at the age of eighteen—without his father's approval, we are told—to spend two years at a British Church Mission Society school in Malta. From there he went to study at the Imperial Medical School in Istanbul, after which he attended the city's Robert College, recently founded by American Protestant missionaries. For five years during the 1860s, Yusuf Diya attended some of the first institutions in the region that provided a modern Western-style education, learning English, French, German, and much else. It was an unusual trajectory for a young man from a family of Muslim religious scholars in the mid-nineteenth century.

Having obtained this broad training, Yusuf Diya filled various roles as an Ottoman government official—translator in the Foreign Ministry; consul in the Russian port of Poti on the Black Sea; governor of districts in Kurdistan, Lebanon, Palestine, and Syria; and mayor of Jerusalem for nearly a decade—with stints teaching at the Royal Imperial University in Vienna. He was also elected as the deputy from Jerusalem to the short-lived Ottoman parliament established in 1876 under the empire's new

---

*Note that Arabic names have been transcribed according to the simplified IJMES system (*International Journal of Middle East Studies*), except where other spelling was preferred by the individuals themselves.

THE KHALIDI LIBRARY

Yusuf Diya al-Din Pasha al-Khalidi

constitution, earning Sultan 'Abd al-Hamid's enmity because he supported parliamentary prerogatives over executive power.[6]

In line with family tradition and his Islamic and Western education, al-Khalidi became an accomplished scholar as well. The Khalidi Library contains many books of his in French, German, and English, as well as correspondence with learned figures in Europe and the Middle East. Additionally, old Austrian, French, and British newspapers in the library show that Yusuf Diya regularly read the overseas press. There is evidence that he received these materials via the Austrian post office in Istanbul, which was not subject to the draconian Ottoman laws of censorship.[7]

As a result of his wide reading, as well as his time in Vienna and other European countries, and from his encounters with Christian missionaries, Yusuf Diya was fully conscious of the pervasiveness of Western anti-Semitism. He had also gained impressive knowledge of the intellectual origins of Zionism, specifically its nature as a response to Christian Europe's virulent anti-Semitism. He was undoubtedly familiar with *Der Judenstaat* by the Viennese journalist Theodor Herzl, published in 1896, and was aware of the first two Zionist congresses in Basel, Switzerland, in 1897 and 1898.[8] (Indeed, it seems clear that Yusuf Diya knew of Herzl from his own time in Vienna.) He knew of the debates and the views of the different Zionist leaders and tendencies, including Herzl's explicit call for a state for the Jews, with the "sovereign right" to control immigration. Moreover, as mayor of Jerusalem he had witnessed the friction with the local population prompted by the first years of proto-Zionist activity, starting with the arrival of the earliest European Jewish settlers in the late 1870s and early 1880s.

Herzl, the acknowledged leader of the growing movement he had founded, had paid his sole visit to Palestine in 1898, timing it to coincide with that of the German kaiser Wilhelm II. He had already begun to give thought to some of the issues involved in the colonization of Palestine, writing in his diary in 1895:

> We must expropriate gently the private property on the estates assigned to us. We shall try to spirit the penniless population across the border by procuring employment for it in the transit countries, while denying it employment in our own country. The property owners will come over to our side. Both the process of expropriation and the removal of the poor must be carried out discreetly and circumspectly.[9]

Yusuf Diya would have been more aware than most of his compatriots in Palestine of the ambition of the nascent Zionist movement, as well as its strength, resources, and appeal. He knew perfectly well that there was no way to reconcile Zionism's claims on Palestine and its explicit aim of Jewish statehood and sovereignty there with the rights and well-being of the country's indigenous inhabitants. It is for these reasons, presumably, that on March 1, 1899, Yusuf Diya sent a prescient seven-page letter to the French chief rabbi, Zadoc Kahn, with the intention that it be passed on to the founder of modern Zionism.

The letter began with an expression of Yusuf Diya's admiration for Herzl, whom he esteemed "as a man, as a writer of talent, and as a true Jewish patriot," and of his respect for Judaism and for Jews, who he said were "our cousins," referring to the Patriarch Abraham, revered as their common forefather by both Jews and Muslims.[10] He understood the motivations for Zionism, just as he deplored the persecution to which Jews were subject in Europe. In light of this, he wrote, Zionism in principle was "natural, beautiful and just," and, "who could contest the rights of the Jews in Palestine? My God, historically it is your country!"

This sentence is sometimes cited, in isolation from the rest of the letter, to represent Yusuf Diya's enthusiastic acceptance of the entire Zionist program in Palestine. However, the former mayor and deputy of Jerusalem went on to warn of the dangers he foresaw as a consequence of the implementation of the Zionist project for a sovereign Jewish state in Palestine. The Zionist idea would sow dissension among Christians, Muslims, and Jews there. It would imperil the status and security that Jews had always enjoyed throughout the Ottoman domains. Coming to his main purpose, Yusuf Diya said soberly that whatever the merits of Zionism, the "brutal force of circumstances had to be taken into account." The most important of them were that "Palestine is an integral part of the Ottoman Empire, and more gravely, it is inhabited by others." Palestine already had an indigenous population that would never accept being superseded. Yusuf Diya spoke "with full knowledge of the facts," asserting that it was "pure folly" for Zionism to plan to take over Palestine. "Nothing could be more just and equitable," than for "the unhappy Jewish nation" to find a refuge elsewhere. But, he concluded with a heartfelt plea, "in the name of God, let Palestine be left alone."

Herzl's reply to Yusuf Diya came quickly, on March 19. His letter was probably the first response by a founder of the Zionist movement to a cogent Palestinian objection to its embryonic plans for Palestine. In it, Herzl established what was to become a pattern of dismissing as insignificant the interests, and sometimes the very existence, of the indigenous population. The Zionist leader simply ignored the letter's basic thesis, that Palestine was already inhabited by a population that would not agree to be supplanted. Although Herzl had visited the country once, he, like most early European Zionists, had not much knowledge of or contact with its native inhabitants. He also failed to address al-Khalidi's well-founded concerns about the danger the Zionist program would pose to the large, well-established Jewish communities all over the Middle East.

Glossing over the fact that Zionism was ultimately meant to lead to

Yusuf Diya to Theodore Herzl: Palestine "is inhabited by others" who will not easily accept their own displacement.

Jewish domination of Palestine, Herzl employed a justification that has been a touchstone for colonialists at all times and in all places and that would become a staple argument of the Zionist movement: Jewish immigration would benefit the indigenous people of Palestine. "It is their well-being, their individual wealth, which we will increase by bringing in our own." Echoing the language he had used in *Der Judenstaat*, Herzl added: "In allowing immigration to a number of Jews bringing their intelligence, their financial acumen and their means of enterprise to the country, no one can doubt that the well-being of the entire country would be the happy result."[11]

Most revealingly, the letter addresses a consideration that Yusuf Diya had not even raised. "You see another difficulty, Excellency, in the existence of the non-Jewish population in Palestine. But who would think of sending them away?"[12] With his assurance in response to al-Khalidi's unasked question, Herzl alludes to the desire recorded in his diary to "spirit" the country's poor population "discreetly" across the borders.[13] It is clear from this chilling quotation that Herzl grasped the importance of "disappearing" the native population of Palestine in order for Zionism to succeed. Moreover, the 1901 charter that he co-drafted for the Jewish-Ottoman Land Company includes the same principle of the removal of inhabitants of Palestine to "other provinces and territories of the Ottoman Empire."[14] Although Herzl stressed in his writings that his project was based on "the highest tolerance" with full rights for all,[15] what was meant was no more than toleration of any minorities that might remain after the rest had been moved elsewhere.

Herzl underestimated his correspondent. From al-Khalidi's letter it is clear that he understood perfectly well that at issue was not the immigration of a limited "number of Jews" to Palestine, but rather the transformation of the entire land into a Jewish state. Given Herzl's reply to him, Yusuf Diya could only have come to one of two conclusions. Either the Zionist leader meant to deceive him by concealing the true aims of the Zionist movement, or Herzl simply did not see Yusuf Diya and the Arabs of Palestine as worthy of being taken seriously.

Instead, with the smug self-assurance so common to nineteenth-century Europeans, Herzl offered the preposterous inducement that the colonization, and ultimately the usurpation, of their land by strangers would benefit the people of that country. Herzl's thinking and his reply to Yusuf Diya appear to have been based on the assumption that the Arabs could ultimately be bribed or fooled into ignoring what the Zionist movement actually intended for Palestine. This condescending attitude toward the intelligence, not to speak of the rights, of the Arab population of Palestine was to be serially repeated by Zionist, British, European, and American leaders in the decades that followed, down to the present day. As for the Jewish state that was ultimately created by the movement Herzl founded, as Yusuf Diya foresaw, there was to be room there for only one people, the Jewish people: others would indeed be "spirited away," or at best tolerated.

YUSUF DIYA'S LETTER and Herzl's response to it are well known to historians of the period, but most of them do not seem to have reflected carefully on what was perhaps the first meaningful exchange between a leading Palestinian figure and a founder of the Zionist movement. They have not reckoned fully with Herzl's rationalizations, which laid out, quite plainly, the essentially colonial nature of the century-long conflict in Palestine. Nor have they acknowledged al-Khalidi's arguments, which have been borne out in full since 1899.

Starting after World War I, the dismantling of indigenous Palestinian society was set in motion by the large-scale immigration of European Jewish settlers supported by the newly established British Mandate authorities, who helped them build the autonomous structure of a Zionist para-state. Additionally, a separate Jewish-controlled sector of the economy was created through the exclusion of Arab labor from Jewish-owned firms under the slogan of "*Avoda ivrit*," Hebrew labor, and the injection of truly massive amounts of capital from abroad.[16] By the middle of the 1930s, although Jews were still a minority of the population, this largely autonomous sector was bigger than the Arab-owned part of the economy.

The indigenous population was further diminished by the crushing repression of the Great 1936–39 Arab Revolt against British rule, during which 14 to 17 percent of the adult male population was killed, wounded, imprisoned, or exiled,[17] as the British employed a hundred thousand troops and air power to master Palestinian resistance. Meanwhile, a massive wave of Jewish immigration as a result of persecution by the Nazi regime in Germany raised the Jewish population in Palestine from just 18 percent of the total in 1932 to over 31 percent in 1939. This provided the demographic critical mass and military manpower that were necessary for the ethnic cleansing of Palestine in 1948. The expulsion then of over half the Arab population of the country, first by Zionist militias and then by the Israeli army, completed the military and political triumph of Zionism.

Such radical social engineering at the expense of the indigenous population is the way of all colonial settler movements. In Palestine, it was a necessary precondition for transforming most of an overwhelmingly Arab country into a predominantly Jewish state. As this book will argue, the modern history of Palestine can best be understood in these terms: as a colonial war waged against the indigenous population, by a variety of parties, to force them to relinquish their homeland to another people against their will.

Although this war shares many of the typical characteristics of other colonial campaigns, it also possesses very specific characteristics, as it was fought by and on behalf of the Zionist movement, which itself was and is a very particular colonial project. Further complicating this understanding is the fact that this colonial conflict, conducted with massive support from external powers, became over time a national confrontation between two new national entities, two peoples. Underlying this feature, and amplifying it, was the profound resonance for Jews, and also for many Christians, of their biblical connection to the historic land of Israel. Expertly woven into modern political Zionism, this resonance has become integral to it. A late-nineteenth-century colonial-national movement thus adorned itself with a biblical coat that was powerfully attractive to Bible-reading Protestants in Great Britain and the United States, blinding them to the modernity of Zionism and to its colonial nature: for how could Jews be "colonizing" the land where their religion began?

Given this blindness, the conflict is portrayed as, at best, a straightforward, if tragic, national clash between two peoples with rights in the same land. At worst, it is described as the result of the fanatical, inveterate hatred of Arabs and Muslims for the Jewish people as they assert their inalienable right to their eternal, God-given homeland. In fact, there is no reason that what has happened in Palestine for over a century cannot be understood as *both* a colonial and a national conflict. But our concern here is its colonial nature, as this aspect has been as underappreciated as it is central, even though those qualities typical of other colonial campaigns are everywhere in evidence in the modern history of Palestine.

Characteristically, European colonizers seeking to supplant or dominate indigenous peoples, whether in the Americas, Africa, Asia, or Australasia (or in Ireland), have always described them in pejorative terms. They also always claim that they will leave the native population better off as a result of their rule; the "civilizing" and "progressive" nature of their colonial projects serves to justify whatever enormities are perpetrated against the indigenous people to fulfill their objectives. One need only refer to the rhetoric of French administrators in North Africa or of British viceroys in India. Of the British Raj, Lord Curzon said: "To feel that somewhere among these millions you have left a little justice or happiness or prosperity, a sense of manliness or moral dignity, a spring of patriotism, a dawn of intellectual enlightenment, or a stirring of duty, where it did not before exist—that is enough, that is the Englishman's justification in India."[18] The words "where it did not before exist" bear repeating. For Curzon and others of his colonial class, the natives did not know what was best for them and could not achieve these things on their own: "You cannot do without us," Curzon said in another speech.[19]

For over a century, the Palestinians have been depicted in precisely the same language by their colonizers as have been other indigenous peoples. The condescending rhetoric of Theodor Herzl and other Zionist leaders was no different from that of their European peers. The Jewish state, Herzl wrote, would "form a part of a wall of defense for Europe in Asia, an outpost of civilization against barbarism."[20] This was similar to the language used in the conquest of the North American frontier, which ended in the nineteenth century with the eradication or subjugation of the continent's entire native population. As in North America, the colonization of Palestine—like that of South Africa, Australia, Algeria, and parts of East Africa—was meant to yield a white European settler colony. The same tone toward the Palestinians that characterizes both Curzon's rhetoric and Herzl's letter is replicated in much discourse on Palestine in the United States, Europe, and Israel even today.

In line with this colonial rationale, there is a vast body of literature dedicated to proving that before the advent of European Zionist colonization, Palestine was barren, empty, and backward. Historical Palestine has been the subject of innumerable disparaging tropes in Western popular culture, as well as academically worthless writing that purports to be scientific and scholarly, but that is riddled with historical errors, misrepresentations, and sometimes outright bigotry. At most, this literature asserts, the country was inhabited by a small population of rootless and nomadic Bedouin who had no fixed identity and no attachment to the land they were passing through, essentially as transients.

The corollary of this contention is that it was only the labor and drive of the new Jewish immigrants that turned the country into the blooming garden it supposedly is today, and that only they had an identification with and love for the land, as well as a (God-given) right to it. This attitude is summed up in the slogan "A land without a people for a people without a land," used by Christian supporters of a Jewish Palestine, as well as by early Zionists like Israel Zangwill.[21] Palestine was *terra nullius* to those who came to settle it, with those living there nameless and amorphous. Thus Herzl's letter to Yusuf Diya referred to Palestinian Arabs, then roughly 95 percent of the country's inhabitants, as its "non-Jewish population."

Essentially, the point being made is that the Palestinians did not exist, or were of no account, or did not deserve to inhabit the country they so sadly neglected. If they did not exist, then even well-founded Palestinian objections to the Zionist movement's plans could simply be ignored. Just as Herzl dismissed Yusuf Diya al-Khalidi's letter, most later schemes for the disposition of Palestine were similarly cavalier. The 1917 Balfour Declaration, issued by a British cabinet and committing Britain to the creation of a national Jewish homeland, never mentioned the Palestinians, the great majority of the country's population at the time, even as it set the course for Palestine for the subsequent century.

The idea that the Palestinians simply do not exist, or even worse, are the malicious invention of those who wish Israel ill, is supported by such fraudulent books as Joan Peters's *From Time Immemorial*, now universally considered by scholars to be completely without merit. (On publication in 1984, however, it received a rapturous reception and it is still in print and selling discouragingly well.)[22] Such literature, both pseudo-scholarly and popular, is largely based on European travelers' accounts, on those of new Zionist immigrants, or on British Mandatory sources. It is often produced by people who know nothing about the indigenous society and its history and have disdain for it, or who worse yet have an agenda that depends on its invisibility or disappearance. Rarely utilizing sources produced from within Palestinian society, these representations essentially repeat the perspective, the ignorance, and the biases, tinged by European arrogance, of outsiders.[23]

The message is also amply represented in popular culture in Israel and the United States, as well as in political and public life.[24] It has been amplified via mass market books such as Leon Uris's novel *Exodus* and the Academy Award–winning movie that it spawned, works that have had a vast impact on an entire generation and that serve to confirm and deepen preexisting prejudices.[25] Political figures have explicitly denied the existence of Palestinians, for example, former Speaker of the House Newt Gingrich: "I think that we've had an invented Palestinian people who are in fact Arabs." While returning from a trip to Palestine in March 2015, the governor of Arkansas, Mike Huckabee, said "There's really no such thing as the Palestinians."[26] To some degree, every US administration since Harry Truman's has been staffed by people making policy on Palestine whose views indicate that they believe Palestinians, whether or not they exist, are lesser beings than Israelis.

Significantly, many early apostles of Zionism had been proud to embrace the colonial nature of their project. The eminent Revisionist Zionist leader Ze'ev Jabotinsky, godfather of the political trend that has dominated Israel since 1977, upheld by Prime Ministers Menachem Begin, Yitzhak Shamir, Ariel Sharon, Ehud Olmert, and Benjamin Netanyahu, was especially clear about this. Jabotinsky wrote in 1923: "Every native population in the world resists colonists as long as it has the slightest hope of being able to rid itself of the danger of being colonised. That is what the Arabs in Palestine are doing, and what they will persist in doing as long as there remains a solitary spark of hope that they will be able to prevent the transformation of 'Palestine' into the 'Land of Israel.'" Such honesty was rare among other leading Zionists, who like Herzl protested the innocent purity of their aims and deceived their Western listeners, and perhaps themselves, with fairy tales about their benign intentions toward the Arab inhabitants of Palestine.

Jabotinsky and his followers were among the few who were frank enough to admit publicly and bluntly the harsh realities inevitably attendant on the implantation of a colonial settler society within an existing population. Specifically, he acknowledged that the constant threat of the use of massive force against the Arab majority would be necessary to implement the Zionist program: what he called an "iron wall" of bayonets was an imperative for its success. As Jabotinsky put it: "Zionist colonisation . . . can proceed and develop only under the protection of a power that is independent of the native population—behind an iron wall, which the native population cannot breach."[27] This was still the high age of colonialism, when such things being done to native societies by Westerners were normalized and described as "progress."

The social and economic institutions founded by the early Zionists, which were central to the success of the Zionist project, were also unquestioningly understood by all and described as colonial. The most important of these institutions was the Jewish Colonization Association (in 1924 renamed the Palestine Jewish Colonization Association). This body was originally established by the German Jewish philanthropist Baron Maurice de Hirsch and later combined with a similar organization founded by the British peer and financier Lord Edmond de Rothschild. The JCA provided the massive financial support that made possible extensive land purchases and the subsidies that enabled most of the early Zionist colonies in Palestine to survive and thrive before and during the Mandate period.

Unremarkably, once colonialism took on a bad odor in the post–World War II era of decolonization, the colonial origins and practice of Zionism and Israel were whitewashed and conveniently forgotten in Israel and the West. In fact, Zionism—for two decades the coddled stepchild of British colonialism—rebranded itself as an anticolonial movement. The occasion for this drastic makeover was a campaign of sabotage and terrorism launched against Great Britain after it drastically limited its support of Jewish immigration with the 1939 White Paper on the eve of World War II. This falling-out between erstwhile allies (to help them fight the Palestinians in the late 1930s, Britain had armed and trained the Jewish settlers it allowed to enter the country) encouraged the outlandish idea that the Zionist movement was itself anticolonial.

There was no escaping the fact that Zionism initially had clung tightly to the British Empire for support, and had only successfully implanted itself in Palestine thanks to the unceasing efforts of British imperialism. It could not be otherwise, for as Jabotinsky stressed, only the British had the means to wage the colonial war that was necessary to suppress Palestinian resistance to the takeover of their country. This war has continued since then, waged sometimes overtly and sometimes covertly, but invariably with the tacit or overt approval, and often the direct involvement, of the leading powers of the day and the sanction of the international bodies they dominated, the League of Nations and the United Nations.

Today, the conflict that was engendered by this classic nineteenth-century European colonial venture in a non-European land, supported from 1917 onward by the greatest Western imperial power of its age, is rarely described in such unvarnished terms. Indeed, those who analyze not only Israeli settlement efforts in Jerusalem, the West Bank, and the occupied Syrian Golan Heights, but the entire Zionist enterprise from the perspective of its colonial settler origins and nature are often vilified. Many cannot accept the contradiction inherent in the idea that although Zionism undoubtedly succeeded in creating a thriving national entity in Israel, its roots are as a colonial settler project (as are those of other modern countries: the United States, Canada, Australia, and New Zealand). Nor can they accept that it would not have succeeded but for the support of the great imperial powers, Britain and later the United States. Zionism, therefore, could be and was both a national and a colonial settler movement at one and the same time.

RATHER THAN WRITE a comprehensive survey of Palestinian history, I have chosen to focus on six turning points in the struggle over Palestine. These six events, from the 1917 issuance of the Balfour Declaration, which decided the fate of Palestine, to Israel's siege of the Gaza Strip and its intermittent wars on Gaza's population in the early 2000s, highlight the colonial nature of the hundred years' war on Palestine, and also the indispensable role of external powers in waging it.[28] I have told this story partly through the experiences of Palestinians who lived through the war, many of them members of my family who were present at some of the episodes described. I have included my own recollections of events that I witnessed, as well as materials belonging to my own and other families, and a variety of first-person narratives. My purpose throughout has been to show that this conflict must be seen quite differently from most of the prevailing views of it.

I have written several books and numerous articles on different aspects of Palestinian history in a purely academic vein.[29] The underpinning of this book, too, is research-based and academic, but it also has a first-person dimension that is usually excluded from scholarly history. Although members of my family have been involved in events in Palestine for years, as have I, as a witness or a participant, our experiences are not unique, in spite of the advantages we enjoyed because of our class and status. One could draw on many such accounts, although much history from below and from other sectors of Palestinian society remains to be related. Nevertheless, in spite of the tensions inherent in this chosen approach, I believe it helps illuminate a perspective that is missing from the way in which the story of Palestine has been told in most of the literature.

I should add that this book does not correspond to a "lachrymose conception" of the past hundred years of Palestinian history, to reprise the great historian Salo Baron's brilliant critique of a nineteenth-century trend in Jewish historical writing.[30] Palestinians have been accused by those who sympathize with their oppressors of wallowing in their own victimization. It is a fact, however, that like all indigenous peoples confronting colonial wars, the Palestinians faced odds that were daunting and sometimes impossible. It is also true that they have suffered repeated defeats and have often been divided and badly led. None of this means that Palestinians could not sometimes defy those odds successfully, or that at other times they could not have made better choices.[31] But we cannot overlook the formidable international and imperial forces arrayed against them, the scale of which has often been dismissed, and in spite of which they have displayed remarkable resilience. It is my hope that this book will reflect this resilience and help recover some of what has thus far been airbrushed out of the history by those who control all of historic Palestine and the narrative surrounding it.

BRITISH MANDATE PALESTINE

Partition Plan, 1947
Arab State
Jewish State
Jerusalem, *corpus separatum*

LEBANON

SYRIA

Lake Tiberius

Haifa

Jenin

Nablus

Tel Aviv
Jaffa

Lydd

Jerusalem

Bethlehem

Gaza

Hebron

Dead Sea

Beersheba

NAQAB

TRANSJORDAN

EGYPT

1

The First Declaration of War, 1917–1939

There are plenty of cases of war being begun before it is declared.

—Arthur James Balfour[1]

At the turn of the twentieth century, before Zionist colonization had much appreciable effect on Palestine, new ideas were spreading, modern education and literacy had begun to expand, and the integration of the country's economy into the global capitalist order was proceeding apace. Production for export of crops like wheat and citrus fruit, capital investment in agriculture, and the introduction of cash crops and wage labor, notable in the rapid spread of orange groves, were changing the face of large sections of the countryside. This evolution went hand in hand with the accumulation of private land ownership by fewer people. Large tracts were coming under the control of absentee landlords—many of whom lived in Beirut or Damascus—at the expense of peasant smallholders. Sanitation, health, and rates of live births were all slowly improving, death rates were in decline, and the population was in consequence increasing more quickly. The telegraph, the steamship, the railway, gaslight, electricity, and modern roads were gradually transforming cities, towns, and even some rural villages. At the same time, travel within the region and beyond was faster, cheaper, safer, and more convenient.[2]

In the 1860s, Yusuf Diya al-Khalidi had to go all the way to Malta and Istanbul to acquire an education along Western lines. By 1914, such an education could be had in a variety of state, private, and missionary schools and colleges in Palestine, Beirut, Cairo, and Damascus. Modern pedagogy was often introduced by foreign missionary schools, Catholic, Protestant, and Orthodox, as well as by the Jewish schools of the Alliance israélite universelle. Partly out of fear that foreign missionaries in league with their great-power patrons would come to dominate the instruction of the younger generation, the Ottoman authorities established a growing network of state schools, which eventually served more students in Palestine than did foreign schools. Although universal access to education and widespread literacy were still far in the future, the changes leading up to World War I offered new horizons and novel ideas to more and more people.[3] The Arab population benefited from these developments.

Socially, Palestine was still heavily rural with a predominantly patriarchal, hierarchical nature, as it largely remained until 1948. It was dominated by narrow urban elites drawn from a few families like my own, who clung to their positions and privileges even as they adapted to new conditions, with younger family members acquiring modern educations and learning foreign languages to maintain their standing and their advantages. These elites controlled the politics of Palestine, although the growth of new professions, trades, and classes meant that in the 1900s there were more avenues of advancement and upward mobility. In the rapidly growing coastal cities of Jaffa and Haifa in particular, change was more visible than in the more conservative inland towns such as Jerusalem, Nablus, and Hebron, as the former witnessed the appearance of a nascent commercial bourgeoisie and an embryonic urban working class.[4]

At the same time, the sense of identity of large parts of the population was also evolving and shifting. My grandfather's generation would have identified—and would have been identified—in terms of family, religious affiliation, and city or village of origin. They would have cherished their descent from revered ancestors; they would have been proud speakers of Arabic, the language of the Qur'an, and heirs to Arab culture. They might have felt loyalty to the Ottoman dynasty and state, an allegiance rooted in custom as well as a sense of the Ottoman state as a bulwark defending the lands of the earliest and greatest Muslim empires, lands coveted by Christendom since the Crusades, lands in which the holy cities of Mecca, Medina, and Jerusalem were located. That loyalty had begun to weaken in the nineteenth century, however, as the religious foundation of the state was diminished, as Ottoman military defeats and territorial losses mounted, and as the ideas of nationalism evolved and spread.

Greater mobility and access to education accelerated these shifts, and the burgeoning press and availability of printed books also played an important role: thirty-two new newspapers and periodicals were established in Palestine between 1908 and 1914, with even more in the 1920s and 1930s.[5] Different forms of identification, such as nationhood, and novel ideas about social organization, including working-class solidarity and the role of women in society, were emerging to challenge previously fixed affiliations. These modes of belonging, whether to a national or class or professional group, were still in formation and involved overlapping ties of loyalty. Yusuf Diya's 1899 letter to Herzl, for example, evokes religious affiliation, Ottoman loyalty, local pride in Jerusalem, and a clear sense of identification with Palestine.

In this first decade of the twentieth century, a large proportion of the Jews living in Palestine were still culturally quite similar to and lived reasonably comfortably alongside city-dwelling Muslims and Christians. They were mostly ultra-Orthodox and non-Zionist, *mizrahi* (eastern) or Sephardic (descendants of Jews expelled from Spain), urbanites of Middle Eastern or Mediterranean origin who often spoke Arabic or Turkish, even if only as a second or third language. In spite of marked religious distinctions between them and their neighbors, they were not foreigners, nor were they Europeans or settlers: they were, saw themselves, and were seen as Jews who were part of the indigenous Muslim-majority society.[6] Moreover, some young European Ashkenazi Jews who settled in Palestine at this time, including such ardent Zionists as David Ben-Gurion and Yitzhak Ben-Zvi (one became prime minister and the other the president of Israel), initially sought a measure of integration into the local society. Ben-Gurion and Ben-Zvi even took Ottoman nationality, studied in Istanbul, and learned Arabic and Turkish.

The much more rapid pace of transformation in the advanced countries of Western Europe and North America compared to the rest of the world during the modern industrial era led many outside observers, including some eminent scholars, to mistakenly claim that Middle Eastern societies, including Palestine, were stagnant and unchanging, or even "in decline."[7] We now know from many indices that this was by no means the case: a growing body of solidly grounded historical work based on Ottoman, Palestinian, Israeli, and Western sources completely refutes these false notions.[8] However, recent scholarship on Palestine in the years before 1948 goes much further than just dealing with the misconceptions and distortions at the heart of such thinking. Whatever it may have looked like to uninformed outsiders, it is clear that by the first part of the twentieth century there existed in Palestine under Ottoman rule a vibrant Arab society undergoing a series of rapid and accelerating transitions, much like several other Middle Eastern societies around it.[9]

MAJOR EXTERNAL SHOCKS have powerful effects on societies, especially on their sense of self. The Ottoman Empire grew increasingly fragile in the early twentieth century, with major territorial losses in the Balkans, Libya, and elsewhere. A long series of wrenching wars and upheavals stretching for nearly a decade started with the Libyan war in 1911–12, followed by the Balkan Wars of 1912–13, and then the extraordinary dislocations of World War I, which led to the empire's disappearance. The four years of that war brought severe shortages, penury, starvation, disease, the requisitioning of draft animals, and the conscription of most working-age men, who were sent to the front. Greater Syria, which included Palestine and present-day Jordan, Syria, and Lebanon, is estimated to have suffered half a million deaths between 1915 and 1918 due to famine alone (which was exacerbated by a plague of locusts).[10]

Hunger and general hardship were only one cause of the dire state of the population. Focused as most observers were on the appalling casualties on the Western Front, few realized that the Ottoman Empire overall was dealt the heaviest wartime losses of any major combatant power, with over three million dead, 15 percent of the total population. Most of these casualties were civilians (the largest single group being the victims of massacres at the behest of the Ottoman authorities in 1915 and 1916—Armenians, Assyrians, and other Christians).[11] Additionally, of the 2.8 million Ottoman soldiers originally mobilized, as many as 750,000 may have died during the war.[12] Arab casualties were correspondingly high, since the army units recruited in Iraq and Greater Syria were heavily represented on bloody battlegrounds such as the Ottoman eastern front against Russia, as well as in Gallipoli, Sinai, Palestine, and Iraq. The demographer Justin McCarthy estimated that after growing by about 1 percent annually until 1914, Palestine's population declined by 6 percent during the war.[13]

The turmoil of the period did not spare even well-off families, such as my own. When my father, Ismail, was born in 1915, four of his adult brothers, Nu'man, Hasan, Husayn, and Ahmad, had been conscripted for service in the Ottoman army. Two of them sustained wounds in the fighting, but all were fortunate to survive. My aunt 'Anbara Salam al-Khalidi remembered harrowing images of starvation and deprivation in the streets of Beirut, where she lived as a young woman.[14] Husayn

Husayn and Hasan al-Khalidi, conscripts in the Ottoman army

al-Khalidi, my uncle, who served as a medical officer during the war, recalled similar heartbreaking scenes in Jerusalem, where he saw the bodies of dozens of people who had starved to death lying in the streets.[15] The wartime exactions of the Ottoman authorities included the hanging, on charges of treason, of my aunt's fiancé, 'Abd al-Ghani al-'Uraysi, alongside many other Arab nationalist patriots.[16]

In 1917 my grandfather Hajj Raghib al-Khalidi, and my grandmother Amira, known to all as Um Hasan, together with the other residents of the Jaffa area, received an evacuation order from the Ottoman authorities. To escape the encroaching dangers of war, they left their home at Tal al-Rish near Jaffa (my grandfather's work as a judge had brought them there from Jerusalem many years earlier) with their four youngest children, my father among them. For several months the family sought refuge in the hill village of Dayr Ghassaneh, east of Jaffa, with members of the Barghouti clan, with whom they had long-standing connections.[17] The village was far enough from the sea to be out of the range of Allied naval guns, and away from the heavy fighting along the coast as the British armies under General Sir Edmund Allenby advanced northward.

From the spring of 1917 through the late fall, the southern parts of the country were the scene of a grinding series of battles between British and Ottoman forces, the latter backed by German and Austrian troops. The fighting involved trench warfare, air raids, and intensive land and naval artillery bombardments. British and imperial units launched a number of major offensives, which slowly pushed back the Ottoman defenders. The fighting spread to the north of Palestine in the winter (Jerusalem, in the center, was captured by the British in December 1917), and continued into early 1918. In many regions, the direct impact of the war caused intense suffering. One of the worst-hit districts comprised Gaza City and the nearby towns and villages, where large areas were pulverized by heavy British shelling during prolonged trench warfare and then the slow Allied advance up the Mediterranean coastline.

Soon after Jaffa fell to the British in November 1917, my grandfather's family returned to their Tal al-Rish home. Another aunt, Fatima al-Khalidi Salam, then an eight-year-old, recalled her father addressing the British troops. "Welcome, welcome," he said in his undoubtedly imperfect English. Um Hasan, who heard this as "Ya waylkum"—"Woe to you!" in Arabic—feared that he had endangered the family by taunting the alien soldiers.[18] Whether Hajj Raghib al-Khalidi welcomed or lamented the arrival of the British, two of his sons were still fighting on the other side, and two were being held as POWs, which placed the family in a perilous position. Two uncles remained with the Ottoman army, which resisted the British in northern Palestine and Syria, until late 1918.

They were among the thousands of men still absent from their homes at war's end. Some had emigrated to the Americas to escape conscription while many, the writer 'Aref Shehadeh (later known as 'Arif al-'Arif) among them, were being held in Allied prisoner of war camps.[19] Others were in the hills, dodging the draft, like Najib Nassar, editor of the outspokenly anti-Zionist Haifa newspaper *al-Karmil*.[20] Meanwhile, there were Arab soldiers who had deserted the Ottoman army and crossed the lines, or who were serving in the forces of the Arab Revolt led by Sharif Husayn and allied with Britain. Still others—such as 'Isa al-'Isa, the editor of *Filastin*, who had been exiled by the Ottoman authorities for his fierce independence with its strong echoes of Arab nationalism—were forced from the relatively cosmopolitan confines of Jaffa to various small towns in the heart of rural Anatolia.[21]

All of these profound material shocks heightened the impact of the wrenching postwar political changes, which obliged people to rethink long-standing senses of identity. By the end of the fighting, people in Palestine and in much of the Arab world found themselves under occupation by European armies. After four hundred years, they were confronted by the disconcerting prospect of alien rule and the swift disappearance of Ottoman control, which had been the only system of government known for over twenty generations. It was in the midst of this great trauma, as one era ended and another began, against a grim background of suffering, loss, and deprivation, that Palestinians learned, in a fragmentary fashion, of the Balfour Declaration.

THE MOMENTOUS STATEMENT made just over a century ago on behalf of Britain's cabinet on November 2, 1917, by the secretary of state for foreign affairs, Arthur James Balfour—what has come to be known as the Balfour Declaration—comprised a single sentence:

> His Majesty's government view with favour the establishment in Palestine of a national home for the Jewish people, and will use their best endeavours to facilitate the achievement of this object, it being clearly understood that nothing shall be done which may prejudice the civil and religious rights of existing non-Jewish communities in Palestine, or the rights and political status enjoyed by Jews in any other country.

If before World War I many prescient Palestinians had begun to regard the Zionist movement as a threat, the Balfour Declaration introduced a new and fearsome element. In the soft, deceptive language of diplomacy, with its ambiguous phrase approving "the establishment in Palestine of a national home for the Jewish people," the declaration effectively pledged Britain's support for Theodor Herzl's aims of Jewish statehood, sovereignty, and control of immigration in the whole of Palestine.

Significantly, the overwhelming Arab majority of the population (around 94 percent at that time) went unmentioned by Balfour, except in a backhanded way as the "existing non-Jewish communities in Palestine." They were described in terms of what they were *not*, and certainly not as a nation or a people—the words "Palestinian" and "Arab" do not appear in the sixty-seven words of the declaration. This overwhelming majority of the population was promised only "civil and religious rights," not political or national rights. By way of contrast, Balfour ascribed national rights to what he called "the Jewish people," who in 1917 were a tiny minority—6 percent—of the country's inhabitants.

Before securing British backing, the Zionist movement had been a colonizing project in search of a great-power patron. Having failed to find a sponsor in the Ottoman Empire, in Wilhelmine Germany, and elsewhere, Theodor Herzl's successor Chaim Weizmann and his colleagues finally met with success in their approach to the wartime British cabinet led by David Lloyd George, acquiring the support of the greatest power of the age. The Palestinians now faced a far more formidable adversary than ever before, with British troops at that very moment advancing northward and occupying their country, troops who served a government that had pledged to implant a "national home" wherein unlimited immigration was meant to produce a future Jewish majority.

The British government's intentions and objectives at the time have been amply analyzed over the past century.[22] Among its many motivations were both a romantic, religiously derived philo-Semitic desire to "return" the Hebrews to the land of the Bible, and an anti-Semitic wish to reduce Jewish immigration to Britain, linked to a conviction that "world Jewry" had the power to keep newly revolutionary Russia fighting in the war and bring the United States into it. Beyond those impulses, Britain primarily desired control over Palestine for geopolitical strategic reasons that antedated World War I and that had only been reinforced by wartime events.[23] However important the other motivations may have been, this was the central one: the British Empire was *never* motivated by altruism. Britain's strategic interests were perfectly served by its sponsorship of the Zionist project, just as they were served by a range of regional wartime undertakings. Among them were commitments made in 1915 and 1916 promising independence to the Arabs led by Sharif Husayn of Mecca (enshrined in the Husayn-McMahon correspondence) and a secret 1916 deal with France—the Sykes-Picot Agreement—in which the two powers agreed to a colonial partition of the eastern Arab countries.[24]

More important than British motivations for issuing the Balfour Declaration is what this undertaking meant in practice for the crystal-clear aims of the Zionist movement—sovereignty and complete control of Palestine. With Britain's unstinting support, these aims suddenly became plausible. Some leading British politicians extended backing to Zionism that went well beyond the carefully phrased text of the declaration. At a dinner at Balfour's home in 1922, three of the most prominent British statesmen of the era—Lloyd George, Balfour, and Secretary of State for the Colonies Winston Churchill—assured Weizmann that by the term "Jewish national home" they "always meant an eventual Jewish state." Lloyd George convinced the Zionist leader that for this reason Britain would never allow representative government in Palestine. Nor did it.[25]

For Zionists, their enterprise was now backed by an indispensable "iron wall" of British military might, in the words of Ze'ev Jabotinsky. For the inhabitants of Palestine, whose future it ultimately decided, Balfour's careful, calibrated prose was in effect a gun pointed directly at their heads, a declaration of war by the British Empire on the indigenous population. The majority now faced the prospect of being outnumbered by unlimited Jewish immigration to a country then almost completely Arab in its population and culture. Whether intended this way or not, the declaration launched a full-blown colonial conflict, a century-long assault on the Palestinian people, aimed at fostering an exclusivist "national home" at their expense.

THE PALESTINIAN REACTION to the Balfour Declaration was late in coming, and initially was relatively muted. Word of the British pronouncement had spread in most other parts of the world immediately following its promulgation. In Palestine, however, local newspapers had been shuttered since the beginning of the war by both government censorship and a lack of newsprint, the result of a tight Allied naval blockade of Ottoman ports. After British troops occupied Jerusalem in December 1917, the military regime banned publication of news of the declaration.[26] Indeed, the British authorities did not allow newspapers to reappear in Palestine for nearly two years. When reports of the Balfour Declaration finally reached Palestine, they trickled in slowly via word of mouth and then through copies of Egyptian newspapers that travelers brought from Cairo.

The bombshell struck a society prostrate and exhausted at this late stage of the war, when survivors of the chaos and displacement were slowly returning to their homes. There is evidence that they reacted with shock to the news. In December 1918, thirty-three exiled Palestinians (including al-'Isa) who had just made their way from Anatolia to Damascus (where their access to news was not restricted) sent an advance letter of protest to the peace conference being convened in Versailles and to the British Foreign Office. They stressed that "this country is our country" and expressed their horror at the Zionist claim that "Palestine would be turned into a national home for them."[27]

Such prospects may have seemed remote to many Palestinians when the Balfour Declaration was issued, at a time when Jews constituted a tiny minority of the population. Nonetheless, some far-sighted individuals, Yusuf Diya al-Khalidi among them, had discerned the danger posed by Zionism early on. In 1914 'Isa al-'Isa wrote, in an astute editorial in *Filastin*, of "a nation threatened with disappearance by the Zionist tide in this Palestinian land, . . . a nation which is threatened in its very being with expulsion from its homeland."[28] Those who felt trepidation about the encroachment of the Zionist movement were alarmed by its ability to purchase large tracts of fertile land from which the indigenous peasants were removed and by its success in increasing Jewish immigration. Indeed, between 1909 and 1914 some forty thousand Jewish immigrants had arrived (although some left soon afterwards) and eighteen new colonies (of a 1914 total of fifty-two) had been created by the Zionist movement on land it had bought mainly from absentee landlords. The relatively recent concentration of private land ownership greatly facilitated these land purchases. The impact on Palestinians was especially pronounced in agricultural communities in areas of intensive Zionist colonization: the coastal plain and the fertile Marj Ibn 'Amer and Huleh valleys in the north. Many peasants in villages neighboring the new colonies had been deprived of their land as a result of the land sales. Some had also suffered in armed encounters with the first paramilitary units formed by the European Jewish settlers.[29] Their trepidation was shared by Arab city dwellers in Haifa, Jaffa, and Jerusalem—the main centers of Jewish population then and now—who observed with mounting concern the stream of Jewish immigrants in the years before the war. After the issuance of the Balfour Declaration, the disastrous implications for the future of Palestine were increasingly apparent to all.

BEYOND DEMOGRAPHIC AND other shifts, World War I and its aftermath accelerated the change in Palestinian national sentiment from a love of country and loyalties to family and locale to a thoroughly modern form of nationalism.[30] In a world where nationalism had been gaining ground for many decades, the Great War provided a global boost to the idea. The tendency was compounded toward the end of the war by Woodrow Wilson in the United States and Vladimir Lenin in Soviet Russia, who both espoused the principle of national self-determination, albeit in different ways and with different aims.

Whatever the intentions of these two leaders, the apparent endorsement of the national aspirations of peoples the world over by ostensibly anticolonial powers had an enormous impact. Clearly, Wilson had no intention of applying the principle to most of those who took them as inspiration for their hopes of national liberation. Indeed, he confessed that he was bewildered by the plethora of peoples, most of whom he had never heard, who responded to his call for self-determination.[31] Nevertheless, the hopes aroused and then disappointed—by Wilson's pronouncements in support of national self-determination, by the Bolshevik Revolution, and by the indifference of the Allies at the Versailles Peace Conference to the demands of colonized peoples for independence—sparked massive revolutionary anticolonial upheavals in India, Egypt, China, Korea, Ireland, and elsewhere.[32] The dissolution of the Romanov, Hapsburg, and Ottoman Empires—transnational dynastic states—was also in large measure a function of the spread of nationalism and its intensification during and after the war.

Political identities in Palestine had certainly evolved prior to the war, in keeping with global shifts and the evolution of the Ottoman state. However, this had happened relatively slowly, within the constraints of the dynastic, transnational, and religiously legitimated empire. The mental map of most of its subjects before 1914 was limited by their having been governed by this political system for so long that it was hard for them to conceive of not living under Ottoman rule. Going into the postwar world, suffering from collective trauma, the people of Palestine faced a radically new reality: they were to be ruled by Britain, and their country had been promised to others as a "national home." Against this could be set their expectations about the possibility of Arab independence and self-determination, promised to Sharif Husayn by the British in 1916—a promise repeated in multiple public pledges thereafter, including in an Anglo-French declaration of 1918, before being enshrined in the Covenant of the new League of Nations in 1919.

One crucial window into Palestinians' perceptions of themselves and their understanding of events between the wars is the Palestinian press. Two newspapers, 'Isa al-'Isa's Jaffa publication, *Filastin*, and *al-Karmil*, published in Haifa by Najib Nassar, were bastions of local patriotism, and critics of the Zionist-British entente and the danger that it posed to the Arab majority in Palestine. They were among the most influential beacons of the idea of Palestinian identity. Other newspapers echoed and amplified the same themes, focusing on the burgeoning, largely closed

Jewish economy and the other institutions created by the Zionist state-building project and supported by the British authorities.

After attending the ceremonial opening of a new rail line in 1929 that connected Tel Aviv to the Jewish settlements and Arab villages to the south, 'Isa al-'Isa wrote an ominous editorial in *Filastin*. All along the route, he wrote, Jewish settlers took advantage of the presence of British officials to make new demands of them, while Palestinians were nowhere to be seen. "There was only one tarbush," he said, "among so many hats." The message was clear: the *wataniyin*, "the people of the country," were poorly organized, while *al-qawm*, "this nation," exploited every opportunity offered them. The title of the editorial summed up the gravity of al-'Isa's warning: "Strangers in Our Own Land: Our Drowsiness and Their Alertness."[33] Another such window is provided by the growing number of published memoirs by Palestinians. Most of them are in Arabic and reflect the concerns of their upper-class and middle-class authors.[34] To find the views of the less well-to-do segments of Palestinian society is more difficult. There is little oral history available from the early decades of British rule.[35]

While sources such as these provide a sense of the evolution of identity among Palestinians, with the increasing use of the terms "Palestine" and "Palestinians," the turning points in this process are hard to pinpoint. A few things can be gleaned from my grandfather's personal trajectory. Hajj Raghib, who had a traditional religious education and who served as a religious official and as a *qadi,* was a close friend of 'Isa al-'Isa (who incidentally was my wife Mona's grandfather), and contributed articles on topics like education, libraries, and culture to *Filastin*.[36] Through Khalidi and al-'Isa family lore we get a sense of the frequent social interactions between the two—one Muslim, the other Greek Orthodox—primarily in the garden of my grandfather's house in Tal al-Rish on the outskirts of Jaffa. In one story, the two men put up with the interminable visit of a boring, conservative local shaykh before returning, after he leaves, to the more convivial pleasure of private drinking.[37] The point is that Hajj Raghib, a religious figure, was part of a circle of leading secular advocates of Palestine as a source of identity.

The history revealed by even a cursory examination of the press,

The al-Khalidi family, Tal al-Rish, circa 1930: Top row from left: Ismail (the author's father), Ya'coub, Hasan (holding Samira), Husayn (holding Leila), Ghalib. Middle row: 'Anbara, Walid, Um Hasan (the author's grandmother), Sulafa, Hajj Raghib (his grandfather), Nash'at, Ikram. Bottom row: 'Adel, Hatim, Raghib, Amira, Khalid, and Mu'awiya.

memoirs, and similar sources generated by Palestinians flies in the face of the popular mythology of the conflict, which is premised on their nonexistence or lack of a collective consciousness. In fact, Palestinian identity and nationalism are all too often seen to be no more than recent expressions of an unreasoning (if not fanatical) opposition to Jewish national self-determination. But Palestinian identity, much like Zionism, emerged in response to many stimuli, and at almost exactly the same time as did modern political Zionism. The threat of Zionism was only one of these stimuli, just as anti-Semitism was only one of the factors fueling Zionism. As newspapers like *Filastin* and *al-Karmil* reveal, this identity included love of country, a desire to improve society, religious attachment to Palestine, and opposition to European control. After the war, the focus on Palestine as a central locus of identity drew strength from widespread frustration at the blocking of Arab aspirations in Syria and elsewhere as the Middle East became suffocatingly dominated by the European colonial powers. This identity is thus comparable to the other Arab nation-state identities that emerged around the same time in Syria, Lebanon, and Iraq.

Indeed, all the neighboring Arab peoples developed modern national identities very similar to that of the Palestinians, and did so without the impact of the emergence of Zionist colonialism in their midst. Just like Zionism, Palestinian and other Arab national identities were modern and contingent, a product of late nineteenth- and twentieth-century circumstances, not eternal and immutable. The denial of an authentic, independent Palestinian identity is of a piece with Herzl's colonialist views on the alleged benefits of Zionism to the indigenous population, and constitutes a crucial element in the erasure of their national rights and peoplehood by the Balfour Declaration and its sequels.

As SOON AS they were able to do so in the wake of World War I, Palestinians began to organize politically in opposition both to British rule, and to the imposition of the Zionist movement as a privileged interlocutor of the British. Palestinians' efforts included petitions to the British, to the Paris Peace Conference, and to the newly formed League of Nations. Their most notable effort was a series of seven Palestine Arab congresses planned by a country-wide network of Muslim-Christian societies and held from 1919 until 1928. These congresses put forward a consistent series of demands focused on independence for Arab Palestine, rejection of the Balfour Declaration, support for majority rule, and ending unlimited Jewish immigration and land purchases. The congresses established an Arab executive that met repeatedly with British officials in Jerusalem and in London, albeit to little avail. It was a dialogue of the deaf. The British refused to recognize the representative authority of the congresses or its leaders, and insisted on Arab acceptance of the Balfour Declaration and the terms of the Mandate that had succeeded it—the antithesis of every substantive Arab demand—as a precondition for discussion. The Palestinian leadership pursued this fruitless legalistic approach for over a decade and a half.

In contrast to these elite-led initiatives, popular dissatisfaction with British support for Zionist aspirations exploded into demonstrations, strikes, and riots, with violence flaring notably in 1920, 1921, and 1929, each episode more intense than the previous one. In every case, these were spontaneous eruptions, often provoked by Zionist groups flexing their muscle. The British repressed peaceful protests and outbreaks of violence with equally harsh severity, but Arab popular discontent continued. By the early 1930s, younger, educated lower-middle- and middle-class elements, impatient with the conciliatory approach of the elite, began to launch more radical initiatives and organize more militant groups. These included an activist network set up throughout the northern parts of the country by a Haifa-based itinerant preacher of Syrian origin named Shaykh 'Iz al-Din al-Qassam, which was clandestinely preparing for an armed uprising, as well as the Istiqlal ("independence") Party, whose name summarized its aims.

All of these efforts took place initially in the shadow of a strict British military regime that lasted until 1920 (one of the congresses was held in Damascus because the British had banned Palestinian political activity), and thereafter under a series of British Mandatory high commissioners. The first of them was Sir Herbert Samuel, a committed Zionist and former cabinet minister who laid the governmental foundations for much of what followed, and who ably advanced Zionist aims while foiling those of the Palestinians.

Well-informed Palestinians were aware of what the Zionists were preaching both abroad and in Hebrew in Palestine to their followers—that unlimited immigration would produce a Jewish majority that would permit a takeover of the country. They had been following the doings and sayings of Zionist leaders via the extensive reportage on the subject in the Arabic press since well before the war.[38] While Chaim Weizmann had, for example, told several prominent Arabs at a dinner party in Jerusalem in March 1918 "to beware treacherous insinuations that Zionists were seeking political power,"[39] most knew that such assertions were strategic and meant to cloak the Zionists' real objectives. Indeed, the Zionist movement's leaders understood that "under no circumstances should they talk as though the Zionist program required the expulsion of the Arabs, because that would cause the Jews to lose the world's sympathy," but knowledgeable Palestinians were not deceived.[40]

While readers of the press, members of the elite, and villagers and city-dwellers who were in direct contact with the Jewish settlers were conscious of the threat, such awareness was far from universal. Similarly, the evolution of the Palestinians' sense of self was uneven. While most people desired Palestinian independence, some entertained the hope that such independence could be secured as part of a larger Arab state. A newspaper briefly published in Jerusalem in 1919 by 'Arif al-'Arif and another political figure, Muhammad Hasan al-Budayri, proclaimed this aspiration in its name: *Suriyya al-Janubiyya*, or Southern Syria. (The publication was quickly suppressed by the British.) A government under Amir Faysal, son of Sharif Husayn, had been established in Damascus in 1918, and many Palestinians hoped their country would become the southern part of this nascent state. However France claimed Syria for itself on the basis of the Sykes-Picot Agreement, and in July 1920, French troops occupied the country, eliminating the newborn Arab state.[41] As Arab countries under mandates or other forms of direct or indirect European control became preoccupied with their own narrow problems, more and more Palestinians realized that they would have to depend on themselves. Arabism and a sense of belonging to the larger Arab world always remained strong, but Palestinian identity was constantly reinforced by Britain's bias in favor of the burgeoning Zionist project.

Changes elsewhere in the Middle East swept a region racked by continued instability. Following a bitter clash with Allied occupying forces, the nucleus of a Turkish republic arose in Anatolia in place of the Ottoman Empire. Meanwhile, Britain failed to impose a one-sided treaty on Iran and withdrew its occupation forces in 1921. France established itself in Syria and Lebanon, after crushing Amir Faysal's state. Egyptians revolting against their British overlords in 1919 were suppressed with great difficulty by the colonial power, which was finally obliged to grant Egypt a simulacrum of independence in 1922. Something analogous occurred in Iraq, where a widespread armed uprising in 1920 obliged the British to grant self-rule under an Arab monarchy headed by the same Amir Faysal, now with the title of king. Within a little more than a decade after World War I, Turks, Iranians, Syrians, Egyptians, and Iraqis all achieved a measure of independence, albeit often highly constrained and severely limited. In Palestine, the British operated with a different set of rules.

IN 1922, THE new League of Nations issued its Mandate for Palestine, which formalized Britain's governance of the country. In an extraordinary gift to the Zionist movement, the Mandate not only incorporated the text of the Balfour Declaration verbatim, it substantially amplified the declaration's commitments. The document begins with a reference to Article 22 of the Covenant of the League of Nations, which states that for "certain communities . . . their existence as independent nations can be provisionally recognized." It continues by giving an international pledge to uphold the provisions of the Balfour Declaration. The clear implication of this sequence is that only one people in Palestine is to be recognized with national rights: the Jewish people. This was in contradistinction to every other Middle Eastern mandated territory, where Article 22 of the covenant applied to the entire population and was ultimately meant to allow for some form of independence of these countries.

In the third paragraph of the Mandate's preamble, the Jewish people, and only the Jewish people, are described as having a historic connection to Palestine. In the eyes of the drafters, the entire two-thousand-year-old built environment of the country with its villages, shrines, castles, mosques, churches, and monuments dating to the Ottoman, Mameluke, Ayyubid, Crusader, Abbasid, Umayyad, Byzantine, and earlier periods belonged to no people at all, or only to amorphous religious groups. There were people there, certainly, but they had no history or collective existence, and could therefore be ignored. The roots of what the Israeli sociologist Baruch Kimmerling called the "politicide" of the Palestinian people are on full display in the Mandate's preamble. The surest way to eradicate a people's right to their land is to deny their historical connection to it.

Nowhere in the subsequent twenty-eight articles of the Mandate is there any reference to the Palestinians as a people with national or political rights. Indeed, as in the Balfour Declaration, the words "Arab" and "Palestinian" do not appear. The only protections envisaged for the great majority of Palestine's population involved personal and religious rights and preservation of the status quo at sacred sites. On the other hand, the Mandate laid out the key means for establishing and expanding the national home for the Jewish people, which, according to its drafters, the Zionist movement was not creating, but "reconstituting."

Seven of the Mandate's twenty-eight articles are devoted to the privileges and facilities to be extended to the Zionist movement to implement the national home policy (the others deal with administrative and diplomatic matters, and the longest article treats the question of antiquities). The Zionist movement, in its embodiment in Palestine as the Jewish Agency, was explicitly designated as the official representative of the country's Jewish population, although before the mass immigration of committed European Zionists the Jewish community comprised mainly either religious or *mizrahi* Jews who in the main were not Zionist or who even opposed Zionism. Of course, no such official representative was designated for the unnamed Arab majority.

Article 2 of the Mandate provided for self-governing institutions; however, the context makes clear that this applied only to the *yishuv*, as the Jewish population of Palestine was called, while the Palestinian majority was consistently denied access to such institutions. (Any later concessions offered on matters of representation, such as a British proposal for an Arab Agency, were conditional on equal representation for the tiny minority and the large majority, and on Palestinian acceptance of the terms of the Mandate, which explicitly nullified their existence— only the first Catch-22 in which the Palestinians would find themselves trapped.) Representative institutions for the entire country on a democratic basis and with real power were never on offer (in keeping with Lloyd George's private assurance to Weizmann), for the Palestinian majority would naturally have voted to end the privileged position of the Zionist movement in their country.

One of the key provisions of the Mandate was Article 4, which gave the Jewish Agency quasi-governmental status as a "public body" with wide-ranging powers in economic and social spheres and the ability "to assist and take part in the development of the country" as a whole.

Beyond making the Jewish Agency a partner to the mandatory government, this provision allowed it to acquire international diplomatic status and thereby formally represent Zionist interests before the League of Nations and elsewhere. Such representation was normally an attribute of sovereignty, and the Zionist movement took great advantage of it to bolster its international standing and act as a para-state. Again, no such powers were allowed to the Palestinian majority over the entire thirty years of the Mandate, in spite of repeated demands.

Article 6 enjoined the mandatory power to facilitate Jewish immigration and encourage "close settlement by Jews on the land"—a most crucial provision, given the importance of demography and control of land throughout the subsequent century of struggle between Zionism and the Palestinians. This provision was the foundation for significant growth in the Jewish population and the acquisition of strategically located lands that allowed for control of the country's territorial backbone along the coast, in eastern Galilee, and in the great fertile Marj Ibn 'Amer valley connecting them.

Article 7 provided for a nationality law to facilitate the acquisition of Palestinian citizenship by Jews. This same law was used to deny nationality to Palestinians who had emigrated to the Americas during the Ottoman era and now desired to return to their homeland.[42] Thus Jewish immigrants, irrespective of their origins, could acquire Palestinian nationality, while native Palestinian Arabs who happened to be abroad when the British took over were denied it. Finally, other articles allowed the Jewish Agency to take over or establish public works, allowed each community to maintain schools in its own language—which meant Jewish Agency control over much of the *yishuv*'s school system—and made Hebrew an official language of the country.

In sum, the Mandate essentially allowed for the creation of a Zionist administration parallel to that of the British mandatory government, which was tasked with fostering and supporting it. This parallel body was meant to exercise for one part of the population many of the functions of a sovereign state, including democratic representation and control of education, health, public works, and international diplomacy. To enjoy all the attributes of sovereignty, this entity lacked only military force. That would come, in time.

To fully appreciate the particularly destructive force of the Mandate for Palestinians, it is worth returning to Article 22 of the Covenant of the League of Nations and looking at a confidential memo written by

Lord Balfour in September 1919. For areas formerly part of the Ottoman Empire, Article 22 ("provisionally") recognized their "existence as independent nations." The background to this article in relation to the Middle East involved repeated British promises of independence to *all* the Arabs of the Ottoman domains during World War I in return for their support against the Ottomans, as well as the self-determination proclaimed by Woodrow Wilson. Indeed, all the other mandated territories in the Middle East ultimately won independence (although both mandatory powers, Britain and France, twisted the rules to maintain the maximum degree of control for the longest possible time).

Only the Palestinians were denied these advantages, while representative institutions and progress toward self-rule were obtained by the Jewish population in Palestine, which benefited uniquely from Article 22 of the covenant. For decades, British officials disingenuously but steadfastly maintained that Palestine had been excluded from wartime promises of Arab independence. However when relevant extracts from the Husayn-McMahon correspondence were revealed for the first time in 1938, the British government was forced to admit that the language used was at the very least ambiguous.[43]

As we have seen, one of the officials most deeply involved in depriving Palestinians of their rights was Britain's foreign secretary, Lord Arthur Balfour. A diffident, worldly patrician and former prime minister and nephew of long-time Tory Prime Minister Lord Salisbury, he had served for five years as Britain's chief secretary in Ireland, the empire's oldest colony, where he was much hated, earning the nickname "Bloody Balfour."[44] Ironically, it was his government that authored the 1905 Aliens Act, meant primarily to keep destitute Jews fleeing tsarist pogroms out of Britain. A confirmed cynic, he nevertheless held a few beliefs, one of which was the utility to the British Empire, and the moral rightness, of Zionism, a cause to which he was enlisted by Chaim Weizmann. In spite of this belief, Balfour was clear-eyed regarding the implications of his government's actions that others preferred to pretend did not exist.

In a confidential September 1919 memo (not publicly known until its publication over three decades later in a collection of documents on the interwar period[45]), Balfour set out for the cabinet his analysis of the complications Britain had created for itself in the Middle East as a result of its conflicting pledges. On the multiple contradictory commitments of the Allies—including those embodied in the Husayn-McMahon correspondence, the Sykes-Picot Agreement, and the Covenant of the League of Nations—Balfour was scathing. After summarizing the incoherence of British policy in Syria and Mesopotamia, he bluntly assessed the situation in Palestine:

> The contradiction between the letter of the Covenant and the policy of the Allies is even more flagrant in the case of the "independent nation" of Palestine than in that of the "independent nation" of Syria. For in Palestine we do not propose even to go through the form of consulting the wishes of the present inhabitants of the country. . . . The four Great Powers are committed to Zionism. And Zionism, be it right or wrong, good or bad, is rooted in age-long traditions, in present needs, in future hopes, of far profounder import than the desires and prejudices of the 700,000 Arabs who now inhabit that ancient land.
>
> In my opinion that is right. What I have never been able to understand is how it can be harmonised with the declaration, the Covenant, or the instructions to the Commission of Enquiry.
>
> I do not think that Zionism will hurt the Arabs; but they will never say they want it. Whatever be the future of Palestine it is not now an "independent nation," nor is it yet on the way to become one. Whatever deference should be paid to the views of those who live there, the Powers in their selection of a mandatory do not propose, as I understand the matter, to consult them. In short, so far as Palestine is concerned, the Powers have made no statement of fact which is not admittedly wrong, and no declaration of policy which, at least in the letter, they have not always intended to violate.

In this brutally frank summary, Balfour set the high-minded "age-long traditions," "present needs," and "future hopes" embodied in Zionism against the mere "desires and prejudices" of the Arabs in Palestine, "who now inhabit that ancient land," implying that its population was no more than transient. Echoing Herzl, Balfour airily claimed that Zionism would not hurt the Arabs, yet he had no qualms about recognizing the bad faith and deceit that characterized British and Allied policy in Palestine. But this is of no matter. The remainder of the memo is a bland set of proposals for how to surmount the obstacles created by this tangle of hypocrisy and contradictory commitments. The only two fixed points in Balfour's summary are a concern for British imperial interests and a commitment to provide opportunities for the Zionist movement. His motivations were of a piece with those of most other senior British officials involved in crafting Palestine policy; none of them were as honest about the implications of their actions.

WHAT DID THESE contradictory British and Allied pledges, and a mandate system tailored to suit the needs of the Zionist project, produce for the Arabs of Palestine in the interwar years? The British treated the Palestinians with the same contemptuous condescension they lavished on other subject peoples from Hong Kong to Jamaica. Their officials monopolized the top offices in the Mandate government and excluded qualified Arabs;[46] they censored the newspapers, banned political activity when it discomfited them, and generally ran as parsimonious an administration as was possible in light of their commitments. As in Egypt and India, they did little to advance education, since colonial conventional wisdom held that too much of it produced "natives" who did not know their proper place. Firsthand accounts of the period are replete with instances of the racist attitudes of colonial officials to those they considered their inferiors, even if they were dealing with knowledgeable professionals who spoke perfect English.

The experience in Palestine was dissimilar to that of most other colonized peoples in this era in that the Mandate brought an influx of foreign settlers whose mission it was to take over the country. During the crucial years from 1917 until 1939, Jewish immigration and the "close settlement by Jews on the land" enjoined by the Mandate proceeded apace. The colonies established by the Zionist movement up and down the coast of Palestine and in other fertile and strategic regions served to ensure control of a territorial springboard for the domination (and ultimately the conquest) of the country, once the demographic, economic, and military balance had shifted sufficiently in favor of the *yishuv*.[47] In short order, the Jewish population tripled as a proportion of the total population, growing from a low of about 6 percent of the whole at the end of World War I to about 18 percent by 1926.

However, in spite of the extraordinary capacity of the Zionist movement to mobilize and invest capital in Palestine (financial inflows to an increasingly self-segregated Jewish economy during the 1920s were 41.5 percent larger than its net domestic product,[48] an astonishing level), between 1926 and 1932 the Jewish population ceased to grow as a proportion of the country's population, stagnating at between 17 and 18.5 percent.[49] Some of these years coincided with the global depression, when Jews leaving Palestine outpaced those arriving and capital inflows decreased markedly. At that point, the Zionist project looked as if it might never attain the critical demographic mass that would make Palestine "as Jewish as England is English," in Weizmann's words.[50]

Everything changed in 1933 with the rise to power in Germany of the Nazis, who immediately began to persecute and drive out the well-established Jewish community. With discriminatory immigration laws in place in the United States, the United Kingdom, and other countries, many German Jews had nowhere to go but Palestine. Hitler's ascendancy proved to be one of the most important events in the modern histories of both Palestine and Zionism. In 1935 alone, more than sixty thousand Jewish immigrants came to Palestine, a number greater than the entire Jewish population of the country in 1917. Most of these refugees, mainly from Germany but also from neighboring countries where anti-Semitic persecution was intensifying, were skilled and educated. German Jews were allowed to bring assets worth a total of $100 million, thanks to the Transfer Agreement reached between the Nazi government and the Zionist movement, concluded in exchange for lifting a Jewish boycott of Germany.[51]

During the 1930s the Jewish economy in Palestine overtook the Arab sector for the first time, and the Jewish population grew to more than 30 percent of the total by 1939. In light of fast economic growth and this rapid population shift over only seven years, combined with considerable expansion of the Zionist movement's military capacities, it became clear to its leaders that the demographic, economic, territorial, and military nucleus necessary for achieving domination over the entire country, or most of it, would soon be in place. As Ben-Gurion put it at the time, "immigration at the rate of 60,000 a year means a Jewish state in all Palestine."[52] Many Palestinians came to similar conclusions.

Palestinians now saw themselves inexorably turning into strangers in their own land, as 'Isa al-'Isa had warned in dire tones in 1929. Over the first twenty years of British occupation, the Palestinians' increasing resistance to the Zionist movement's growing dominance had found expression in periodic outbreaks of violence, which occurred in spite of commitments by the Palestinian leadership to the British to keep their followers in line. In the countryside, sporadic attacks, often described by the British and the Zionists as "banditry," bespoke the popular anger at Zionist land purchases, which often resulted in the expulsion of peasants from lands they considered to be theirs that were their source of livelihood. In the cities, demonstrations against British rule and the expansion of the Zionist para-state grew larger and more militant in the early 1930s.

Trying to maintain control of events, the elite notables organized a pan-Islamic conference while sending several delegations to London and coordinating various forms of protest. These leaders, however, unwilling to confront the British too openly, withstood Palestinian calls for a full boycott of the British authorities and a tax strike. They remained unable to see that their timid diplomatic approach could not possibly convince any British government to renounce its commitment to Zionism or to acquiesce in the Palestinians' demands.

In consequence, these elite efforts failed to halt the march of the Zionist project or to advance the Palestinian cause in any way. Nevertheless, in response to growing Palestinian agitation, and especially following the outbreaks of violent unrest, different British governments were obliged to reexamine their policies in Palestine. The result was a variety of commissions of inquiry and white papers. These included the Hayward Commission in 1920, the Churchill White Paper in 1922, the Shaw Commission in 1929, the Hope-Simpson Report in 1930, the Passfield White Paper in 1930, the Peel Commission in 1937, and the Woodhead Commission in 1938. However, these policy papers recommended only limited measures to placate the Palestinians (most of which were countermanded by the government in London under pressure from the Zionists) or proposed a course of action that only compounded their deep sense of injustice. The eventual result was an unprecedented, country-wide violent explosion in Palestine starting in 1936.

THE FRUSTRATION OF the Palestinian population at their leadership's ineffective response over fifteen years of congresses, demonstrations, and futile meetings with obdurate British officials finally led to a massive grassroots uprising. This started with a six-month general strike, one of the longest in colonial history, launched spontaneously by groups of young, urban middle-class militants (many of them members of the Istiqlal Party) all over the country. The strike eventually developed into the great 1936–39 revolt, which was the crucial event of the interwar period in Palestine.

In the two decades after 1917, the Palestinians had been unable to develop an overarching framework for their national movement such as the Wafd in Egypt or the Congress Party in India or Sinn Fein in Ireland. Nor did they maintain an apparently solid national front as some other peoples fighting colonialism had managed to do. Their efforts were undermined by the hierarchical, conservative, and divided nature of Palestinian society and politics, characteristic of many in the region, and further sapped by a sophisticated policy of divide and rule adopted by the mandatory authorities, aided and abetted by the Jewish Agency. This colonial strategy may have reached its peak of perfection in Palestine after hundreds of years of maturation in Ireland, India, and Egypt.

The British policies meant to divide the Palestinians included co-opting factions of their elite, setting members of the same family, such as the Husaynis, against one another, and inventing out of whole cloth "traditional institutions" to serve their purposes. Examples of these British creations were the position of grand mufti of all Palestine (traditionally, there had been four muftis of Jerusalem, not all of Palestine: one each for the Hanafi, Shafi'i, Maliki, and Hanbali rites) and the Supreme Muslim Council to administer Muslim community affairs. The British had nominated Hajj Amin al-Husayni as grand mufti and head of the council after he pledged to Sir Herbert Samuel during a sort of job interview that he would maintain order (which he did for the better part of fifteen years).[53] His appointment served two purposes. One was to create an alternative leadership structure to the nationalist Arab Executive of the Palestinian congresses, which was headed by the mufti's cousin, Musa Kazim Pasha al-Husayni, and thus also to instigate friction between the two men. The other was to enforce the idea that, besides the Jewish people, with its national characteristics, the Arab population of Palestine had no national nature and consisted only of religious communities. These measures were meant to distract the Palestinians from demanding democratic, nationwide representative institutions, to divide the national movement, and to prevent the creation of a single national alternative to the Mandate and its Zionist charge.[54]

Although the tactics of divide and rule were fairly successful until the mid-1930s, the six-month general strike of 1936 constituted a popular and spontaneous explosion from the bottom up that took the British, the Zionists, and the elite Palestinian leadership by surprise, and that obliged the latter to put aside its divisions, at least nominally. The result was the creation of the Arab Higher Committee, which was set up to lead and represent the entire Arab majority, although the British never recognized the AHC as representative. The committee was made up entirely of men, all people of substance, and all members of the Palestinian elite in its service, landowning, and merchant wings. The AHC tried to take charge of the general strike, but unfortunately their most important achievement was to broker an end to it in the fall of 1936 at the request of several Arab rulers, who were essentially acting at the behest of their patrons, the British. They promised the Palestinian leadership that the British would provide redress for their grievances.

The disappointing outcome of this intervention came in July 1937, when a Royal Commission under Lord Peel charged with investigating the unrest in Palestine proposed to partition the country, creating a small Jewish state in about 17 percent of the territory, from which over two hundred thousand Arabs would be expelled (expulsion was euphemized as "transfer"). Under this scheme, the rest of the country was to remain under British control or be handed over to Britain's client, Amir 'Abdullah of Transjordan, which from a Palestinian perspective amounted to much the same thing. Once again, the Palestinians had been treated as if they had no national existence and no collective rights.

The Peel Commission's satisfaction of the basic Zionist aims of statehood and removal of the Palestinians, albeit not in the whole of Palestine, combined with its denial of their fervently desired goal of self-determination, goaded the Palestinians into a much more militant stage of their uprising. The armed revolt that broke out in October 1937 swept the country. It was only brought under control two years later through a massive use of force, just in time for crack British military units (by then there were a hundred thousand troops in Palestine, one for every four adult Palestinian men) to be redeployed to fight World War II. The revolt achieved remarkable temporary successes but ultimately produced debilitating results for the Palestinians.

Of all the services Britain provided to the Zionist movement before 1939, perhaps the most valuable was the armed suppression of Palestinian resistance in the form of the revolt. The bloody war waged against the country's majority, which left 14 to 17 percent of the adult male Arab population killed, wounded, imprisoned, or exiled,[55] was the best illustration of the unvarnished truths uttered by Jabotinsky about the necessity of the use of force for the Zionist project to succeed. To quash the uprising, the British Empire brought in two additional divisions of troops, squadrons of bombers, and all the paraphernalia of repression that it had perfected over many decades of colonial wars.[56]

The refinements of callousness and cruelty employed went well beyond summary executions. For possession of a single bullet, Shaykh Farhan al-Sa'di, an eighty-one-year-old rebel leader, was put to death in 1937. Under the martial law in force at the time, that single bullet was sufficient to merit capital punishment, particularly for an accomplished guerrilla fighter like al-Sa'di.[57] Well over a hundred such sentences of execution were handed down after summary trials by military tribunals, with many more Palestinians executed on the spot by British troops.[58] Infuriated by rebels ambushing their convoys and blowing up their trains, the British resorted to tying Palestinian prisoners to the front of armored cars and locomotives to prevent rebel attack, a tactic they had pioneered in a futile effort to crush resistance of the Irish during their war of independence from 1919 to 1921.[59] Demolitions of the homes of imprisoned or executed rebels, or of presumed rebels or their relatives, was routine, another tactic borrowed from the British playbook developed in Ireland.[60] Two other imperial practices employed extensively in repressing the Palestinians were the detention of thousands without trial and the exile of troublesome leaders.

The explosive reaction to the Peel Commission's partition recommendation culminated in the assassination of the British district commissioner for Galilee, Captain Lewis Andrews, in October 1937. In response to this direct challenge to British authority, the Mandate authorities deported virtually the entire Palestinian nationalist leadership, including the mayor of Jerusalem, Dr. Husayn al-Khalidi, my uncle. With four others (he and another two were members of the AHC) he was sent to the Seychelles Islands, an isolated location in the Indian Ocean that the British Empire frequently chose for exiling nationalist opponents.[61] The men were held in a heavily guarded compound for sixteen months, deprived of visitors and outside contact. Their fellow prisoners in the Seychelles included political leaders from Aden in Yemen and Zanzibar. Other Palestinian leaders were exiled to Kenya or South Africa, while a few, including the mufti, managed to escape and made their way to Lebanon. Still others were confined, generally without trial, in more than a dozen of what the British themselves called "concentration camps," most notably that in Sarafand. Among them was another uncle of mine, Ghalib, who like his older brother was involved in nationalist activity deemed to be anti-British.

Just before his arrest and exile, Husayn al-Khalidi, who served on the AHC and as Jerusalem's elected mayor for three years before he was removed by the British, encountered Major General Sir John Dill, the officer in command of the British forces in Palestine. In his memoirs, my uncle recalls telling the general that the only way to end the violence was to meet some of the Palestinians' demands, specifically stopping Jewish immigration. What would be the effect of arresting the Arab leadership? Dill wanted to know. A senior Arab figure had told him that such arrests would end the revolt in days or weeks. My uncle set him straight: the revolt would only accelerate and spread out of control. It was the Jewish Agency that wanted the arrests, and al-Khalidi knew that the Colonial Office was considering it, but solving the Palestine question would not be so simple.[62]

My uncle had been right. In the months after his exile and the mass arrests of others, the revolt entered its most intense phase, and British forces lost control of several urban areas and much of the countryside,

Members of the Higher Arab Committee in exile in the Seychelles Islands, 1938. Dr. Husayn is seated on the left.

which were taken over and governed by the rebels.[63] In the words of Dill's successor, Lieutenant General Robert Haining, in August 1938, "The situation was such that civil administration of the country was, to all practical purposes, non-existent."[64] In December, Haining reported to the War Office that "practically every village in the country harbours and supports the rebels and will assist in concealing their identity from the Government Forces."[65] It took the full might of the British Empire, which could only be unleashed when more troops became available after the Munich Agreement in September 1938, and nearly a year more of fierce fighting, to extinguish the Palestinian uprising.

Meanwhile, deep differences had appeared among the Palestinians. Some, aligned with Amir 'Abdullah of Jordan, quietly welcomed the Peel Commission's recommendation of partition, as it favored attaching to Transjordan the part of Palestine that would not be transformed into the new Jewish state. Most Palestinians, however, strongly opposed all aspects of the recommendations—whether the partition of their country, the establishment in it of a Jewish state, however small, or the expulsion from that state of most of its Arab population. Thereafter, as the revolt reached its height in late 1937 and early 1938, an even more intense internecine conflict among Palestinians followed a bitter split between those loyal to the mufti, who favored no compromise with the British, and the mufti's opponents, led by the former Jerusalem mayor Raghib al-Nashashibi, who were more conciliatory. In the view of 'Isa al-'Isa, inter-Palestinian disputes, which resulted in hundreds of assassinations in the late 1930s, gravely sapped the strength of the Palestinians. He himself was forced into exile to Beirut in 1938 after his life was threatened and his house in Ramleh burned with the loss of all his books and papers. This was undoubtedly the work of the mufti's men, and it left him deeply bitter.[66] If at the outset the revolt "was directed against the English and the Jews," he wrote, it was "transformed into a civil war, where methods of terrorism, pillage, theft, fire and murder became common."[67]

IN SPITE OF the sacrifices made—which can be gauged from the very large numbers of Palestinians who were killed, wounded, jailed, or exiled—and the revolt's momentary success, the consequences for the Palestinians were almost entirely negative. The savage British repression, the death and exile of so many leaders, and the conflict within their ranks left the Palestinians divided, without direction, and with their economy debilitated by the time the revolt was crushed in the summer of 1939. This put the Palestinians in a very weak position to confront the now invigorated Zionist movement, which had gone from strength to strength during the revolt, obtaining lavish amounts of arms and extensive training from the British to help them suppress the uprising.[68]

As war clouds loomed in Europe in 1939, however, momentous new global challenges to the British Empire combined with the impact of the Arab Revolt to produce a major shift in London's policy, away from its previous full-throated support of Zionism. While the Zionists had been delighted by Britain's decisive smashing of Palestinian resistance, this new shift confronted their leaders with a critical situation. As Europe slid inexorably toward another world war, the British knew that this conflict would be fought, like the previous one, in part on Arab soil. It was now imperative, in terms of core imperial strategic interests, to improve Britain's image and defuse the fury in the Arab countries and the Islamic world at the forcible repression of the Great Revolt, particularly as these areas were being deluged with Axis propaganda about British atrocities in Palestine. A January 1939 report to the cabinet recommending a change of course in Palestine stressed the importance of "winning the confidence of Egypt and the neighbouring Arab states."[69] The report included a comment from the secretary of state for India, who said that "the Palestine problem is not merely an Arabian problem, but is fast becoming a Pan-Islamic problem"; he warned that if the "problem" was not dealt with properly, "serious trouble in India must be apprehended."[70]

After the failure of a conference held in the spring of 1939 at St. James's Palace in London involving representatives of the Palestinians, the Zionists, and the Arab states, Neville Chamberlain's government issued a White Paper in an attempt to appease outraged Palestinian, Arab, and Indian Muslim opinion. This document called for a severe curtailment of Britain's commitments to the Zionist movement. It proposed strict limits on Jewish immigration and on land sales (two major Arab demands) and promised representative institutions in five years and self-determination within ten (the most important demands). Although immigration was in fact restricted, none of the other provisions was ever fully implemented.[71] Moreover, representative institutions and self-determination were made contingent on approval of all the parties, which the Jewish Agency would never give for an arrangement that would prevent the creation of a Jewish state. The minutes of the cabinet meeting of February 23, 1939, make it clear that Britain meant to withhold the substance of these two crucial concessions from the Palestinians, as the Zionist movement was to have effective veto power, which it would obviously use.[72]

The Palestinians might have gained an advantage, albeit a slight one, had they accepted the 1939 White Paper, in spite of its flaws from their perspective. Husayn al-Khalidi, for one, did not believe that the British government was sincere in any of its pledges.[73] He stated acidly that he knew at the St. James's Palace conference, which he was brought out of exile in the Seychelles to attend, that Britain "never seriously intended for one moment to be faithful to its promises." From the first sessions, it was clear to him that the conference was a means "to gain time, and to drug the Arabs, no more and no less . . . to please the Arabs so they would stop their revolution," and give the British "time to catch their breath as war clouds gathered."[74] He nevertheless came around to favoring a flexible and positive response to the White Paper, as did other Palestinian leaders such as Musa al-ʿAlami and Jamal al-Husayni, the mufti's cousin.[75] In the end, however, the mufti, after indicating that he was inclined toward acceptance, insisted on outright refusal, and his position carried the day. After the St. James's Palace conference, the British once again sent Husayn al-Khalidi into exile, this time to Lebanon. When he saw how the revolt had degenerated in the face of massive British repression and how dire the situation was in Palestine, he argued for halting the resistance. But here, too, his views were overruled.[76]

In any case, it was already too late. The Chamberlain government had only a few months left in office when it issued the White Paper, Britain was at war very soon afterward, and Winston Churchill, who succeeded Chamberlain as prime minister, was perhaps the most ardent Zionist in British public life. More important, as World War II turned into a truly global conflict with the Nazi invasion of the Soviet Union and the entry of the United States into the war after Pearl Harbor, a new world was about to be born in which Britain would at best be a second-class power. The fate of Palestine would no longer be in its hands. But as Dr. Husayn bitterly noted, by this point Britain had already more than done its duty to its Zionist protégé.

LOOKING BACK IN his three-volume memoirs written in Beirut in 1949 (during one of the many periods of exile he endured), my uncle believed that the primary problem faced by the Palestinians during the Mandate was the British.[77] He deplored the bad faith and ineptitude of the leaders of the Arab states, and he directed balanced and mostly even-keeled criticism at the failures of the Palestinian leadership, including at times his own. He saw clearly the impact of the Zionist movement's single-minded focus on complete domination of Palestine and the competence and sheer deceitful audacity of its leaders, many of whom he knew personally. But like most of his generation and class, Dr. Husayn reserved his true spleen for the British and their hostility toward the Palestinians.

He knew many of their officials well—he had served as a senior medical officer under the Mandate administration before becoming mayor of Jerusalem. He later dealt with them as a negotiator at the St. James's Palace conference in 1939 and then in Jerusalem through the fighting of 1947–48, when he was one of the few Palestinian leaders to remain in the holy city (many were still in British-ordered exile). He apparently got on with a few British officials, and the English he had learned at the Anglican St. George's School in Jerusalem and the American University of Beirut served him well in his dealings with them, but his resentment of the hypocrisy, haughtiness, and duplicity of British officialdom in general was boundless.[78] He took T. E. Lawrence ("of Arabia") as a perfect example of British perfidy (although he was careful to contrast Lawrence's frank description in *Seven Pillars of Wisdom* of his deception and betrayals of the Arabs with the honesty and uprightness of the British teachers and missionaries he knew in Jerusalem before the war).[79]

It was their consistent support for the Zionists that most angered Dr. Husayn. Even if British officials in Palestine became convinced of the unsustainable manifold costs of maintaining the iron wall to protect the Zionist project (whose leaders were often ungrateful for all that was done for them), their recommendations were almost invariably countermanded in London. At least until 1939, the Zionists were able to place their supporters, or sometimes their leaders, like the formidable Chaim Weizmann, at the elbow of key British decisionmakers in Whitehall, some of whom were also fervent Zionists. Dr. Husayn notes caustically that when official British commissions came out to Palestine to investigate the situation in the 1920s and 1930s, any conclusions they reached that were favorable to the Arabs were countered by Zionist lobbying in London, where an extraordinary degree of intimacy prevailed between Zionist leaders and senior British political figures.[80]

'Isa al-'Isa also wrote his memoirs in exile in Beirut soon after the 1948 war. His view of the interwar period differs in many respects from my uncle's. Unlike Dr. Husayn, al-'Isa had fallen out bitterly with the mufti after the Peel Commission report in 1937, and he suffered personally from the subsequent split in the Palestinian leadership. If in al-'Isa's view this internal division gravely harmed the Palestinians, so did backward social relations and lack of education among the Arabs, and above all the unwavering focus of the Zionists, backed by the British, on supplanting the indigenous population, a topic on which he had been writing eloquently for many decades. He had no love for the British nor they for him, but in his analysis the central problem was Zionism, compounded by Palestinian and Arab weakness. Fittingly, his critiques in poetry and prose of the Arab rulers after 1948 were scathing, and his descriptions of them, especially Amir 'Abdullah, are far from complimentary.

Two further things must be said in conclusion about the revolt and about Britain's repression of it. The first is that it proved the clearsightedness of Ze'ev Jabotinsky and the self-delusion of many British officials. The Zionists' colonial enterprise, aimed at taking over the country, necessarily had to produce resistance. "If you wish to colonize a land in which people are already living," Jabotinsky wrote in 1925, "you must find a garrison for the land, or find a benefactor who will provide a garrison on your behalf. . . . Zionism is a colonizing venture and, therefore, it stands or falls on the question of armed forces."[81] At least initially, only the armed forces provided by Britain could overcome the natural resistance of those being colonized.

Much earlier, the King-Crane Commission, sent out in 1919 by President Woodrow Wilson to ascertain the wishes of the peoples of the region, had come to similar conclusions as those of Jabotinsky. Told by representatives of the Zionist movement that it "looked forward to a practically complete dispossession of the present non-Jewish inhabitants of Palestine" in the course of turning Palestine into a Jewish state, the commissioners reported that none of the military experts they consulted "believed that the Zionist program could be carried out except by force of arms," and all considered that a force of "not less than 50,000 soldiers would be required" to execute this program. In the end, it took the British more than double that number of troops to prevail over the Palestinians in 1936 through 1939. In a cover letter to Wilson, the commissioners presciently warned that "if the American government decided to support the establishment of a Jewish state in Palestine, they are committing the American people to the use of force in that area, since only by force can a

Jewish state in Palestine be established or maintained."[82] The commission thereby accurately predicted the course of the subsequent century.

The second point is that both the revolt and its repression, and the consequent successful implantation of the Zionist project, were the direct, inevitable results of the policies set out in the Balfour Declaration, and the belated implementation of the declaration of war that Balfour's words embodied. Balfour did "not think that Zionism will hurt the Arabs," and initially seemed to believe there would be no significant reaction to the Zionists taking over their country. But in the words of George Orwell, "sooner or later a false belief bumps up against solid reality, usually on a battlefield,"[83] which is precisely what happened on the battlefield in the Great Revolt, to the Palestinians' lasting detriment.

AFTER 1917, THE Palestinians found themselves in a triple bind, which may have been unique in the history of resistance to colonial-settler movements. Unlike most other peoples who fell under colonial rule, they not only had to contend with the colonial power in the metropole, in this case London, but also with a singular colonial-settler movement that, while beholden to Britain, was independent of it, had its own national mission, a seductive biblical justification, and an established international base and financing. According to the British official responsible for "Migration and Statistics," the British government was not "the colonizing power here; the Jewish people are the colonizing power."[84] Making matters worse was that Britain did not rule Palestine outright; it did so as a mandatory power of the League of Nations. It was therefore bound not just by the Balfour Declaration but also by the international commitment embodied in the 1922 Mandate for Palestine.

Time and time again, expressions of deep Palestinian dissatisfaction, in the form of protests and disturbances, caused British administrators on the spot and in London to recommend modifications in policy. However, Palestine was not a crown colony or any other form of colonial possession where the British government was free to act as it pleased. If it appeared that Palestinian pressure might force Britain to violate the letter or the spirit of the Mandate, there was intensive lobbying in the League's Permanent Mandates Commission in Geneva to remind it of its overarching obligations to the Zionists.[85] Thanks to Britain's faithfulness to these obligations, by the end of the 1930s it was too late to reverse the transformation of the country or to change the lopsided balance of forces that had developed between the two sides.

The great initial disadvantage under which the Palestinians labored was compounded by the Zionist organization's massive capital investments, arduous labor, sophisticated legal maneuvers, intensive lobbying, effective propaganda, and covert and overt military means. The Jewish colonists' armed units had developed semi-clandestinely, until the British allowed the Zionist movement to operate military formations openly in the face of the Arab revolt. At this point, the Jewish Agency's collusion with the mandatory authorities reached its peak. There is a consensus among objective historians that this collusion, supported by the League of Nations, severely undermined any possibility of success for the Palestinians' struggle for the representative institutions, self-determination, and independence they believed were their right.[86]

What the Palestinians might have done to get out of this triple bind is an impossible question to answer. Some have argued that they should have abandoned the preferred legalistic approach of their conservative leadership of mounting empty protests and fruitlessly sending delegations to London, to appeal to British goodwill and "fair-mindedness." Instead, this thesis suggests, they should have broken completely with the British, refused to cooperate with the Mandate (as had the Congress Party with the Raj in India or Sinn Fein with the British in Ireland), and, failing all else, they should have followed the path of their Arab neighbors and risen up in arms much sooner than they ultimately did.[87] In any case, they had very few good choices in the face of the powerful triad of Britain, the Zionist movement, and the League of Nations Mandate. Moreover, they had no serious allies, besides the support of amorphous, inchoate Arab public opinion, which was solidly behind them even before 1914 but all the more so as the interwar period wore on. No Arab country (except Saudi Arabia and Yemen), however, enjoyed full independence; indeed all of them were largely still under the thumb of the British and the French, and none had fully democratic institutions, such that this pro-Palestinian opinion could express itself fully.

When the British left Palestine in 1948, there was no need to create the apparatus of a Jewish state *ab novo*. That apparatus had in fact been functioning under the British aegis for decades. All that remained to make Herzl's prescient dream a reality was for this existing para-state to flex its military muscle against the weakened Palestinians while obtaining formal sovereignty, which it did in May 1948. The fate of Palestine had thus been decided thirty years earlier, although the denouement did not come until the very end of the Mandate, when its Arab majority was finally dispossessed by force.

The Second Declaration of War,
1947–1948

Partition both in principle and in substance can only be
regarded as an anti-Arab solution.
                    —United Nations Special Commission on Palestine,
                                        Minority Report[1]

A few months before he died in 1968, my father, sensing that he had little
time left, sat with me in our dining room and told me of a message he
had been asked to deliver two decades earlier. I was a nineteen-year-old
college student at this time; he bade me to listen carefully.

   In 1947, my father, Ismail Raghib al-Khalidi, returned to Palestine for
the first time in eight years. He had left in the fall of 1939 for graduate
study at the University of Michigan and thereafter at Columbia University in New York, and had remained in the United States during World
War II, working at the Office of War Information as an Arabic-language
broadcaster to the Middle East. During the war, my grandmother in
Jaffa would stay up until after midnight to listen to the radio to hear her
youngest son, whom she had not seen for years.[2] At the time of his return
visit to Palestine, he was serving as secretary of the newly formed Arab-
American Institute (my Lebanese-born mother worked there, too—it
was where my parents had met).[3] The institute had been set up by a group
of notable Arab-Americans under the direction of Professor Philip Hitti,

of Princeton, to raise American awareness of the situation in Palestine,[4] and a Middle Eastern tour to introduce its work to the leaders of the newly independent Arab states had brought my father to Jerusalem.[5]

His brother, Dr. Husayn Fakhri al-Khalidi, the former mayor of Jerusalem, was older by twenty years. In view of the great age of their father and of Dr. Husayn's eminence, Ismail and the three other younger siblings, Ghalib, Fatima, and Ya'coub, had been placed under the charge of Dr. Husayn, who oversaw discipline, money, and other matters.[6] Another older brother, Ahmad, who was a widely recognized educator, writer, and the head of the Government Arab College in Jerusalem, was in charge of their education. In spite of the twenty-year age difference and Dr. Husayn's reputation for severity, he and my father were close, as is evidenced by their correspondence while Husayn was imprisoned by the British in the Seychelles Islands. In diaries written while he was in exile, Dr. Husayn complains at one point about the execrable English of a letter

Ismail al-Khalidi, broadcasting to the Middle East for the United Nations.

he received from my father ("his writing is dreadful") and hopes that studying at the American University of Beirut would improve it. It did.[7] Photos show that Dr. Husayn was a dignified and formidable-looking man, but by the late 1940s he was worn, and much thinner than he had been before his nearly seven years of imprisonment and exile (while in the Seychelles he lost twenty-four pounds). As one of the few Arab leaders still in Jerusalem in late 1947, a time of great crisis for the Palestinians, he was intensely busy. Yet he summoned his youngest brother, and my father responded with alacrity.

Dr. Husayn knew that Ismail was going to Amman at the behest of the Arab-American Institute to see King 'Abdullah of Transjordan, and he wanted to send him a personal but official message. When my father heard its contents, he blanched. On behalf of Dr. Husayn and the Arab Higher Committee of which he was the secretary, Ismail was to tell the king that while the Palestinians appreciated his offer of "protection" (he had used the Arabic *wisaya,* literally "tutelage" or "guardianship"), they were unable to accept. The implicit meaning of the message was that were the Palestinians to succeed in escaping the British yoke, they did not want to come under that of Jordan (which, given pervasive British influence in Amman, meant much the same thing). They aspired to control their own fate.

My father weakly protested that passing on this most unwelcome news would ruin his visit, which was meant to gain the king's support for the work of the Arab-American Institute. Dr. Husayn cut him off. Other envoys had brought King 'Abdullah the same message repeatedly but he had refused to listen. Given the importance of family ties, he would be obliged to believe it coming from Dr. Husayn's own brother. He curtly told Ismail to do as he had been asked and ushered him out of the office. My father left with a heavy heart. Respect for his older brother obliged him to transmit the message, but he knew that his visit to Amman would not end well.

King 'Abdullah received his guest and listened politely but without great interest to Ismail's enthusiastic report of how the Arab-American Institute was working to change American opinion on Palestine, which, even then, was overwhelmingly pro-Zionist and largely ignorant of the Palestinian cause. For decades, the king had attached his fortunes to those of Great Britain, which subsidized his throne, paid for and equipped his troops, and officered his Arab Legion. By contrast, the United States seemed far away and insignificant, and the king appeared manifestly unimpressed. Like most Arab rulers at the time, he failed to appreciate the postwar role of the United States in world affairs.

Having carried out the main part of his mission, my father then hesitantly conveyed the message Dr. Husayn had entrusted to him. The king's face registered anger and surprise, and he abruptly stood up, compelling everyone else in the room to stand as well. The audience was over. Exactly at that moment, a servant entered, announcing that the BBC had just broadcast the news of the UN General Assembly's decision in favor of the partition of Palestine. It happened that my father's meeting with the king had coincided with the assembly's historic vote on November 29, 1947, on Resolution 181, which provided for partition. Before stalking out of the room, the king turned to my father and said coldly, "You Palestinians have refused my offer. You deserve what happens to you."

WHAT HAPPENED IS, of course, now well known. By the summer of 1949, the Palestinian polity had been devastated and most of its society uprooted. Some 80 percent of the Arab population of the territory that at war's end became the new state of Israel had been forced from their homes and lost their lands and property. At least 720,000 of the 1.3 million Palestinians were made refugees. Thanks to this violent transformation, Israel controlled 78 percent of the territory of former Mandatory Palestine, and now ruled over the 160,000 Palestinian Arabs who had been able to remain, barely one-fifth of the prewar Arab population. This seismic upheaval—the Nakba, or the Catastrophe, as Palestinians call it—grounded in the defeat of the Great Revolt in 1939 and willed by the Zionist state-in-waiting, was also caused by factors that were on vivid display in the story my father told me: foreign interference and fierce inter-Arab rivalries. These problems were compounded by intractable Palestinian internal differences that endured after the defeat of the revolt, and by the absence of modern Palestinian state institutions. The Nakba was only finally made possible, however, by massive global shifts during World War II.

The outbreak of war in 1939 put an end to the wrangling over the British White Paper and brought a relative lull after the upheavals of the revolt. Still, for three years, until the battles of al-Alamein and Stalingrad in the fall of 1942, the danger of Nazi panzers arriving from Libya or through the Caucasus was ever present. Jewish immigration slowed significantly as a result of the White Paper and wartime conditions, while Zionist leaders, enraged at what they perceived as Whitehall's abandonment of its commitments to Zionism, shrewdly looked to engineer a diplomatic realignment away from Britain and toward new patrons. However, during this lull, the Zionists were able to continue to build up their military capabilities. Under pressure from the Zionist movement and with support from British prime minister Winston Churchill, a Jewish Brigade Group of the British army was formed in 1944, providing the already considerable Zionist military forces with training and combat experience, offering a vital advantage in the conflict to come.

By contrast, although a wartime boom in Palestine enabled some recovery from the damage caused to the Arab economy by the revolt, the Palestinians remained fragmented politically, with many of their leaders still in exile or in British detention, and failed to make sufficient preparations for the brewing storm. Over twelve thousand Palestinian Arabs volunteered for the British army during World War II (while many others like my father did war work for the Allies), but unlike the Jewish soldiers from Palestine, they never constituted a single unit, and there was no Palestinian para-state to take advantage of the experience they had garnered.[8]

The end of the world war brought a new phase of the colonial assault on Palestine, launched by the arrival in the Middle East of two great powers that had previously played small regional roles: the United States and the USSR. An empire that had never fully acknowledged its colonial nature and whose domain had been restricted to the Americas and the Pacific, after Pearl Harbor the United States suddenly became not just a global power but the preeminent one. Starting in 1942, American ships, troops, and bases arrived in North Africa, Iran, and Saudi Arabia. They have not left the Middle East since. Meanwhile, the USSR, which had turned inward after the Bolshevik revolution, spreading its ideology but avoiding projecting its strength, had the largest land army in the world as a result of the war, would liberate half of Europe from the Nazis, and became increasingly assertive in Iran, Turkey, and other areas to its south.

Led by the dominant political figure in the *yishuv*, David Ben-Gurion, the Zionist movement presciently foresaw the shift in the global balance of power. The key event in this realignment was the proclamation in 1942 at a major Zionist conference held at the Biltmore Hotel in New York of what was called the Biltmore Program.[9] For the first time, the Zionist movement openly called for turning all of Palestine into a Jewish state: the exact demand was that "Palestine be established as a Jewish Common-wealth." As with the "national home," this was another circumlocution for full Jewish control over the entirety of Palestine, a country with a two-thirds Arab majority.[10] It was no coincidence that this ambitious program was proclaimed in the United States and in New York in particular, then and now the city with the largest Jewish population in the world.

Before long, the Zionist movement had mobilized many American politicians and much of public opinion around this objective. This was a result both of this movement's unceasing and effective public relations efforts, which the Palestinians and the fledgling Arab states were unable to match, and of widespread horror at the revelation of the destruction of most of European Jewry by the Nazis in the Holocaust.[11] After President Harry Truman endorsed the goal of a Jewish state in a majority Arab land in the post-war years, Zionism, once a colonial project backed by the declining British Empire, became part and parcel of the emerging American hegemony in the Middle East.

Following the war, two crucial events that occurred in quick succes-sion were emblematic of the obstacles ahead for the Palestinians. Their relations with many of the Arab regimes were already fraught because of the Arab rulers' alignment with Britain, going back to their intervention to end the 1936 general strike and their involvement in the failed 1939 St. James's Palace Conference. Things grew worse in March 1945 when, under the aegis of Great Britain, six Arab states formed the Arab League. In his memoirs, Dr. Husayn describes the Palestinians' bitter disappoint-ment that the member states decided to remove references to Palestine from the League's inaugural communiqué and to retain control over the choice of Palestine's representative.[12]

The Egyptian prime minister blocked Musa al-'Alami, the Palestinian emissary, from attending the League's founding conference, but reversed his decision immediately when al-'Alami secured a letter from Brigadier Clayton, a British intelligence officer in Cairo, who authorized his participation. Although the Alexandria Protocol of October 1944, whereby Egypt, Iraq, Syria, Lebanon, and Transjordan originally agreed to create the League, had stressed the importance of the "cause of the Arabs of Palestine," while "regretting the woes that have been inflicted on the Jews of Europe," these states were barely independent of their former colonial masters.[13] Britain in particular had a powerful influence on the foreign policy of all of them, and British hostility toward any independent Palestinian initiative had not abated. This meant that the Palestinians could not count on any significant support from these weak and dependent Arab regimes.

More far-reaching in its consequences was the formation of the Anglo-American Committee of Inquiry in 1946. This body was established by the British and US governments to consider the urgent and pitiful situation of Jewish Holocaust survivors, a hundred thousand of whom were confined to displaced-persons camps in Europe. The American and Zionist preference was for these unfortunates to be granted immediate entry to Palestine (neither the US nor the UK being willing to accept them), in effect negating the thrust of the 1939 White Paper.

The Palestinian case was presented to the committee by Albert Hourani (later to become perhaps the greatest historian of the modern Middle East), who, with colleagues in the newly formed Palestinian Arab Office, had produced a large quantity of materials that was transmitted in written and oral form.[14] Their main effort was embodied in Hourani's testimony,[15] which offered a prescient description of the devastation and chaos that the creation of a Jewish state would wreak on Palestinian society and sow throughout the Arab world. He warned the committee that "in the past few years responsible Zionists have talked seriously about the evacuation of the Arab population, or part of it, to other parts of the Arab world."[16] The implementation of the Zionist program, he said, "would involve a terrible injustice and could only be carried out at the expense of dreadful repressions and disorders, with the risk of bringing down in ruins the whole political structure of the Middle East."[17] The multiple military coups by Arab officers who had fought in Palestine and then overthrew regimes in Syria, Egypt, and Iraq from 1949 to 1958, the eruption of the Soviet Union into the affairs of the Middle East in the mid-1950s, and the expulsion of Britain from the region can all be seen as aftershocks of the earthquake that Hourani had foreseen. At the time, these outcomes may have seemed far-fetched to the twelve American and British committee members who heard Hourani's testimony.

Reflecting the new balance of power between Britain and the United States, the committee ignored the case made by the Arabs and the preference of the British government, which was to continue to limit Jewish immigration to Palestine to avoid antagonizing the country's Arab majority and the populations of the newly independent Arab states. The committee came to conclusions that mirrored precisely the desires of the Zionists and the Truman administration, including the recommendation to admit a hundred thousand Jewish refugees to Palestine. This signified that the 1939 White Paper was indeed a dead letter, that Britain no longer had the decisive voice in Palestine, and that it was the United States that would become the predominant external actor there and eventually in the rest of the Middle East.

BOTH EVENTS SHOW clearly that at this advanced stage of the struggle to retain control of their homeland, the Palestinians had not developed effective Arab allies or the apparatus of a modern state, despite their intense patriotic feeling and the formation of a national movement strong enough to briefly pose a threat to British control of Palestine during the revolt. This absence meant that they were facing the well-developed para-state of the Jewish Agency without having a central state system themselves; this proved to be a fatal weakness militarily, financially, and diplomatically.

Unlike the Jewish Agency, which had been granted vital arms of governance by the League of Nations Mandate, the Palestinians had no foreign ministry, no diplomats—as my father's story attests—nor any other government department, let alone a centrally organized military force. They had neither the capacity to raise the necessary funding, nor international assent to creating state institutions. When Palestinian envoys had managed to meet with foreign officials, whether in London or Geneva, they were condescendingly told that they had no official standing, and that their meetings were therefore private rather than official.[18] The comparison with the Irish, the only people to succeed in (partially) freeing themselves of colonial rule between World Wars I and II, is striking. In spite of divisions in their ranks, their clandestine parliament, the Dail Eirann, their nascent branches of government, and their centralized military forces ultimately out-administered and outfought the British.[19]

During these critical years leading up to the Nakba, Palestinian disarray in regard to institution-building was profound. The rudimentary nature of the organizational structures available to the Palestinians is clear from the recollections of Yusif Sayigh, who was appointed as the first director-general of the newly created Arab National Fund in 1946.[20] The fund had been established by the Arab Higher Committee in 1944 to serve as a state treasury and an equivalent to the Jewish National Fund, which by then was almost half a century old. By the mid-1930s, the JNF was annually collecting $3.5 million for the colonization of Palestine in the United States alone, part of much larger sums it regularly channeled from all over the world to support the Zionist project.[21]

The Arab National Fund only began its task of collecting resources after Sayigh was appointed and developed a structure for its efforts. Sayigh recounted the many difficulties he faced in his work, from setting up a country-wide network from scratch to accepting donations to the difficulties of moving about the countryside as the security situation in Palestine deteriorated. By mid-1947, in a little over a year, the fund had managed to raise 176,000 Palestine pounds (over $700,000 at the time), an impressive sum given the relative poverty of the population. It paled in contrast to the fundraising muscle of the Zionist movement, however. When, against Sayigh's advice, a member of the fund's board, 'Izzat Tannous, boasted to the press about the sum, Sayigh and his colleagues learned the next day of a gift of a million Palestine pounds ($4 million) to the JNF by a rich Jewish widow from South Africa.

Sayigh's portrayal of the Arab Higher Committee—the Palestinian leadership body formed in 1936, disbanded by the British in 1937, and reconstituted after the war—is equally harsh, a tableau of disorganization and infighting. It should be remembered that the AHC had been outlawed and all its leaders had been imprisoned or exiled by the British during the revolt or were forced to flee the country to escape arrest. Some, like the mufti, were exiled permanently, while others, among them Dr. Husayn, the mufti's cousin Jamal al-Husayni, and Musa al-'Alami, were only allowed to return to Palestine many years later, after being exiled in different countries.[22] However, their return did not solve the problem. Sayigh describes the situation when the committee, which had no bureaucratic apparatus, was suddenly faced with the daunting task of documenting the Palestinian case to the Anglo-American Committee of Inquiry. Sayigh wrote:

> Now the Arab Higher Committee realized it didn't have the intellectual skills among its members. Indeed it had no structure at all. When Jamal Husseini left the office in the afternoon, he locked the door and put the key in his pocket. There was no secretariat, absolutely no secretariat. One or two people to make coffee. Not even a secretary who would take notes or type. It was that empty, the whole thing.[23]

The situation was in fact even worse, given the deep political and personal differences that divided its members and the inter-Arab rivalries that swirled around the AHC. All of these ills crippled the potential of another new organization formed in the immediate postwar era, the Arab Office, which the AHC had tasked with making the Palestinian argument to the Anglo-American Committee. Set up as the nucleus of a Palestinian foreign ministry and supported mainly by the pro-British Iraqi government headed by Nuri al-Sa'id, the Arab Office had both a diplomatic and informational mission, with the goal of making the Palestinian cause better known.

In contrast to the disarray of the other bodies, the Arab Office housed an extraordinary and highly motivated group of men (I have not seen an account of a single woman involved with its work). They included Musa al-'Alami, its founder; the noted educator Darwish al-Miqdadi; the lawyer Ahmad Shuqayri, who became the first head of the PLO; the future historian Albert Hourani and his younger brother, Cecil; and younger men such as the economist Burhan Dajani; Wasfi al-Tal, later the Jordanian prime minister; and my cousin, Walid Khalidi, who also went on to become a renowned academic. It was this group that put together the remarkably cogent, prescient (and ignored) presentation delivered to the Committee of Inquiry by Albert Hourani.

With its resources of talent, the Arab Office held promise to fill the function of a professional diplomatic service, such as would obviate the need, for example, for Dr. Husayn to use his young brother as an envoy. Advanced modern states do occasionally use personal envoys to convey messages alongside more conventional channels, but the Palestinians had been allowed no such channels by the British Mandate. However, this condition also arose partly from the strongly patriarchal, hierarchical, and fractious nature of their politics, especially before the era of mass-based political parties. But the Arab Office failed to remedy this condition: Yusuf Sayigh's and Walid Khalidi's recollections attest to the challenges that hamstrung the Palestinians at every turn, ultimately undermining efforts to establish competent bodies to represent them internationally. Moreover, by 1947 al-ʿAlami and Dr. Husayn, the two Palestinian leaders perhaps best suited to deal with matters of diplomatic representation, were no longer allies. Walid Khalidi describes how al-ʿAlami's high-handedness alienated colleagues,[24] for which there is ample evidence in Dr. Husayn's memoirs. More important, al-ʿAlami's closeness to the pro-British Iraqi regime provoked the suspicions of many Palestinian figures.

These inter-Palestinian differences, exacerbated by the rivalries between the newly independent Arab states, are described by Dr. Husayn in painful detail. As he shows, much of the pre-war polarization between partisans and opponents of the mufti, Hajj Amin al-Husayni, dating to the revolt and before, continued into the postwar era. The polarization was intensified by Britain's unremitting opposition to both the mufti and any independent Palestinian political entity, which they feared— probably rightly—would be hostile to Britain. This hostility to much of the Palestinian leadership was echoed by most Arab governments, over which the UK still had great influence. Britain's deft behind-the-scenes management of Palestine's representation at the Arab League's founding conference in March 1945 provides a striking example of that influence. Musa al-ʿAlami, who did finally attend the conference, was an able law-yer, according to Dr. Husayn, and spoke well in defense of the Palestinian cause, but he was also very much in the confidence of the British, who sent him on diplomatic missions on their behalf all over the region in 1945–46, at one point providing him with a British bomber for trips to Saudi Arabia, Iraq, and other Arab countries.[25]

Convinced that Britain, which did not have the best interests of the Palestinians at heart, had too much influence on al-'Alami via its support for the Arab Office, Dr. Husayn publicly criticized its performance, implicitly criticizing al-'Alami. One day in 1947 he received a visit in his Jerusalem office from a colonel of British military intelligence, who after a general discussion spoke highly of al-'Alami and of the Arab Office's work for the Arab cause and for "greater understanding and closeness between the Arab and British peoples." Dr. Husayn, whose hostility to Britain had intensified after the crushing of the Great Revolt and his own years of British-imposed exile, kept his views to himself but was puzzled by the visit. When he continued to disparage the Arab Office publicly for its failure to coordinate with the Arab Higher Committee, his military visitor returned.

This time the colonel remained standing while bluntly delivering his message: "We respect the Director of the Arab Offices, and have full confidence in him, and we want you to cooperate with him." Dr. Husayn responded coldly: "Your respect for him and your confidence in him is your business, not mine. My cooperation or noncooperation with him is my concern, not yours. Good morning, Colonel." From the moment al-'Alami was admitted to the Arab League, Dr. Husayn notes bitterly, "he became a representative of the British government, and not that of the Arabs of Palestine."[26]

Musa al-'Alami had also managed to earn the distrust of Hajj Amin al-Husayni, the still-exiled mufti, who after relocating to Cairo from Germany in 1946 had immediately reengaged in Palestinian politics. From his places of exile, he could no longer control events in Palestine, but he was still considered the paramount leader and for a time he continued to exercise influence, in spite of the lasting damage his presence in Nazi Germany during the war had done to the Palestinian cause. Al-'Alami had initially been acceptable to all concerned as the head of the Arab Office because he was not aligned with any Palestinian faction (it helped that his sister was married to the mufti's cousin, Jamal al-Husayni). However, by 1947 that nonalignment came to irk the mufti, who prized loyalty above all other virtues. Yusif Sayigh, whose work with the Arab National Fund involved meeting the mufti several times, was positively inclined toward him, but he nevertheless understood the profound limitations of the mufti's traditional style of leadership.

The basic weakness of the mufti was that he thought that the merit of the cause he was working for, namely setting up an independent Palestine, saving Palestine from takeover by the Zionists, was enough in itself. Because it was a just cause, he did not build a fighting force in the modern sense. . . . I think part of it was that he feared a big organization, he felt that he could not control a big organization. He could control an entourage, people to whom he whispered and who'd whisper to him. A big organization would have to be decentralized to a certain point, and he would lose touch. And perhaps he would have to depend on them, and they would depend less on him. Perhaps he was afraid that some leading young fighter would emerge who would be charismatic and would take away some of the loyalty and support that was his.[27]

Much in this acute analysis of the patriarchal nature of the mufti's approach applied to the entire generation of men of his class born during the late Ottoman era who dominated the Palestinian leadership, and for that matter politics in most of the Arab world. There were nascent political parties with a diverse social base in Palestine and elsewhere, such as the Syrian National Party to which Sayigh belonged. But except for Egypt, where the Wafd, a genuine mass-based political party, had dominated the country's politics since 1919, nowhere had these formations developed to the point that they eclipsed the "politics of the notables," as Albert Hourani masterfully described it in a famous 1968 essay.[28]

Having been financed primarily by Iraq's Nuri al-Sa'id and his British-backed government, the Arab Office eventually alienated other Arab states, notably Egypt and Saudi Arabia, which both aspired to pan-Arab leadership. Their leaders, as well as those of Syria and Lebanon, suspected—probably correctly—that the creation of the Arab Office was a vehicle for Iraq's regional ambitions. Other such vehicles included a project for federation among the countries of the Fertile Crescent—

Iraq, Syria, Lebanon, Jordan, and Palestine—behind which Nuri's rivals feared lurked his patron, Great Britain.[29] The Arab states' opposition, expressed through the Arab League in Cairo, itself under Egyptian influence, gravely undermined the authority and capacity of the Arab Office, ultimately further weakening the Palestinians.

Meanwhile King 'Abdullah of Transjordan had his own ambitions to dominate as much as possible of Palestine, having done his best to come to terms with both the Zionists and his British backers over his plans for the country. As Avi Shlaim reports in *Collusion Across the Jordan*, his account of this era, extensive clandestine contact took place between King 'Abdullah and Jewish Agency leaders (later Israeli prime ministers) Moshe Sharett and Golda Meir.[30] As the United Nations moved toward partition of Palestine, the king repeatedly met with them secretly in the hope of reaching an accord in which Jordan would incorporate the part of Palestine to be designated for its Arab majority. The king confidently gave them his assurances that the Palestinians would come around and assent to his rule.* Thus 'Abdullah, unlike Iraq's Nuri, had no use for any form of independent Palestinian leadership or for a body like the Arab Office that would serve as their diplomatic arm.

Beyond the strength and broad external support enjoyed by the Zionists, in contrast with the weakness and fragmentation of the Palestinian national movement, the newly independent Arab states—Iraq, Transjordan, Egypt, Syria, and Lebanon—were frail and fraught with rancorous disunity and the Palestinians had to contend with their dueling ambitions. In his attempt to impose his tutelage on the Palestinians, King 'Abdullah was in competition with Egypt's King Farouq and King 'Abd al-'Aziz ibn Sa'ud of Saudi Arabia. Other Arab leaders occasionally entertained complex, ambiguous, and surreptitious contacts with the Zionist movement, often to the detriment of the Palestinians.

At the same time, many Arab rulers continued to lean heavily on personal relations with undependable British advisors, even as British power was waning. King 'Abdullah, his brother King Faisal of Iraq and his successors there, and King 'Abd al-'Aziz ibn Sa'ud relied on British

---

*The king's confidence suddenly evaporated in late 1947. My father's story explains why.

officials, current or former, whose positions were ambiguous (one such was the commander of 'Abdullah's army, Lieutenant General Sir John Bagot Glubb, known as Glubb Pasha). In some cases these rulers were obliged by treaty to have such advisors, all of whom owed their primary loyalty to Great Britain, not to the Arab leaders they advised. This was also the case with the foreign diplomats from whom the Arab leaders accepted counsel and sometimes orders. The British ambassador's residence in Amman abutted the royal palace, providing for a short trip through the back garden to offer guidance to the king.[31] At times, such advice was quite muscular. In 1942, Ambassador Sir Miles Lampson, unhappy with the Egyptian government of the day, ordered British tanks to surround Abdeen Palace in Cairo, entered the palace grounds in his Rolls-Royce, had the palace doors shot open, and commanded King Farouq to appoint Britain's choice of prime minister. This same prime minister, Mustafa Nahhas Pasha, was the one who refused to allow Musa al-'Alami to represent Palestine at the Arab League. But the quick reversal of his decision by a British intelligence officer showed where the real power resided in Cairo. However much Arab leaders may have wished to demonstrate their postwar independence, the poor, backward states they led were entangled in a thick web of dependency, based on unequal treaties, continued foreign military occupation, and external control of their natural and other resources.

In relation to the newly powerful United States, the Arab leaders— many of them chosen by their European overlords for their pliability— demonstrated feebleness combined with a striking lack of expertise and global awareness. King 'Abd al-'Aziz of Saudi Arabia, who had farsightedly signed a crucial agreement with American oil companies in 1933 to the detriment of British oil interests, met with an ailing Franklin D. Roosevelt on board a US warship in the spring of 1945, weeks before the American leader's death. He received reassuring pledges directly from the president that the United States would do nothing to harm the Arabs of Palestine and would consult with the Arabs before taking any action there.[32] These promises were casually disregarded by Roosevelt's successor, Harry Truman, but because of the Saudi regime's economic and military dependency on the United States, the king refrained from protesting or exerting influence decisively in favor of the Palestinians. Nor did any of his six sons who succeeded him. This dependency, and the ignorance of generation after generation of Arab rulers about the workings of the American political system and international politics, would consistently deprive the Arab world of any possibility of resisting American influence or shaping US policy.

By contrast, the Zionist movement applied a highly developed understanding of global politics. Complementing its origins in Europe among well-educated, assimilated Jews such as Theodor Herzl and Chaim Weizmann, the movement also drew on deep roots and extensive connections in the United States—established decades before my father's meeting with King 'Abdullah. David Ben-Gurion and Yitzhak Ben-Zvi, later the second president of Israel, had spent several years at the end of World War I working for the Zionist cause in the United States, where Golda Meir had lived since childhood. Meanwhile, no members of the Palestinian leadership had ever visited the United States. (My father was the first of his family to do so.) Compared with the sophisticated grasp the Zionist leadership had of European and other Western societies, of which most of them were natives or citizens, Arab leaders had at best a limited understanding of the politics, societies, and cultures of the countries of Europe, to say nothing of the nascent superpowers. The Palestinian and Arab disunity conveyed by the accounts of my father, Dr. Husayn, Yusif Sayigh, and Walid Khalidi, the intrigue and infighting they describe, were ultimately disastrous, not just for the plan for the Arab Office to represent the Palestinians internationally, but also for their prospects in the climactic conflict of 1947–48. They entered this fateful contest woefully unprepared both politically and militarily, and with a fragmented and dispersed leadership. Moreover, they had little external support except from the deeply divided and unstable Arab states, still under the influence of the old colonial powers, and which had poor and largely illiterate populations. This was in stark contrast to the international standing and the strong, modern para-state built up by the Zionist movement over several decades.

SINCE 1917, THE Palestinian national movement had been faced with the antagonistic tandem of Britain and its protégé, the Zionist project. But the *yishuv* had grown more and more hostile to its British patron after the passage of the 1939 White Paper. This hostility erupted with assassinations of British officials, such as that by the Stern gang in 1944 of Lord Moyne, the resident minister in Egypt, and was followed by a sustained campaign of violence against British troops and administrators in Palestine. This culminated in the 1946 blowing up of the British HQ, the King David Hotel, with the loss of ninety-one lives. The British soon found themselves unable to master the armed opposition of virtually the entire *yishuv*, whose potent military and intelligence organizations they had themselves reinforced during the Great Revolt and World War II. Reeling from deep postwar economic and financial problems and the unwinding of the centuries-old Indian Raj, Great Britain finally capitulated in Palestine.

In 1947, the Clement Attlee government dumped the problem of Palestine into the lap of the new United Nations, which formed a UN Special Commission on Palestine (UNSCOP) to provide recommendations for the future of the country. At the UN, the dominant powers were the United States and the Soviet Union, a development the Zionist movement had shrewdly anticipated with its diplomatic efforts toward both, but which left the Palestinians and the Arabs flat-footed. The postwar realignment of international power was apparent in the workings of UNSCOP and in its majority report in favor of partitioning the country in a manner that was exceedingly favorable to the Jewish minority, giving them over 56 percent of Palestine, against the much smaller 17 percent for the Jewish state envisioned by the 1937 Peel partition plan. It was visible as well in the pressure that went into fashioning General Assembly Resolution 181, which resulted from the UNSCOP majority report.

The November 29, 1947, passage in the UN General Assembly of Resolution 181, which called for dividing Palestine into a large Jewish state and a smaller Arab one, with an international *corpus separatum* encompassing Jerusalem, reflected the new global balance of power. The United States and USSR, which both voted in favor of the resolution, now clearly played the decisive role in sacrificing the Palestinians for a Jewish state to take their place and control over most of their country. The resolution was another declaration of war, providing the international birth certificate for a Jewish state in most of what was still an Arab-majority land, a blatant violation of the principle of self-determination enshrined in the UN

Charter. The expulsion of enough Arabs to make possible a Jewish majority state necessarily and inevitably followed. Just as Balfour did not think that Zionism would hurt the Arabs, it is doubtful that when Truman and Stalin pushed through UNGA 181 they or their advisors paid much heed to what would happen to the Palestinians as a consequence of their vote.

Meanwhile, the creation of a Jewish state was no longer the outcome sought by Britain. Infuriated by the violent Zionist campaign that had driven it from Palestine, and not wishing to further alienate the Arab subjects of its remaining Middle Eastern empire, Britain abstained in the partition resolution vote. From the 1939 White Paper onward, British policymakers had recognized that their country's predominant interests in the Middle East lay with the independent Arab states and not with the Zionist project that Britain had nurtured for over two decades.

With the UN partition decision, the Zionist movement's military and civil structures were backed by both of the nascent superpowers of the postwar era and could prepare to take over as much of the country as possible. The catastrophe that ensued for the Palestinians was thus the product not only of their own and Arab weaknesses and of Zionist strength, but also of events as far afield as London, Washington, DC, Moscow, New York, and Amman.

LIKE A SLOW, seemingly endless train wreck, the Nakba unfolded over a period of many months. Its first stage, from November 30, 1947, until the final withdrawal of British forces and the establishment of Israel on May 15, 1948, witnessed successive defeats by Zionist paramilitary groups, including the Haganah and the Irgun, of the poorly armed and organized Palestinians and the Arab volunteers who had come to help them. This first stage saw a bitterly fought campaign that culminated in a country-wide Zionist offensive dubbed Plan Dalet in the spring of 1948.[33] Plan Dalet involved the conquest and depopulation in April and the first half of May of the two largest Arab urban centers, Jaffa and Haifa, and of the Arab neighborhoods of West Jerusalem, as well as of scores of Arab cities, towns, and villages, including Tiberias on April 18, Haifa on April 23, Safad on May 10, and Beisan on May 11. Thus, the ethnic cleansing of Palestine began well before the state of Israel was proclaimed on May 15, 1948.

Jaffa was besieged and ceaselessly bombarded with mortars and harassed by snipers. Once finally overrun by Zionist forces during the first weeks of May, it was systematically emptied of most of its sixty thousand Arab residents. Although Jaffa was meant to be part of the stillborn Arab state designated by the 1947 Partition Plan, no international actor attempted to stop this major violation of the UN resolution. Subjected to similar bombardments and attacks on poorly defended civilian neighborhoods, the sixty thousand Palestinian inhabitants of Haifa, the thirty thousand living in West Jerusalem, the twelve thousand in Safad, six thousand in Beisan, and 5,500 in Tiberias suffered the same fate. Most of Palestine's Arab urban population thus became refugees and lost their homes and livelihoods.

In April 1948, when the Haganah and other Zionist paramilitary units overran the Arab neighborhoods of West Jerusalem, the Arab Fund's main office in the Qatamon district was seized and its director, Yusif Sayigh, was taken prisoner. Only a few weeks earlier, Sayigh had traveled to Amman to ask King 'Abdullah for help to prevent the imminent fall of the Arab districts of West Jerusalem. However, the Jordanian consul-general in Jerusalem told the king by telephone, in Sayigh's presence, that there was no such danger, declaring: "Your Majesty! Who is telling you

Jaffa in 1948, emptied during Plan Dalet

these stories that Jerusalem is about to fall to the Zionists? Nonsense!"[34] In consequence, 'Abdullah turned down Sayigh's request and the prosperous West Jerusalem Arab neighborhoods were overrun. Sayigh spent the rest of the war in a POW camp, although he was not connected to the military.

Scenes of flight unfolded in smaller towns and villages in many parts of the country. People fled as news spread of massacres like that on April 9, 1948, in the village of Dayr Yasin near Jerusalem, where one hundred residents, sixty-seven of them women, children, and old people, were slaughtered when the village was stormed by Irgun and Haganah assailants.[35] A day earlier, the strategic nearby village of al-Qastal had fallen to Zionist forces during a battle in which the Palestinian commander of the Jerusalem area, 'Abd al-Qadir al-Husayni, died leading his fighters.[36] He too had just returned from a fruitless trip to an Arab capital, in this case Damascus, to beg for arms from an Arab League committee. 'Abd al-Qadir was the most competent and respected of Palestinian military leaders (especially after so many had been killed, executed, or exiled by the British during the Great Revolt). His death was a crushing blow to the Palestinian effort to retain control of the approaches to Jerusalem, areas that were supposed to fall to the Arab state under the partition plan.

In this first phase of the Nakba before May 15, 1948, a pattern of ethnic cleansing resulted in the expulsion and panicked departure of

Yusuf Sayigh, POW, at left

about 300,000 Palestinians overall and the devastation of many of the Arab majority's key urban economic, political, civic, and cultural centers. The second phase followed after May 15, when the new Israeli army defeated the Arab armies that joined the war. In belatedly deciding to intervene militarily, the Arab governments were acting under intense pressure from the Arab public, which was deeply distressed by the fall of Palestine's cities and villages one after another and the arrival of waves of destitute refugees in neighboring capitals.[37] In the wake of the defeat of the Arab armies, and after further massacres of civilians, an even larger number of Palestinians, another 400,000, were expelled and fled from their homes, escaping to neighboring Jordan, Syria, Lebanon, and the West Bank and Gaza (the latter two constituted the remaining 22 percent of Palestine that was not conquered by Israel). None were allowed to return, and most of their homes and villages were destroyed to prevent them from doing so.[38] Still more were expelled from the new state of Israel even after the armistice agreements of 1949 were signed, while further numbers have been forced out since then. In this sense the Nakba can be understood as an ongoing process.

Among those displaced in 1948 were my grandparents, who had to leave their Tal al-Rish home where my father and most of his siblings were born. Initially my grandfather, now eighty-five years old and frail, stubbornly refused to leave his house. After his sons took most of the family to shelter in Jerusalem and Nablus, he remained there alone for several weeks. Fearing for his safety, a family friend from Jaffa ventured to the house during a lull in the fighting to retrieve him. He left unwillingly, lamenting that he could not take his books with him. Neither he nor his children ever saw their home again. The ruins of my grandparents' large stone house still stand abandoned on the outskirts of Tel Aviv.[39]

THE NAKBA REPRESENTED a watershed in the history of Palestine and the Middle East. It transformed most of Palestine from what it had been for well over a millennium—a majority Arab country—into a new state that had a substantial Jewish majority.[40] This transformation was the result of two processes: the systematic ethnic cleansing of the Arab-inhabited areas of the country seized during the war; and the theft of Palestinian

The ruins of the Khalidi family home at Tal al-Rish

land and property left behind by the refugees as well as much of that owned by those Arabs who remained in Israel. There would have been no other way to achieve a Jewish majority, the explicit aim of political Zionism from its inception. Nor would it have been possible to dominate the country without the seizures of land. In a third major and lasting impact of the Nakba, the victims, the hundreds of thousands of Palestinians driven from their homes, served to further destabilize Syria, Lebanon, and Jordan—poor, weak, recently independent countries—and the region for years thereafter.

In the immediate aftermath, however, Transjordan's King 'Abdullah was a beneficiary of the war. Memorably described as a "falcon in a canary's cage," 'Abdullah had always wanted to rule over a larger domain with more subjects than small, sparsely populated Transjordan, which had a population of barely 200,000 when he arrived there in 1921.[41] Thereafter he sought to expand his territory through a variety of means. The most obvious direction was westward, into Palestine, whence the king's lengthy secret negotiations with the Zionists to reach an accommodation that would give him control of part of the country. To further this aim, 'Abdullah privately approved the 1937 Peel Commission's recommendation to partition Palestine (the only Arab leader to do so), which would have annexed part of the Arab section to Transjordan. Both the king and the British opposed allowing the Palestinians to benefit from the 1947 partition or the war that followed, and neither wanted an independent Arab state in Palestine. They had come to a secret agreement to prevent this, via sending "the Arab Legion across the Jordan River as soon as the Mandate ended to occupy the part of Palestine allotted to the Arabs."[42] This goal meshed with that of the Zionist movement, which negotiated with 'Abdullah to achieve the same end. However, when the stubborn but disorganized resistance of the Palestinians was overcome in the spring of 1948 in the context of the country-wide Zionist offensive and the Arab armies then entered Palestine, the Arab Legion, which was the instrument of 'Abdullah's expansionist ambitions, took the lead in opposing the advances of the new Israeli army. Under strong British influence, the legion was armed and trained by Britain, commanded by British officers, and had more combat experience than any other Middle Eastern military; it succeeded in keeping Israel from conquering the West Bank and East Jerusalem, retaining the area for 'Abdullah while denying it to the Palestinians. As the historian Avi Shlaim noted, "It is hardly an exaggeration to say that" British Foreign Secretary Ernest Bevin "colluded directly with the Transjordanians and indirectly with the Jews to abort the birth of a Palestinian Arab state."[43]

The rest of the newly independent Arab countries faced grim prospects after the 1948 war, not only because of the influx of Palestinian refugees. They had lost the battle over the partition of Palestine at the UN in 1947, and then lost the 1948 war as their armies were defeated, one by one, by the superior forces of the new Israeli state. Notwithstanding the widely accepted assertion that the Israeli army was dwarfed by seven invading Arab armies, we know that in 1948 Israel in fact outnumbered and outgunned its opponents. There were only five regular Arab military forces in the field in 1948, as Saudi Arabia and Yemen did not have modern armies to speak of. Just four of these armies entered the territory of Mandatory Palestine (the minuscule Lebanese army never crossed the frontier); and two of these—Jordan's Arab Legion and Iraq's forces—were forbidden by their British allies from breaching the borders of the areas allocated to the Jewish state by partition, and thus carried out no invasion of Israel.[44]

Having faced their first major international test, the Arab states had failed it with disastrous consequences. Thus began a string of decisive military defeats by what rapidly became a potent Israeli military machine, defeats that continued through the 1982 Lebanon War. They led to a series of regional shocks that fully bore out Albert Hourani's grim predictions in 1946. As a result, the Arab countries, which had been struggling to throw off the chains of poverty, dependency, foreign occupation, and indirect control, now had to confront both daunting new internal challenges and other problems caused by their powerful and aggressive new neighbor, Israel.

Finally, the Palestine war confirmed the eclipse of Great Britain in the Middle East and its replacement by the dueling superpowers, the United States and the Soviet Union. Despite their already tense postwar rivalry, both had supported the partition of Palestine and the creation of a Jewish state, albeit for different reasons. Once the state of Israel was established, they both recognized it and offered crucial military support, which was instrumental in its victory. Neither attempted to do anything to help in the creation of the Arab state foreseen in the partition resolution, nor did they act to prevent the elimination of that state via the tacit collaboration of Israel, Jordan, and Britain.[45]

Notwithstanding these similarities, the support of the two superpowers for Israel was different in motives, duration, and nature. Stalin and his colleagues in the Soviet leadership soon soured on a state that they had assumed would be a socialist protégé of the USSR. They had expected that Israel would serve as a progressive counterweight to what Moscow saw as Britain's pawns, the reactionary British-aligned Arab monarchies of Jordan, Iraq, and Egypt, and that it would fully align with the USSR. By 1950, however, when Israel chose neutrality during the Korean War while moving closer to the United States, it was clear that this would not happen. It did not take long for relations between the two countries to cool considerably. By 1955, the Soviet Union had developed close links with several Arab states, while Israel had secretly aligned itself with the old colonial powers, Britain and France, against one of the USSR's new

Arab allies, Egypt. Thus the Soviet honeymoon with Zionism and Israel proved to be ephemeral.

Israel's relationship with the United States proceeded on entirely different lines. Unlike the domains of the Russian tsars, which were one of the great crucibles of the virulent European anti-Semitism that gave birth to Zionism, the United States had always been seen as a tolerant refuge for persecuted Jews fleeing from Eastern Europe, 90 percent of whom migrated there. Between 1880 and 1920, the American Jewish population grew from a quarter of a million to four million, with the majority of new immigrants coming from Eastern Europe.[46] Modern political Zionism developed deep roots in the United States, both within the Jewish community and among many Christians. With Hitler's rise to power in Germany in the early 1930s, Zionism won over influential segments of US public opinion. The revelations of the horrors of the Holocaust were decisive in confirming the validity of the Zionists' call for a Jewish state and in discomfiting and silencing their opponents, within the Jewish community and outside it.

These shifts in opinion during and after World War II were enough to change the calculations of many American politicians. President Harry Truman, predisposed to Zionism through personal friendships and the influence of his closest advisors, was convinced that outright support of its aims was a domestic political necessity.[47] In November 1945, only nine months after Roosevelt had met and pledged his support to Ibn Sa'ud, Truman bluntly revealed the motivations behind this major shift when a group of American diplomats presciently warned him that an overtly pro-Zionist policy would harm US interests in the Arab world. "I am sorry, gentlemen," he said, "but I have to answer to hundreds of thousands who are anxious for the success of Zionism. I do not have hundreds of thousands of Arabs among my constituents."[48]

Initially, the State Department, the Pentagon, and the CIA—what would become the permanent foreign-policy establishment of the new global American imperium—were opposed to Truman's and his advisors' determined partisanship for Zionism and the new state of Israel. Yet Truman, who did not come from a patrician background, had no higher education (he was the last US president without a college degree), and was inexperienced in foreign affairs, was not intimidated by the foreign policy establishment he had inherited. At the outset of the postwar era, respected figures, from Secretary of State George Marshall down to Dean Acheson, George Kennan, and other senior officials at State and the other departments, argued that support for the new Jewish state would harm American strategic, economic, and oil interests in the Middle East in the context of the emerging Cold War. But in the first book to examine carefully newly available government documents from this period, the political scientist Irene Gendzier shows that the outlook of key elements within the bureaucracy changed within a matter of months. After Israel's stunning military victories, many bureaucrats and military officers, and with them the US oil industry, quickly came to appreciate the possible utility of the Jewish state for US interests in the region.[49]

The main reasons driving this shift were economic and strategic, related to Cold War considerations and the vast energy resources of the Middle East. Militarily, the Pentagon came to see Israel as a potentially powerful ally. Moreover, neither policymakers nor the oil companies perceived Israel as a threat to US oil interests, given Saudi complaisance over Palestine (at the height of the 1948 war, as Israeli troops overran most of the country and expelled hundreds of thousands of Palestinians, Marshall found cause to thank King Ibn Sa'ud for his "conciliatory manner" regarding Palestine).[50] Thereafter, Saudi Arabia never rocked the boat where the close American-Israeli relationship was concerned. Indeed, it was seen by the Saudi royal family as completely compatible with the intimate American-Saudi connection that went back to the first oil exploration and exploitation deal of 1933.[51]

During its first decades, however, Israel did not receive the massive levels of American military and economic support that came to be routine starting in the early 1970s.[52] Moreover, at the UN, the United States often took positions that were at odds with those of Israel, including voting for repeated Security Council condemnations of Israeli military actions.[53] During the Truman administration, and indeed until the 1967 war, while generally favorable toward and supportive of the Jewish state, US policymakers gave relatively little consideration to Israel per se. American leaders, from Truman on down, gave even less consideration to the Palestinians.

IN SHOCK, DEFEATED, dispersed, and temporarily leaderless, most Palestinians were only dimly aware of the global shifts that had left their homeland in ruins. The older generation, who over decades had come to see Britain as the primary enabler of Zionism, continued with great bitterness to regard it as the main source of their misfortunes. Palestinians also harshly criticized the failures of their own leadership, and expressed deep disgust over the performance of the Arab states and the incapacity of their armies to preserve more than 22 percent of Arab Palestine.[54] This was combined with anger at Arab rulers for their disunity, and even worse, the complicity of some—notably King 'Abdullah of Jordan—with Israel and the great powers. Thus 'Isa al-'Isa, writing after the Nakba from his place of exile in Beirut, skewered the Arab rulers:

> Oh little kings of the Arabs, by the grace of God
> Enough feebleness and infighting
> Once upon a time our hopes were on you
> But all our hopes were dashed.[55]

For these many reasons, in the bleak new reality after the Nakba, more than a million Palestinians faced a world turned utterly upside down. Wherever they were, whether inside Palestine or not, they experienced profound social disruption. For the majority, this meant destitution—the loss of homes, jobs, and deeply rooted communities. Villagers lost their land and livelihoods and urbanites their properties and capital, while the Nakba shattered the power of the country's notables together with their economic base. The discredited mufti would never regain his prewar authority, nor would others of his class. Social upheavals in much of the Arab world, often triggered by military-backed revolutions, would replace the notable class with younger leaders drawn from more diverse social strata. The Nakba produced the same result among the Palestinians.

Even those who were able to avoid impoverishment had been severed from their place in the world. This was the case for my aged grandparents, who were abruptly uprooted from their routines and from their home, losing most of their possessions. They were very fortunate by comparison with many others. Until they died in the early 1950s, they always had a solid roof over their heads, although they were obliged to move among the homes of their children, who were now scattered from Nablus and Jerusalem in the West Bank to Beirut, Amman, and Alexandria. After their visit in 1947, my parents had gone back to New York for my father to continue his studies, intending to return to Palestine when he finished. Neither of them ever saw Palestine again.

For all Palestinians, no matter their different circumstances, the Nakba formed an enduring touchstone of identity, one that has lasted through several generations. It marked an abrupt collective disruption, a trauma that every Palestinian shares in one way or another, personally or through their parents or grandparents. At the same time as the Nakba provided a new focus for their collective identity, it broke up families and communities, dividing and dispersing Palestinians among multiple countries and distinct sovereignties. Even those still inside Palestine, whether refugees or not, were subject to three different political regimes: Israel, Egypt (for those in the Gaza Strip), and Jordan (for those on the West Bank and in East Jerusalem). This condition of dispersal, *shitat* in Arabic, has afflicted the Palestinian people ever since. My own family is typical in that I have cousins in Palestine and in a half dozen Arab countries, and almost as many in Europe and the United States. Each of these separate Palestinian collectives faced a range of restrictions on movement, held a variety of identity documents or none at all, and were obliged to operate under different conditions, laws, and languages.

The small minority of Palestinians, about 160,000, who had managed to avoid expulsion and remained in the part of Palestine that had become Israel were now citizens of that state. Israel's government, dedicated above all to serving the country's new Jewish majority, viewed this remaining population with deep suspicion as a potential fifth column. Until 1966, most Palestinians lived under strict martial law and much of their land was seized (along with that of those who had been forced from the country and were now refugees). This stolen land, an expropriation deemed legal by the Israeli state, including the bulk of the country's arable areas, was given to Jewish settlements or the Israel Lands Authority, or placed under the control of the JNF, whose discriminatory charter prescribed that such property could only be used for the benefit of the Jewish people.[56]

This provision meant that dispossessed Arab owners could neither buy back nor lease what had once been their property, nor could any other non-Jew. Such moves were crucial to the transformation of Palestine from an Arab country to a Jewish state, since only about 6 percent of Palestinian land had been Jewish-owned prior to 1948. The Arab population inside Israel, isolated by military travel restrictions, was also cut off from other Palestinians and from the rest of the Arab world. Accustomed to being a substantial majority in their own country and region, they suddenly had to learn to make their way as a despised minority in a hostile environment as subjects of a Jewish polity that never defined itself as a state of all its citizens. In the words of one scholar, "by virtue of Israel's definition of itself as a Jewish state and the state's exclusionary policies and laws, what was conferred on Palestinians was in effect second-class citizenship." Most significantly, the martial regime under which the Palestinians lived granted the Israeli military near-unlimited authority to control the minutiae of their lives.[57]

Displaced Palestinians who now lived outside the borders of the state of Israel—indeed the majority of the Palestinian people—were refugees (as were some who remained inside Israel). Those who had fled to Syria, Lebanon, and Jordan sorely taxed those countries' limited relief capacities. Initially, most of them found themselves in refugee camps managed by the United Nations Relief and Works Agency. Most refugees with means, employable skills, or relatives in Arab countries did not register with UNRWA or found other housing, and others were eventually able to move out of the camps and integrate in cities like Damascus, Beirut, Sidon, and Amman. Palestinians who never stayed in the camps or who swiftly made their way out of them tended to be better off, educated, and urbanized. Over time, others followed, and a large majority of refugees and their descendants came to live outside these camps.

In Jordan, home to 2.2 million refugees registered with UNRWA—the largest single group—only 370,000 still remain in camps, as do only a quarter of the 830,000 registered refugees in the West Bank. Fewer than a quarter of the 550,000 refugees in Syria lived in camps before the civil war there, as do less than half of the 470,000 Palestinian refugees in Lebanon. The proportion is approximately the same among the 1.4 million registered refugees in the cramped territory of the Gaza Strip, which came under Egyptian control until 1967. Thus although five and a half million Palestinian refugees and their descendants are registered with UNRWA, most of them, about four million, and many others who never registered with the UN, do not live in refugee camps today.

In 1950, King ʿAbdullah realized his aspiration to enlarge his small kingdom, now called Jordan rather than Transjordan, by annexing the West Bank, an annexation that was recognized only by his closest allies, the UK and Pakistan. At the same time, the king extended Jordanian citizenship to all Palestinians within his newly expanded domain. This generous measure, which applied to the overwhelming majority of the Palestinian refugees living in exile in the Arab world and in the West Bank, belies a repeated assertion by Israel that the Arab states prevented the refugees from integrating, obliging them to remain in camps as a useful political weapon.

While the old Palestinian political and economic elite had been discredited, some of its members, notably those who had opposed the mufti—for example, Raghib al-Nashashibi, once the mayor of Jerusalem—adjusted rapidly to their new circumstances under the Hashemite monarchy. A few even took positions in the Jordanian government in Amman. Other Palestinians remained unreconciled and bitter at having lost their chance at self-determination, and worse, being subjected to their old antagonist King ʿAbdullah. Although Jordan's Arab Legion, backed by Britain, had been the only army to hold its own against Israel's forces in 1948, preventing more of Palestine from falling under Israeli control, the price for being saved in this way—Hashemite rule over the West Bank and East Jerusalem—was steep. ʿAbdullah's fealty to the hated British colonial masters, his opposition to Palestinian independence, and his widely rumored contacts with the Zionists all counted against him. My father, who had experienced ʿAbdullah's attitude firsthand, refused to accept a Jordanian passport after his British Palestine Mandate passport expired. He eventually obtained a Saudi passport, through the intercession of his brother Dr. Husayn, who had met the Saudi foreign minister (and later king), Faysal ibn ʿAbd al-ʿAziz, at the St. James's Palace conference in London in 1939.

Ultimately, King 'Abdullah paid the highest price for his dealings with Israel.[58] In July 1951 he was assassinated in the broad esplanade of the Haram al-Sharif in Jerusalem as he was leaving the al-Aqsa Mosque after Friday prayers.[59] His assassin, caught soon after and rapidly tried and executed, was reputedly linked to the former mufti of Jerusalem—the mufti's offices had long been located in and around the rectangular Haram, a paramount locus of Palestinian identity. Rather than interring the slain king in a chamber adjoining the Haram next to the resting place of his father, Sharif Husayn of Mecca, it was decided to bury him in his capital, Amman.

The killing further embittered relations between the Jordanian regime and Palestinian nationalists, who were seen by the rulers of the newly expanded kingdom as irresponsible, dangerous radicals, and elements of instability. The monarchy thereafter exploited the existing cleavages between many Jordanians and the country's new Palestinian citizens, who now constituted a majority of the population. Many Jordanians nevertheless came to see the Hashemite regime as an undemocratic and repressive bastion of imperial interests, one that served as a friendly buffer protecting the eastern frontier of the Jewish state. Although a sizeable segment of Palestinians would eventually become prosperous and reliable pillars of Jordanian society, the tension between the regime and its Palestinian subjects endured for decades, eventually exploding into armed conflict in 1970.

Palestinians who took refuge in Lebanon also became involved in the politics of the host country, although the number of refugees and their proportion of the total population were much smaller than in Jordan. Mainly Muslim, the Palestinians were never considered for Lebanese citizenship because this would have upset the country's precarious sectarian balance, engineered by the French mandatory authorities to allow the Maronite Christians to dominate. Some Lebanese Sunni, Druze, Shi'ite, and left-wing politicians who were sympathetic to their cause in time came to see the Palestinians as useful allies in their efforts to reshape Lebanon's sectarian political system. However, any commitment to the Palestine cause did not extend to integrating the Palestinians, who in any case still clung to the hope of returning to their homeland. Opposition to *tawtin*, or permanent resettlement in Lebanon, was thus an article of faith for both Lebanese and Palestinians.

The residents of Palestinian refugee camps were kept under close surveillance by the Deuxième Bureau, the Lebanese army's intelligence service, with tough restrictions on their employment and ownership of property. At the same time, UNRWA's provision of services in Lebanon and elsewhere, notably universal education and vocational training, enabled Palestinians to become among the most highly educated people in the Arab world. The proficiencies thus acquired facilitated their emigration, especially to the oil-rich Arab countries that badly needed skilled labor and professional expertise. Still, in spite of the safety valve provided by UNRWA's services, which channeled many young Palestinians away from the refugee camps, nationalism and irredentism were widespread among all classes and communities. As Palestinians began to emerge from the shock of the Nakba and organize politically, their activities led to further polarization among the Lebanese along sectarian and political lines, and eventually to clashes with the authorities in the late 1960s.

A smaller number of Palestinian refugees ended up in Syria, some in camps and others in Damascus and other cities, fewer in Iraq, and fewer still in Egypt. In these larger and more homogeneous countries, the limited groups of Palestinian refugees did not have a destabilizing effect. Refugee camps were established in Syria, but Palestinians there also had certain advantages. They received many benefits of Syrian citizenship, such as the right to own land and access to state education and government employment, but were denied nationality, passports (as in Lebanon, they received refugee travel documents), and the right to vote. Palestinians in Syria thus achieved a high degree of social and economic integration while retaining their legal status as refugees.

In time, as the Arab Gulf countries, Libya, and Algeria developed their oil industries, and were able to keep a higher proportion of their oil and gas revenues, many Palestinians became resident there and played a major role in building up these countries' economies, government service, and education systems. Like the characters in the short novel *Men in the Sun*, by the Palestinian writer Ghassan Kanafani, however, they did not always find this route easy, for it often involved alienation, isolation, and, as when Palestinians attempted to cross frontiers with their refugee papers, even tragedy.[60] Living in the Arab Gulf countries did not bring with it citizenship or permanent residency: the ability of Palestinians to stay in these places was dependent on employment, even if they had been there most of their lives.

Regardless of the degree of Palestinian integration, the populations of all the Arab states felt great and continuing concern about the question of Palestine, both out of broad sympathy for the people and because the humiliating defeat of 1948 had brought home their own weakness, vulnerability, and instability. Indeed, in his memoir *Philosophy of the Revolution,* Gamal Abdel Nasser, the leader of Egypt's 1952 uprising, muses on how the idea of overthrowing the old regime was in the forefront of the minds of officers fighting in the 1948 war in Palestine: "We were fighting in Palestine, but our dreams were in Egypt."[61]

Beyond helping to provoke such upheavals, the military defeat in 1948 made its Arab neighbors deeply fearful of Israel, whose powerful army continued to launch devastating strikes as part of a strategy of disproportionate reprisals for refugee incursions, aimed at forcing Arab governments to crack down on Palestinian irredentism.[62] These Israeli attacks regularly came up at meetings of the UN Security Council (meetings that my father attended in the 1950s and 1960s in his capacity as a member of the UN's Political and Security Council Affairs division), where Israel's actions were often condemned.[63] The reports that the council received from the UN truce observers were starkly different, not only from Israeli government statements but also from the skewed coverage in the American media.[64]

This volatile dynamic along their borders resulted in the peculiar situation wherein Arab leaders often raised the question of Palestine because of popular pressure but refrained from actually doing anything about it, out of fear of Israel's might and the disapproval of the great powers. The Palestine issue thus became a political football exploited at will by opportunistic politicians, as each sought to outbid the other in proclaiming their devotion to it. Palestinians witnessing this cynical game eventually realized that if anything was to be done about their cause, they would have to do it themselves.

IN THE AFTERMATH of the 1948 war, the Palestinians were virtually invisible, hardly covered in the Western media and rarely allowed to represent themselves internationally. They and their sacred cause were invoked by Arab governments, but they themselves played almost no independent role. The Arab states presumed to speak for the Palestinians in inter-Arab forums, but given the division and disarray among them and the many distractions they faced, they did not do so with a unified voice. At the United Nations and elsewhere, the Palestine question was generally subsumed under the rubric of the "Arab-Israeli conflict," and the Arab states took the lead, feebly representing Palestinian interests. Immediately after the Nakba, several former members of the AHC, under Ahmad Hilmi Pasha, including my uncle Husayn, attempted to establish a government-in-exile for the Arab state that was specified in the partition resolution. They set up a Government of All Palestine in Gaza, but it failed to win the support of key Arab states, notably Jordan, which yet again did not want the Palestinians to have independent representation, and it garnered no international recognition.[65] The effort came to nothing.

The mufti and a few of the notables lingered on, some in exile, some in retirement, and some serving the monarchy in Amman. Several of the old leaders were involved in the brief six-month democratic opening in Jordan in 1956–57 represented by the nationalist government of Sulayman al-Nabulsi. These leaders included my uncle Dr. Husayn, who served as foreign minister in the nationalist government and then as prime minister for ten days after al-Nabulsi was dismissed and before King Hussein appointed a pliable government that imposed martial law. The 1956 elections that brought al-Nabulsi to power were, as one unfriendly British diplomat admitted, "the first approximately free ones in the history of Jordan" (and they may have been the last), but his government faced the unremitting hostility of Britain and of the Hashemite monarchy.[66] With the exception of this brief episode, none of the Palestinian old guard ever again played an important role in politics. It is striking, moreover, that after leadership passed to a new generation of Palestinians and a new class, almost none of the prominent figures were drawn from the notable families that had dominated Palestinian politics before the Nakba.*

---

*The sole exception in this period was the late Faysal Husayni, whose prominence was a result of his courage, political acumen, militant activism within Fatah, and his

The few political formations such as trade unions and other non-elite groupings like the Istiqlal Party that had developed in Mandatory Palestine were irrevocably shattered by the Nakba. The only exception was the remnant of the Palestinian Communist Party, which before 1948 had a largely Arab membership and a mainly Jewish leadership. This became the core of the Israeli Communist Party, which from the 1950s onward developed into a Jewish-Arab vehicle for the political aspirations of many Palestinian citizens of Israel, as purely Arab formations were banned by the military regime in place until 1966. The party's activities were confined to the Israeli system, however, and for several decades it had little impact on Palestinians elsewhere. There was thus a sort of political tabula rasa among Palestinians after 1948.

Into this post-Nakba political vacuum stepped the Arab states, many of which, as in Jordan under King 'Abdullah, had already tried to bring the Palestinians under their control. However, they were much more concerned with their own agendas, with avoiding conflict with their powerful and aggressive Israeli neighbor, and with ingratiating themselves with Israel's great power patrons. Rather than being allies of the Palestinians in their resistance to the low-level war being waged on them, the Arab governments hindered their efforts, and sometimes were complicit with the Palestinians' enemies. The prime example was Jordan, which after King 'Abdullah's annexation of the West Bank firmly repressed expressions of Palestinian nationalism, but other Arab states also prevented Palestinians from organizing or launching attacks against Israel.

Spurred by the unwillingness or inability of the Arab states and the international community to reverse the disastrous consequences of 1948,

---

repeated arrests by Israel. Faysal, with whom I worked closely during the Madrid and Washington Palestinian-Israeli negotiations in 1991–93, confronted armed settlers and the Israeli security forces that protected them when they took over Palestinian homes in Jerusalem. His preeminence in Jerusalem was due to these qualities and not family connections, although his father was the beloved military leader 'Abd al-Qadir al-Husayni, who was killed in battle in April 1948. He was also related to the mufti and to Jamal al-Husayni and was the grandson of Musa Kazim Pasha al-Husayni, a mayor of Jerusalem removed from his post by the British. His grandfather had led the Palestinian national movement until his death at eighty-four in 1934, months after British policemen beat him with truncheons during a demonstration in Jaffa.

Palestinian activism in various forms revived in the bleak post-Nakba environment. Small groups engaged in militant activity primarily aimed at mobilizing Palestinians to recover primary responsibility for their own cause by taking up arms against Israel. This started spontaneously and consisted mainly of uncoordinated raids on Israeli border communities. It took several years before such largely inchoate forms of clandestine armed action coalesced into a visible trend and emerged from obscurity with the formation of organizations like Fatah in 1959.

Beyond dealing with Israel's opposition to any Palestinian attempt to redress the status quo, Palestinians had to confront the Arab host governments, notably those of Jordan, Lebanon, and Egypt. These states were deeply reluctant to countenance attacks on their neighbor, given their profound military weakness vis-à-vis the Jewish state. Even when the new Palestinian movements did manage to establish themselves, they had to fend off attempts by some Arab states to bend them to their purposes. The formation of the Palestine Liberation Organization by the Arab League in 1964 at the behest of Egypt was a response to this burgeoning independent Palestinian activism and constituted the most significant attempt by Arab states to control it.

The Egyptian government was in part reacting to its bitter experience in the period leading up to the 1956 Suez War. In the wake of the 1952 revolution, the military regime had eschewed an expensive rearmament program, even though the defeat in Palestine had in part been a function of the Egyptian army's inadequate and outmoded weaponry. Instead, the regime focused on domestic economic and social development, with the wide-scale electrification and irrigation promised by building the Aswan Dam, investment in industrialization, extending and expanding K–12 and higher education, and state-led economic planning. Egypt sought foreign economic aid for these efforts from all possible sources, while trying to remain nonaligned as the Cold War developed.[67]

At the beginning of his regime, Gamal Abdel Nasser sought in particular to avoid provoking Israel, Egypt's powerful neighbor. This effort was undermined by the aggressive policies of Israeli leaders, especially Prime Minister David Ben-Gurion,[68] and by the growing Palestinian militancy within the Gaza Strip. The large, concentrated refugee population there provided an ideal environment for the growth of this militancy, as confirmed in accounts by founders of the Fatah movement who were based in Gaza, among them Yasser 'Arafat (Abu 'Ammar), Salah Khalaf (Abu Iyad), and Khalil al-Wazir (Abu Jihad). Years afterward, they talked about the obstacles—including arrest, torture, and harassment—that post-coup Egyptian intelligence placed in the way of their efforts to organize against Israel.[69]

Thus a Palestinian campaign of sporadic but often lethal attacks on Israel was launched despite heavy-handed repression by the Egyptian military and its intelligence services, which tightly controlled the Gaza Strip. Israel's retaliation for the casualties inflicted by Palestinian cross-border infiltrators, known as *feda'iyin* (meaning "those who sacrifice themselves"), was massive and disproportionate, and the Gaza Strip bore the brunt of these attacks. No neighboring country was immune to them, however. In October 1953, Israeli forces in the West Bank village of Qibya carried out a massacre following an attack by *feda'iyin* that killed three Israeli civilians, a woman and her two children, in the town of Yehud. Israeli special forces Unit 101, under the command of Ariel Sharon, blew up forty-five homes with their inhabitants inside, killing sixty-nine Palestinian civilians.[70] The raid, which was condemned by the UN Security Council,[71] was launched despite the unceasing efforts of Jordan (then in control of the West Bank) to prevent armed Palestinian activity, which included imprisoning and even killing would-be infiltrators. Jordanian troops were often deployed in ambushes against Palestinian militants, and were under orders to fire on anyone attempting to enter Israel.[72]

The Israeli leadership struggled over the policy of disproportionate force in 1954 and 1955, with then defense minister Ben-Gurion taking a bellicose position against the more pragmatic, nuanced stance of Prime Minister Moshe Sharett. Ben-Gurion believed that only the unremitting application of force would oblige the Arab states to make peace on Israel's terms. In Sharett's view, this aggressive approach needlessly provoked the Arabs and foreclosed opportunities for compromise.[73] (Like Ben-Gurion, though, Sharett was reluctant to give up any of the territory Israel had gained in 1948 or to allow any significant return of Palestinian refugees to their homes.) In March 1955, Ben-Gurion proposed a major attack on Egypt and the occupation of the Gaza Strip.[74] The Israeli cabinet rejected the proposal, only to acquiesce in October 1956 after Ben-Gurion replaced Sharett as prime minister and his militant ethos won out. Transmitted through acolytes such as Moshe Dayan, Yitzhak Rabin, and Ariel Sharon, Ben-Gurion's belligerent policies have pervaded the Israeli government's dealings with its neighbors ever since.

In the buildup to this 1956 attack, Israel carried out a series of large-scale military operations against Egyptian army and police posts in the Gaza Strip.[75] These culminated with assaults in which thirty-nine Egyptian soldiers were killed in Rafah in February 1955 and another seventy-two in Khan Yunis six months later, with more soldiers killed in further operations, along with many Palestinian civilians.[76] The manifest weakness of its army finally forced Egypt to abandon nonalignment and try to purchase arms first from the UK and the US. When that effort failed, Egypt in September 1955 agreed to a massive arms deal with a Soviet client, Czechoslovakia. Unable to respond to Israeli attacks, and embarrassed before Egyptian and Arab public opinion, the government meanwhile ordered its military intelligence services to help the Palestinian militants they had previously suppressed to launch operations against Israel. The response to this new development was not long in coming, and it was devastating. Thus a few bloody raids launched in the early 1950s by small Palestinian militant groups, actions taken against the wishes of most Arab governments, ultimately led to Israel launching the Suez War of October 1956. Israel did not do so alone, and its partners had their own reasons for attacking Egypt.

Old-school imperialists in office in Britain and France were enraged by Egypt's nationalization of the Franco-British Suez Canal Company, which was carried out in retaliation for the cancellation by the US secretary of state of a planned World Bank loan to build the Aswan Dam. In addition, France sought to end Egypt's support for Algerian rebels, who had been offered military training and a diplomatic and broadcasting platform in Cairo.[77] Meanwhile, the Conservative government of Anthony Eden in London chafed at the demand by Egypt's new regime that Britain end its military presence there (which had lasted seventy-two years). The British were also infuriated by Egypt's support for nationalist challenges to Britain's position in Iraq, the Gulf, Aden, and other parts of the Arab world. These challenges drove both countries to join Israel in its full-scale invasion of Egypt in October 1956.[78]

This second major Arab-Israeli war had a number of peculiarities. Unlike Israel's other conventional wars, in 1948, 1967, 1973, and 1982, which had multiple Arab protagonists, the Suez war was fought against only one Arab country. It was preceded by the Protocol of Sèvres, a secret agreement between Israel and the old colonial powers, France and Britain, that was drawn up a few days before the war began. Sèvres marked the end of the estrangement between Britain and the Zionist movement that went back to the White Paper of 1939. The war involved a further reversal of alliances: Israel's patrons in 1947–48, the United States and Soviet Union, ultimately sided with Egypt.

Once the secret Sèvres accord was negotiated, the tripartite offensive was launched under the pretext that Anglo-French forces were intervening only to separate the combatants. The Egyptian army was decisively and rapidly defeated. Despite the foregone conclusion of a military contest between a powerful Israel backed by two European powers against a weak Third World country that had barely absorbed its new Soviet weapons, the political results were not favorable to the aggressors. President Dwight Eisenhower was furious at Britain and France for not consulting with Washington and for launching what looked like (and was) a neocolonial intervention at just the moment when Soviet tanks were crushing the Hungarian uprising of 1956. The Soviets were angered at this imperialist attack on their new Egyptian ally, but relieved at the distraction from their repression of the revolt in Budapest.

Operating in tandem in the Middle East as they had in 1948, and notwithstanding their intense Cold War rivalry, the United States and the Soviet Union took a harsh stand against the tripartite alliance. The Soviets threatened to use nuclear weapons, the United States warned that it would cut off economic aid to its allies, and both swiftly pushed through a UN General Assembly resolution demanding immediate withdrawal. (A resolution in the Security Council was impossible because of the certainty of an Anglo-French veto.) This intense pressure from the superpowers forced Israel, France, and Britain to end the occupation of Egyptian territory and of the Gaza Strip. Israel did try to drag its feet, not withdrawing the last of its forces from the Sinai Peninsula and Gaza Strip until early 1957. The aggressors had been rolled back, the US and

USSR had shown who was boss in the Middle East, and Nasser became a pan-Arab hero, but the Palestinian residents of the Gaza Strip, most of them refugees, had suffered greatly.

As the occupying Israeli troops swept through the Gaza towns and refugee camps of Khan Yunis and Rafah in November 1956, more than 450 people, male civilians, were killed, most of them summarily executed.[79] According to a Special Report by the director-general of UNRWA, in the first massacre, which took place in Khan Yunis and the neighboring refugee camp on November 3, 275 men were shot. One week later on November 12 in the Rafah camp, 111 were killed. Another 66 were shot between November 1 and 21.[80] I was present once when Muhammad El-Farra, who represented Jordan at the UN, recalled how several of his cousins who lived in Khan Yunis had been rounded up and executed.[81] Israel's claim, that the Palestinian deaths were the result of clashes with troops searching for *feda'iyin*, was decisively debunked by the UNRWA report. The civilians were killed after all resistance had ceased in the Gaza Strip, apparently as revenge for the raids into Israel before the Suez War. Given the precedent of 1948 and the civilian massacres at Dayr Yasin and at least twenty other locations,[82] as well as the high civilian casualties in the raids of the early 1950s, such as that at Qibya, the gruesome events in the Gaza Strip were not isolated incidents. They were part of a pattern of behavior by the Israeli military. News of the massacres was suppressed in Israel and veiled by a complaisant American media.

The events of 1956 were an early installment of the heavy price that the people of Gaza paid and still pay in the continuing war on the Palestinians. The French historian Jean-Pierre Filiu chronicles a total of twelve major Israeli military campaigns against Gaza, going back to 1948, some being full-fledged occupations and some constituting all-out warfare.[83] The major wars between Israel and the Arab states often obscured how Gaza was targeted, as interstate conflicts directly involving the great powers invariably received more attention. It is not surprising that the Gaza Strip should have been the target in this way: it was the crucible of the resistance of Palestinians to their dispossession after 1948. Most of the founding leaders of Fatah and the PLO emerged from the cramped quarters of the narrow coastal ship; the militant Popular Front for the Liberation of Palestine drew its most fervent support there; and later on it was the birthplace and stronghold of Islamic Jihad and Hamas, the most strenuous advocates of armed struggle against Israel.

Only a few years after the Nakba, the shock and humiliation it had caused Palestinians gave way to a desire to resist the powers ranged against them, in spite of the formidable odds. This led to the sequence of lethal armed raids that constituted both a direct response to the Nakba and a continuation of a pre-1948 strain of militancy. The raids triggered disproportionate Israeli retaliatory attacks on the neighboring Arab states, which ultimately led to the Suez War. Its genesis, sparked by Palestinian resistance to being supplanted in their homeland, was directly rooted in the Palestine question. The same had been true of the war of 1948.

Both clashes are thought of almost exclusively in terms of a contest between the armies of Israel and those of its Arab neighbors. However, the refusal of the Palestinians to acquiesce in their dispossession dragged Arab states that were otherwise preoccupied, and that were neither seeking nor ready for war with Israel, into confrontations that rapidly escalated out of control. In October 1956, these escalating confrontations provided the opportunity for a devastating and long-planned Israeli first strike. Despite their manifest weakness, the dispersed, defeated Palestinians, written out of history by the victors of 1948, largely ignored or muzzled by the Arab governments, and sacrificed on the altar of the great powers' global ambitions, repeatedly managed to upset the regional status quo that was so unfavorable to them. The consequences for doing so in 1956, in Gaza and elsewhere, were grave. They were to be graver still in the next round.

The Third Declaration of War, 1967

I was trying to see how an event is made and unmade, as ultimately it only exists via what one says about it, since it is properly
speaking fabricated by those who spread its renown.

—Georges Duby[1]

On a bright, sunny morning early in June 1967, I walked out of Grand
Central Station in Manhattan, en route from our family home in Mount
Vernon to my father's office in the United Nations building. The Six-Day
War was raging in the Middle East, and the news reports indicated that
the Egyptian, Syrian, and Jordanian air forces had been wiped out in a
first strike by Israel. I dreaded the prospect of another crushing Israeli
victory, but even with my limited exposure to military strategy, I knew
that an army in the desert without air cover would be easy pickings for
any air force, especially one as powerful as Israel's.

Out on Forty-second Street, I noticed a commotion. Several people
on the sidewalk were holding the corners of a large bedsheet, which was
weighed down with a heap of coins and bills. Others were coming from
every direction to throw in more money. I stopped momentarily to watch
and realized that the people were soliciting contributions for Israel's war
effort. It struck me that while my family and many others were preoccupied with the fate of Palestine, lots of New Yorkers were just as worried

about the outcome for Israel. They sincerely believed that the Jewish state was in danger of extinction, as did many Israelis, alarmed by the empty threats of certain Arab leaders.

President Lyndon B. Johnson knew otherwise. When Abba Eban, Israel's foreign minister, told Johnson at a meeting in Washington, DC, on May 26 that Egypt was about to launch an attack, the president asked his secretary of defense, Robert McNamara, to set the record straight. Three separate intelligence groups had looked carefully into the matter, McNamara said, "and it was our best judgment that an attack was not imminent." "All of our intelligence people are unanimous," Johnson added, that if Egypt were to attack, "you will whip hell out of them."[2] As Washington knew, Israel's military in 1967 was far superior to the militaries of all the Arab states combined, as it was in every other contest between them.

Government documents published since then have confirmed these judgments. US military and intelligence sources predicted a crushing victory by Israel in any and all circumstances, given the mastery enjoyed by its armed forces.[3] Five years after the 1967 war, five Israeli generals echoed the US assessment, stating in different venues that Israel was not imperiled by annihilation.[4] On the contrary: its forces were much stronger than the Arab armies in 1967, and the country was never in any danger of losing a war, even if the Arabs had struck first.[5] Yet the myth prevails: in 1967, a tiny, vulnerable country faced constant, existential peril, and it continues to do so.[6] This fiction has served to justify blanket support of Israeli policies, no matter how extreme, and despite its repeated rebuttal even by authoritative Israeli voices.[7]

The war unfolded much as the CIA and Pentagon had foreseen. A lightning first strike by the Israeli air force destroyed most Egyptian, Syrian, and Jordanian warplanes on the ground. This gave Israel complete air superiority, which, in that desert region, in that season, provided an absolute advantage to its ground forces. Israeli armored columns thus were able to conquer the Sinai Peninsula and the Gaza Strip, the West Bank, including Arab East Jerusalem, and the Golan Heights in six days.

If the reasons for Israel's decisive victory in June 1967 are clear, the factors that led to the war are less so. A key cause was the rise of militant Palestinian commando groups. The Israeli government had recently begun to divert the waters of the Jordan River to the center of the country despite great Arab popular distress and even greater impotence on the part of the Arab regimes. On January 1, 1965, Fatah launched an attack to sabotage a water-pumping station in central Israel. This was intended as a strike of symbolic significance, the first of many, designed to show that the Palestinians could act effectively when the Arab governments could not, and to embarrass those governments and force them to act. Fatah was regarded with suspicion by Egyptian officials as a loose cannon, recklessly provoking Israel at a time when Egypt was heavily engaged in military intervention in a civil war in Yemen and in building up its economy.

This was at the height of what the scholar Malcolm Kerr called "the Arab Cold War," when Egypt led a coalition of radical Arab nationalist regimes opposed to the conservative bloc headed by Saudi Arabia. The flash point of their rivalry was Yemen, where a revolution against the monarchy in 1962 led to a civil war in which much of Egypt's military became entangled.

Given Israel's overwhelming military superiority, and the fact that more than sixty thousand Egyptian troops and much of its air force were tied down in the Yemeni civil war, Egypt's provocation of Israel in May 1967—by moving troops into the Sinai Peninsula and requesting the removal of UN peacekeeping forces—appears illogical. But Egypt was responding to an upsurge of Palestinian guerrilla raids on Israel from bases provided by the radical new Syrian regime that had come to power in 1966, to which Israel had reacted by attacking and threatening Syria. The Egyptian leadership felt obliged to answer this challenge to maintain its prestige in the Arab world.[8] Whatever its motives, Egypt's moves in Sinai constituted overt incitement of Israel. Moreover, they provided the *casus belli* that allowed the Israeli military to launch a long-planned first strike, one that smashed three Arab armies and changed the face of the Middle East.[9]

EVERY MORNING DURING the war, I headed down to the UN—changing my route to avoid the bedsheet fundraisers—to my father's thirty-fifth-floor office, with its panoramic view of the East River and Queens. He worked in the division of Political and Security Council Affairs and one of his jobs was to report on the council's Middle East deliberations. So he sat in on Security Council meetings whenever the Arab-Israeli conflict was discussed, which meant about half of its sessions during the decade and a half that he worked there, until he died in 1968. At his office, I listened to the radio, read the news, and generally tried to make myself useful until the council was called into session. I was then able to sit in the visitors' gallery while my father would take his seat in the last row, behind the assistant secretary general in charge of his division. This particular official, by some arcane early Cold War deal that perhaps went back to Yalta, was always a Russian, a Byelorussian, or a Ukrainian.[10]

The council had been in formal or informal session repeatedly since the crisis had begun in earnest the preceding month. During the six days of the war itself, the council held eleven sessions, many of them running into the early hours of the morning. The pace and the workload were grueling, and my father, who with his colleagues had to spend many hours preparing materials for the council and secretary general and then drafting reports on each session, looks haggard and drawn in photos taken at that time.[11]

By Friday June 9, the fifth day of the war, Israeli forces had decisively defeated the Egyptian and Jordanian armies and occupied the Gaza Strip, the Sinai Peninsula, the West Bank, and Arab East Jerusalem. Early that morning Israel had begun storming the Golan Heights, routing the Syrian army, and was advancing rapidly along the main road toward Damascus. The council had ordered comprehensive cease-fires on June 6 and 7, but Israeli forces entering Syria ignored these resolutions, even as their government loudly proclaimed its adherence to them. By that night in the Middle East (still afternoon in New York) Israel's forces were approaching the key provincial capital of Quneitra, beyond which stood only the flat Hauran plain between their armored columns and the Syrian capital, just forty miles away.

Early in the council's session, which started at 12:30 pm, the Soviet Union proposed a draft of a third and more urgent cease-fire resolution. At this point, after the humiliating defeat of the Soviet-equipped Egyptian army and the seizure of the Golan Heights, the Soviets were desperate to protect their Syrian clients from further reverses, especially from an Israeli march on Damascus. The urgency was reflected in the

The UN Security Council, 1967. Ismail al-Khalidi, with his pipe, is second from right in the back row.

increasingly testy interventions in the debate by Ambassador Nikolai Fedorenko, the Soviet representative. The resolution, SC 235, which passed unanimously at about 1:30 pm, demanded of all the parties to the conflict "that hostilities should cease forthwith." Unusually, it also called on the UN secretary-general to "arrange immediate compliance" with the cease-fire and report back to the council "not later than two hours from now."[12]

As the session wore on into the afternoon, I fidgeted nervously, waiting for the secretary-general's confirmation of compliance with the cease-fire. This would signal that the fighting had been brought to an end and the Israeli advance had been halted. But as the minutes ticked by, fresh reports kept coming in of Israeli troops getting closer and closer to Damascus. It seemed as if the council might have been on the point of taking some action to enforce its demand for an immediate cease-fire when Ambassador Arthur Goldberg, the US representative, asked for an adjournment. After a desultory discussion, the council agreed to adjourn for two hours, and the delegations slowly filed out of the chamber.

I rushed down to meet my father, expecting him to explain why the council had agreed to allow another two hours of delay. Goldberg wanted to consult with his government, my father told me flatly. I was incredulous. How much consultation was needed to impose a cease-fire resolution? With a strange, bitter smile, my father responded dispassionately in Arabic. "Don't you understand?" he said. "The Americans are giving the Israelis a little more time."

Thanks to Ambassador Goldberg's maneuver to delay implementation of the June 9 cease-fire resolution for a few extra hours, the Israeli advance into Syria did not stop, and it continued until the following afternoon. By then, the Security Council had spent nine more hours in acrimonious debate stretching over three more sessions and running into the early hours of June 10. Throughout, Goldberg had reprised his delaying tactics.

Minor though the incident was, the ambassador's performance betokened a major shift in the United States' policies toward Israel. What we had witnessed that day was evidence of a new Middle Eastern axis in action—the armored spearheads on the ground were Israeli, while the diplomatic cover was American. It is an axis that is still in place today, over a half century later. The shift, which had been underway for some time, was mainly due to global factors, notably the impact of the Cold War and the Vietnam War on the region and on US policy, but also to significant personal and political considerations in Washington, DC. Evolving in parallel were Israel's external alliances, whereby it decisively moved away from its patrons of the 1950s and early 1960s, France and Britain (with whose weapons it fought the 1956 and 1967 wars), to a complete alignment with the United States. All of these factors had coalesced by June 1967, before the start of the war, when the Israeli government sought and received a green light from Washington to launch a preemptive attack on the air forces of Egypt, Syria, and Jordan.

If the Balfour Declaration and the Mandate constituted the first declaration of war on the Palestinian people by a great power, and the 1947 UN resolution on the partition of Palestine represented the second one, the aftermath of the 1967 war produced the third such declaration.

It came in the form of SC 242, a resolution crafted by the United States and approved on November 22, 1967. US policy toward Israel and Palestine had not followed a straight line in the twenty years between the passage of these two resolutions. In the years that followed the 1948 war, the Truman and Eisenhower administrations had tried rather tepidly and without success to persuade Israel to offer some concessions to its defeated adversaries. Their efforts focused on the return to their homes of the 750,000 or so Palestinian refugees, whose property had been seized by Israel, and on reducing the expansive borders Israel had achieved through its victories in the 1948 war. These feeble American attempts petered out in the face of the obduracy of David Ben-Gurion, who rejected concessions on both points.[13]

The Truman, Eisenhower, and Kennedy administrations maintained close relations with Israel, extending economic aid to the new state, although they did not see it as a principal element in their regional policies and did not approve of all of its actions. Eisenhower had forced Israel's withdrawal from Sinai and the Gaza Strip after the 1956 Suez War, and later Kennedy tried and failed to prevent Israel from developing nuclear weapons.[14] In the early 1960s Kennedy came to see Arab nationalism and Egypt's Nasser as a bulwark against communism, which was the prime American concern in the Middle East. This was in part because of events in Iraq, where the regime of 'Abd al-Karim Qasim was supported by the Iraqi Communist Party and the USSR, but vigorously opposed by Egypt and its nationalist allies.

With Kennedy's assassination and the advent of the Johnson administration in December 1963, new elements intervened. As the war in Southeast Asia intensified, Johnson's government was ever more inclined to see other parts of the world in rigid Cold War terms. Partly in consequence, US-Egyptian relations deteriorated markedly as the Yemeni civil war that had begun in 1962 turned into a major regional conflict. The USSR and its allies backed the Yemeni Republican regime, which relied upon a large Egyptian expeditionary force, while the United States, Britain, Israel, and their allies upheld the Saudi-supported Royalists. By 1967, US relations with Egypt were much colder than they had been under Kennedy, and the Middle East was polarized along lines of the Arab Cold War, with Egypt and Saudi Arabia as its antagonistic poles.

This conflict increasingly ran parallel to the larger global Cold War, but it had its own regional specificities. These included an ideological struggle not between communism and capitalism, but rather between the authoritarian Arab nationalism promoted by Egypt and the political Islam, centered on Wahhabism and absolute monarchy, that was purveyed by Saudi Arabia under King Faysal.

The realignment of American Middle Eastern priorities was also affected by President Johnson's long-standing and overt sympathy for Israel: as Senate majority leader in 1956, he had opposed Eisenhower's pressure on Israel to withdraw from Sinai and the Gaza Strip. Johnson was also relatively unfamiliar with Middle Eastern and other global realities. By contrast, Kennedy, the worldly and wealthy son of an ambassador, had visited Palestine in the early summer of 1939, when he was a twenty-two-year-old Harvard student, and sent his father a letter in which he demonstrated a reasonably good grasp of the facts and a skeptical assessment of the main arguments of both sides in the conflict. This skepticism made Kennedy less susceptible than most American politicians to the pressures applied by Israel's supporters.[15]

Lyndon Johnson, on the other hand, came from a much more modest background and his primary interests had revolved around domestic politics. His strong affinity with Zionism and Israel was reflected in his circle of close friends and advisors, which included such supporters of Israel as Abe Fortas, whom he made a Supreme Court Justice,[16] Arthur Goldberg, McGeorge Bundy, Clark Clifford, and the brothers Eugene and Walter Rostow. All were devoted backers of the Jewish state whose sympathies had to some extent been held in check by Kennedy.[17] Other avid Israel boosters who were personally close to Johnson were also major donors to the Democratic Party, such as Abraham Feinberg and Arthur Krim,[18] and the latter's wife, Dr. Mathilde Krim, a renowned scientist who had once smuggled weapons and explosives for the Revisionist Zionist terror group, the Irgun.[19] Although Johnson had inherited most of Kennedy's foreign-policy advisors, they had considerably more prominence in an administration led by a president with less experience and assurance in world affairs than Kennedy had. These political and personal factors combined in the three years leading up to the 1967 war to prepare the way for the ensuing shift in US policy.

Israel, for its part, had been stung by the strong American opposition to its 1956 Suez adventure. As it prepared in 1967 for a first strike against the Arab air forces, its leaders were determined to get prior American approval for their action, which they indeed obtained. A crucial exchange took place at a meeting in Washington on June 1, 1967, during which Major General Meir Amit, the head of the Mossad, Israel's external intelligence agency, told Secretary of Defense McNamara that he was going to recommend to his own government that Israel launch an attack. He asked the secretary for assurances that the United States would not react negatively. According to Amit, McNamara replied "All right," said he would tell the president, and asked only how long the war would last and what Israeli casualties might be.[20] Johnson and McNamara had already heard from their military and intelligence advisors that the Arabs were not going to attack, and that in any case Israel was likely to win an overwhelming victory. The Israeli military now had the green light it needed to launch a long-planned preemptive strike.[21]

The United States facilitated Israel's first strike in other ways. At a small meeting of Arab UN officials and diplomats after the war, Muhammad El-Farra, Jordan's ambassador, told the group that he felt he had been the victim of American duplicity in the run-up to the war.[22] Ambassador Goldberg, he said, had conveyed to Arab ambassadors that the United States was mediating with Israel to defuse the crisis and would restrain it from attacking, while he urged them to counsel restraint to their governments. The Johnson administration had given Israel the go-ahead for its surprise attack, El-Farra said, just before Egypt's vice-president arrived in Washington for negotiations to resolve the crisis. The Arab ambassadors had been used to deceive their governments, he felt, while Israel prepared its first strike with US approval.

No less important was that given this shift in US policy, Israel could count on President Johnson and his advisors to prevent a repetition of the pressure that had forced a withdrawal from its 1956 conquests. This was a complete transformation of the US stance in 1956 on Israeli control of conquered Arab territory, and its ramifications were disastrous for the Palestinians. The result of this new tolerance for Israeli territorial gains was Security Council Resolution 242. Its text was largely drafted by the British permanent representative, Lord Caradon, but in essence, it distilled the views of the United States and Israel and reflected the weakened position of the Arab states and their Soviet patron after the crushing June defeat. Although SC 242 stressed the "inadmissibility of the acquisition of territory by war," it linked any Israeli withdrawal to peace treaties with the Arab states and the establishment of secure frontiers. In practice, this meant that any withdrawals would be both conditional and delayed, given the Arab states' reluctance to engage in direct negotiations with Israel. Indeed, in the case of the West Bank, East Jerusalem, and the Golan Heights, full withdrawals have not taken place for over half a century, in spite of decades of sporadic indirect and direct negotiations.

Moreover, by linking Israel's withdrawal from Occupied Territories to the creation of secure and recognized boundaries, SC 242 allowed for the possibility of enlarged Israeli borders to meet the criterion of security, as determined by Israel. This nuclear-armed regional superpower has subsequently deployed an extraordinarily expansive and flexible interpretation of the term. Finally, the ambiguous language of SC 242 left open another loophole for Israel to retain the territories it had just occupied: the resolution's English text specifies "withdrawal from territories occupied" in the 1967 war rather than "from *the* territories occupied." Abba Eban pointedly stressed to the Security Council that his government would regard the original English-language text as binding, rather than the equally official French version, whose wording (*"des territoires occupés"*) does not permit this ambiguity.[23] In the half century since, with American help, Israel has driven a coach and horses through this linguistic gap, which has permitted it to colonize the occupied Palestinian and Syrian territories, some of which—East Jerusalem and the Golan Heights—it has formally annexed, and to maintain its unending military control over them. Repeated United Nations condemnations of these moves, unsupported by even a hint of sanctions or any genuine pressure on Israel, have over time amounted to tacit international acceptance of them.

The United States was now more squarely on the side of Israel than it had been previously, which meant the abandonment of the semblance of balance shown at times by the Truman, Eisenhower, and Kennedy administrations. This was the beginning of what became the classical period of the Arab-Israeli conflict, lasting until the end of the Cold War, during which the United States and Israel developed a unique full-scale (albeit informal) alliance, based essentially on Israel showing itself in 1967 as a reliable partner against perceived Soviet proxies in the Middle East.

For the Palestinians, this near-total alignment brought another forceful intervention by a great power to the detriment of their rights and interests, and gave a renewed international imprimatur to a further stage in their dispossession. As in 1947, a new international legal formula harmful to the Palestinians came via the medium of a UN resolution, and as with the Balfour Declaration of 1917, the key document contains not a single mention of Palestine or the Palestinians.

Security Council Resolution 242 treated the entire issue as a state-to-state matter between the Arab countries and Israel, eliminating the presence of Palestinians. The text does not refer to the Palestinians or to most elements of the original Palestine question; instead it contains a bland reference to "a just solution of the refugee problem." If the Palestinians were not mentioned and were not a recognized party to the conflict, they could be treated as no more than a nuisance, or at best as a humanitarian issue. Indeed, after 1967, their existence was acknowledged mostly under the rubric of terrorism purveyed by Israel and eventually adopted by the United States.

By its omissions, Resolution 242 consecrated a crucial element of Israel's negationist narrative: since there were no Palestinians, the only genuine issue was that the Arab states refused to recognize Israel and wielded a phantom "Palestine problem" as a pretext for this refusal. In the discursive battle over Palestine, which Zionism had dominated since 1897, UNSC 242 gave validity to this brilliant fabrication, delivering a powerful blow to the displaced and occupied Palestinians. Only two years later, in 1969, Israeli Prime Minister Golda Meir famously proclaimed that "there were no such thing as Palestinians . . . they did not exist," and that they never had existed.[24] She thereby took the negation characteristic of a settler-colonial project to the highest possible level: the indigenous people were nothing but a lie.

Perhaps most important, Resolution 242 effectively legitimated the 1949 armistice lines (since known as the 1967 borders or the Green Line) as Israel's de facto boundaries, thereby indirectly consenting to its conquest of most of Palestine in the 1948 war. The failure to refer to core issues dating back to 1948 extended to ignoring the right of the Palestinian refugees to return to their homes and obtain compensation, another blow to their aspirations. With Resolution 242, the UN was walking away from its own commitment to these rights, consecrated by the General Assembly in Resolution 194 in December 1948. Once again, the Palestinians were being dealt with by the great powers in a cavalier fashion, their rights ignored, deemed not worthy of mention by name in the key international decision meant to resolve the conflict and determine their fate. This slight further motivated the Palestinians' reviving national movement to put its case and cause before the international community.

Thanks in large part to SC 242, a whole new layer of forgetting, of erasure and myth-making, was added to the induced amnesia that obscured the colonial origins of the conflict between Palestinians and the Zionist settlers. The resolution's exclusive focus on the results of the 1967 war made it possible to ignore the fact that none of the underlying issues resulting from the 1948 war had been resolved in the intervening nineteen years. Along with the expulsion of the Palestinian refugees, the refusal to allow them to return, the theft of their property, and the denial of Palestinian self-determination, these included the legal status of Jerusalem and Israel's expansion beyond the 1947 partition frontiers. As for the core problems arising from the original usurpation of Palestine, SC 242 did not even refer to them, much less offer any solutions. Yet the resolution henceforth became the benchmark for resolving the entire conflict, nominally accepted by all parties, even as it passed over the basic aspects of the conflict in silence. In view of the resolution's perverse genesis, it is not surprising that over fifty years after it was adopted, UNSC 242 remains unimplemented and the essence of the struggle over Palestine remains unaddressed.

Indeed, SC 242 exacerbated the problem. Confining the conflict to its post-1948 state-to-state dimensions made it possible to split the challenges facing Israel into separate bilateral state-to-state compartments, each of which could be dealt with in isolation, as Israel and the United States preferred, while ignoring the most difficult and uncomfortable questions. Instead of being obliged to confront a (nominally) unified Arab position and engage the tough issues relating to the Palestinians,

Israel now had the far easier task of dealing on a bilateral basis with the grievances of individual Arab states whose territory it had occupied, while sidelining the Palestinians.

In Israel's effort to divide its enemies and deal with them separately, the United States was of enormous help, using its power and influence to play on the Arab states' weaknesses and rivalries. This was seen as being in the US interest, too. Characteristically, Henry Kissinger put this pithily, speaking of another Middle Eastern crisis: "The end result would be exactly what we have worked all these years to avoid: it would create Arab unity."[25] The United States had multiple reasons to prevent such unity, primarily to fend off threats to its regional dominance, and in particular to the fragile oil autocracies of the Gulf with which it was closely aligned. Following the push by the United States and Israel for bilateral settlements, Egypt in the 1970s and then Jordan in the 1990s negotiated separate peace treaties with Israel. These countries were thereby removed from the conflict, leaving Israel in an even stronger position to deal with its more intractable foes, the Syrians, the Lebanese, and of course the Palestinians. To most people in the Arab world, however, the stark contrast between Arab normalization with Israel and the misery that its colonization and occupation inflicted on the Palestinians inevitably undermined any faith in an American-sponsored peace process.[26]

In and of itself, SC 242 did not force the Arab states to accept the bilateralization and fragmentation of the conflict. Other factors were at work, among them the impact of Egypt's defeat in 1967, its subsequent withdrawal from Yemen, both of which marked the end of its attempt to assert regional hegemony. Egypt's diminution left its rival Saudi Arabia as the dominant actor in the Arab world, a situation that continues to the present day. The failure of the Arab socialist model adopted by the authoritarian nationalist regimes, and the pronounced regional weakness of the USSR, also played a role in their capitulation. At different times, encouraged by the United States, the Arab countries walked into the trap of separate settlements with open eyes, eventually abandoning any semblance of unity or even minimal coordination. Even the Palestinians, represented by the PLO, eventually traveled down the path laid out in SC 242. Only a few years after the Arab states accepted 242 and the bilateral approach as a basis for a resolution of the conflict, the PLO leadership followed.[27]

There is another side to the story of what happened in 1967, however. For all the harm the war and SC 242 did to the Palestinians, they ultimately served as the spark to their reviving national movement, which had been declining since the defeat of the 1936–39 revolt. The process of revival had started well before the 1967 war, of course, playing a crucial role in precipitating that and the 1956 war. Still, 1967 marked an extraordinary resurgence of Palestinian national consciousness and resistance to Israel's negation of Palestinian identity, a negation made possible by the complicity of much of the world community. In the words of one seasoned observer: "A central paradox of 1967 is that by defeating the Arabs, Israel resurrected the Palestinians."[28]

THE RESURRECTION OF the idea of Palestine faced an uphill battle in the wake of the 1967 war in most parts of the world. The year after the war, I joined a tiny demonstration to protest the appearance of Golda Meir, who had been invited to speak at Yale Law School. She was rapturously received by a large and appreciative audience, while, as I recall it, our demonstration consisted of a total of four protestors: myself, a Lebanese-American friend, a Sudanese graduate student, and one American who had lived in the Middle East. That scene accurately represented the balance between Israel and Palestine in American opinion. The Zionist narrative enjoyed complete dominance while the very word "Palestine" was almost unmentionable.

In Beirut, on the other hand, where I now spent the summers with my mother and brothers, I was witness to an important resurgence of Palestinian political agency. Writers and poets both throughout the Palestinian diaspora and living inside Palestine—Ghassan Kanafani, Mahmoud Darwish, Emile Habibi, Fadwa Touqan, and Tawfiq Zayyad, together with other gifted and engaged artists and intellectuals—played a vital role in this renaissance, culturally and politically. Their work helped to reshape a sense of Palestinian identity and purpose that had been tested by the Nakba and the barren years that followed. In novels, short stories, plays, and poetry, they gave voice to a shared national experience of loss, exile, alienation. At the same time, they evinced a stubborn insistence on the continuity of Palestinian identity and steadfastness in the face of daunting odds.

These different facets are evident in one of the best-known of these works, Emile Habibi's *The Pesssoptimist*, a brilliant novella that traces the tragicomic tale of its protagonist, Sa'id, using his fate to portray the plight of the Palestinians and their resilience. The work's full title, *The Strange Incidents Around the Disappearance of Sa'id Father of Nahs, the Pessoptimist*, conveys the essential paradox of the Palestinian situation: happiness, expressed in the name Sa'id, which means happy, and calamity, or *Nahs*. Both are contained in the portmanteau word "pessoptimist."[29]

Among the literary figures whose ideas and images played a major role in the revival of Palestinian identity, Kanafani was perhaps the most prominent prose writer and the most widely translated.[30] His five novellas, notably *Men in the Sun* (1963) and *Return to Haifa* (1969), are widely popular, perhaps because they depict so vividly the dilemmas faced by Palestinians: the travails of exile and the pain of life in post-1967 Palestine, now entirely under Israeli control. The novellas encouraged Palestinians to confront their dire predicament and forcefully resist the powers that oppressed them. *Return to Haifa* stressed the importance of armed struggle while at the same time poignantly depicting an Israeli Holocaust survivor living in the home of a Palestinian family that returns to visit after 1967.

Kanafani was also a prolific journalist, steeped in Palestinian resistance literature—indeed, he may have coined the term in a collection he published under that title[31]—and he had been deeply involved in politics since his late teens. Born in Acre in 1936, he and his family had been forced to flee their home during the Zionist offensive of May 1948, first settling in Damascus. When I met him in Beirut, he was thirty-three years old and the editor of *al-Hadaf*, the weekly magazine of the radical Popular Front for the Liberation of Palestine, of which Kanafani was also the public spokesman. He won others over not only with his literary talent, but also with his manifest intelligence, his self-deprecating and sardonic sense of humor, and his pleasant, open demeanor and ready smile. In light of his literary renown and militant activism, he was a significant

The funeral of Ghassan Kanafani, who was assassinated in a car bombing by the Mossad, Beirut, July 1972

figure in the revived Palestinian national movement. For the same reason, he was a target of the PFLP's enemies, the foremost being the Israeli government and its intelligence services.

In July 1972, Kanafani was assassinated in a car bombing by the Mossad, together with his seventeen-year-old niece, Lamis Najm.[32] His enormous funeral, which I attended, drew what seemed to be hundreds of thousands of people mourning him. It was the first of many funerals of Palestinian leaders and militants that I would attend during my fifteen years in Beirut.*

The reshaping and revival of Palestinian identity that Kanafani, Darwish, Zayyad, Touqan, Habibi and others helped to spark with their literary output went in tandem with the rise of new political movements and armed groups. After 1948, Palestine had ceased to exist on the map, with

---

*Kanafani was pursued even in death. An English stage adaptation of *Return to Haifa* was commissioned by the Public Theater in New York but never produced. Members of its board opposed staging work by Kanafani, who had been dubbed a terrorist.

most of the country absorbed into Israel and the rest under the control of Jordan and Egypt. Palestinians had almost no voice, no central address, and no champions other than the bickering, self-interested Arab states. The Zionist movement's deepest desire had been to transform Palestine into Israel and replace the country's indigenous inhabitants with Jewish immigrants. After 1948, it appeared as if the Palestinians had largely disappeared, both physically and as an idea.

The Palestinians of course had not disappeared in the years after 1948. The collective trauma of the Nakba had perversely cemented and reinforced their identity, and the small irredentist militant groups that arose in the 1950s had already had a significant impact on the Middle East, having played a role in triggering both the 1956 and 1967 wars. These groups were founded by young middle-class and lower-middle-class radicals, many of whom saw themselves as the progeny of Shaykh 'Iz al-Din al-Qassam, whose death in battle with the British had been one of the sparks of the 1936 revolt and who remained a revered symbol of heroic armed militancy. They continued after 1956 to work to reestablish the Palestinians as a regional force and to represent their rights and interests. In the 1960s, these efforts culminated in two main trends. One was led by the Movement of Arab Nationalists, a pan-Arab organization founded largely by Palestinians, which gave birth in 1967 to the Marxist PFLP. The other was headed by a group formally established in Kuwait in 1959, and which in 1965 publicly announced itself as Fatah. The origins of both go back to the late 1940s and early 1950s, when their first leaders were university students or recent graduates.

MAN was founded by George Habash, a physician trained at the American University of Beirut who had experienced the Nakba as a young man in Lydd, a town that was depopulated after 1948, resettled with Jewish immigrants, and renamed Lod. Habash set up MAN together with a group of other young Palestinians and Arabs, most of them middle-class professionals like himself and his closest collaborator, Wadi' Haddad, another AUB-trained physician. Habash and his colleagues argued for Arab unity around the question of Palestine as the sole means to reverse the results of the Nakba. After Nasser's Egypt became the standard-bearer for Arab nationalism in the mid-1950s, a close alignment between MAN and the Egyptian regime developed.

MAN profited greatly from this alliance, becoming a pan-Arab political force, implanted in countries from Libya and Yemen to Kuwait, Iraq, Syria, and Lebanon. Egyptian foreign policy benefited as well from its connection with MAN's widespread network of young militants.[33]

Habash, Haddad, and their comrades' view of Palestine as the central issue for the Arab world had in large measure been imparted to them at the American University of Beirut by the historian and intellectual Constantin Zureiq through a student organization, Al-'Urwa al-Wuthqa, of which Zureiq was the mentor and to which my father belonged.[34] This influential Syrian-born, Princeton-trained professor of history did much to spread the ideas of Arab nationalism and the centrality of the Palestine issue in lectures to his students in Beirut and to people across the Arab world through his writings. His short eighty-six-page book, *The Meaning of the Catastrophe*, was one of the first post-mortems of the 1948 defeat, written while the war was ongoing, and featured perhaps the first use of the word *nakba* in this context.[35] Zureiq argued in it for rigorous, introspective self-criticism of Arab weaknesses and failures, and for Arab coordination and unity as the only means of overcoming the effects of the 1948 disaster. My father studied with Zureiq at the AUB in the late 1930s and was strongly influenced by him; several of Zureiq's historical and political books, some inscribed by the author, were in my father's library. When I first met Zureiq in the early 1970s in Beirut at the Institute for Palestine Studies, of which he was a cofounder, he urged me and other young historians associated with the IPS to focus on the future. This was more important than history, he seemed to imply, which had already been written by him and his generation.

Faced by an upsurge of activist, nationalist sentiment, spurred by Fatah's first military operation (carried out in January 1965), and feeling the need to keep up with one of its core constituencies, MAN was forced to move away from its broad Arab nationalist stance and concentrate more on Palestine. The defeat of Egypt and Syria in 1967 put the last nail in the coffin of MAN's reliance on the Arab regimes to resolve the question of Palestine.[36] The result was the formation of the PFLP by Habash and his colleagues in 1967. Although it was not the largest Palestinian group, the PFLP rapidly became the most dynamic, a stature it maintained for several years. It carried out multiple airplane hijackings in that short time; these were masterminded by Wadi' Haddad, as were most of what it called its "external operations," seen as terrorist attacks by much of the world.

Much of the prestige that the group enjoyed among Palestinians was due to the image and integrity of Habash, who was respected even by his political rivals. He was known as *al-Hakim*, the doctor, which he was, but the term is also used for someone who is wise, and it was applied to Habash in both senses. He was a riveting speaker, especially in small groups, where his articulate and intellectual approach and his approachable and pleasant affect made the greatest impact. He spoke softly but firmly, with no trace of demagoguery. As I witnessed in south Lebanon in the early 1970s, Habash could keep an audience rapt for hours, in spite of the complexity of his ideas. With its Marxist-Leninist affinity, the PFLP was popular among students, the educated, the middle class, and particularly those drawn to leftist politics. It also had a dedicated following in the refugee camps, where its radical message resonated strongly with the Palestinians who had suffered the most.

Fatah, by contrast, was decidedly nonideological in its political approach, when compared to the PFLP and other avowedly leftist Palestinian groups. At the time of its founding, Fatah represented a reaction both to the Arab nationalist orientation of groups like MAN and the Baath Party, and to communist, leftist, and Islamist groups like the Muslim Brotherhood, which argued for societal change before other problems, notably that of Palestine, could be addressed. Fatah's call for direct and immediate action by Palestinians, as well as its broad-tent nonideological stance, was one of the factors that rapidly enabled it to become the largest political faction. Some of the details are hazy, but we know that Fatah was founded in Kuwait in 1959 by a group of Palestinian engineers, teachers, and other professionals, headed by Yasser 'Arafat. The core of the group had coalesced earlier in the Gaza Strip and in the universities of Cairo, where it competed with MAN for leadership of the Union of Palestinian Students.

Salah Khalaf—Abu Iyad—once told me an emblematic story about 'Arafat and university politics in Cairo. In danger of losing a student election the following day to MAN, 'Arafat said he had an idea and took Khalaf to visit someone he knew at the Egyptian Interior Ministry. They sat drinking tea and coffee and making small talk until the man had to leave his office for a moment, at which point 'Arafat leaped up, went behind the official's desk, did something furtive, and returned to his seat. When the man returned, the two took their leave. Khalaf objected that they hadn't once brought up the imminent election. 'Arafat told him to go home: the problem was solved. The next day, Khalaf glumly went to the union office to wait out the election only to find an official-looking notice on the door, stamped by Egypt's Ministry of the Interior, ordering the election postponed. This was 'Arafat's doing, and he used the delay, Khalaf said, to enroll Palestinian students studying at al-Azhar University, many of whom were blind, and none of whom had been courted for their votes by the competing factions. When the election was finally held, they voted en bloc for the Fatah list, securing its victory.

Fatah's main, indeed only, focus was the Palestinian cause. To further this end, Fatah called for a campaign of direct armed action against Israel, which it launched on January 1, 1965, with its sabotage attack on the water-pumping station in central Israel. Like much of what Fatah did in this era, the act was more symbolic than effective. Nonetheless, Egyptian officials considered Fatah to be dangerously adventurist at a time when Egypt could ill afford such provocations across its borders. While MAN and other groups made excuses for the inaction of the nationalist regimes they were associated with, Fatah deliberately tried to show up the Arab states for their lack of true commitment to Palestine. This posture infuriated the regimes (especially since Fatah's fervent rhetoric was not matched by much effective armed action), but it went over well with most Palestinians, who were frustrated by the Arab states' lack of engagement. It was also attractive to many Arab citizens, who supported the Palestinians and shared their frustrations.

This appeal to public opinion over the heads of the Arab regimes via direct action against Israel was one of the great secrets to the early success of the Palestinian resistance groups, especially Fatah. They spoke to the widespread sense among Arabs that an injustice had been done in Palestine and that their governments were doing nothing substantive about it. In the years during which this appeal was effective, throughout the 1960s and 1970s, the support for the Palestinian resistance by a broad sector of public opinion served to restrain even undemocratic

Arab governments. However, that restraint had severe limits, which were reached when Palestinian militancy threatened the Arab states' domestic status quo or provoked Israel to take action.

In the meantime, the small militant groups went from strength to strength, and it became clear that a full-scale revival of the Palestinian national movement was underway. By the mid-1960s, this coalescing movement threatened to seize the initiative in the conflict with Israel from the Arab states, and indeed helped to precipitate the events that led to the 1967 war. For all their rhetoric, most of the Arab states (Syria being the exception under the ultraradical regime in power from 1966 to 1970) were preoccupied with other issues and were deeply reluctant to challenge a status quo that heavily favored Israel, whose demonstrated military power they regarded with trepidation. While in the West, Israel still retained its image as a beleaguered victim of Arab hostility, this was far from how it was seen in the Arab world, which instead viewed its decisive military victories and potential possession of nuclear weapons as evidence of towering strength.

To co-opt and control the rising tide of Palestinian nationalist fervor, the Arab League, under Egypt's leadership, founded the Palestine Liberation Organization in 1964. This was meant to be a tightly controlled subsidiary of Egyptian foreign policy that would channel and manage Palestinian enthusiasm for striking against Israel, but this attempt to keep the Palestinians under Arab tutelage rapidly unraveled. In the immediate wake of the 1967 war, the militant Palestinian resistance groups took over the PLO, sidelining its Egypt-oriented leadership. 'Arafat, as the head of Fatah, the largest of these groups, soon became chairman of the PLO Executive Committee, a post he retained, among others, until his death in 2004.

Henceforth, the Arab states were obliged to take account of an independent Palestinian political actor, based mainly in the countries bordering Israel, a situation that had already proved problematic for these states and that would eventually become a source of great vulnerability for the Palestinian movement. The rise of this independent actor further complicated the strategic situation of the border states, notably Egypt and Syria, while it constituted a grave domestic problem for Jordan and Lebanon, both of which had large, restive Palestinian refugee populations.

For Israel, the reemergence of the Palestinian national movement as a force in the Middle East and increasingly on the global stage constituted a great irony: its victory in 1967 had helped to precipitate even more intransigent Palestinian resistance. This constituted a sharp reversal of one of Israel's great successes of the 1948–1967 period, in which the very issue of Palestinian nationhood had almost been fully eclipsed in both arenas. The return of the Palestinians, whose disappearance would have signified a final victory for the Zionist project, was a most unwelcome apparition for Israel's leaders, as unwelcome as the return of any indigenous population would be for a settler-colonial enterprise that believed it had dispensed with them. The comforting idea that "the old will die and the young will forget"—a remark attributed to David Ben-Gurion, probably mistakenly—expresses one of the deepest aspirations of Israeli leaders after 1948. It was not to be.

While the Palestinian resurgence posed little or no threat to Israel in strategic terms (although the attacks by militant groups did create serious security problems), it constituted an entirely different kind of challenge on the discursive level, one that was existential. The ultimate success of the Zionist project as hard-line Zionists defined it depended in large measure on the replacement of Palestine by Israel. For them, if Palestine existed, Israel could not. Israel was in consequence obliged to focus its powerful propaganda machine on a new target, while still having to counter the efforts of the Arab states. Since from the Zionist vantage point the name Palestine and the very existence of the Palestinians constituted a mortal threat to Israel, the task was to connect these terms indelibly, if they were mentioned at all, with terrorism and hatred, rather than with a forgotten but just cause. For many years, this theme was the core of a remarkably successful public relations offensive, especially in the United States.

Finally, the reemergence of the Palestine question posed a problem for US diplomacy, which with SC 242 had chosen to ignore it and act as if the Palestinians did not exist. For a decade thereafter, the United States strove to keep its head in the sand, even as much of the international community began to extend to the Palestinian movement some degree of recognition. This US stance was in keeping with pronounced Israeli preferences, and it was made possible by the inadequate representation by the Palestinians of their own cause in the US arena, and the weakness of pro-Palestinian sentiment in American public opinion. At the same time, administrations from that of Nixon onward also gave various forms of covert and overt support to military action directed against the PLO by Israel, Jordan, Lebanese factions, and Syria.

By MANAGING TO impose themselves on the map of the Middle East in spite of the best efforts of Israel, the United States, and many Arab governments, the Palestinians succeeded in reacquiring something long denied to them, what Edward Said called the "permission to narrate." This meant the right to tell their story themselves, taking back control of it not only from Israel's omnipresent narrative in the West, in which the Palestinians scarcely figured except as villains (as in *Exodus,* for example), but also from the Arab governments. For many years, the Arab states had taken charge of the Palestinian side of the story as their own, relating it feebly as a conflict between Israel and themselves over borders and refugees.[37]

One aspect of the rapid ascent in the fortunes of their national movement that has been overlooked is the effectiveness of the Palestinians' communications strategy in the Arab countries, in the developing world, and to a lesser extent in Europe and the West. At the UN, where Third World countries by the 1960s had a much bigger presence, this translated into a more favorable environment for the Palestine cause. In consequence, the historic gap between the Zionists' success in shaping world public opinion and Palestinian ineptness in this sphere began to narrow, partly due to an increase in the number of Palestinians steeped in Western culture or with experience in other parts of the globe.

In the Arab world, the movement received an enormous boost in March 1968, nine months after the war, in Karameh, a small Jordanian town (whose name by fortuitous coincidence means "dignity"). In Israel's biggest military operation since the war, about fifteen thousand troops with armor, artillery, and air support crossed the Jordan River to eliminate a concentration of Palestinian fighters based in and around Karameh. The attackers unexpectedly met fierce resistance from the Jordanian army and the PLO, which inflicted between one hundred to two hundred casualties on the seemingly invincible Israeli army, and forced it to abandon a number of damaged tanks, armored personnel carriers, and other equipment.

In the wake of the disastrous war barely a year earlier, this relatively small engagement, in which the Israelis seemed to leave the battlefield in disarray, electrified the Arab world and revolutionized the image of the Palestinians. Although it was Jordanian artillery and armor, positioned in the hills overlooking the Jordan River valley, which undoubtedly inflicted the most damage on Israel's forces, the Palestinians fighting inside Karameh reaped most of the glory from this episode. The battle of Karameh proved to be a godsend to the propaganda of the Palestinian resistance movement, which effectively publicized the clash as a stand for Arab dignity, trampled underfoot as it had been by the failures of the Arab regimes. As a result, the Palestinian resistance was lionized throughout the Arab world.

The irony of this self-presentation was that at its height, the PLO never posed any kind of military challenge to Israeli forces, which defeated all the Arab armies in the field in every one of their conventional wars. Even when PLO forces fought well defensively, as at Karameh, they were rarely capable of going head-to-head for very long with one of the most experienced, well-trained, and best-equipped militaries in the world. Moreover, from the beginning of the Palestinian armed struggle in the 1960s until the PLO later renounced this approach, they never were able to develop a successful guerrilla war strategy that might have countered the superiority of Israel's conventional forces or the limitations of being based in Arab countries vulnerable to Israeli military pressure.

In fact, the PLO's greatest success in its heyday during the late 1960s and 1970s came in the realm of diplomacy, despite the United States' refusal to engage with the Palestinians. This was visible not only in the Arab world and the Eastern Bloc, which extended limited support to the PLO from the late 1960s onward, but also in much of the Third World, many countries of Western Europe, and even at the UN, Resolution 242 notwithstanding. In the General Assembly, the PLO could now muster majorities that were immune to the veto that the US wielded in the Security Council. There and in other arenas, the PLO achieved a high level of diplomatic recognition, even succeeding to some small degree in isolating Israel. The PLO was recognized by the Arab League in 1974 as the sole legitimate representative of the Palestinian people, while simultaneously opening PLO missions in more than one hundred countries. The invitation to Yasser 'Arafat to speak before the UN General Assembly that same year was the greatest diplomatic success in Palestinian history, after so many decades of nonrecognition by the League of Nations, the UN, and the great powers.

There were different reasons for these limited triumphs. This was an era when successful national liberation movements in Algeria, southern Africa, and Southeast Asia garnered support, including among young people, in the West. The PLO's anticolonial and Third-World revolutionary appeal also resonated with China, the Soviet Union and its satellites, with Third World countries, and among those countries' representatives at the UN.[38] In most of the newly independent countries of Asia and Africa, the Palestinians were seen as another people struggling against a colonial-settler project backed by the Western powers; they therefore deserved the sympathy of those who themselves had just thrown off the colonial yoke. At the height of the Vietnam War, these themes had great appeal to disaffected youth in Europe and the United States. Finally, the PLO succeeded to some extent in galvanizing the Palestinian and Arab diaspora in the Americas, who became advocates for the national cause.

Yet all of these efforts had severe limitations. Among them were the PLO's failure to devote sufficient energy, talent, and resources to diplomacy and information, despite the gains made in these areas. Nor did the PLO work hard enough at understanding their target audiences, the most crucial of them being the United States and Israel. There, the PLO ultimately failed to overcome a more effective competing narrative generated by Israel and its supporters that equated "Palestinian" with "terrorist."[39] The PLO's incapacity to understand the importance of these two vital arenas started with its top leadership. Respected Palestinian-American academics in the United States, notably Edward Said, Ibrahim Abu-Lughod, Walid Khalidi, Hisham Sharabi, Fouad Moughrabi, and Samih Farsoun, repeatedly tried to impress on Palestinian leaders that they needed to take American public opinion into account and devote to it sufficient resources and energy, but to no avail.

At a 1984 meeting in Amman of the Palestine National Council

(PNC), the PLO's governing body, a US-based group in which I participated strove to make this point to Yasser 'Arafat. He agreed to meet
us and listened courteously until, after only a couple of minutes, an aide
came in and whispered in his ear. We were hurriedly ushered out while
'Arafat received one Abu al-'Abbas, the leader of the Palestine Liberation
Front, a tiny, insignificant faction that caused great damage to the Palestinian cause (but was on Iraq's payroll). Our audience was over and
the opportunity for us Palestinian-Americans to make the case for the
importance of appealing to US public opinion evaporated. In the PLO
leadership's misplaced priorities, the inter-Arab balancing act at which
'Arafat excelled was more pressing than was furthering the Palestine
cause with the public of the preeminent global superpower.

Notwithstanding this failure, the Palestinian cause did make some
progress in the United States after 1967. This was largely thanks to the
efforts of the same group of Palestinian-American academics, who were
effective in putting the Palestinian narrative before college campuses,
the alternative media, and other sectors of public opinion. Edward Said
in particular had an outsized impact, articulately making a case for the
Palestinians in ways that his audiences had never heard before. While
he and his Palestinian-American colleagues were unable to achieve a
breakthrough with the mainstream media, which by and large continued to repeat the Israeli line, they laid the groundwork for an increased
understanding of the Palestinian perspective in future years.

As the PLO appeared to go from one diplomatic and propaganda victory to another after 1967, these successes did not go uncontested, each
one provoking ferocious opposition from its many foes. Israel's raid on
Karameh was one of its first efforts to counter the PLO's growing status;
a devastating raid on the Beirut airport in 1968 was another. In 1970, the
PFLP's aircraft hijackings and Palestinian excesses in Jordan precipitated
a disastrous confrontation with the Hashemite regime that the resistance
movement was in no position to win. Facing superior force, and having
lost some popular sympathy, the movement was driven from Amman
that year in what became known as Black September, and then completely expelled from Jordan in the spring of 1971. One of the casualties
of the Jordan debacle was the aura of successful dynamism that some
components of the movement, notably the PFLP, had maintained until

that point. The resistance movement's pattern of recklessly provoking its enemies, alienating its hosts, and ultimately being expelled was to be repeated in Beirut eleven years later.

Meanwhile, Israel carried out further punishing attacks on Syria and Lebanon, countries from which the Palestinians continued to launch military operations. These included a major ground incursion into south Lebanon in 1972, an aerial bombardment in 1974 of the Nabatiya Palestinian refugee camp in Lebanon, which was completely destroyed and never rebuilt, and an invasion that resulted in the long-term occupation of parts of south Lebanon in 1978. All these moves against the PLO benefited from strong US support: both the Israeli and Jordanian militaries received American arms, and both countries were able to count on full US diplomatic backing.

The United States reacted to the increased visibility of the PLO and to what seemed to be a unified Arab bloc in another way, as well. Given the USSR's support for the PLO and the Arab bloc, President Nixon and his national security advisor and later secretary of state, Henry Kissinger, expended great efforts to weaken the Soviet Union's links to what they saw as its Arab clients in the Middle East. The centerpiece of this Cold War strategy was the American attempt to prise Egypt away from the USSR, align it with the US, and induce it to agree to a separate peace settlement with Israel. When this American-led initiative finally succeeded in the late 1970s, under the Carter administration, it had the effect of splitting the (nominally) unified Arab front and leaving the Palestinians and other Arab actors to face Israel in a much weaker position. In all of this, the United States stuck to the lines laid down in SC 242, which excluded the Palestinians from any share in the negotiations for a settlement. US policymakers were guided by their hostility to the PLO because of its militancy and its alignment with the USSR, but also by Israel's intense opposition to discussion of any aspect of the Palestine question.

Thereafter, the PLO was trapped in a dilemma: how could it achieve Palestinian national aspirations through participation in a Middle East peace settlement when the internationally recognized terms for such a settlement, SC 242, negated these aspirations? It was a dilemma remarkably similar to that posed by the Balfour Declaration and the Palestine

Mandate: in order to be recognized, the Palestinians were required to accept an international formula designed to negate their existence.

THE SMALL MILITANT groups that relaunched the Palestinian national movement in the 1950s and early 1960s put forward simple objectives for their struggle. For them, Palestine had long been an Arab land with an Arab majority. Its people had been unjustly dispossessed of their homes, their property, their homeland, and their right of self-determination. These groups' main purpose was to return the Palestinian people to their homeland, restore their rights, and oust those whom they saw as usurpers. The term "return" was central, as it has been for Palestinians ever since. Most felt no sense that there were now two peoples in Palestine, each with national rights; to them Israelis were no more than settlers, foreign immigrants to their country. This position exactly mirrored that of most Israelis, for whom there was only one people with national rights in Eretz Yisrael, the Land of Israel, and that was the Jewish people, while the Arabs were no more than transient interlopers. In the Palestinian reading of the day, Israel was a colonial-settler project that the West had helped create and supported (which was largely true), and the Israeli Jews were part of a religious group only, not a people or a nation (which the successful creation of a powerful nation-state with a strong national identity had already shown to be false). At this point, the Palestinians had not come to terms with the reality of a new national entity in Palestine, in part because this had happened at their expense and at a ruinous cost to them.

The culmination of this thinking about the objectives of the Palestinian struggle was articulated in the National Charter (*al-mithaq al-watani*), adopted by the PLO in 1964. The charter stated that Palestine was an Arab country where national rights belonged only to those residing there before 1917 and their descendants. This group included Jews then resident in Palestine, but not those who had immigrated after the Balfour Declaration, who would therefore be obliged to leave. From this perspective, liberation involved the reversal of everything that had taken place in Palestine since the Balfour Declaration, the British Mandate, the partition of the country, and the Nakba. It meant turning back the clock and refashioning Palestine into an Arab country once more. Although the ideas the charter embodied were reflective of much, perhaps most, Palestinian sentiment at the time, it was adopted by a body created by the Arab League, not one that was elected by or represented the Palestinians.

These objectives would change rapidly with shifting circumstances and the transformations of Palestinian politics after 1964. With the takeover of the PLO by Fatah and the other resistance groups in 1968, the national movement formulated a new objective, advocating the idea of Palestine as a single democratic state for all its citizens, both Jews and Arabs (some iterations referred to a secular democratic state). This was meant to supersede the aims laid down in the National Charter, recognizing that Israeli Jews had acquired the right to live in Palestine and could not be made to leave. The change was also meant to refashion the PLO's image and appeal to Israelis, who were treated by the 1964 National Charter as if they did not exist. The statement that Jews and Arabs living in Palestine were entitled to be equal citizens of the country represented a major evolution of the movement's thinking. However, the single democratic state proposal did not recognize the Israelis as a people with national rights, nor did it accept the legitimacy of the state of Israel or of Zionism.

Over time, this new objective came to be broadly accepted among Palestinians and was embodied in successive authoritative pronouncements of PLO policy via resolutions of the PNC. In the end, it superseded the charter and rendered it obsolete, yet these fundamental changes were resolutely ignored by the PLO's opponents, who continued to harp on the charter's original provisions for decades to come. The change also achieved little traction with most Israelis and failed to convince many in the West. Again, the inability of the PLO leadership to understand how important these audiences were, and its unwillingness to devote sufficient resources to explaining the significance of this evolution in order to win them over, doomed any effort to convince others of the validity of these aims.

More important, achieving an objective of this magnitude would require the dissolution of Israel with a new state of Palestine taking its place. This would mean overturning what since 1947 had become an international consensus around the existence of Israel as a Jewish state, as specified by the wording of GA 181. Only a revolutionary shift in the balance of forces both within Israel and globally could accomplish such an end, something that the Palestinians could hardly achieve or even contemplate on their own. And they could not count on their brothers in the Arab regimes. Radical Arab states such as Syria, Iraq, and Libya continued to talk a big game where the Palestine cause was concerned, but their rhetoric was empty. What these states actually did was to sabotage the PLO by sponsoring nihilistic terrorist groups, such as the Abu Nidal organization, which assassinated numerous PLO leaders and killed Israelis and Jews indiscriminately. As for the other key Arab states, Egypt and Jordan, with the support of Saudi Arabia, had by 1970 accepted SC 242, and Syria followed in 1973. This major development (unacknowledged by Israel), amounted to those states' de facto recognition of Israel, at least within the 1949 armistice lines. The dissonance between this crucial shift by several major Arab states and the PLO's position was to have grave consequences for the Palestinians.

Changes in regional circumstances led many PLO leaders to consider a further modification of their objectives. A number of factors exerted an influence: the PLO's inability to sustain an effective guerrilla campaign against Israel after the loss of its bases in Jordan; the Arab states' growing acceptance of the conflict with Israel not as existential but as a state-to-state confrontation over frontiers; and Arab and international pressure on the PLO to conform to more limited objectives. At the Arab League's summit in Khartoum in 1967, the League had declared that there would be no peace, no recognition, and no negotiations with Israel (the "three nos" that were much repeated in Israeli propaganda). In reality, Egypt and Jordan welcomed mediation with Israel through UN special envoy Gunnar Jarring and later via US Secretary of State William Rogers. The Khartoum summit notwithstanding, the most powerful Arab country bordering Israel had, by accepting SC 242, conceded in principle that its neighbor had a right to secure and recognized boundaries. It remained only for the Arab states and Israel to negotiate those boundaries and the other terms of a settlement. The Jordanian crackdown on the Palestinians in September 1970, although provoked by the PFLP aircraft hijackings, was meant among other things to punish the Palestinians for not accepting the new limitations of the key Arab states' aims.

Starting in the early 1970s, members of the PLO responded to these pressures, in particular to the urging of the Soviet Union, by floating the idea of a Palestinian state alongside Israel, in effect a two-state solution. This approach was notably promoted by the Democratic Front for the Liberation of Palestine (which had split off from the PFLP in 1969), together with Syrian-backed groups, discreetly encouraged by the leadership of Fatah. Although there had been early resistance to the two-state solution by the PFLP and some Fatah cadres, in time it became clear that 'Arafat, among other leaders, supported it. This marked the beginning of a long, slow process of shifting away from the maximalist objective of the democratic state, with its revolutionary implications, to an ostensibly more pragmatic aim of a Palestinian state alongside Israel, to be achieved via negotiations on the basis of SC 242.

THE PATH TOWARD these radical modifications was not an easy one for the PLO. Only after some of the most severe blows inflicted on the Palestinian national movement since the Nakba did the PLO come to accept a two-state approach based on SC 242. These blows came in quick succession during the Lebanese civil war, which began formally in April 1975. However, for the Palestinians the war began two years earlier, on April 10, 1973, with the assassination of three PLO leaders in their homes in West Beirut by Israeli commandos led by Ehud Barak (later Israel's prime minister).[40] The crowds of Palestinians and Lebanese attending the funerals of the poet and PLO spokesman Kamal Nasser and Fatah leaders Kamal 'Adwan and Abu Yusuf Najjar were immense. As I walked with the masses of mourners, I was not surprised to see that they were even larger than those for Ghassan Kanafani.

These four men were among the scores of Palestinian leaders and cadres who fell victim to the assassination squads of the Mossad. It is true that nominally Palestinian groups murdered other Palestinian figures, including three members of the Fatah Central Committee and the PLO ambassadors in London and to the Socialist International. These groups served as agents of the three dictatorial Arab regimes—those of Hafez al-Asad in Syria, Saddam Hussein in Iraq, and Mu'ammar al-Qaddhafi in Libya—that were loud in their proclamation of support for the Palestinian cause but harsh in their treatment of the PLO. These regimes were patrons at different times of the gunmen of the Abu Nidal organization, which did most of this killing, and other small splinter groups.

While the impact of these assassinations by Israel and the hostile Arab powers is a mark of the extraordinarily difficult path trodden by the Palestinian national movement, there is an important distinction between them. The Arab states that used such means wanted to bend the PLO to their will, even by using brute force, as when the Asad regime sent troops to confront the PLO in Lebanon in 1976. However, they operated on the basis of cold, calculating raison d'état. They did not want to destroy the PLO or to extinguish the Palestine cause. Israel's case was quite different, as this was always its objective. Its long-standing policy of liquidating Palestinian leaders, inherited from the Zionist movement during the late Mandate period, aimed at eliminating the Palestinian reality, demographically, ideationally, and politically. Assassinations were thus a central element in Israel's ambition to transform the entire country, from the river to the sea, from an Arab to a Jewish one. To use Baruch Kimmerling's term once again, this was an example of politicide in its most literal form.

As evidence of the extent of the campaign of liquidations, we have two new accounts of it, one of them based on classified Israeli intelligence and military material. Among much else that is new, it contains sensational revelations about repeated attempts to assassinate Yasser 'Arafat.[41] The pretext that such killings were a blow against "terrorism" simply do not wash when the target is the leader of a national movement, unless the aim is to destroy that movement. Leaders of other anticolonial movements were invariably vilified by their colonial masters in similar terms—terrorists, bandits, and murderers—whether they were Irish, Indian, Kenyan, or Algerian. Similarly, Israel's demonization of the PLO as "terrorist" served as a justification for its eradication. The private statements of Israeli Defense Minister Ariel Sharon in 1982 about Palestinian "terrorists" in Beirut could not be clearer on this point.[42]

The justification of assassinations as necessary protection against terrorists, who would kill if not killed first, also rings hollow when many of those killed—Ghassan Kanafani and Kamal Nasser, for example, or PLO representatives abroad such as Mahmoud Hamshari and Wael Zu'aytir—were intellectuals and advocates for the Palestine cause, rather than military personnel. Their artistic ventures were supplementary and linked to their political activities: Kanafani was a gifted novelist and painter, Nasser a poet, Zu'aytir a writer and budding translator. These were not "terrorists," but the most prominent voices of a national movement, voices Israel was determined to stifle.

In Lebanon, the assassinations of Nasser, 'Adwan, and Najjar in April 1973 were followed one month later by an armed confrontation with the Lebanese army during which the air force strafed the Palestinian Sabra and Shatila refugee camps in the southern suburbs of Beirut. Throughout the remainder of the Lebanese civil war, which dragged on until 1990, Palestinian refugee camps and population centers were a frequent target: besieged, devastated, the scenes of massacres and forced expulsions. Tal al-Za'tar, Karantina, Dbaye, Jisr al-Basha, 'Ain al-Hilwa, Sabra, and Shatila—Palestinians in all these places suffered such atrocities. The war also brought horrific massacres of Lebanese Christians by factions of the PLO and its Lebanese allies, notably at Damour in January 1976 where hundreds of Christians were killed, and the town was sacked and looted.

Tal al-Za'tar was the largest, poorest, and most isolated of the Palestinian refugee camps in the Beirut area, with a population of about twenty thousand Palestinians and perhaps ten thousand impoverished Lebanese, mainly Shi'ites from the south. It was located in the East Beirut suburb of Dikwaneh, which was inhabited largely by Lebanese Maronites sympathetic to the right-wing anti-Palestinian Phalangist Party. I was living in Beirut with my wife, Mona, in the years leading up to the civil war, first working on my doctoral dissertation, and then teaching at the Lebanese University and the American University of Beirut. With a group of friends—Palestinian graduate students and residents of Tal al-Za'tar—we had opened the first preschool in the camp, backed by Jamiyat In'ash al-Mukhayam, a Lebanese-Palestinian charitable organization.

Relations between the camp and its surroundings became increasingly fraught as the situation in Lebanon deteriorated, and by May 1973 it was clear that Tal al-Za'tar and the nearby Dbaye and Jisr al-Basha refugee camps, as well as the Palestinian community in the Karantina area, were in decidedly hostile territory. Their neighbors deeply resented the presence of heavily armed Palestinian militiamen in the camps. In these perilous circumstances, we were all concerned about the safety of the small children in the preschool, so we dug a shelter beneath the center. Several other groups, and eventually the PLO, also built shelters, which saved many lives when the war broke out in earnest in 1975.

One Sunday in April that year, Mona and I were having lunch in Tal al-Za'tar, at the home of the parents of our friend Qasim, when we heard that there had been an incident on the road that led to the camp, which ran through the mainly Maronite suburb of 'Ain al-Rummaneh. We were advised to leave immediately. Driving back to West Beirut in our old VW Beetle, we spotted a small bus stopped at an awkward angle in the middle of the road. It had just been ambushed on its way back to Tal al-Za'tar by Phalangist militiamen, who had killed all of its twenty-seven passengers. It transpired that the Phalangists had taken revenge for a shooting at a Maronite church nearby where their leader, Pierre Gemayel, had been present.[43] Thus began the fifteen-year Lebanese civil war.

We were never able to return to Tal al-Za'tar. Besieged by what came to be called the Lebanese Forces, headed by Pierre Gemayel's son, Bashir, the camp was overrun in August 1976 and its entire population was expelled. Perhaps two thousand people were killed in what was probably the largest single massacre during the entire war. Some died during the siege, some when they fled the camp, and some at LF checkpoints, where Palestinians were picked up and taken away to be murdered. Two of the teachers from our preschool were killed in this way, as was Jihad, Qasim's eleven-year-old niece, who was kidnapped and murdered at a roadblock together with her mother.

The LF carried out the Tal al-Za'tar massacre with Israel's covert support. Years later, in 1982, facing parliamentary attacks by Labor Party leaders, Ariel Sharon upheld his conduct during the notorious Sabra and Shatila massacres in September of that year (in which over one thousand civilians were killed) by pointing to the Israeli government's support for the Phalangists at the time of the 1976 killings in Tal al-Za'tar.[44] In a secret meeting of the Knesset Defense and Foreign Affairs Committee, Sharon revealed that Israel's military intelligence officers, who were on the spot at the time of the Tal al-Za'tar massacre, reported that the Phalangists were killing people "with the weapons we supplied and the forces we helped them build."[45] Sharon went on to say to Shimon Peres, leader of the opposition Labor Party, which had been in power in 1976:

> You and us are acting according to the same moral principles. . . . The Phalangists murdered in Shatila and the Phalangists murdered in Tal Za'atar [sic]. The link is a moral one: should we get involved with the Phalangists or not. You supported them and continued to do so after Tal Za'atar.[46]

While Israeli military and intelligence officers may not have been inside the camps, as Sharon pointed out to the Knesset committee, they were present at the command posts from which both operations were directed. According to Hassan Sabri al-Kholi, the horrified Arab League mediator in Lebanon, who was present in the LF operations room and tried to halt the 1976 massacre as it was taking place, Israeli officers and two Syrian liaison personnel, Colonel 'Ali Madani and Colonel Muhammad Kholi, were there at the time.[47] Few images are more symbolic of the odds faced by the Palestinians during the Lebanon War than that of Israeli and Syrian officers—whose coexistence in Lebanon had been brokered by Henry Kissinger to "break the back" of the PLO[48]—looking on as LF commanders directed a massacre at a Palestinian refugee camp. But as Kissinger said in another context, "Covert action should not be confused with missionary work."[49]

The war in Lebanon had multiple protagonists, Lebanese and non-Lebanese, each one with different objectives, but for a number of them the PLO was a major target. To those Lebanese who opposed the PLO, most of them Maronite Christians, their resistance to the armed Palestinian presence was carried out in the name of Lebanese nationalism and independence. As most Palestinian refugees in Lebanon were Sunni Muslims, and because the secular PLO was allied with Lebanese leftist and Muslim groups, the Maronites feared a disruption of the country's sectarian political system, which the French Mandate had rigged in their favor in the early 1920s.

To Syria, Lebanon was a vital strategic arena it sought to dominate, a potential point of vulnerability in the conflict with Israel, and the site of its struggle with the PLO over leadership of the Arab front against Israel. These became crucial issues for Damascus as Egypt moved inexorably toward a separate peace with Israel and in effect became the US client state it has been ever since. While losing its Egyptian ally, Syria needed to find another counterweight to Israel, and domination of Lebanon, the Palestinians, and Jordan may have seemed like the only viable option. The boundless mistrust between the Syrian president Hafez al-Asad and the PLO's 'Arafat exacerbated the situation, as did the PLO's backing of Lebanese leftist formations, which were thereby enabled to take a position more independent of Damascus.

For the Israeli government, indirect and direct involvement in the Lebanon War furnished a welcome opportunity to acquire Lebanese clients, develop a new sphere of influence, and weaken Syria and its allies. Most important, the war provided an opening to retaliate against the PLO's sporadic attacks on Israelis, undermining and perhaps crippling it. This would also neutralize the threat that Palestinian nationalism posed to Israel's permanent control of the Occupied Territories, where millions more restive Palestinians had come under Israel's rule after 1967. The PLO's attacks launched from Lebanon, which often targeted civilians, gave different Israeli governments all the provocation they needed to justify interventions against their northern neighbor. Israeli methods ranged from direct support in the form of arms and training for the PLO's foes, notably the LF (which received equipment worth $118.5 million and training for 1,300 militiamen, according to an official Israeli source[50]), to the assassinations and car bombings that killed Palestinian leaders and countless civilians. Senior Israeli military and intelligence personnel recounted details of some of these operations in a book in which the chapter on Lebanon is entitled "A Pack of Wild Dogs."[51] The reference is to how Israeli operatives described their allies in the LF, which they employed for many of the most gruesome of these lethal operations.

The United States supported Israel's goals in Lebanon under Nixon, Ford, and Kissinger, and later under Carter, Vance, and Brzezinski, as well as during the Reagan administration. The two essential objectives of US Middle East policy were to woo the most important Arab state,

Egypt, away from the Soviet Union, while not allowing the Middle East conflict to complicate détente with the USSR. This required steering Egypt toward acceptance of Israel. Egypt's complete alignment with the US would let American leaders claim that they had won the Cold War in the Middle East while establishing a Pax Americana. Given the magnitude and importance to Washington of these strategic objectives, the PLO's opposition was a relatively minor obstacle, and there were plenty of Middle Eastern parties that were happy to help the United States by acting against it.

With the explicit approval of the United States, one of these parties, Syria, launched a direct military assault on the PLO in Lebanon in 1976 as the civil war there was already underway. While Washington and Syria were working toward an understanding about this intervention, Kissinger clarified US objectives: "We could let the Syrians move and break the back of the PLO." This was, he said, "a strategic opportunity which we shall miss."[52] In the end, the United States did not let the opportunity slip away, and Syrian troops engaged in pitched battles with Palestinian commandos in Sidon and the Shouf Mountains and elsewhere. This Syrian intervention was only made possible after Kissinger persuaded Israel not to oppose it, via a tacit agreement on "red lines" that set geographical limits to the Syrian advance.[53]

THE INVOLVEMENT OF the United States in hostilities against the Palestinians long preceded its green light to Syria in 1976. Henry Kissinger had no place for the PLO or for the resolution of the Palestinian problem in his Cold War–driven framework for the Middle East. For him, the Palestinians—in league with the Soviets and "radical" Arab regimes—were at worst a hindrance to be removed, and at best a problem to be ignored. In furtherance of the American Cold War aims and in his single-minded pursuit of these goals, Kissinger was instrumental in negotiating three important disengagement agreements between Israel and Egypt and Syria after the 1973 war, which were precursors to a separate Egyptian-Israeli peace treaty. To achieve this, Kissinger sought only to contain the Palestine issue, prevent it from interfering with his diplomacy, and render it manageable, if necessary by the use of force exerted by a range of proxies.

This was the case in Jordan from the late 1960s until 1971, and later in Lebanon in the early to mid-1970s, when the PLO opposed Egypt's US-encouraged drift toward a direct settlement with Israel. In both cases, Kissinger colluded with America's local allies to crush the Palestinian movement. Standing behind all of them, in the shadows, often indirectly responsible, was the United States.

Still, Kissinger admitted in his memoirs that the Palestinians' "fate was, after all, the origin of the crisis," and as anyone who followed his long career can attest, he was nothing if not a pragmatist.[54] Even as he was negotiating the terms of Syria's military intervention against the Palestinians in 1975, Kissinger also authorized covert, indirect talks with the PLO. These contacts were necessarily clandestine because of a pledge the secretary of state had made in a secret US-Israel Memorandum of Agreement in September that year. According to this pledge, the United States promised not to "recognize or negotiate with the Palestine Liberation Organization" until the PLO recognized Israel's "right to exist," abjured from the use of force (coded as terrorism), and accepted SC Resolutions 242 and 338 (which, passed in 1973, reaffirmed SC 242 and called for "negotiations . . . between the parties concerned under appropriate auspices," meaning a multilateral peace conference, later convened at Geneva).[55]

Notwithstanding this clandestine promise to Israel, soon after Kissinger asked President Gerald Ford to approve US contact with the PLO. He argued that "There would be no change in our position toward the PLO on the Middle East question but we have no commitment to Israel not to talk to the PLO exclusively about the situation in Lebanon."[56] Ostensibly, the purpose of these contacts was to ensure the security of the US embassy in Beirut and of American citizens during the Lebanese civil war, which the PLO undertook to do. Over several subsequent years, there was extensive coordination between intelligence personnel from the two sides about such security, provided by the PLO. When these dealings became known, Israel's response was harshly critical, but the US government affirmed their limited nature. However, US-PLO contacts rapidly expanded well beyond these original limited aims to encompass the general political situation in Lebanon. In 1977, the US ambassador in Beirut, Richard Parker, was tasked with maintaining contacts regarding a variety of political issues through intermediaries affiliated with the PLO, among them a professor at the AUB and a prominent Palestinian businessman.

There can be little question that despite Kissinger's justification, US discussions with the PLO violated the terms of the 1975 Memorandum of Agreement with Israel.[57] Once the Israeli government discovered what was going on, it reacted forcefully to this betrayal, as they saw it. In January 1979, Israeli agents in Beirut assassinated Abu Hassan Salameh, the key PLO figure involved in these contacts, by bombing his car, causing a "huge explosion" that resulted in a "ball of fire." Salameh had been the head of Yasser 'Arafat's personal security service, Force 17, and Israel claimed that he had been involved in the 1972 attack on Israeli athletes at the Munich Olympics. However, an account based on interviews with Israeli intelligence officers involved in the operation states that "the Mossad eventually reached the conclusion that 'cutting this channel was important . . . to give the Americans a hint that this was no way to behave towards friends.'"[58] The assassination did not end the contacts, although they became even more deeply shrouded in secrecy, as both the United States and the PLO took the heavy-handed Israeli hint.

In 1978, John Gunther Dean, Parker's successor as ambassador to Lebanon, was ordered to continue the channels of communication, which broadened to include the first direct interactions between American and PLO officials and came to address an even wider range of political topics. Among these were the terms for PLO acceptance of SC 242 and for US recognition of the PLO; the inclusion of the PLO in peace negotiations; the Iranian Islamic revolution; and freeing American hostages being held in Tehran. For at least four years, the United States was clandestinely negotiating with the PLO, its pledge to Israel notwithstanding.

Dean was the target of an assassination attempt in 1980. The Front for the Liberation of Lebanon from Foreigners claimed responsibility, but this group was later identified in interviews with Israeli intelligence sources as an Israeli-controlled operation.[59] Dean always maintained that Israel was behind the attempt to kill him, and this evidence, in addition to Israel's assassination of several Palestinians involved in contacts with the United States, appears to bear out Dean's claim.[60]

Correspondence with the State Department during 1979, to which

Dean provided me access, illustrates the extent of these US-PLO contacts in ways that are not fully reflected in the official State Department documentary series *Foreign Relations of the United States*.[61] They include, for example, extensive exchanges on PLO efforts to free American hostages held in the embassy in Tehran (a number of whom were apparently released at least in part because of Palestinian intercession with the Iranian revolutionary regime). While the contacts began via intermediaries, they led to direct meetings between Dean and, among others, Brigadier Sa'd Sayel (Abu al-Walid)—a former Jordanian army officer, the PLO's chief of staff, and its senior military officer.[62] He, too, was later assassinated, perhaps by Syrian agents or possibly by those of Israel.

As important as the extent and range of the exchanges was their tenor. The Palestinian intermediaries involved talked at length with Dean and one of his colleagues about terms for the PLO's acceptance of SC 242 (it was willing to do this with some reservations) and how that could lead to official, open US-Palestinian contacts. Agreement on this matter was never reached. The Palestinians involved repeatedly relayed the PLO's desire for recognition from Washington of its efforts on behalf of US interests, but Dean was authorized only to express his government's gratitude for the provision of security to American institutions. The United States never offered the political recompense for these services that the Palestinian leadership apparently expected.

WHILE AMERICAN CONTACTS were ongoing with the PLO in Beirut, President Jimmy Carter's administration, working to hold a multilateral Middle East peace conference in Geneva, issued a joint communiqué with the USSR in October 1977. The communiqué broke ground, referring to participation of all parties to the conflict, including "those of the Palestinian people." A statement made by Carter some months earlier, calling for a homeland for the Palestinians, signaled a different tone in Washington. However, under pressure from the newly elected Likud government in Israel, led by Menachem Begin, and from Egypt's Anwar Sadat, the administration soon abandoned its push for a comprehensive settlement and the inclusion of the Palestinians in negotiations.[63] Instead, it adopted the bilateral Camp David process, resulting in the separate Egyptian-Israeli peace treaty of 1979.

This process was specifically designed by Begin to freeze out the PLO, allow unimpeded colonization of the Occupied Territories occupied in 1967, and put the Palestine issue on hold, which is where it remained for over a decade. While Sadat and American officials feebly protested this sidetracking of the Palestinian issue, whose importance Carter had stressed at the outset of his presidency, in the end they acquiesced. For Sadat, the treaty restored the Sinai Peninsula to Egypt. For Begin, the unilateral Egyptian peace strengthened Israel's control of the rest of the Occupied Territories and permanently removed Egypt from the Arab-Israeli conflict. For the United States, the treaty completed Egypt's shift from the Soviet to the American camp, defusing the most dangerous aspects of the superpower conflict in the Middle East.

Given the vital importance of these national goals to all three parties, Begin was allowed to dictate the terms where Palestine was concerned at Camp David and in the 1979 peace treaty.[64] All of this was apparent to the PLO leadership, and the later phases of their indirect interaction with the United States government reflected their increasing bitterness. They saw that the PLO's cooperation in Lebanon, far from having been reciprocated, was in fact repaid with further isolation of the organization by the United States and its Israeli ally.

Although under Carter the United States had come close to endorsing the Palestinians' national rights and their involvement in negotiations, the two sides found themselves farther apart than ever. Camp David and the Israeli-Egyptian peace treaty signaled US alignment with the most extreme expression of Israel's negation of Palestinian rights, an alignment that was consolidated by Ronald Reagan's administration. Begin and his successors in the Likud, Yitzhak Shamir, Ariel Sharon, and then Benjamin Netanyahu, were implacably opposed to Palestinian statehood, sovereignty, or control of the occupied West Bank and East Jerusalem. Ideological heirs of Ze'ev Jabotinsky, they believed that the entirety of Palestine belonged solely to the Jewish people, and that a Palestinian people with national rights did not exist. At most, autonomy might be possible for the "local Arabs," but this autonomy would apply only to people, not to the land. Their explicit aim was to transform the entirety of Palestine into the Land of Israel.

Via the treaty with Egypt, Begin ensured that nothing would interfere with the implementation of the Likud vision. The foundation he had cannily laid down, which was adopted by the United States, formed the basis of everything that would follow.[65] Future negotiations would be restricted to the terms of self-rule for an infinitely extendable interim period and exclude any discussion of sovereignty, statehood, Jerusalem, the fate of refugees, and jurisdiction over the land, water, and air of Palestine. Meanwhile, Israel set about reinforcing its colonization of the Occupied Territories. In spite of occasional meek American and Egyptian protestations, the conditions imposed by Begin set the ceiling of what the Palestinians were allowed to negotiate for.

In the wake of the 1979 peace treaty, conditions became even worse for the Palestinians. The Lebanon War ground on, destroying much of the country, exhausting its people, and debilitating the PLO. At different stages, the PLO found itself facing the Israeli, Syrian, and Lebanese armies, as well as Lebanese militias supported covertly by an array of states, including Israel, the United States, Iran, and Saudi Arabia. Nevertheless, after all this and despite an Israeli incursion in 1978—the Litani Operation—which left a swath of south Lebanon under the control of its proxy, the South Lebanese Army, the PLO was still standing. Indeed, it remained the strongest force in large parts of Lebanon, those that were not in the hands of foreign armies or their proxies, including West Beirut, Tripoli, Sidon, the Shouf Mountains, and much of the south. It would take one more military campaign to dislodge the PLO, and in 1982, American Secretary of State General Alexander Haig agreed to Ariel Sharon's plans for Israel to finish off the organization and with it Palestinian nationalism.

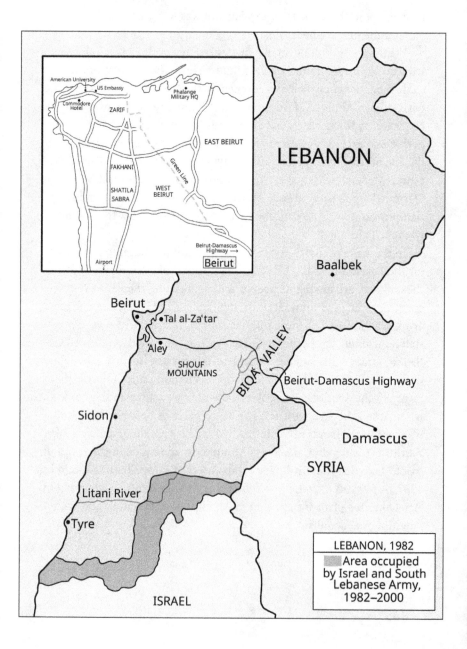

LEBANON

Baalbek

Beirut
Tal al-Zaʻtar
ʻAley
SHOUF
MOUNTAINS
BIQAʻ VALLEY
Beirut-Damascus Highway
Sidon
Damascus
SYRIA
Litani River
Tyre
ISRAEL

American University
US Embassy
Commodore Hotel
ZARIF
Phalange Military HQ
EAST BEIRUT
FAKHANI
Green Line
SHATILA SABRA
WEST BEIRUT
Beirut-Damascus Highway →
Airport
Beirut

LEBANON, 1982
Area occupied
by Israel and South
Lebanese Army,
1982–2000

The Fourth Declaration of War,
1982

The attack or bombardment of towns, villages, habitations or dwellings which are undefended is prohibited.
    —Article 25, Annex to the Hague Convention, July 29, 1899[1]

You are afraid to tell our readers and those who might complain to you that the Israelis are capable of indiscriminately shelling an entire city.
    —*New York Times* Beirut Bureau Chief
    Thomas Friedman to his editors[2]

By 1982, Beirutis had lived through many years of war. They were used to the sound of explosions and had learned from experience to distinguish among them. On June 4 that year, a Friday, I was in a meeting of the admissions committee at the American University of Beirut, where I had been teaching for the past six years. It seemed like a routine end of the week. Suddenly, we heard the thunderous sound of what must have been multiple two-thousand-pound bombs exploding in the distance. We quickly recognized the gravity of what was happening, and the meeting broke up immediately. This aerial bombardment was the opening salvo in Israel's 1982 invasion of Lebanon directed against the PLO. Everyone in the country had long been expecting it, and most had been dreading it.

Our two daughters, Lamya, who was five and a half, and Dima, then almost three, were at kindergarten and nursery school in different places. With the screeching roar of supersonic warplanes diving to attack in the background (one of the most terrifying sounds on earth), I rushed to my car to pick the girls up from their schools. Everyone on the road that day drove with the heedless abandon they always displayed when the fighting started up again in Beirut—that is, they drove only slightly more recklessly than usual.

My wife, Mona, then in her fourth month of pregnancy, was at work at WAFA, the PLO's Palestine News Agency, where she was chief editor of its English-language bulletin. As best as I could tell, the colossal explosions rocking the Lebanese capital seemed to be coming from the teeming Fakhani district of West Beirut a couple of miles away. Adjacent to the Sabra and Shatila refugee camps, the WAFA office was located there, as were most of the PLO's information and political offices. The site of the explosions was soon confirmed by radio reports.

The Beirut telephone system, never very reliable and even less so after seven years of war, was so overloaded that I could not get through to Mona. I had no way to reach her and no idea of what was happening. I hoped she had taken shelter in the basement of the rundown WAFA building. Luckily, the AUB was close to the girls' schools. Mona and I were always anxious about being able to reach them quickly whenever the on-again, off-again fighting began. During the first few years of the intermittent war in Lebanon, we had never been afraid for ourselves, but there was constant worry once the girls started going to school.

Our daughters, and later our son, were born in Beirut in the midst of the war, and by virtue of the fact of having parents who were politically involved (as were almost all of the 300,000 or so Palestinians in Lebanon), they were seen as terrorists by the Israeli government and some others, as were Mona and I. To my distress, those most likely to label us in this way were now preparing to invade the city. Although it could almost have been a normal Beirut Friday school pickup, even with the shuddering explosions in the distances, I knew that our lives would not be normal for quite a while. I soon had the girls safely at home, and my mother and I calmed them as well as we could against the relentless thunderous noise outside.

When Mona finally got home, I learned that in spite of the heavy aerial bombardment, she had decided not to heed advice to go down to a basement shelter. From her experience over many years of war, she knew that a prolonged assault (as that one was) would mean she could be stuck there and separated from the girls for many hours. So instead she slipped out of the office and started off for home. With everyone in the street running away from the bombing and no cars or taxis in sight, she ran, too. A breathless mile or so away, near the UNESCO offices, she found a cab willing to stop and take her the rest of the way safely. This experience had no apparent effect on the baby she was carrying, our son Ismail, who was born a few months later, although for a very long time after, he remained extremely sensitive to loud sounds.

On that Friday, Israeli warplanes bombed and flattened dozens of buildings, including a sports stadium near the Fakhani neighborhood, on the pretext that they housed PLO offices and facilities. The intense bombardment of targets in Beirut and the south of Lebanon that continued into the next day were the prelude to a massive ground assault starting on June 6, which ultimately led to Israel's occupation of much of

The Fakhani district, West Beirut, June 1982. WAFA was located there, as were most of the PLO's information and political offices.

Lebanon. The offensive culminated in a seven-week siege of Beirut that finally ended with a cease-fire on August 12. During the siege, entire apartment buildings were obliterated and large areas devastated in the western half of the already badly damaged city. Nearly fifty thousand people were killed or wounded in Beirut and the rest of Lebanon, while the siege constituted the most serious attack by a regular army on an Arab capital since World War II. It was not to be equaled until the US occupation of Baghdad in 2003.

The 1982 invasion of Lebanon was a watershed in the conflict between Israel and the Palestinians. It was the first major war since May 15, 1948, to mainly involve the Palestinians rather than the armies of the Arab states. Palestinian *feda'iyin* had faced Israeli troops in combat from the mid-1960s on, in Karameh in Jordan, in southern Lebanon in the late 1960s and the 1970s, notably in the 1978 Litani Operation, and in a furious exchange of fire across the Lebanese-Israeli border in the summer of 1981. In spite of the repeated attempts to uproot the PLO, however, it had built up such a position of strength in Lebanon both politically and militarily that relatively limited operations of this nature had made only a minimal impact.

The invasion in 1982 was of an entirely different order in terms of its aims, scale, and duration, the heavy losses involved, and its long-range impact. Israel's war on Lebanon had multiple objectives, but what distinguished it was its primary focus on the Palestinians and its larger goal of changing the situation inside Palestine. While the general scheme for the war was approved by Prime Minister Menachem Begin and the Israeli cabinet, they were often kept in the dark by the invasion's architect, defense minister Ariel Sharon, regarding both his real goals and his operational plans. Although Sharon wanted to expel the PLO and Syrian forces from Lebanon and create a pliable allied government in Beirut to transform circumstances in that country, his chief objective was Palestine itself. From the perspective of proponents of Greater Israel such as Sharon, Begin, and Yitzhak Shamir, destroying the PLO militarily and eliminating its power in Lebanon would also put an end to the strength of Palestinian nationalism in the occupied West Bank, Gaza Strip, and East Jerusalem. These areas would thereby become far easier for Israel to control and ultimately annex. Former Israeli chief of staff Mordechai

Gur, speaking to a secret session of a Knesset committee at the outset of the war, approvingly summed up its purpose: in "the Occupied Territories, in the final analysis the idea was to limit the [PLO] leadership's influence in order to provide us with greater freedom of action."[3]

In scale, the Israeli invasion of Lebanon involved the equivalent of eight divisions (well over 120,000 troops, a large proportion of them reservists), the country's largest mobilization since the 1973 war.[4] For the first couple of weeks of the war, this massive force engaged in intermittent but fierce battles with a few thousand Palestinian and Lebanese fighters in southern Lebanon, and in ferocious combat with two divisions of Syrian armor and infantry in the Biqa' Valley and the mountains of the Shouf and Metn districts east of Beirut. On June 26, Syria accepted a cease-fire (which explicitly excluded the PLO) and sat on the sidelines for the rest of the war. The subsequent siege of Beirut involved air and artillery bombardments of the city and sporadic ground combat solely with the forces of the PLO and its Lebanese allies.

During the ten weeks of fighting from early June through mid-August, 1982, according to Lebanese official statistics, more than nineteen thousand Palestinians and Lebanese, mostly civilians, were killed, and more than thirty thousand wounded.[5] The strategically located 'Ain al-Hilwa Palestinian refugee camp near Sidon, the largest in Lebanon with over forty thousand residents, was almost entirely destroyed after its population offered fierce resistance to the Israeli advance. In September a similar fate befell the twin Sabra and Shatila camps in the Beirut suburbs, scene of an infamous and grisly massacre after the fighting had supposedly ended. Beirut and many other areas in the south and the Shouf Mountains sustained severe damage, while Israeli forces periodically cut off water, electricity, food, and fuel to the besieged Western part of the Lebanese capital as they intermittently, but at times very intensively, bombarded it from air, land, and sea. The official Israeli toll of military casualties during the ten weeks of war and siege totaled more than 2,700, with 364 soldiers killed and nearly 2,400 wounded.[6] The invasion of Lebanon and the subsequent lengthy occupation of the southern part of the country—which ended only in 2000—involved Israel's third-highest military casualty toll among the six major wars in its seventy-plus-year history.[7]

THROUGHOUT THE TEN weeks of bombardment and the siege of West Beirut, my family—Mona, our two daughters, my mother, Selwa, my younger brother Raja, and I—stayed together in our apartment in the built-up Zarif neighborhood of West Beirut. The front lines had come uncomfortably close to my mother's home in the southern suburb of Haret Hreik, forcing her and my brother to move in with us. When we were able to visit their apartment after the fighting ended, we found that the kitchen had suffered a direct hit from an Israeli artillery shell.

Being together meant that each of us in the family knew where the others were at all times, and we could help keep up our general morale, despite the many privations of the siege—caring for two little children cooped up at home, coping with the acute shortages of water, electricity, and fresh food and the stench of burning garbage, which we withstood along with hundreds of thousands of other West Beirutis. We had endured years of civil war, weathering heavy bombardments and even Israeli air attacks, but this siege, with its volume of Israeli artillery fire from land and sea and the relentless aerial bombing, was far more intense and ferocious.

During this existential crisis for the Palestinian cause, which felt to many of us as if life and death hung in the balance, I acted as an off-the-record source for Western journalists, with some of whom I had become friends over the years. Free from the obligation to present the PLO's official line, but still in close touch with colleagues at WAFA, where I had once worked, I was able to provide my own frank assessment of events. Meanwhile, Mona continued to edit the WAFA English-language news bulletin, although given her pregnancy it was now far too dangerous for her to go to the old office in the Fakhani neighborhood, and she had to work remotely.[8]

It was fortunate for the presentation of the Palestinian point of view that Beirut had always been the journalistic nerve center of much of the Middle East (as well as the center for espionage), with most journalists located in the Western part of the city. Among them were veteran war correspondents who had covered the Arab-Israeli and Lebanese conflicts for many years and were mostly immune to obvious propaganda,

The author, on the right, helping out at a press briefing at the Commodore Hotel, Beirut

whether be it the unsubtle messaging of the PLO, the harsh rhetoric of the Maronite Lebanese Front, the formulaic bluster of the Syrian regime, or the slick, devious *hasbara* that Israel had mastered. Because of their presence in Beirut, the course of the war was well covered by the international media.

The previous July, Israel and the PLO had engaged in an intense two-week exchange of fire across the border, with Israel's aviation and artillery pounding south Lebanon and PLO rocket and artillery units hitting targets across northern Israel.[9] In consequence, large numbers of Lebanese and Palestinian civilians had been forced to flee their homes, while Israelis in Galilee were confined to shelters or fled. This fierce fighting culminated in a July 25, 1981, cease-fire negotiated by US presidential envoy Ambassador Philip Habib, which, remarkably, held for the next ten months with very few violations.[10] However, it was clear that the Begin government and Ariel Sharon were not satisfied with this outcome.

Warnings of Israeli war preparations had reached Lebanese and Palestinian leaders, the media, and others. One of these warnings was delivered in a spring 1982 briefing for researchers that I attended at the Institute for Palestine Studies. It was delivered by Dr. Yevgeny Primakov, who was director of the Soviet Oriental Institute and reputed to be a senior officer of the KGB. Primakov was blunt: Israel would soon attack Lebanon, the United States would support it fully, and the USSR did not have the capability to prevent the attack or to protect its Lebanese and Palestinian allies. Moscow, he said, would be hard pressed to prevent the war from extending to Syria or to preserve its main regional ally, the Syrian regime. We were told that he had said much the same things to the PLO leadership.[11]

So none of us should have been surprised when the war started with the bombing of Beirut on June 4, 1982, although the scope and scale of what followed was much greater than I and others expected. By contrast, Yasser 'Arafat and other PLO leaders had long understood that when war came, Sharon would push his army all the way to Beirut. They had clearly been preparing for this eventuality, stockpiling ammunition and supplies, moving offices and files, and preparing shelters and backup command centers.[12] Starting on June 6, Israel's immense armored columns, often preceded by amphibious and helicopter landings of commandos, pushed northward rapidly beyond Sidon along the coast toward Beirut. Other Israeli armored units simultaneously advanced through the Shouf Mountains in the center of the country, while still others fought up the Biqa' Valley to the east. The invading force of eight divisions enjoyed absolute superiority in numbers and equipment on all fronts, as well as complete control of the air and sea. Although difficult terrain or heavily built-up areas combined with determined resistance could briefly hinder such a forceful offensive, only very heavy Israeli casualties would have potentially slowed if not stopped it.

Thus on June 13, Israeli troops arrived at the strategic Khaldeh intersection on the coast road just south of Beirut, where Palestinian, Lebanese, and Syrian combatants were eventually overwhelmed.[13] Israeli tanks and artillery soon after appeared near the presidential palace in Ba'abda and in other suburbs in the eastern part of the capital. West Beirut was now encircled, and the siege was about to begin. Following the Israeli offensive that drove Syrian forces out of the mountain towns overlooking Beirut and into a separate cease-fire, the PLO was alone in the field with its allies in the Lebanese National Movement. The siege was tightening, Israeli forces bombarded West Beirut seemingly at will, and there was no prospect of relief or meaningful support from any quarter.

In certain cases, the Israeli shelling and bombing were carefully targeted, sometimes on the basis of good intelligence. All too often, however, that was not the case. Scores of eight- to twelve-story apartment buildings were destroyed in airstrikes all over the western part of the city, especially in the Fakhani–Arab University district, hitting many empty PLO offices as well as residential homes. Many of the buildings that were leveled there and elsewhere—along the shore in the Raouché neighborhood, for example, where my cousin Walid's apartment was destroyed by an artillery shell—had no plausible military utility.

Although his editors at the *New York Times* removed the offending word from his article, reporter Thomas Friedman at one point described the Israeli bombardment as "indiscriminate."[14] He was referring specifically to the sporadic shelling of neighborhoods like the area around the Commodore Hotel, where he and most journalists were staying, and which certainly contained nothing whatsoever of military interest.[15] The only possible objective of such blanket bombardment was to terrorize the population of Beirut and turn it against the PLO.

In spite of this firestorm, and even with Israel's extensive aerial surveillance capabilities and its many hundreds of agents and spies planted in Lebanon[16] (the war took place before the age of the reconnaissance drone), not one of the PLO's several functioning underground command and control posts or its multiple communications centers, was ever hit. Nor was a single PLO leader killed in the attacks, although many civilians died when the Israeli air force missed its targets. This is surprising, given just how extensive were Israel's efforts to liquidate them.[17] Israel's leaders were clearly unconcerned about killing civilians trying to do so: after an air attack in July 1981 destroyed a building in Beirut with heavy civilian casualties, Begin's office had stated that "Israel was no longer refraining from attacking guerrilla targets in civilian areas."[18] 'Arafat himself was a prime target. In an August 5 letter to Ronald Reagan, Begin wrote that "these days" he felt as if he and his "valiant army" were "facing

'Berlin' where, amongst innocent civilians, Hitler and his henchmen hide in a bunker deep beneath the surface."[19] Begin often drew such parallels between 'Arafat and Hitler: if 'Arafat was another Hitler, then killing him was certainly permissible and justified, whatever the cost in civilian lives.[20]

One of Israel's most notorious supposed spies, known to Beirutis as Abu Rish ("father of the feather": he sometimes wore a feather in his cap), often camped out opposite my mother-in-law's apartment building in the Manara district of West Beirut, and sometimes even in her lobby. His eccentric appearance was familiar to passersby and to my daughters, watching him from the balcony above, who remember him more than thirty-five years later.[21] Some Beirutis reported seeing him later guiding Israeli troops, although that may have been an urban legend.

In an interview with me in Tunis two years after the war, chief of PLO intelligence Abu Iyad (Salah Khalaf) helped explain why Israel may have failed to hit some of its intended targets, for all its vaunted intelligence services. During the siege, the PLO had managed to obtain a continuous flow of fuel, food supplies, and munitions by transferring them across lines controlled by a branch of the mainly Maronite Lebanese Front, which was allied with Israel. It was a simple matter of money, he said in his rumbling, low smoker's voice—and the systematic use of double agents, the employment of whom might have also had something to do with the high survival rate of PLO leaders. "But one should never trust a double agent," he told me. "Anyone you can buy can be bought again." In a cruel irony, it was a double agent who had been turned again who assassinated Abu Iyad in Tunis in 1991.[22]

Toward the end of the siege, on August 6, I was near a half-finished eight-story apartment building a few blocks from where we lived when a precision-guided munition demolished it.[23] I had stopped to drop off a friend at his parked car not far from the building. I had almost reached home as planes swooped down, and I heard a huge explosion behind me. Later I saw that the entire building was flattened, pancaked into a single mound of smoking rubble. The structure, which had been full of Palestinian refugees from Sabra and Shatila, had reportedly just been visited by 'Arafat. At least one hundred people, probably more, were killed— most of them women and children.[24] Days later, my friend told me that immediately after the air attack, just as he got into his car, shaken but

Zarif, West Beirut, August 6, 1982: "I heard a huge explosion behind me. Later I saw that the entire building was flattened, pancaked into a single mound of smoking rubble."

unhurt, a car bomb exploded nearby, presumably having been set to kill the rescuers who were helping families trying to find their loved ones in the rubble. Such car bombs—a weapon of choice for the Israeli forces besieging Beirut, and one of their most terrifying instruments of death and destruction—were described by one Mossad officer as "killing for killing's sake."[25]

This dirty war continued until the PLO was forced to agree to evacuate Beirut, under intense pressure from Israel, the United States, and their Lebanese allies, and in the absence of meaningful support from any Arab government.[26] The exit negotiations took place primarily via Ambassador Habib's exchanges with Lebanese intermediaries, but also involved France and some Arab governments, notably Saudi Arabia and Syria. Until the end, and despite some shifts in the American cast of characters and attitude toward Israel, the United States remained committed to achieving Israel's core war aim: the defeat of the PLO and its expulsion from Beirut.

Israel demanded complete and virtually unconditional PLO withdrawal from the city, an aim which the United States fully endorsed. Employing Cold War tropes that they knew would resonate in Washington, Begin and Sharon had early on convinced President Reagan and his administration that the PLO was a terrorist group aligned with the evil Soviet empire and that its elimination would be a service to both the United States and Israel. All US diplomacy during the war flowed from that shared conviction. The PLO thus faced not only fierce military pressure from Israel, but also unremitting diplomatic coercion from Israel's US ally. That coercion was intense and constant, and it was accompanied by Israeli and American campaigns of disinformation and deception about the course of the negotiations, designed to sap Palestinian and Lebanese morale and precipitate a quick surrender.

Meanwhile, the United States also provided indispensable material support to its ally, to the tune of $1.4 billion in military aid annually in both 1981 and 1982. This paid for the myriad of US weapons systems and munitions deployed in Lebanon by Israel, from F-16 fighter-bombers to M-113 armored personnel carriers, 155mm and 175mm artillery, air-to-ground missiles, and cluster munitions.

Beyond the intertwined roles of Israel and the United States, one of the shabbiest and most shameful subsidiary aspects of the war was the capitulation of the leading Arab regimes to American pressure. Their governments loudly proclaimed their support for the Palestinian cause, but did nothing to back the PLO as it stood alone, but for its Lebanese allies, against Israel's military onslaught, and as an Arab capital was besieged, bombarded, and occupied. They did no more than issue pro forma objections as the United States championed Israeli demands to expel the PLO from Beirut. The Arab League foreign ministers, meeting on July 13 in preparation for the Arab summit later that year, proposed no action in response to the war, which by then had been ongoing for over five weeks. Instead, the Arab states meekly acquiesced.

This was notably true of Syria and Saudi Arabia, which had been chosen by the Arab League to represent the Arab position on a mission to Washington during the summer of 1982. Such Arab governmental opposition as there was to the war was cheaply bought off with flimsy American promises to issue a brand-new US–Middle East diplomatic initiative, eventually unveiled on September 1 and later dubbed the Reagan Plan. The initiative would have placed a limit on Israeli settlements and created an autonomous Palestinian authority in the West Bank and Gaza Strip, but it ruled out a sovereign Palestinian state in these territories. The Reagan Plan, which the United States never forcefully promoted and which was effortlessly torpedoed by the Begin government, ultimately went nowhere.

Among Arab public opinion, however, the invasion of Lebanon and siege of Beirut, whose gripping televised images were widely broadcast, provoked great shock and anger. Yet nowhere was there enough popular pressure on any of the repressive and undemocratic Arab governments to force an end to Israel's siege of an Arab capital or secure better terms for the PLO's withdrawal. There were few mass demonstrations and little open unrest in most of the heavily policed Arab cities. Ironically, perhaps the largest demonstration in the Middle East provoked by the war took place in Tel Aviv, in protest against the Sabra and Shatila massacres.

Israelis might have fought the war and suffered casualties, but once again Palestinians found that the foe on the battlefield was backed by a great power from the outset. The decision to invade Lebanon was made by Israel's government, but it could not have been implemented without the explicit assent given by Secretary of State Alexander Haig or without American diplomatic and military support, combined with the utter passivity of the Arab governments. The green light that Haig gave to Israel, for what was supposedly "a limited operation," was as bright as could be. On May 25, ten days before the offensive began, Sharon met with Haig in Washington and laid out his ambitious war plan in explicit detail. Indeed, Sharon gave Haig a much fuller picture than he later presented to the Israeli cabinet. Haig's only response was that there "must be a recognizable provocation," one that would be "understood internationally."[27] Soon after, the attempted assassination of Israel's ambassador in London, Shlomo Argov (by the anti-PLO Abu Nidal group), provided just such a provocation.[28]

Sharon explained to Haig that Israel's forces would eradicate the PLO presence in Lebanon, including all the "terrorist organizations," the military structures, and the political headquarters, which were located in Beirut. (This element of the plan alone belied Sharon's description of a "limited operation.") Israel would also expel Syria from Lebanon "as a byproduct"—although Sharon piously insisted that he did not "want war with Syria"—and install a puppet Lebanese government. The exposition was clear, as was the "green light from Haig for a limited operation," noted by the American diplomat who recorded this as the meeting's outcome.[29]

WHILE THE PLO knew it could expect little support from the Arab regimes in power in 1982, the organization had counted on a sympathetic response from the Lebanese people. However, the PLO's heavy-handed and often arrogant behavior in the preceding decade and a half had seriously eroded popular support for the Palestine cause in general and especially for the Palestinian presence in Lebanon. In a typical incident that occurred near the Institute for Palestine Studies, located in Beirut's genteel Verdun neighborhood, the guards for a senior PLO leader, Colonel Abu Za'im, who himself was hardly a paragon, shot and killed a young Lebanese couple in their car late one night when they failed to stop at a checkpoint hastily erected near his apartment.[30] Given PLO indiscipline, no one was punished for these deaths. Such inexcusable acts were all too common.

Palestinian operations in Lebanon were supposedly constrained within a formal framework—the Cairo Agreement, adopted in 1969—which had given the PLO control of Palestinian refugee camps and freedom of action in much of south Lebanon. But the heavily armed PLO had become an increasingly dominant and domineering force in many parts of the country. Ordinary Lebanese people were aggrieved that this oppressive Palestinian presence had only intensified as the long civil war dragged on. The creation of what amounted to a PLO mini-state in their country was ultimately unsustainable, as it was intolerable to many Lebanese. There was also deep resentment of the devastating Israeli attacks on Lebanese civilians that were provoked by Palestinian military actions. The PLO's assaults in Israel were often directed at civilian targets and visibly did little to advance the Palestinian national cause, if indeed they did not harm it. Inevitably, all these factors turned important sectors of the Lebanese population against the PLO. An inability to see the intensity of the hostility prompted by its own misbehavior and flawed strategy was among the gravest shortcomings of the PLO during this period.

So it was that when the moment of truth came in 1982, the PLO suddenly found itself bereft of support from many of its traditional allies, including three key groups. These were the Syrian-aligned Amal movement, headed by Nabih Berri, and its large Shi'ite constituency in south Lebanon and the Biqa' Valley (although young Amal militiamen nevertheless fought valiantly alongside the PLO in many areas); the strategically located Druze fiefdom of Walid Jumblatt in the Shouf Mountains, southeast of Beirut; and the Sunni urban populations of Beirut, Tripoli, and Sidon. The backing of Sunni political leaders had been essential to defending the Palestinian political and military presence in Lebanon since the 1960s.[31]

It is not hard to understand the reasoning of these leaders and the communities they represented. Southerners, most of them Shi'ites, had suffered more than any other Lebanese from the PLO's actions. Besides its own violations and transgressions against the population in the south, the PLO's very presence had exposed them to Israeli attacks, forcing many to flee their villages and towns repeatedly. It was understood by all that Israel was intentionally punishing civilians to alienate them from the Palestinians, but there was nevertheless much bitterness against the PLO as a result.

Walid Jumblatt, whose reasoning was similar, later related that he had no choice but to bow before the overwhelming force of Israel's advance into the Druze region of the Shouf. He may have felt that assurances given by Druze officers in the Israeli army would secure a measure of protection for his community. He came to regret his decision when, starting in late June 1982, the Israeli military and security services supported the penetration of undisciplined and vengeful Maronite militias into Druze-dominated regions like 'Aley and Beit al-Din, where they committed more of the atrocities for which they were notorious.[32]

For the Sunnis, in particular those in West Beirut, the bombardment and siege of the Lebanese capital put an end to their staunch support for the PLO, which they had seen as a vital ally against the domination of the Lebanese state by the Maronites and the armed power of their militias. Some may have been stirred by Palestinian calls to turn Beirut into another Stalingrad or Verdun, but most were aghast at the prospect of the city being devastated by Israeli artillery and airstrikes. Defiance of

Israel was all well and good, but not at the cost of the avoidable destruction of their homes and property. This was a crucial shift: without the support of Beirut's largely Sunni population, together with its many Shi'a residents, prolonged resistance by the PLO to the Israeli offensive was ultimately futile.

These calculations led to a severe erosion of the already weakening support for the PLO, which diminished further during the early days of the fighting, when the south and the Shouf were overrun, Beirut was bombarded and encircled, Syria dropped out of the war, and Philip Habib relayed Israel's harsh demands for the PLO's immediate and unconditional evacuation. A few more weeks into the war, however, the leaders of the three Lebanese Muslim communities changed their position significantly and became more supportive of the PLO. This shift came after the PLO consented to withdraw from Beirut in exchange for ironclad guarantees for the protection of the civilians who would be left behind.

On July 8, the PLO presented its Eleven-Point Plan for withdrawal of its forces from Beirut. This plan called for establishing a buffer zone between Israeli forces and West Beirut, coupled with a limited withdrawal of the Israeli army, the lasting deployment of international forces, and international safeguards for the Palestinian (and Lebanese) populations, which would be left behind virtually without defenses once the PLO's fighters had departed.[33] On the strength of this plan, the Lebanese Muslim leaders were convinced that the PLO was sincere in its willingness to depart as a move to save the city. Also, they were deeply disconcerted by mounting evidence of Israel's overt backing for the mainly Maronite LF, since it underlined the vulnerability of their communities in a post-PLO Lebanon dominated by Israel and its militant allies.

These concerns had been reinforced by the arrival of the LF militias in the Shouf in late June, and the widespread massacres, abductions, and murders that they carried out there and in the areas of the south under Israeli control.[34] At this stage, after seven years of civil war, such sectarian slaughter was commonplace, and the PLO's forces had served as a primary defender of the country's Muslims and leftists. The Sunni, Shi'a, and Druze leaders therefore redoubled their backing for the PLO's demands in its Eleven-Point Plan.

There is a vital thread of US responsibility that must be followed to understand what happened next. The consequences were not just the result of decisions by Sharon, Begin, and other Israeli leaders, or of the actions of Lebanese militias who were Israel's allies. They were also the direct responsibility of the Reagan administration, which, under pressure from Israel, stubbornly refused to accept the need for any formal safeguards for civilians, rejected the provision of international guarantees, and blocked the long-term deployment of international forces that might have protected noncombatants. Instead, to secure the PLO's evacuation, Philip Habib, operating via Lebanese intermediaries, provided the Palestinians with solemn, categorical written pledges to shield the civilians in the refugee camps and neighborhoods of West Beirut. Typed on plain paper without letterhead, signatures, or identification, these memos were transmitted to the PLO by Lebanese Prime Minister Shafiq al-Wazzan and later enshrined in the records of the Lebanese government. The first of these memos, dated August 4, cited "US assurances about the safety of . . . the camps." The second, two days later, said: "We also reaffirm the assurances of the United States as regards safety and security . . . for the camps in Beirut."[35] An American note of August 18 to the Lebanese foreign minister enshrining these pledges stated that

> Law-abiding Palestinian non-combatants remaining in Beirut, including the families of those who have departed, will be authorized to live in peace and security. The Lebanese and US governments will provide appropriate security guarantees . . . on the basis of assurances received from the government of Israel and from the leaders of certain Lebanese groups with which it has been in contact.[36]

These assurances were taken by the PLO to constitute binding commitments, and it was on their basis that it agreed to leave Beirut.

On August 12, after epic negotiations, final terms were reached for the PLO's departure. The talks were conducted while Israel carried out a second day of the most intense bombardment and ground attacks of the entire siege. The air and artillery assault on that day alone—over a month after the PLO had agreed in principle to leave Beirut—caused more than five hundred casualties. It was so unrelenting that even Ronald Reagan was moved to demand that Begin halt the carnage.[37] Reagan's diary relates that he called the Israeli prime minister during the ferocious offensive, adding, "I was angry—I told him it had to stop or our entire future relationship was endangered. I used the word holocaust deliberately & said the symbol of his war was becoming a picture of a 7 month old baby with its arms blown off."[38] This sharp phone call impelled Begin's government to halt its rain of fire almost immediately, but Israel refused to budge on the crucial issue of international protection for the Palestinian civilian population as a quid pro quo for the PLO's evacuation.

The departure from Beirut of thousands of the PLO's militants and fighting forces between August 21 and September 1 was accompanied by a broad outpouring of emotion in West Beirut. Weeping, singing, ululating crowds lined the routes as convoys of trucks carried the Palestinian militants to the port. They watched as the PLO was forced to evacuate the Lebanese capital, with its leaders, cadres, and fighters going to an unknown destiny. They ended up scattered by land and sea over a half dozen Arab countries.

The men and women bound for an uncertain exile, some for the second or third time in their lives, were seen as heroes by many Beirutis for having stood up for ten weeks—with no external support to speak of—to the most powerful army in the Middle East. As their convoys rolled through Beirut, no one was aware that a sudden and unilateral American decision, taken under Israeli pressure, meant that the international forces supervising the evacuation—American, French, and Italian troops—would be withdrawn as soon as the last ship left. Israeli obduracy and US acquiescence had left the civilian population unprotected.

In the Zarif neighborhood where we lived, only a few buildings had been severely damaged, so we managed to survive the siege of Beirut physically unscathed (although I worried about the lasting effect the war might have on our two young daughters[39]). Once PLO forces were gone and the siege was lifted, life slowly began to return to normal, even though Israeli troops still ringed West Beirut and tension remained very high. This seeming normalcy ended soon enough, and we would learn that those assurances delivered to the PLO were not worth the plain white paper they were written on.

On September 14, President-elect Bashir Gemayel, commander of the

LF and leader of the Phalangists, was assassinated in a huge bomb blast that destroyed a Phalangist headquarters. This was the trigger for Israel's forces immediately to enter and occupy the western part of the city—despite promises to the United States that it would not do so—where the PLO had previously been headquartered and where its LNM allies were still located. The following day, as Israeli troops swept into West Beirut quickly overpowering scattered and fitful resistance from fighters of the LNM, my family and I feared for our safety, as did other Palestinians with connections to the PLO—that is, nearly all Palestinians in Lebanon. They included not only refugees registered and born in Lebanon, but also people with foreign citizenship, work permits, and legal residence like ourselves.

Uppermost in all our minds was the Phalangist massacre in the Tal al-Za'tar refugee camp in 1976 where two thousand Palestinian civilians had been slaughtered. In light of the Israeli-LF alliance, the PLO had specifically cited Tal al-Za'tar in its Eleven-Point Plan and during the negotiations over its evacuation. Our fears were of course compounded by the murders that had been carried out by the LF forces in areas recently occupied by Israel, and by Israel's depiction of the PLO as terrorists, with no distinction made between militants and civilians.

The morning after Gemayel's assassination, amid the sound of heavy gunfire, we heard, through the open windows of our apartment, the approaching roar of diesel engines and the clanking of tank treads. The din was produced by the Israeli armored columns advancing into West Beirut. We knew that we had to get to safety quickly. I was fortunate to reach Malcolm Kerr, the president of the AUB and a good friend, who immediately let us take refuge in a vacant faculty apartment.[40] Mona, my mother, my brother, and I loaded our girls and a few hastily packed things into two cars and sped to the university just before Israeli troops arrived at its gates.

The next day, September 16, I was sitting with Kerr and several of my AUB colleagues on the veranda of his residence when a breathless university guard came to tell him that Israeli officers at the head of a column of armored vehicles were demanding to enter the campus to search for terrorists. Kerr rushed off to the university entrance, where, he later told us, he rejected the officers' demands. "There are no terrorists on the AUB campus," he said. "If you're looking for terrorists, look in your own army for those who've destroyed Beirut."

Thanks to Malcolm Kerr's courage, we were temporarily safe in a faculty apartment at the AUB, but we soon heard that others were at that moment in mortal peril. On the same night, September 16, Raja and I were perplexed as we watched a surreal scene: Israeli flares floating down in the darkness in complete silence, one after another, over the southern reaches of Beirut, for what seemed like an eternity. As we saw the flares descend, we were baffled: armies normally use flares to illuminate a battlefield, but the cease-fire had been signed a month earlier, all the Palestinian fighters had left weeks ago, and any meager Lebanese resistance to the Israeli troops' arrival in West Beirut had ended the previous day. We could hear no explosions and no shooting. The city was quiet and fearful.

The following evening, two shaken American journalists, Loren Jenkins and Jonathan Randal of the *Washington Post*, among the first Westerners to enter the Sabra and Shatila refugee camps, came to tell us what they had seen.[41] They had been with Ryan Crocker, who was the first American diplomat to file a report on what the three of them witnessed: the hideous evidence of a massacre. Throughout the previous night, we learned, the flares fired by the Israeli army had illuminated the camps for the LF militias—whom it had sent there to "mop up"—as they slaughtered defenseless civilians. Between September 16 and the morning of

This *Doonesbury* cartoon captured the Israeli government's expansive view of who might be a terrorist. The reference to "7,000 baby terrorists" always made me think of my two little daughters.

September 18, the militiamen murdered more than thirteen hundred Palestinian and Lebanese men, women, and children.[42]

The flares that had so puzzled my brother and me are described from a very different perspective in *Waltz with Bashir*, a film and book coauthored by Ari Folman. An Israeli soldier during the siege of Beirut, Folman was stationed on a rooftop at the time of the massacre with a unit that launched the flares.[43] In *Waltz with Bashir*, Folman refers to concentric circles of responsibility for the mass murder that was facilitated by this act, suggesting that those in the outer circles were also implicated. In his mind, "the murderers and the circles around them were one and the same."[44]

The statement is as true of the war as a whole as it is of the massacres in Sabra and Shatila. A commission of inquiry set up after the events, chaired by Israeli Supreme Court Justice Yitzhak Kahan, established the direct and indirect responsibility of Begin, Sharon, and senior Israeli military commanders for the massacres.[45] Most of those named lost their posts as a result of both the inquiry and the general revulsion in Israel over the massacres. However, documents released by the Israel State Archives in 2012[46] and the unpublished secret appendices to the Kahan Commission[47] reveal even more damning evidence of these individuals' culpability, which was far greater than the original 1983 report lays out. The documents expose long-deliberated decisions by Sharon and others to send the practiced Phalangist killers into the Palestinian refugee camps, with the aim of massacring and driving away their populations. They also show how American diplomats were repeatedly browbeaten by their Israeli interlocutors and failed to stop the slaughter that the US government had promised to prevent.

According to these documents, after the entire PLO military contingent had left Beirut at the end of August 1982, Begin, Shamir, Sharon, and other Israeli officials falsely asserted that some two thousand Palestinian fighters and heavy weaponry remained in the city, in violation of the evacuation accords.[48] Shamir made the claim in a meeting with an American diplomat on September 17,[49] even though the United States government knew for certain that this was not the case—Sharon himself told the Israeli cabinet a day earlier that "15,000 armed terrorists had been withdrawn from Beirut."[50] Moreover, Israeli military intelligence undoubtedly knew that this number included every single regular PLO military unit in Beirut.

Sadly, American diplomats did not challenge Israeli leaders on their spurious figures. Indeed, the documents show that US officials had difficulty standing up to the Israelis over anything to do with their occupation of West Beirut. When Moshe Arens, Israel's ambassador in Washington, was obliged to listen to a series of harsh talking points read to him that were drafted by Secretary of State George Shultz (who by then had taken over from Haig)—accusing Israel of "deception" and demanding the immediate withdrawal of its troops from West Beirut—Arens responded with scorn. "I am not sure you guys know what you are doing," he told Lawrence Eagleburger, the deputy secretary of state, and called the American points "a fabrication" and "completely false." Eagleburger suggested that the State Department might issue a statement calling Israel's occupation of West Beirut "contrary to assurances," at which point Arens's deputy, the thirty-three-year-old Benjamin Netanyahu, weighed in: "I would suggest you delete this," he said. "Otherwise you give us no choice but to defend our credibility by setting the record straight. We'll end up in a shooting war with each other." After listening to an aside from Netanyahu in Hebrew, Arens added, "I think that is right."[51] Rarely in history has a junior diplomat of a small country spoken thus to a senior representative of a superpower, and been supported in doing so.

On September 17, as the massacres Loren Jenkins and Jon Randal described to us continued, Philip Habib's assistant, Ambassador Morris Draper, was instructed by Washington to press Shamir and Sharon for a commitment to leave West Beirut. Sharon, characteristically, escalated things. "There are thousands of terrorists in Beirut," he told Draper. "Is it your interest that they will stay there?" Draper did not demur at this false assertion, but when the exasperated US envoy said to the assembled Israeli officials, "We didn't think you should have come in [to West Beirut]. You should have stayed out," Sharon bluntly told the ambassador: "You did not think, or you did think. When it comes to our security, we have never asked. We will never ask. When it comes to existence and security, it is our own responsibility and we will never give it to anybody to decide for us." After Draper mildly challenged Sharon on another claim involving "terrorists," Israel's defense minister flatly said, "So we'll kill them. They will not be left there. You are not going to save them. You are not going to save these groups of the international terrorism [*sic*]."[52] Sharon could not have been more chillingly explicit. Unbeknown to Draper or the US government, at that very moment the LF militias that Sharon's forces had sent into the refugee camps were carrying out the killing of which he spoke—but of unarmed old people, women, and children, not supposed terrorists. If Sharon's forces did not carry out the actual slaughter, they had nonetheless armed the LF to the tune of $118.5 million, trained them, sent them to do the job, and illuminated and facilitated their bloody task with flares.

That Sharon's intention to use the LF in this way was premeditated stands out in scores of pages of the secret appendices to the commission's report. Sharon; the army chief of staff, Lieutenant General Rafael Eitan; the chief of military intelligence, Major General Yehoshua Saguy; the head of the Mossad, Yitzhak Yofi; and Yofi's deputy and successor, Nahum Admoni—all knew full well of the atrocities perpetrated by the LF earlier in the Lebanese war.[53] They also knew of the lethal intentions of Bashir Gemayel and his followers toward the Palestinians.[54] While those named vigorously denied such knowledge to the Kahan Commission, the evidence that it collected and kept secret is damning, and it informed the commission's decisions. Nonetheless, the killings in Sabra and Shatila were not just the result of the LF militias' thirst for revenge or even of these Israeli commanders' premeditation. As with the war itself, these deaths were also the direct responsibility of the US government.

In planning for the invasion of Lebanon, Israel's leaders had been wary of repeating the fiasco of 1956, when their country had attacked Egypt without US approval and been forced to back down. Having learned from this bitter experience, Israel only went to war in 1967 after receiving the backing of its American ally. Now, in 1982, launching this "war of choice," as many Israeli commentators called it, was entirely dependent on the green light given by Alexander Haig, a point confirmed by well-informed Israeli journalists soon after the war.[55] The new and fuller details revealed in previously unavailable documents make the case clearly: Sharon told Haig exactly what he was about to do in great detail, and Haig gave his endorsement, amounting to another US declaration of war on the Palestinians. Even after a public outcry over the deaths of so many Lebanese and Palestinians civilians, after the televised images of the bombardment of Beirut, after the Sabra and Shatila massacres, American support continued undiminished.

In terms of what Ari Folman called the outer circles of responsibility, American culpability for Israel's invasion extends even further than Haig's green light: the United States supplied the lethal weapons-systems that killed thousands of civilians and that were manifestly not used in keeping with the exclusively defensive purposes mandated by American law. Sharon explicitly forewarned US officials that this would happen. According to Draper's later recollections, after he and Habib met with Sharon in December 1981, he reported to Washington that in Israel's planned attack "we were going to see American-made munitions being dropped from American-made aircraft over Lebanon, and civilians were going to be killed."[56] Moreover, the Israeli high command and intelligence services were not the only ones who were aware of the murderous propensities of the LF toward Palestinian civilians. Their American counterparts were just as knowledgeable about the LF's bloody track record.

Because of this knowledge, because of American backing for Israel and tolerance of its actions, its supplies of arms and munitions for use against civilians, its coercion of the PLO to leave Beirut and refusal to deal directly with it, and its worthless assurances of protection, the 1982 invasion must be seen as a joint Israeli-US military endeavor—their first war aimed specifically against the Palestinians. The United States thereby stepped into a position similar to that played by Britain in the 1930s, helping to repress the Palestinians by force in the service of Zionist ends. However, the British were the leading party in the 1930s, while in 1982 it was Israel that called the tune, deployed its might, and did the killing, while the United States played an indispensable but supporting role.

AFTER WE LEARNED of the massacres in Sabra and Shatila, we knew that it was not safe for us to remain in Beirut, especially with our two small children and with Mona about to have a third. Our journalist friends put us in touch with Ryan Crocker, the senior American political officer and the only US diplomat still at the embassy in West Beirut.[57] Crocker not only offered to arrange our evacuation as US citizens, he would also escort us out of Israeli-occupied Beirut in an armored vehicle belonging to the embassy. But he could take us only to the Israeli-Syrian lines between Bhamdoun and Sofar in the Lebanese mountains, because of reports of the presence of Iranian Revolutionary Guards in Syrian-controlled territory. When I told him that we had to get farther than that, to nearby Shtaura in the Biqa' Valley, whence we could take a taxi to Damascus, he assented. Crocker was as good as his word. On September 21, the day Amin Gemayel was elected president of Lebanon in place of his assassinated brother, we left Beirut with him and a driver, crossed the Israeli and LF lines, reached Shtaura, and went on to Damascus by taxi.

Once there, however, instead of taking us to our hotel, the driver deposited us at one of the many offices of the Syrian intelligence services. There Mona, now seven months pregnant, my brother, and I were treated to several hours of detention, punctuated by separate interrogations of each of us that featured such penetrating questions as "Did you see any Israeli soldiers in Beirut?" The Syrian security apparatus fortunately did not interrogate my sixty-seven-year-old mother or our two little daughters, and eventually we were released, after which we went to our hotel, and then left Damascus as quickly as we could.[58] We flew to Tunis, where we reunited with some of our Palestinian friends from Beirut who had been evacuated there. In Tunis, I first developed the ideas that eventually became my book about the decisions taken by the PLO during the 1982 war, *Under Siege*, and began discussions with some of the PLO leaders whom I later interviewed for the book. We then went on to Cairo, where Mona and I both had family, and we realized how badly the war had affected the girls: they went into a wild panic when they heard the screeching rumble of trolley cars in an adjacent street, thinking they were Israeli tanks.

As soon as the Israeli army withdrew from West Beirut and the airport opened, we went back to the city. Mona insisted on having our third child delivered by the same obstetrician who had delivered our two daughters (and whose father had delivered Mona herself over thirty years earlier). Our son Ismail was born in November 1982,[59] and I returned to teaching at the AUB and continued to work at the IPS. After a tense few months marked by the suicide bombing of the US embassy in the spring of 1983, we left Beirut for what we expected would be just a year away.

But the Lebanese civil war erupted in force once again, and we never returned to our Beirut home.[60]

THE POLITICAL IMPACT of the 1982 war was enormous. It brought about major regional changes that affect the Middle East to this day. Among its most significant lasting results were the rise of Hizballah in Lebanon and the intensification and prolongation of the Lebanese civil war, which became an even more complex regional conflict. The 1982 invasion was the occasion of many firsts: the first direct American military intervention in the Middle East since US troops had briefly been sent into Lebanon in 1958, and Israel's first and only attempt at forcible regime change in the Arab world. These events in turn engendered an even fiercer antipathy toward Israel and the United States among many Lebanese, Palestinians, and other Arabs, further exacerbating the Arab-Israeli conflict. These were all consequences that flowed directly from the choices made by Israeli and US policymakers in launching the 1982 war.

The war also provoked intense reactions, including widespread revulsion against its results among important segments of Israeli society, leading to the rapid growth of the Peace Now movement, which had been founded in 1978. It also produced the first significant and sustained negative American and European perceptions of Israel since 1948.[61] For many weeks, the international media widely disseminated disturbing images of intense civilian suffering in besieged and bombarded Beirut, the first and only Arab capital to be attacked and then occupied by Israel in this way. No amount of sophisticated propaganda by Israel and its supporters sufficed to erase these indelible images, and as a result, Israel's standing in the world was severely tarnished. The entirely positive image that Israel had assiduously cultivated in the West had been appreciably harmed, at least temporarily.

The Palestinians garnered considerable international sympathy as a result of the siege. In another first, they at least partially shed the terrorist label Israeli propaganda had successfully affixed to them, and appeared to many as David facing Israel's Goliath-like military juggernaut. But in spite of this limited improvement in their international image, they failed to obtain sufficient support, whether from the Arab states, the USSR, or others, to counterbalance the grimly determined backing of the Reagan administration for Israel's key war aim of dislodging the PLO from Lebanon.

With the PLO's evacuation from Beirut, the Palestinian cause appeared to have been gravely weakened, and Sharon seemed to have achieved all of his core objectives. However, the paradoxical result of these events was gradually to shift the center of gravity of the Palestinian national movement away from the neighboring Arab countries, where it had been relaunched in the 1950s and 1960s, moving it back inside Palestine. It was there that the First Intifada broke out five years later, in December 1987, with results that shook both Israeli and world public opinion. As the Nakba had done decades earlier, this stinging defeat produced a new and different form of resistance by the Palestinians to the multipronged war being waged against them. Sharon and Begin had launched the invasion to defeat the PLO and demoralize the Palestinians, thereby freeing Israel to absorb the Occupied Territories, but the end result was to spur their resistance and relocate it inside Palestine.

As for those who played a key part in the events of the summer of 1982, for many of them misgivings and regret seemed to dominate their recollections. In interviews with me in 1983 and 1984, Morris Draper and Robert Dillon, the US ambassador to Lebanon at the time, expressed deep remorse for their role in the negotiations with the PLO. Both felt bitterly deceived by Sharon and Begin, who they said had given the United States explicit commitments that Israeli forces would not enter West Beirut. Philip Habib pulled no punches, saying that his government had been deceived not only by Israel, but also by its own secretary of state: "Haig was lying. Sharon was lying" he said to me.[62] The recently released Israeli documents confirm that a great deal of deception, and perhaps even more self-deception, were going on in Beirut, Washington, and Jerusalem in the spring and summer of 1982.

Senior French diplomats I interviewed who were involved in the negotiations over the PLO's evacuation from Lebanon expressed regrets about their failure to get a better deal; they were bitter about their inability to obtain international security guarantees for the Palestinian civilian population and for the long-term stationing of multinational forces to protect the Palestinian civilian population. They regretted the United

States' unilateral handling of the negotiations and its efforts to restrict the involvement of international representatives. At the time, they had warned repeatedly and presciently that the course being followed by the United States would lead to a tragic outcome, but in the end the French government did nothing to prevent it.

Within the PLO, its leaders were angry at their betrayal by the United States, which had failed to protect the camps. They expressed sorrow and even a sense of guilt at not having secured ironclad guarantees for the safety of those they left behind. Abu Iyad, who had argued through-out the siege for a tougher negotiating position, explicitly charged the PLO leadership with failing its own people, a judgment that was shared by many Palestinians. A few others held similar opinions. Beyond expressing deep regret at the outcome, Abu Jihad [Khalil al-Wazir] was otherwise taciturn and unrevealing. Unsurprisingly, 'Arafat was the least self-critical.[63]

For the United States, its insistence on monopolizing Middle East diplomacy and its furtherance of Israel's ambitions did not serve American interests well. This was glaringly attested to by subsequent events, which included the suicide bombings of the US Embassy in Beirut, the US Marines barracks, and of the French troops, who had returned to an ill-defined mission in the city soon after the Sabra and Shatila massacres. Within months, the battleship USS *New Jersey* was firing shells the size of Volkswagen Beetles into the Shouf Mountains where Druze militias (supported by Syria) were battling the LF (supported by Israel),[64] and the United States became embroiled in a shooting war that few Americans, including many of those directly involved, fully understood.

Hizballah, which grew out of the Lebanese maelstrom, became a deadly foe of the United States and Israel. In considering its rise, few have noted that many of the young men who founded the movement and carried out its lethal attacks on American and Israeli targets had fought alongside the PLO in 1982. They had remained after the PLO fighters left, only to see hundreds of their fellow Shi'ites massacred alongside the Palestinians in Sabra and Shatila. The people killed in the US Embassy bombing, the Marines who died in their barracks, and the many other Americans kidnapped or assassinated in Beirut—among them Malcolm Kerr and several of my colleagues and friends at the AUB—largely victims of attacks by the groups that became Hizballah, paid the price for the perceived collusion between their country and the Israeli occupier. Within Folman's circles of responsibility, the Lebanese who were directly and indirectly responsible for the massacres paid perhaps the highest price. Bashir Gemayel and his lieutenant Elie Hobeika were both assassinated, as were several others, and the senior LF leader (and eventually president of the political party it became) Samir Geagea spent eleven years in prison for crimes committed during the Lebanese war, although not for any related to the 1982 invasion. Of the PLO leaders who made the fateful decisions that led to the tragedy in Sabra and Shatila, Abu Jihad and Abu Iyad were both assassinated, the former by Israel and the latter probably by an Iraqi agent. 'Arafat died after being besieged by Israeli troops in his headquarters in Ramallah.[65] None of them was ever held responsible for the outcomes of the 1982 war.

Most of the Israeli decisionmakers involved, including Begin, Sharon, and several senior generals, endured humiliation or loss of office as a result of the Kahan Commission report and the condemnation within Israel following the massacres. However, none of them suffered criminal penalties or any other serious sanction. Indeed, the head of Israel's Northern Command, Major General Amir Drori, who was in charge of the invasion forces, served out his term in command and then went off for a year's study leave in Washington, DC. Both Shamir and Sharon, as well as Netanyahu, went on to serve as prime ministers of Israel.

By contrast, none of the American officials involved were ever held responsible for any of their acts, whether their collusion with Israel in launching and waging the 1982 war, or the failure of the United States to honor its pledges regarding the security of Palestinian civilians. Many of them—including Reagan, Haig, and Habib—are now dead. All have so far escaped judgment.

The Fifth Declaration of War, 1987–1995

They make a desert and call it peace.

—Tacitus[1]

The Palestinian uprising, or intifada, which broke out in December 1987 was a perfect example of the law of unintended consequences.[2] Ariel Sharon and Menachem Begin had launched the invasion of Lebanon to quash the power of the PLO, and thereby end Palestinian nationalist opposition in the occupied West Bank and Gaza to the absorption of those territories into Israel. This would complete the colonial task of historic Zionism, creating a Jewish state in all of Palestine. The 1982 war did succeed in weakening the PLO, but the paradoxical effect was to strengthen the Palestinian national movement in Palestine itself, shifting the focus of action from outside to inside the country. After two decades of a relatively manageable occupation, Begin and Sharon, two fervent partisans of the Greater Israel ideal, had inadvertently sparked a new level of resistance to the process of colonization. Opposition to Israel's landgrab and military rule has erupted within Palestine repeatedly and in different forms ever since.

The First Intifada, as it became known, erupted spontaneously all over the Occupied Territories, ignited when an Israeli army vehicle struck a truck in the Jabalya refugee camp in the Gaza Strip, killing four

Palestinians. The uprising spread very quickly, although Gaza was the crucible and remained the most difficult area for Israel to bring under control. The intifada generated extensive local organization in the villages, towns, cities, and refugee camps, and came to be led by a secret Unified National Leadership. The flexible and clandestine grassroots networks formed during the intifada proved impossible for the military occupation authorities to suppress.

After a month of escalating unrest, in January 1988, Defense Minister Yitzhak Rabin ordered the security forces to use "force, might, and beatings."[3] His "iron fist" policy was carried out through the explicit practice of breaking the demonstrators' arms and legs and cracking their skulls, as well as beating others who aroused the soldiers' ire. Within a short time, widely televised images of heavily armed soldiers brutalizing teenage Palestinian protestors created a major media backlash in the United States and elsewhere, showing Israel in its true light as a callous occupying power. Only five years after the media coverage of the siege and bombing of Beirut, this exposure dealt another blow to the image of a country largely dependent on complaisant American public opinion.

In spite of the harmful impact of the 1982 war on Israel's standing, the country's shrewd public relations efforts had succeeded in re-anesthetizing much of US public opinion.[4] But unlike the televised air and artillery bombardments of Lebanon, which ended after ten weeks, the violence of the intifada ground on, year after brutal year, from December 1987 through 1993, winding down somewhat during the Gulf War and the peace conference organized by the United States in Madrid in October 1991. During this time, the uprising produced gripping scenes of street battles between young Palestinian protestors and Israeli troops, who were supported by armored personnel carriers and tanks. The iconic image from this period was of a small Palestinian boy hurling a stone at a huge Israeli tank.

"If it bleeds it leads," the saying goes, and television viewers were riveted by repeated tableaus of wrenching violence, which inverted the image of Israel as a perpetual victim, casting it as Goliath against the Palestinian David. This was a constant drain on Israel, not only in terms of the pressure on its security forces, but also and perhaps more significant, in terms of its reputation abroad, in some ways its most vital asset.

Even Rabin, the man in charge, realized the importance of this political factor. A flattering *New York Times* interview with Rabin opened by claiming that "Palestinian rioters have been winning the public relations battle against Israel in the world press, Defense Minister Yitzhak Rabin conceded today, stressing that the army is confronting something new and complex: a widespread uprising born of decades of Palestinian frustrations."[5]

At the time that the First Intifada broke out, the occupation of the West Bank and Gaza Strip had been in place for two decades. Taking advantage of a situation of relative calm, Israel began the colonization of the Occupied Territories immediately after the 1967 war, eventually creating over two hundred settlements, from cities of 50,000 residents to flimsy prefabricated clusters housing a few dozen settlers. For years, Israeli experts had assured their leaders and the public that the Palestinians living under what they called "an enlightened occupation" were content and fully under control. The eruption of massive grass-roots resistance belied this notion. It was true that some Palestinians, intimidated by Israeli might and by a round of mass expulsions of more than 250,000 of their number after the 1967 war,[6] had seemed to acquiesce at first to the new order imposed on them. It was also true that incomes in the West Bank and Gaza Strip rose significantly as tens of thousands of Palestinians were newly allowed to work in Israel.

By 1976, however, alienation had intensified. Any expression of nationalism—flying the Palestinian flag, displaying the Palestinian colors, organizing trade unions, voicing support for the PLO or any other resistance organization—was severely suppressed, with fines, beatings, and jail. Detentions and imprisonment usually featured torture of detainees. Protesting the occupation publicly or in print could lead to the same result or even to deportation. More active resistance, especially that involving violence, invited collective punishment, house demolitions, imprisonment without trial under the rubric of "administrative detention" that could last for years, and even extrajudicial murder. That year, mayoral candidates backed by the PLO won municipal elections in Nablus, Ramallah, Hebron, and al-Bireh, as well as in other towns. A number of the mayors were deported in 1980, accused of incitement, and others were removed from office by the military occupation authorities in the spring of 1982, provoking widespread unrest. This was done in the lead-up to the invasion of Lebanon as part of Ariel Sharon's comprehensive campaign to uproot the PLO.

One aspect of that campaign was an attempt to create local collaborationist groups, the "village leagues," a project that never got off the ground because of widespread Palestinian refusal to cooperate with the occupation after the mayors' removal. Sharon's chosen instrument for this policy was a so-called Israeli Arabist, Menachem Milson, a professor of Arabic and a reserve colonel in the Israeli army.[7] For a person to wear these two hats was not unusual: most senior academic Middle East specialists in Israel doubled as reserve officers in military intelligence or other branches of the security services, engaged in spying on and oppressing the people they studied the rest of the time.[8]

Meanwhile, a new generation of Palestinians had come of age having known nothing but military occupation, and they were anything but acquiescent. These young people came out in public expressions of support for the PLO in East Jerusalem, the West Bank, and the Gaza Strip, in spite of the risk of doing so. The years preceding the intifada were marked by mass demonstrations by young Palestinians more fearless than their elders and by intensifying repression by Israeli security forces, whose superiors seemed heedless of the cumulative effect of the brutality they were ordering.

Given all the signs of growing unrest, the uprising should have come as no surprise to the Israeli authorities. Yet their swift response was ill-conceived, heavy-handed, and disproportionate. The systematic brutality of the soldiers, most of them young draftees, toward the population they were charged with controlling was not only the result of frustration or even fear. Rabin's orders to "break bones" set the tone, but the excessive violence was also rooted in constant societal anti-Palestinian indoctrination, grounded in the dogmatic idea that Israel would be overwhelmed by the Arabs if its security forces did not deter them by force, since their supposedly irrational hostility to Jews was otherwise uncontrollable.[9]

The intifada had been underway for nearly a year and a half when I took my first trip to Palestine since 1966, at which time the West Bank had been under Jordanian rule.[10] During a visit to Nablus with some University of Chicago colleagues, after leaving my cousin Ziyad's home one evening, we found ourselves in the winding streets of the Old City, caught in a clash between young protestors and the Israeli troops who were chasing them, firing rubber bullets and tear gas. The soldiers did not catch any of the demonstrators, but they did eventually manage to disperse them. It was clear at that moment that there could be no lasting victory for Israel's forces in this kind of cat-and-mouse urban unrest. The young protestors could reappear at any moment somewhere else in the labyrinth of narrow alleys. Of course, the troops could simply kill them, and that happened all too frequently. From the beginning of the First Intifada to the end of 1996—nine years, including six when the intifada was ongoing—Israeli troops and armed settlers killed 1,422 Palestinians, almost one every other day. Of them, 294, or over 20 percent, were minors sixteen and under. One hundred and seventy-five Israelis, 86 of them security personnel, were killed by Palestinians during the same period.[11] That eight-to-one casualty ratio was typical, something one would not have known from much of the American media coverage.

On another occasion, I was driving through Gaza City on the way to visit my cousin Huda, wife of Dr. Haydar 'Abd al-Shafi, head of the Palestinian Red Crescent in Gaza. In the slow crawl of a traffic jam, our car passed a heavily armed Israeli patrol, the soldiers in the jeep holding their weapons at the ready. They were fidgety and nervous, and in their faces I saw a quality I had noticed in the Israeli troops in occupied Beirut in 1982: they were afraid. Their vehicles moved at a snail's pace through heavily populated built-up areas where the entire community loathed the occupation that the soldiers embodied and enforced. Soldiers of a regular army, no matter how heavily armed, will never feel secure in such circumstances.

Rabin and others recognized the inherent problems that I saw on the streets of Nablus and Gaza. According to Itamar Rabinovich, Rabin's biographer, close collaborator, and tennis partner, the First Intifada brought the veteran general to the realization that a political solution was necessary.[12] Nonetheless, he held fast to the deterrent effect of brutality. "The use of force," Rabin said, "including beatings, undoubtedly has brought about the impact we wanted—strengthening the population's fear of the Israel Defense Forces."[13] Maybe so, but this brutality did not put an end to the uprising.

Nablus Casbah, the First Intifada, 1988. There could be no lasting victory for Israel's forces in this kind of cat-and-mouse urban unrest.

The intifada was a spontaneous, bottom-up campaign of resistance, born of an accumulation of frustration and initially with no connection to the formal political Palestinian leadership. As with the 1936–39 revolt, the intifada's length and extensive support was proof of the broad popular backing that it enjoyed. The uprising was also flexible and innovative, developing a coordinated leadership while remaining locally driven and controlled. Among its activists were men and women, elite professionals and businesspeople, farmers, villagers, the urban poor, students, small shopkeepers, and members of virtually every other sector of society. Women played a central role, taking more and more leadership positions as many of the men were jailed and mobilizing people who were often left out of conventional male-dominated politics.[14]

Along with demonstrations, the intifada involved tactics ranging from strikes, boycotts, and withholding taxes to other ingenious forms of civil disobedience. Protests sometimes turned violent, often ignited by soldiers inflicting heavy casualties with live ammunition and rubber bullets used against unarmed demonstrators or youths throwing stones. Nevertheless, the uprising was predominantly nonviolent and unarmed, a crucially important factor that helped mobilize sectors of society in addition to the young people protesting in the streets while showing that the entirety of Palestinian society under occupation opposed the status quo and supported the intifada.

The First Intifada was an outstanding example of popular resistance against oppression and can be considered as being the first unmitigated victory for the Palestinians in the long colonial war that began in 1917. Unlike the 1936–39 revolt, the intifada was driven by a broad strategic vision and a unified leadership, and it did not exacerbate internal Palestinian divisions.[15] Its unifying effect and largely successful avoidance of firearms and explosives—in contrast to the Palestinian resistance movement of the 1960s and 1970s—helped to make its appeal widely heard internationally, leading to a profound and lasting positive impact on both Israeli and world public opinion.

This was no accident: the intifada was explicitly aimed not only at mobilizing Palestinians and Arabs, but also at shaping Israeli and world perceptions. That this was a key objective was clear from many of the tactics used, and also from the sophisticated and effective communications strategies of those who were able to explain to international audiences what the intifada meant. These included articulate and worldly activists and intellectuals inside Palestine, such as Hanan 'Ashrawi, Haydar 'Abd al-Shafi, Raja Shehadeh, Iyad al-Sarraj, Ghassan al-Khatib, Zahira Kamal, Mustafa Barghouti, Rita Giacaman, Raji Sourani, and many others. Those outside of Palestine, among them Edward Said and Ibrahim Abu Lughod, had a similar impact. By the early 1990s, the unified Palestinian stance had successfully made it clear that the occupation was untenable, at least as it had functioned in its first two decades.

For all of the First Intifada's achievements, there was a hidden internal danger in its success and in the emergence of an effective local leadership with articulate, attractive spokespersons. A grassroots movement that supersedes established political elites constitutes a challenge to their power. After the PLO's defeat in Lebanon in 1982, the organization was stuck in a sterile and debilitating exile in Tunis and other Arab capitals, with its energy directed at an initially fruitless attempt to win US acceptance as an interlocutor and Israeli acceptance as a partner to a settlement. The PLO was taken by surprise by the outbreak of a grassroots-led uprising and lost no time trying to co-opt and profit from it.

Since most of those who had risen up in revolt in the Occupied Territories saw the PLO as their legitimate representative and its leaders as the embodiment of Palestinian nationalism, this posed few problems at the outset. The population of the Occupied Territories, who had watched from a distance the sacrifices of the PLO's militants in Jordan during Black September and in Lebanon throughout the civil war and the Israeli invasion, felt they were now shouldering part of the national burden. They were proud that Palestinians under occupation were taking the lead in the struggle for liberation.

The problem with this development was the short-sightedness and limited strategic vision of the PLO's leaders in Tunis. Many of them did not fully understand the nature of the occupation regime or the complex social and political situation of the Palestinians in the West Bank and Gaza Strip after two decades of Israeli control. Indeed, most of these leaders had not been inside Palestine since 1967 or earlier. Their understanding of Israeli society and politics was far more limited than the Palestinians who had lived under and watched Israeli rule, many of whom had learned Hebrew in their jobs inside Israel or while serving time in prison (a fifth of the Palestinian population under occupation had passed through these prisons). The consequence was increasingly intrusive management of the intifada by remote control from Tunis, as the PLO came to dominate what had been a popular resistance movement. It issued directives and ran things from a distance, often ignoring the views and preferences of those who had initiated the revolt and had led it successfully.

This problem became considerably more acute after Israel's assassination of Abu Jihad in April 1988, some four months after the intifada began. Abu Jihad, 'Arafat's closest lieutenant, had been a leading figure in Fatah since the beginning and had long been in charge of dealing with the Occupied Territories or, as his department was called, *al-Qita' al-Gharbi*, the Western Sector (presumably to conceal its true purpose).

Abu Jihad had his failings, but he was a close observer of the situation inside Palestine and was deeply knowledgeable about both Palestinians and Israelis there. His assassination, which was a result of the Israeli leadership's mounting frustration at their inability to master the intifada, deprived the PLO of one of its key figures, whose role could not easily be filled by another.[16] Abu Jihad's killing was part of Israel's decades-long policy of systematic liquidation of top Palestinian organizers, particularly the effective ones among them.[17]

The loss of Abu Jihad and the lack of expertise in Tunis was not the only reason for the PLO's problems in dealing with the intifada. Following the 1982 war, Fatah had weathered a major Syrian-sponsored mutiny among its remaining cadres in Northern and Eastern Lebanon (from which they had not been evacuated in 1982) and in Syria, led by two senior military commanders, Colonel Abu Musa and Colonel Abu Khalid al-'Amleh. This was the most serious internal challenge to Fatah's leadership since its founding, and it constituted another element in the largely covert offensive against the Palestinian national movement carried out by Arab regimes, in this case Syria.[18]

The Fatah mutiny was bitter and costly and intensified the concern of 'Arafat and his colleagues about the emergence of rivals, especially those under the influence of hostile regimes. The concern was well founded, given the efforts by the movement's adversaries to create alternatives, such as the village leagues in the Occupied Territories. Notably, Hamas, founded in 1987 (and initially discreetly supported by Israel with the objective of weakening the PLO[19]), was already beginning to develop into a formidable competitor. This alarm at the possibility of being superseded was at the root of the PLO leadership's jealousy of the intifada's local leaders, especially as their following grew within Palestine and the global media came to view them positively. 'Arafat's resentment became an increasing problem as the intifada progressed and as the PLO's long-desired prize—a place at international negotiations as the legitimate representative of the Palestinian people—appeared to come within its reach.

JUST AS THEY had a weak understanding of the reality inside the Occupied Territories and Israel, the PLO's leaders had never grasped the full measure of the United States. Even after 1982, they remained ill-informed about the country and its politics, with the exception of a few second-rank figures, such as Nabil Sha'ath and Elias Shoufani, who had been educated in the United States but were unable to influence 'Arafat and his partners.[20] Some senior PLO leaders, such as Faruq al-Qaddumi (Abu Lutf), head of the Political Department (effectively foreign minister), attended sessions of the UN General Assembly in New York every fall, but they were legally restricted to a travel radius of twenty-five miles from Columbus Circle. In any case, they mostly stayed put in their luxury hotels for the duration of their visits. They ventured out infrequently to see Arab diplomats or to speak to Palestinian community groups, but made few public appearances and did not engage with American groups or the New York media. They certainly never undertook the all-points diplomatic and public relations campaigns of Israeli officials, who were ubiquitous on TV and at regional gatherings at all times, and especially when the annual meetings of the General Assembly came around.

The failure to take advantage of the Palestinian presence at the UN amounted to willfully ignoring the people, the elites, and the media of the greatest power on earth and the mainstay of Israel, an approach that dated back to 1948 and before. As I saw in 1984, 'Arafat gave more importance to meeting the leader of a minor PLO faction linked to Iraq than to listening to expert advice about swaying public opinion in the United States. The situation had not improved since then. A simplistic view of the structures of government and decision-making in Washington led the PLO to pin all its hopes on winning the US government's recognition as the legitimate Palestinian interlocutor; American good offices for a fair deal with the Israelis would surely follow. This attitude carried a trace of the naive faith of earlier generations of Palestinian leaders (shared by many Arab rulers to this day) that a personal appeal to a British colonial secretary or prime minister, a US secretary of state or president, could solve the problem. This illusory view of the personal element in power relations may have been grounded in the experience of dealing with mercurial, all-powerful dictators and absolute monarchs in the Arab world.

It was also partly shaped by the experience of the Arab monarchs, who saw US Secretary of State George Shultz (who had headed Bechtel, a major contractor in the Gulf), and later President George H. W. Bush and his secretary of state, James Baker (Texans with past links to the oil industry), as "pro-Arab." Indeed, as with most other US policy-makers since Roosevelt, these men were closely tied to the Arab petro-monarchies, but this did not translate into sympathy for the Arabs generally or for the Palestinians in particular, or into a critical attitude toward Israel.

These flawed understandings were at the root of the PLO's failure to engage seriously with US public opinion and become involved in peace negotiations through the late 1980s. However, in 1988, buoyed by the international impact of the intifada, the organization redoubled its efforts, culminating in the Palestinian Declaration of Independence adopted at a meeting of the Palestine National Council in Algiers on November 15. Drafted largely by Mahmoud Darwish, who was aided by Edward Said and the respected intellectual Shafiq al-Hout, the document formally abandoned the PLO's claim to the entirety of Palestine, accept-ing the principles of partition, a two-state solution, and a peaceful reso-lution to the conflict. An accompanying political communiqué accepted SC 242 and SC 338 as the basis for a peace conference.

These were major political shifts for the PLO, the culmination of an evolution toward acceptance of Israel and advocacy of a Palestinian state alongside it that had begun in the early 1970s, although these changes were unacknowledged by its Israeli adversaries. A more significant shift was yet to come. On December 14 that year, 'Arafat accepted US con-ditions for entering a bilateral dialogue. In his statement, he explicitly accepted Resolutions 242 and 338, recognized the right of Israel to exist in peace and security, and renounced terrorism.[21] This capitulation to American conditions finally obtained for the PLO the long-sought open-ing with Washington, but it neither moved the Israelis to agree to deal with the organization nor led to peace negotiations, at least not for three more years.

The reasons for this were simple. Beyond the PLO's other misas-sumptions about the United States, its leaders failed to grasp the lack of American concern, even its disdain, for their interests and aims (this incomprehension is hard to fathom in light of the painful betrayal of American promises to safeguard the refugee camps in Beirut in 1982). Most important, though, was their inability to understand how intimately the policies of the United States and Israel were linked. Kissinger's secret 1975 commitments locked US policymakers' feet in cement where dealing with the Palestine question was concerned. The PLO might not have known that Israel had effectively secured veto power over US positions in any peace talks,[22] but there had been enough credible leaks in the press and elsewhere about these secret agreements (mainly from Israelis, who were understandably eager to publicize them).[23] There had also been embarrassing incidents as when Andrew Young, ambassador to the UN, was forced to resign after meeting with a PLO official.

The general terms of US commitments to Israel should have been clear to an informed observer. This 'Arafat and his colleagues definitely were not. The intifada had delivered to them a gift of inestimable value, a store of moral and political capital. The popular revolt had revealed the limits of the military occupation, damaged Israel's international standing, and improved that of the Palestinians. For all the effectiveness of the PLO in its first decades in putting Palestine back on the global map, it can be argued that the intifada had a more positive impact on world opinion than the organization's generally ineffective efforts at armed struggle ever had. The director of the Mossad at the time, Nahum Admoni, confirmed this, saying "The Intifada caused us a lot more political harm, damage to our image, than everything that the PLO had succeeded in doing throughout its existence."[24] Trading on this significant new asset enabled the PLO leadership to abandon formally its strategy of armed struggle from bases outside Palestine, which in any case was increasingly impossible after 1982, and in their hands had never had much chance of success, if it was not actually harmful to the Palestinian cause.

Even before 1982, many in the PLO understood that the time had come to end the armed struggle. While still based in Lebanon, its leaders had tasked the distinguished Pakistani intellectual Eqbal Ahmad, a close friend of Edward Said and a friend of mine, with assessing their military strategy. Ahmad had worked with the Front de libération nationale in Algeria in the early 1960s, had known Frantz Fanon, and was a renowned Third World anticolonial thinker. After visiting PLO bases in south Lebanon he returned with a critique that disconcerted those who had asked his advice. While in principle a committed supporter of armed struggle against colonial regimes such as that in Algeria, Ahmad had strong criticisms of the ineffective and often counterproductive way in which the PLO was carrying out this strategy.

More seriously, on political rather than moral or legal grounds, he questioned whether armed struggle was the right course of action against the PLO's particular adversary, Israel. He argued that given the course of Jewish history, especially in the twentieth century, the use of force only strengthened a preexisting and pervasive sense of victimhood among Israelis, while it unified Israeli society, reinforced the most militant tendencies in Zionism, and bolstered the support of external actors.[25] This was in distinction to Algeria, where the FLN's use of violence (including women using "baskets to carry bombs, which have taken so many innocent lives" in the accusatory words of a French interrogator in the 1966 Gillo Pontecorvo film *The Battle of Algiers*) ultimately succeeded in dividing French society and eroding its support for the colonial project. Ahmad's critique was profound and devastating, and not welcomed by the PLO's leaders, who still publicly proclaimed a devotion to armed struggle even as they were moving away from it in practice. Beyond his acute understanding of the deep connection between Zionism and the long history of persecution of Jews in Europe, Ahmad's analysis shrewdly perceived the unique nature of the Israeli colonial project.[26]

The mainly nonviolent intifada in Palestine enabled 'Arafat to take account, albeit belatedly, of Ahmad's view, and at the same time to respond positively to a prime US condition for dialogue: renouncing armed resistance, deemed to be terrorism by the United States and Israel. However, the results of the PLO's naïveté regarding the United States soon became apparent. In and of themselves, recognition by the United States and a seat at the negotiating table were unexceptionable aims. Every anticolonial movement, whether in Algeria, Vietnam, or South Africa, desired its foes to accept its legitimacy and to negotiate with it for an honorable end to the conflict. In all these cases, however, an honorable outcome meant ending occupation and colonization and ideally reaching a peaceful reconciliation based on justice. That was the primary object of the negotiations sought by other liberation movements. But instead of using the intifada's success to hold out for a forum framed in terms of such liberatory ends, the PLO allowed itself to be drawn into a process explicitly designed by Israel, with the acquiescence of the United States, to prolong its occupation and colonization, not to end them.

The PLO desperately pursued admission to supposed peace negotiations whose narrow parameters were from the outset restricted by SC 242 in ways that were enormously disadvantageous to the Palestinians. SC 242 includes no mention of the Palestine question, or of the Arab state specified in UNGA Resolution 181 in 1947, or of the return of refugees mandated by UNGA Resolution 194 of 1948. With its carefully drafted wording about withdrawal from "territories occupied" in 1967 (rather than "*the* territories occupied"), 242 effectively gave Israel a chance to expand its pre-1967 borders further. Whether they realized it or not, by accepting Resolution 242 as the basis for any negotiations, 'Arafat and his colleagues had set themselves an impossible task.

They also failed to understand the need to continue to put pressure on one's adversaries: with the end of armed struggle and the waning of the intifada in the early 1990s, this became less and less possible. Once talks finally began, in Madrid in the fall of 1991, the PLO tried to put a halt to the intifada (it did not stop, but petered out a few years later), as if launching negotiations were the end of the process rather than the beginning. Added to the fact that the United States could never be an honest broker given the commitments it had undertaken, Israel also had its own independent positions. Thus any concessions made by the PLO to the United States did not necessarily bind Israel or make it more willing to deal with the organization. In fact, when at the end of the Reagan administration the United States finally began a dialogue with the PLO following its 1988 declaration, Israel became even more intransigent.

Furthermore, the PLO did not seem to comprehend the full import of the 1978 Camp David deal and subsequent 1979 Egyptian-Israeli peace treaty, in which Menachem Begin had struck a ruinous bargain over Palestine with Anwar Sadat and Jimmy Carter. Also, the decline of the USSR meant that the PLO lost an intermittent and inconsistent patron that had provided military and diplomatic support and had championed its inclusion in negotiations under far less onerous terms than those demanded by the United States and Israel.[27] By the end of 1991, however, the USSR had disappeared, and the United States was left as the sole international guarantor and sponsor of any Palestinian-Israeli process.

Another grave blow to the PLO's standing was the profound miscalculation made by Yasser 'Arafat and most of his colleagues regarding the 1990–91 Gulf War. Almost immediately after Iraq's invasion and occupation of Kuwait in August 1990, the Gulf states, together with virtually every other major Arab power, including Egypt and Syria, joined the US-led international coalition to forcibly reverse Saddam Hussein's gross violation of the sovereignty of a member state of the Arab League. This was in keeping with the consistent preference of postcolonial states in Asia, Africa, and the Middle East for the preservation of colonial borders and the states that had grown up within them. Instead of firmly supporting Kuwait against Iraq, 'Arafat tried to steer a "neutral" course, offering to mediate between the two sides. His suggestion was ignored by all concerned, as were the mediating efforts of more powerful actors such as the USSR, which fruitlessly sent its senior Middle East envoy to Baghdad.[28]

There were multiple reasons for the PLO's bizarre decision to essentially support Iraq, a move that made the organization a pariah among the Gulf states on which it depended for financial support and harmed it in innumerable other ways. First among these reasons was 'Arafat's long-standing and fierce antipathy toward Hafez al-Asad's overbearing Syrian regime (an antipathy that was richly reciprocated) and his reflexive search for a counterweight. One of 'Arafat's signature slogans, "*al-qarar al-Filastini al-mustaqill*"—"the independent Palestinian decision"—was usually brandished in response to Syrian efforts to coerce, constrain, and dominate the PLO. While Egypt had once served to balance the pressures exerted by the Asad regime, that role was no longer possible after Sadat's separate peace with Israel. The only other plausible counterweight had of necessity been Syria's rival, Iraq. In the wake of Sadat's apostasy, the PLO had become increasingly dependent on Iraqi political, military, and financial patronage, especially after the Syrian regime sought to undermine 'Arafat's leadership by masterminding the fratricidal rebellion against him in 1982.

This dependency subjected 'Arafat and the PLO to intense pressure to conform to Iraqi policies, which were dictated by the vagaries of Saddam Hussein, a thuggish despot who was ignorant, mercurial, and brutal. To keep the PLO in line, the Iraqi regime frequently punished it. Among the many tools for this purpose, Baghdad had at its disposal various nominally Palestinian splinter groups like Abu Nidal's terrorist network, the Ba'thist Arab Liberation Front, and the Palestine Liberation Front, headed by Abu al-'Abbas. All these tiny groups lacked a popular base and were essentially extensions of the fearsome Iraqi intelligence services (although, as we have seen, Abu Nidal's guns for hire were also at times clandestinely employed by the Libyan and Syrian regimes, and were deeply penetrated by other intelligence services). Any one of them could carry out operations designed to undermine the PLO or attack its leaders to force it back into line with the Iraqi regime. Indeed, for a time, Abu Nidal's gunmen murdered almost as many PLO envoys and leaders in Europe as did the Mossad. These fronts for several Arab regimes also specialized in spectacular terror operations against Israeli and Jewish civilians, such as the Abu Nidal group's 1985 Rome and Vienna airport massacres and its bloody 1986 assault on an Istanbul synagogue, or the PLF's 1985 attack on the *Achille Lauro* cruise liner.

Their dependency on Iraq apart, 'Arafat and others wildly overestimated Iraqi military capacities in 1990–91. They had an inflated judgment of Iraq's ability to withstand the onslaught by the US-led coalition that was clearly coming after the invasion of Kuwait. This delusional view (Iraq had been unable to defeat Iran in eight years of war) was widespread in various parts of the Arab world. In the months before the inevitable US-led counteroffensive began, otherwise intelligent, well-informed people in Palestine, Lebanon, and Jordan loudly pronounced their certainty that war would not come, but if it did, Iraq would prevail. 'Arafat was in some measure carried along by a popular tide, as large segments of Arab public opinion shared this fantasy. Many supported Saddam Hussein's landgrab as a nationalist blow against "colonially imposed frontiers" (as if most of the frontiers and states in the Arab East had not also been colonially imposed). Saddam was seen by those thus deluded as a great Arab hero, a new Saladin (the original Saladin had come from Tikrit, Hussein's birthplace), who could surely defeat the United States and its allies.

The one exception to the PLO's consensus of idiocy was its intelligence chief, Abu Iyad, among the brightest and most grounded of its senior leaders. He understood that the chosen course would lead to disaster and fought fiercely against the decision to back Iraq, provoking tempestuous arguments with 'Arafat. As well as the obvious reasons for his stance, he was concerned with safeguarding the prosperous Palestinian community in Kuwait, which was several hundred thousand strong. Both he and 'Arafat had lived and worked in Kuwait for years and he had close ties to the community, which furnished one of the PLO's most solid popular and financial bases anywhere in the world. Moreover, Kuwait itself was supportive toward the PLO and was the only Arab country where Palestinians had relative freedom of expression. They ran their own schools and could organize to help the PLO as long as they took care not to interfere in Kuwaiti politics. Abu Iyad argued that 'Arafat's failure to oppose Saddam's suicidal invasion of Kuwait would weaken the PLO and condemn Palestinians there to the destruction of their community and another forced displacement.

It all played out exactly as Abu Iyad had foreseen, but he paid for his temerity (he had reportedly even criticized Saddam Hussein in person).[29] He was assassinated in Tunis on January 14, 1991, three days before the US-led offensive began. The gunman was acting for the Abu Nidal network (and by extension undoubtedly for Iraq), which the PLO intelligence services under Abu Iyad had hunted for years. The loss of Abu Iyad, coming three years after the killing of Abu Jihad, left no one in the top Fatah echelons with the stature or will to stand up to 'Arafat—a situation that only enhanced his inclination to high-handedness.

The consequences of 'Arafat's ill-considered decision were not long in coming, beginning with the tragic uprooting of hundreds of thousands of Palestinians from Kuwait after the country's liberation. The Gulf states halted all financial support to the PLO, which was ostracized in many Arab countries, including some of those that had agreed to host its cadres after the 1982 evacuation from Beirut. Thus after the 1990–91 Gulf War, the PLO found itself more friendless and alone than perhaps at any stage in its history. The icebergs on which 'Arafat and his comrades were afloat were melting fast, and they were desperately eager to jump to solid ground.

It happened that this crisis coincided with a moment of American triumphalism, with the victory in Iraq and the end of the Soviet Union. In George H. W. Bush's State of the Union speech in January 1991, he hailed the "new world order" and the "next American century." The Bush administration was determined to take advantage of the opportunity that

Saddam's folly had given them to shape and define this new world order, one that in their view necessitated a resolution of the Arab-Israeli conflict. Israeli and American diplomats knew that the PLO's negotiating position was severely weakened. It was in this context that Secretary of State James Baker began planning for a peace conference to be held in Madrid in October 1991, hoping to jump-start direct Israeli-Arab talks and determine the future of Palestine. When 'Arafat and his colleagues were eventually offered a proxy seat at the negotiating table, they were under so much pressure and so eager to leave their precarious perches in Tunis and elsewhere, that they failed to assess their vast disadvantage. The setbacks that followed, in the negotiations at Madrid, Washington, Oslo, and thereafter, were thus to a large extent rooted in the PLO's epic miscalculation over Kuwait.

In the summer of 1991 while doing research in Jerusalem, I paid a casual visit to Faysal Husayni, a relative by marriage who, until his untimely death in Kuwait, was the foremost Palestinian leader in Jerusalem and also a senior figure in Fatah. I had gone to consult on a minor problem among some of my cousins (I have a large and occasionally fractious family in Jerusalem). Faysal unexpectedly asked if I would agree to serve as an advisor to the Palestinian delegation to a peace conference to be convened by the United States. I knew that at the behest of the PLO, Husayni, Hanan 'Ashrawi, Haydar 'Abd al-Shafi, and others were in discussions with James Baker over the ground rules for the conference and the formation of the delegation. I also knew that Yitzhak Shamir, Israel's prime minister, was implacably opposed to the PLO's participation in any negotiations and to the creation of a Palestinian state, so I was confident that the conference would never take place. I acquiesced to Faysal's request without giving it much thought, thanked him for his advice on our family problem, and took my leave.

I found myself in Madrid a few months later, in late October 1991, having failed to account for Baker's tenacity or the desperation of the PLO leadership in Tunis. At the outset of the conference, the dignified speech by the head of the Palestinian delegation, 'Abd al-Shafi, and the effective media appearances by 'Ashrawi gave many Palestinians the impression that their cause was at last getting traction and that the sacrifices of the intifada were not in vain. However, various clouds hung over the conference and over all the subsequent bilateral negotiations with the Israelis in Madrid and later in Washington. The PLO had, via Baker, acquiesced to Shamir's condition that there would be no independent Palestinian representation at a conference that aimed to determine the fate of Palestine. So I was attached as an advisor to a joint Jordanian-Palestinian delegation.

Of course, the Palestinians' exclusion from an independent role in decisions about their lives was nothing new (the Palestinian delegation was eventually allowed to separate from that of Jordan). But Israel's veto extended to the choice of Palestinian representatives, and it blocked the participation of anyone connected to the PLO, or from Jerusalem, or from the diaspora (which drastically narrowed the field of available delegates). Thanks to Baker's intervention, leaders excluded by these terms, such as Husayni, 'Ashrawi, and Sari Nuseibeh, as well as advisors and legal and diplomatic experts, such as Raja Shehadeh, Camille Mansour, and me, were allowed to join the delegation, but were barred from the formal talks with the Israelis. The humiliation of a procedure whereby Israel decreed with whom it would negotiate and in what configuration had not deterred the PLO. More humiliation was to come.

As well as dictating who could talk, the Shamir government determined what could be talked about. The limitations regarding Palestine that Begin had insisted on in the Camp David Accords and the 1979 peace treaty with Egypt were now applied to the three-day Madrid conference and the many subsequent months of discussions in Washington: for the Palestinians only self-rule was on the table, whether under the rubric of "autonomy" or that of "interim self-government." Every item of essence—Palestinian self-determination, sovereignty, the return of refugees, an end to occupation and colonization, the disposition of Jerusalem, the future of the Jewish settlements, and control of land and water rights—was disallowed. Instead, these issues were postponed, supposedly for four years, but in fact until a future that never came: the fabled "final status" talks that were supposed to be completed by 1997 (this deadline was later extended to 1999 in the Oslo Accords) were never concluded. In the meanwhile, during an interim phase intended to last only until then, Israel was allowed to do exactly as it pleased in all these domains. Thus throughout the 1990s, the Palestinian negotiators at Madrid and elsewhere operated under imposed rules restricting discussion to the terms of their ongoing colonization and occupation. The prospect of future relief from this interim phase was dangled before them by the sponsors of the Madrid conference, but Palestinians in the Occupied Territories are still living in that temporary interim state over a quarter of a century later.

The United States was ostensibly cosponsoring the conference with the USSR, which was about to go out of existence and whose backing was nominal: in fact, Baker and Bush made all the decisions. Washington's ground rules were embodied in a carefully drafted letter of invitation to all parties, which included delegations from Syria, Lebanon, and Jordan.[30] In a solemn commitment in the letter of invitation, the United States pledged to "act as an honest broker in trying to resolve the Arab-Israeli conflict" in a "comprehensive" fashion.[31] Detailed separate US letters of assurance were also given to each of the delegations. In that addressed to the Palestinians, the United States committed itself to "encourage all sides to avoid unilateral acts that would exacerbate local tensions or make negotiations more difficult or preempt their final outcome," and stressed that "no party should take unilateral actions that seek to predetermine issues that can only be resolved through negotiations."[32] The United States never made good on these commitments, failing to prevent an unending series of unilateral Israeli actions, from settlement expansion and the closure of Jerusalem to West Bankers and Gazans, to the erection of a massive new network of walls, security barriers, and checkpoints.

When they arrived in Madrid, none of the other members of the Palestinian delegation knew of Gerald Ford's 1975 explicit commitment to Rabin to avoid presenting any peace proposals of which Israel disapproved, and nor did I.[33] We were all aware of the 1978 Camp David Accords, of the US bias in favor of Israel, and of the partiality of many American diplomats, but we did not know of the degree to which Kissinger had tethered his successors to an Israeli platform. Had I understood how heavily the deck was stacked and that the United States was bound in this way by a formal commitment—which meant that Israel effectively determined both its own position and that of its sponsor—I probably would not have gone to Madrid or spent much of the next two years engaged in the Washington talks. Even if I had been able to share this knowledge with the delegation (who were all from the Occupied Territories with no diplomatic experience, but who eventually proved to be formidable negotiators), it would have made little difference.

All the important decisions on the Palestinian side were made by the PLO leaders in Tunis. So desperate were they to be brought into the negotiation process and to escape their isolation, that even had they known how tightly bound the United States was to follow the Israeli line, I believe they would likely have still made the mistakes they ended up making in the talks. With few allies regionally or globally, little ability to put pressure on Israel, and a limited understanding of the nature of the occupation or of the arcane legal issues involved, they had essentially chosen to put all their eggs in the basket of a US government obliged to express only points of view preapproved by Israel. Most important, they had little patience for the pettifogging legal detail that negotiations with experienced Israeli diplomats necessitated, or for a long-term strategy that might have worn down Israel's stubbornness on key issues involving control of territory, the expansion of settlements, and Jerusalem.

In bringing all the parties together, the Madrid conference served its function of starting a comprehensive negotiation process. It was followed by several different tracks: the three Arab states, Syria, Lebanon, and Jordan, proceeded to bilateral talks with Israel on final peace treaties. Meanwhile, the Palestinian track, decoupled from that of Jordan, involved ten rounds of discussions over a year and a half with Israeli representatives at the State Department in Washington. These remained rigidly restricted to the subject of limited self-rule in the West Bank and Gaza. Among many obstacles that prevented progress in Washington—the PLO leadership's flawed direction of the talks, the deceptive role of the United States, and Israel's obduracy on Palestinian rights—was the fact that while the Palestinian negotiators and their advisors gradually developed legal and diplomatic expertise, the leaders in Tunis had no understanding of its crucial importance in the process.

This was all the more important given the distorted part played by many of the American personnel involved. Several were loath to push the

Israelis on any issue of substance—such as settlement expansion and the status of Jerusalem during the interim period, or the scope of the jurisdiction the Palestinians were to have over the areas and populations that would become nominally autonomous. Whatever the issue at hand, the US representatives considered the Israeli position, as they read it, to be the ceiling of what was feasible or could be discussed. We knew that they coordinated closely with their Israeli peers, and some of them took the formal (but secret) US commitment to Israel to an extreme. American negotiator Aaron David Miller later regretfully used the term "Israel's lawyer" to describe his stance and that of many of his colleagues.[34] Aptly, the term was apparently coined by Henry Kissinger, who knew a thing or two about American advocacy of Israeli policy.[35]

Quite different in this respect from any of his subordinates was James Baker, a man with extraordinarily fine political instincts and an acute sense of the ways to deploy power. He and Bush understood the benefit to the US in the post–Cold War moment of a comprehensive resolution of the Arab-Israeli conflict and intuited that reaching a lasting agreement would require putting pressure on Israel. Baker also had enough backbone and a close enough relationship with the president to ignore the limitations on US freedom of action negotiated in 1975 by Kissinger, or at least to interpret these limitations loosely in light of what they saw as the US national interest. They had done this to get the negotiations started: when Shamir stonewalled the administration's initial effort to sponsor a conference, Baker was not afraid to confront the Shamir government publicly, saying, "When you're serious about peace, call us" and offering the White House phone number.[36] Baker pushed relentlessly for Palestinian participation at Madrid, in the teeth of stubborn opposition from Shamir. Those of us who met Baker sensed that he had sympathy for the predicament of Palestinians under occupation and understood our frustration at the absurd restraints imposed by the Shamir government. This sympathy was in part the result of his prolonged interactions with Husayni, 'Ashrawi, 'Abd al-Shafi, and their colleagues during meetings to prepare for the conference.

But Baker was only able, or willing, to do so much. Among the most important things he did not do was restrain Israeli actions that systematically changed the status quo in Palestine while negotiations were underway. These included continuous building of settlements and barring residents of the rest of the Occupied Territories from entering Jerusalem. Both were grave violations of the US commitments embodied in Baker's letter of assurance. In the Palestinian view, by these actions Israel was preemptively eating the cake that the two sides were supposed to be dividing, while exploiting the prohibition on the Palestinian delegates that prevented them from talking about final status issues. Although the Bush administration's impatience with Shamir's obstructionism and the ceaseless pace of colonization of the West Bank led it to withhold ten billion dollars in loan guarantees that Israel sought for the resettlement of Russian Jews, this had little or no effect on the Israeli government.[37] More than this Washington would not do.

In any case, Baker was gone from the State Department ten months after Madrid, drafted in August 1992 to run Bush's failing presidential campaign. From that point on, the junior officials who had been firmly under Baker's control while he was secretary of state took over the shop, and they did not have his stature, his steely will in dealing with Israel, his even-handedness, or his vision. This situation went on for the remaining few months of the Bush administration and then became worse under Bill Clinton, who won election in November that year, and his two undistinguished secretaries of state, Warren Christopher and Madeleine Albright. No one at the top of the new administration had the same view of the process, of Israel, or of the Palestine issue as had Bush and Baker, and all were strongly under the influence of the officials they inherited from the Bush administration, especially Dennis Ross.

Many members of this group of experts had a strong personal affinity for Labor Zionism and deep admiration for Rabin (which was also true of Bill Clinton), who became prime minister in June 1992. They had made their reputations and careers by working the so-called peace process, which had been dragging on since the 1978 Camp David summit. The rise of these peace-process professionals marked the demise of a generation of so-called Arabists in the State Department and other branches of government. The latter were mainly veterans of lengthy government service in the Middle East with extensive language capabilities, who brought to their jobs a deep understanding of the region and of the US's position in it. They were often vilified by flacks of such lobbies as the American

Israel Public Affairs Committee (AIPAC) as being anti-Israel, which was a fiction—in fact they simply did not represent an Israel-centric view, unlike most of those who eventually succeeded them.[38]

Their successors were men—they were all men—who had been involved in this issue to the exclusion of almost everything else: Disraeli's "the East is a career" became "the peace process is a career." They generally had academic expertise—Dennis Ross, Martin Indyk, Daniel Kurtzer, and Miller all had PhDs[39]—but they had not spent years serving in the Middle East, nor did they have any particular sympathy for the region or its peoples, except for Israel. Several of them later served as US ambassadors, Kurtzer to Egypt and Israel and Indyk to Israel, others as assistant secretary of state for the Middle East, head of policy planning at the State Department, and in the National Security Council.

The doyen of these peace-process professionals and by far the most partisan was Dennis Ross. As one senior State Department official said of him: "Ross's bad habit is pre-consultation with the Israelis."[40] Another was even more scathing: Ross, he said, was prone to "preemptive capitulations to red lines," referring to Israel's red lines.[41] Over the decades that he dealt with this dossier, Ross's deep and abiding commitment to Israel only become more apparent, especially after he left government service in 2011 (he had been in and out of public office since the mid-1970s). Thereafter he became a lobbyist for Israel in all but name, as head of the Jewish People Policy Planning Institute, a body founded and funded by the Jewish Agency, and as a distinguished fellow at the AIPAC-supported Washington Institute for Near East Policy, which he cofounded together with Martin Indyk. The other cofounder of WINEP, Martin Indyk, had also previously worked for AIPAC and became a key figure in the negotiations during the Clinton administration (which arranged rapid approval of US citizenship for this Australian national so that he could take up a government post in 1993).[42]

The overt bias of Dennis Ross and some of his colleagues was obvious in all of our interactions. Their key characteristic was that they accepted Israel's stated public positions as the limit of what was admissible in terms of US policy. For Ross and others, this outlook was rooted in their core beliefs. Indeed, Ross took his partiality to Israel even further, making his own assessments of what Israel would not accept and therefore what the

US could not countenance. These assessments often proved to be wrong. He deemed recognition of the PLO and its involvement in negotiations unacceptable to Israel, even though Rabin in fact eventually agreed to these terms. During one stalemate in Washington, the US side, which had steadfastly refused to put forward its own ideas, agreed to offer what it called a "bridging proposal." Proudly presented by Ross, this bridge to nowhere was even less forthcoming than the last position informally put forward by the Israelis themselves.[43] Ross's bias was apparent at another point in the talks, when in my hearing he threatened that if the Palestinian delegation did not accept a contentious point being pressed on them by Israel, Washington would get their "friends in the Gulf" to lean on them.

The obstacles posed by Israel were of a completely different nature. While Shamir was prime minister, there was constant squabbling over procedure and a painful dialogue of the deaf as far as substance was concerned. In particular, Israel was wedded to Begin's vision, enunciated at Camp David in 1978, of autonomy for the people but not the land. This was in keeping with the Israeli right's view—indeed the core of the Zionist doctrine—that only one people, the Jewish people, had a legitimate right to existence and sovereignty in the entirety of the land, which was called Eretz Israel, the land of Israel, not Palestine. The Palestinians were, at best, interlopers. In practice, this meant that when the Palestinians argued for broad legal and territorial jurisdiction for the future self-governing authority, they were met with a firm refusal from Israeli negotiators. Similarly, there was a refusal to limit settlement activity in any way. This was not surprising. Famously, Shamir was reported as saying that he would have dragged out the talks for ten more years while "vastly increasing the number of Jewish settlers in Israeli-occupied territory."[44]

After a Labor-led coalition replaced Shamir's government, Rabin, now prime minister, wavered between prioritizing the Syrian or the Palestinian track. Ever the strategist, he realized that one of the advantages of reaching a deal with Syria was that it would put the Palestinians in a weaker position, making them easier to deal with. Rabin also felt that an agreement on the Syrian front was more strategically significant, relatively straightforward, and achievable. He was probably right about the last point, and he and Hafez al-Asad nearly managed to reach an agreement.[45]

As evidence of his seriousness in regard to Syria, Rabin appointed Itamar Rabinovich as chief negotiator on the Syrian track (and concurrently as Israel's ambassador to the US). A reserve colonel in the Israeli army, where he had been a senior intelligence officer, and a prominent academic with deep expertise on Syria, Rabinovich was an ideal choice for this position. His appointment led to what he himself described as "some progress" with the Syrians, although in the end the two sides could not come to terms, separated mainly by a disagreement over the disposition of a few strategic square miles of the shoreline on the eastern side of the Sea of Galilee. This fairly uncomplicated but weighty problem was considerably amplified by the intense opposition in several quarters in Israel (and among its most fervent supporters in the US) to any withdrawal from the Golan Heights, a step which Rabin was prepared to contemplate. In the midst of the negotiations, I happened to attend a talk in Chicago where Rabinovich failed utterly to convince Israel's hardline supporters among the group that a deal with Syria was both feasible and desirable. This irrational opposition, I pointed out to Rabinovich, was something Israel had created for itself by its prior demonization of a Syria with which he and Rabin were now convinced that Israel could reach an agreement.

By contrast to his relatively flexible approach to Syria and his appointment of a highly suitable envoy, Rabin changed little in Israel's core approach to the Palestinians at the negotiating table. He kept in place the chief of the Israeli delegation, Elyakim Rubinstein, an experienced diplomat and later a Supreme Court justice, who was tough as nails in his dealings with us. There were some shifts in Israel's positions—on Palestinian elections, the contiguity of the West Bank and Gaza Strip, and a few other matters—but the central element in Rubinstein's brief remained restricted to the most rigidly limited form of self-rule and nothing more. There was palpable disappointment within the Palestinian delegation, and in Tunis, when we realized that Israel's change of government did not herald a substantive change of views. We should not have been surprised. In a speech given in 1989, Rabin had made clear his commitment to Begin's Camp David approach, including autonomy but no independent state for the Palestinians.[46] Six years later in October 1995, less than a month before he was assassinated, Rabin told the Knesset that any Palestinian "entity" to be created would be "less than a state."[47]

IN SPITE OF the discouraging signs in Washington in January 1992, while Shamir was still in office, the Palestinian delegation put forward the outline of a proposal for a Palestinian Interim Self-Governing Authority, or PISGA, as we called it, which we foresaw as the stepping stone to a state. An enhanced and more substantive version was presented in March. Its core idea was the creation of a Palestinian governmental entity, whose authority was to be derived from its election by the people, including Palestinian residents of the West Bank, Jerusalem, the Gaza Strip, those displaced from these areas in 1967, as well as those deported since then by Israel. Following the election, the Israeli military government and its occupation bureaucracy, the euphemistically named Civil Administration, would transfer all powers to this new authority, after which these Israeli bodies would withdraw. The authority would have complete jurisdiction (but neither sovereignty nor full security control) over the air, land, and water of the entirety of the Occupied Territories, including settlements (but not settlers), and over all their Palestinian inhabitants. Israel would have been obliged to freeze settlement activity and withdraw its troops "to redeployment points along the borders of the occupied Palestinian territories" when this authority came into being.[48]

Although the PISGA proposal constituted a genuine effort to envisage a transition from occupation to independence, it was ultimately a vain attempt to do an end run around the limitations that constrained the negotiations and the restricted forms of self-rule that Israel was prepared to countenance. These essentially reserved all powers over security, land, water, airspace, population registers, movement, settlements, and most other matters of importance for Israel. There were many reasons for the PISGA proposal's failure, the main one being the doctrine that was at the root of the Palestinians' displacement: the Zionist doctrine of the exclusive Jewish right to the entirety of Palestine. Jurisdiction, as it was broadly envisaged in the PISGA proposal, contradicted that core doctrine from which everything else flowed; it came far too close to the no-no of sovereignty to be acceptable to Rubinstein and his political bosses, be they Yitzhak Shamir or Yitzhak Rabin.

Tunis formed another obstacle. Although the PLO leadership had approved the proposal, I sensed a distinct lack of enthusiasm for the concepts it embodied. They failed to promote it internationally, in the Arab world, or in Israel, even though such promotion might have provided it with some momentum. Perhaps they knew the Israeli government would never accept it, and they were overly eager for an acceptable deal, any deal. Or their tepid response may have been due to jealousy of a delegation that had actually produced a complex and carefully crafted plan instead of simply reacting to whatever was presented by their adversaries, as the PLO had done since the beginning of the process and still does to this day.

This problem was exacerbated by the deep tensions running between the PLO in Tunis and the Palestinians from the Occupied Territories, many of them veteran leaders of the intifada, who were the official members of the delegation. We were all aware of this tension, and we saw it flare into open dispute on occasion. Many of us were present in Faysal Husayni's Washington hotel suite during furious phone exchanges between him and 'Arafat. The Israelis were also aware of the tension and happy to exploit it. In 1993, they suddenly changed the ground rules and allowed the direct participation of Husayni, 'Ashrawi, and others (including us advisors) who had been excluded from the formal negotiations. This may have seemed like a gracious concession, but as Rabin told Clinton during a meeting, his goal in so doing was to sow divisions among the Palestinians in the hope that "a local leader could stand up to Arafat."[49] These divide-and-rule tactics, which Rabin had employed when he was defense minister, are standard procedure for any colonial ruler, but they did not matter in the end. After rejecting our PISGA proposal, the delegation in Washington received no serious counterproposal from the Israelis that would have meaningfully changed the colonial status quo inside Palestine. In consequence, the Washington talks proved fruitless.

Something fundamental did eventually change in the Israeli position, although we had only an inkling of this shift during our time in Washington. After more than a year and a half of stalemate and frustration, we learned that an important secret exchange had taken place between the

Haydar 'Abd al-Shafi, Hanan 'Ashrawi (concealed by a camera), and Faysal Husayni swamped by the press at the Madrid Peace Conference, 1991. The author is at the back, looking off to the right.

PLO and Israel. During the last round of talks with the Israelis in Washington in June 1993, 'Ashrawi and I were tasked with drafting a document overnight to serve as the basis for a briefing on this exchange that we were to give the next day to diplomats representing the American sponsors. When I heard what we were supposed to tell them, I was surprised. The PLO and Israel, we learned, had reached a confidential understanding whereby PLO cadres and forces "possibly including officers of the Palestine Liberation Army," were to be allowed to enter the Occupied Territories and take up duties there as security forces. This was a revelation to those of us who were to deliver the briefing. If true, it meant that the PLO and Israel had been engaged in covert, direct negotiations (there had been rumors to this effect), and that they had already reached a tentative understanding on the issue paramount to both Rabin and 'Arafat: security.

We later learned that this breakthrough was the result of the opening of an undisclosed negotiating track that was completely separate from the secret Oslo talks and has never received the same degree of fame. This was only one of several tracks that Rabin authorized while keeping the existence of each one hidden from those involved in the others.[50] The leading protagonists in the parallel Oslo negotiations, Israeli Foreign Minister Shimon Peres and Ahmad Quray' (Abu al-'Ala'), had richly deserved reputations as relentless self-promoters, and it was to be expected that they would ensure that their story obliterated any other, which is just what happened.[51] By contrast, Rabin and 'Arafat used confidential intermediaries to come to a quiet understanding on the key issue of security, which was an essential precondition and the basis for the success of the better-known and more exhaustive Oslo process that was simultaneously underway.

These security talks took place entirely outside the limelight, in a location that is still secret, via discreet envoys, and little is known about them to this day. They were headed on Israel's side by a former chief of military intelligence who had also served as the first coordinator for dealing with the Palestinians under occupation, Maj. Gen. (ret.) Shlomo Gazit. Rabin seemed to repose full confidence only in senior serving, reserve, and retired officers such as Gazit and Rabinovich.[52] 'Arafat had the same inclination, and thus Gazit's opposite number was Nizar 'Ammar, a senior officer in the late Abu Iyad's intelligence services, who later served as commander of the security forces of the Palestinian Authority.[53] 'Arafat had clearly authorized the briefing that Hanan, my colleagues, and I were about to give. I knew that because, incredulous that the Israelis had contemplated accepting such expansive terms, we sent a draft to Tunis which somewhat toned down what we had been told to say. We immediately got back emendations in 'Arafat's unmistakable handwriting restoring the draft to full strength.

On June 23, 1993, we briefed Dan Kurtzer and Aaron David Miller, and they were incredulous as well, even though we had not been authorized to say explicitly that a formal agreement existed (which was true: at best, it was an informal, albeit significant, understanding). Hanan 'Ashrawi said that to provide for security, the Palestinians needed to "draw on external resources," for example "officers in the PLA" with relevant experience. I added that "Israeli security managers" understood that such individuals were a necessity. One of the American diplomats quickly grasped that something "may have been going on in communications between Israelis and Palestinians," but he doubted that such an arrangement would fly "unless you have an understanding with the

Israelis." I tried to reassure them, saying that "We don't think we'll have a problem agreeing on this" with Israel. "Well, for the first time we are speechless," Kurtzer said, while Miller added "this security presentation is otherworldly."[54]

These savvy US diplomats undoubtedly knew that covert channels had been established between the two sides, but they found it hard to imagine that the PLO and Israel had been able to agree on anything so sweeping. They may have been chagrined as well, as this information went against everything they and Dennis Ross believed and had always told their superiors at the State Department and in the White House: the Israelis would never deal directly with the PLO, let alone allow PLA forces into the Occupied Territories to take charge of security. Whatever their reaction, though, it was no longer up to the Americans.

This important shift resulted from the lesson Rabin had learned from the intifada: that Israel could no longer control the Occupied Territories solely by the use of force. In consequence, he was willing to do some things differently than Begin and Shamir while continuing the military occupation and the colonization of what remained of Palestine (indeed, spending on the settlements was curbed under Rabin's government but overall settlement activity increased). To this end, Rabin authorized direct contact with the PLO, but held fast to the narrow option of limited self-rule. In time, these clandestine contacts led Rabin to accept the return of most of the PLO's leaders and cadres to Palestine in the context of mutual recognition between the two sides, which was the basis of the Declaration of Principles between Israel and the PLO that was signed on the White House lawn in September 1993. By this agreement, Israel recognized the PLO as representative of the Palestinian people and the PLO recognized the state of Israel.

While Rabin had done something no other Israeli leader had ever done by formally conceding that there was a Palestinian people, accepting the PLO as their representative, and opening negotiations with it, obtaining in return its recognition of the state of Israel, this exchange was neither symmetrical nor reciprocal. Israel had not recognized a Palestinian state or even made a commitment to allow the creation of one. This was a peculiar transaction, whereby a national liberation movement had obtained nominal recognition from its oppressors, without achieving liberation, by trading its own recognition of the state that had colonized its homeland and continued to occupy it. This was a resounding, historic mistake, one with grave consequences for the Palestinian people.

BY JUNE 1993, three months before the ceremonial signing on the White House lawn, the Washington talks were no longer the primary site for negotiations between the PLO and Israel. The most important of the various covert, direct lines of communication that had opened up between the two parties was in Oslo. The two sides wished to escape the attention of our American hosts and the media, although that was a subsidiary reason for the shift. Once Rabin and 'Arafat had found that a direct deal was possible, they assigned various emissaries to explore the possibilities further. The talks in Oslo were authorized by the two leaders but were supervised on the Israeli side by Shimon Peres and on the Palestinian by Mahmud 'Abbas (Abu Mazin).

It was there that the Declaration of Principles, which came to be called Oslo I, was worked out and where the details of the agreement between the two sides were tied up. The problem with the agreement was that the devil is in the details, and the personnel the PLO sent to Oslo were not strong on details. Indeed, they did not have the linguistic or legal or other expertise necessary to comprehend exactly what the Israelis were doing. After initial rounds of exploratory discussions led on the Israeli side by two academics, the Palestinians then found themselves up against a formidable and expert Israeli negotiating team including individuals with vast international legal experience such as Joel Singer (another former colonel in the Israeli military).

This team was assembled by Shimon Peres, who was no more prepared to see the Palestinians as equals or to countenance Palestinian statehood and sovereignty than were Rabin or Shamir. The Palestinian envoys at Oslo were simply out of their league, lacking resources and training, none of them having been in occupied Palestine for decades, and having failed to study and absorb the results of our ten rounds of negotiations with Israel. The deteriorating situation of the Palestinian population in the Occupied Territories after Oslo since the mid-1990s has been in large measure the result of the choice of envoys whose performance at Oslo was inept, and of 'Arafat and his colleagues' willing-ness to sign the defective agreements they drew up.[55]

When we first saw the text of what had been agreed in Oslo, those of us with twenty-one months of experience in Madrid and Washington grasped immediately that the Palestinian negotiators had failed to under-stand what Israel meant by autonomy. What they had signed on to was a highly restricted form of self-rule in a fragment of the Occupied Territo-ries, and without control of land, water, borders, or much else. In these and subsequent accords based on them, in force until the present day with minor modifications, Israel retained all such prerogatives, indeed amounting to virtually complete control over land and people, together with most of the attributes of sovereignty. This was exactly what our PISGA proposal had sought to avoid by attributing robust jurisdiction over people and land to an autonomous, elected Palestinian authority. As a result of their failure to see the importance of these vital assets, the Palestinian negotiators at Oslo had fallen into trap after trap that we had managed to avoid. In effect, they ended up accepting a barely modified version of the Begin autonomy plan, to which both the Shamir and Rabin governments held firm.

After Israel's rejection of the PISGA proposal, our delegation had refused to accept self-rule à la Begin. The delegates from the Occupied Territories knew what self-rule Israeli style would mean in practice, as did the advisors to the delegation, who lived in or had spent exten-sive time in Palestine. Given the refusal of both the Shamir and Rabin governments to countenance a permanent settlement freeze or to end military rule, we knew that they were offering cosmetic changes only while intending to maintain the status quo of occupation into the indef-inite future. This is why we dug in our heels in Washington and why the PLO should have ordered its envoys in Oslo to stand firm against such a Begin-style deal, which Edward Said rightly called "an instrument of Palestinian surrender, a Palestinian Versailles."[56]

I am convinced that rejecting Israel's bare-bones offer in Washington and Oslo would have been the right course. Had the PLO taken such a tough stance, the outcome would not have been worse than the loss of land, resources, and freedom of movement suffered by the Palestinians since 1993. On balance, a failure to reach a deal would have been better than the deal that emerged from Oslo. Occupation would have continued, as it has anyway, but without the veil of Palestinian self-government, without relieving Israel of the financial burden of governing and administering a population of millions, and without "security coordination"—the worst outcome of Oslo—whereby the PA helps Israel police the restive Palestinians living under its military regime as their lands are gradually appropriated by Israeli colonizers.

There is also the small chance that Rabin might have been forced to concede better terms. Whether such hypothetical terms might have led to a truly sovereign Palestinian state is impossible to say. However, just as the PLO felt compelled to secure a deal, Rabin too felt the need to produce an agreement, especially after progress on the Syrian track stalled. According to Itamar Rabinovich, by August 1993, Rabin "felt pressure" to make a dramatic move, given the stalemate after a year of negotiations with Syria and the Palestinians, and the instability of the coalition government he headed.[57] That move might have been in the direction of a better deal for the Palestinians.

This outcome does not seem likely, however, since Rabin proved to be constrained by his limitations and biases: an ingrained preoccupation with security, which in the Israeli lexicon has an all-encompassing meaning of complete domination and control of the adversary; and a deep disdain for Palestinian nationalism and the PLO in particular, which he had fought for much of his career. This disdain was evident on Rabin's face when he shook 'Arafat's hand in Washington in September 1993. He also had to take account of the ferocious opposition to any genuine agreement with the Palestinians from the fervent religious-nationalist partisans of the Greater Land of Israel. He was right to fear this potent group. One of its adherents, Yigal Amir, killed him in 1995, and they have dominated Israeli politics ever since.

YASSER 'ARAFAT RETURNED to Palestine in July 1994 and I visited him soon after in his new headquarters overlooking the sea in Gaza. He was ecstatic to be back in his homeland after nearly thirty years and to have escaped from the gilded cage that had been his lot in Tunis. He did not seem to realize that he had moved from one cage to another. I had come to express my deep concern about the deteriorating situation in Arab East Jerusalem, where I had been living. Israel had closed the city off to Palestinians from the rest of the Occupied Territories and had begun erecting a series of walls and massive fortified border checkpoints to regulate their entry.

There were many worrying signs that things were getting worse for the Palestinian population of Jerusalem, with draconian restrictions on the entry of West Bankers and Gazans starving the economy of the Arab part of the city, and an acceleration of land seizure, home demolitions, and exile of Jerusalemites whom Israel arbitrarily deemed had lost their residency. 'Arafat brushed aside my concerns. I soon realized that my visit was a waste of time. He was still afloat on a wave of euphoria, enjoying the homage of worshipful delegations from all over Palestine. He was in no mood to hear bad news, and in any case, he airily indicated, any problems would soon be resolved. I received precisely the same brushoff later that day when I expressed similar concerns to Abu Mazin, also newly arrived in Gaza.

It was clear to me that 'Arafat and Abu Mazin optimistically assumed that what their envoys had been unable to obtain for the Palestinians at Oslo they would manage to extract from Israel in subsequent negotiations. 'Arafat was presumably relying on his legendary skill at maneuvering, with which he had for decades dealt with the Arab regimes, eventually wearing out the patience of many of their monarchs and dictators. But the Israelis were not in the least susceptible to the legerdemain for which 'Arafat was famous. They stuck grimly to their guns, and later accords were just as one-sided as Oslo I.

The Interim Agreement on the West Bank and the Gaza Strip, or Oslo II as it is known, was agreed upon by the two sides in 1995 and completed the ruinous work of Oslo I. It carved both regions into an infamous patchwork of areas—A, B, and C—with over 60 percent of the territory, Area C, under complete, direct, and unfettered Israeli control. The Palestinian Authority was granted administrative and security control in the 18 percent that constituted Area A, and administrative control in the 22 percent of Area B while Israel remained in charge of security there. Together, Areas A and B comprised 40 percent of the territory but housed some 87 percent of the Palestinian population. Area C included all but one of the Jewish settlements. Israel also kept full power over entering and leaving all parts of Palestine and held exclusive control of the population registers (meaning that it decided who had residency rights and who could live where). Settlement construction was able to continue apace, Jerusalem was further severed from the West Bank, and Palestinians from the Occupied Territories were increasingly barred from entering Israel. Eventually, scores of military checkpoints and hundreds of miles of walls and electrified fences carved the West Bank into a series of isolated islands and scarred the landscape.

It soon became impossible to do what I and many Palestinians had done regularly and without difficulty: drive to Ramallah from Jerusalem in under half an hour, or travel quickly to Gaza from the West Bank. I will never forget the lone Israeli soldier, tipped back on a chair, his weapon on his lap, who lazily waved us through the ramshackle checkpoint that marked the entry to the Gaza Strip as we entered on my first visit there after the Oslo Accords. With the new checkpoints and walls and the need for hard-to-obtain Israeli permits to pass through them, with Israel blocking free movement among the West Bank, Gaza, and East Jerusalem, and with the introduction of roads forbidden to Palestinian travel, the progressive constriction of Palestinian life, especially for Gazans, was underway. 'Arafat and his colleagues in the PLO leadership, who sailed through the checkpoints with their VIP passes, did not seem to know, or care, about the increasing confinement of ordinary Palestinians.

Most PLO personnel soon moved from Tunis and elsewhere to the Occupied Territories, where they took positions, usually the top ones, in the security forces and in the institutions of the PA. The authority had supposedly been set up as the interim body for self-rule in the Occupied Territories, to be supplanted in a few years by a permanent form of governance after final status negotiations—which never happened. The PLO carried out its wholesale relocation as if liberation had already occurred, instead of keeping part, if not most, of the PLO apparatus outside Palestine until the outcome of the Oslo Accords was clear. Only the Political Department—its foreign ministry—and a few other offices remained in Tunis or in other countries. On a human level, it was easy to sympathize with the wish to return home after a lengthy exile as well as the desire to escape the unwelcoming Arab capitals to which the PLO had been consigned since 1982. It also made sense for the organization's people to live among their popular political base, the segment located inside Palestine, after they had been cut off from most Palestinian communities.

But there was a hidden peril in bringing most of the PLO to the still Occupied Territories. 'Arafat and his colleagues had effectively put themselves in a cage, at the mercy of a military regime that remained in place and largely unchanged. In an ominous sign, Israel tried to prevent some of the PLO's personnel from living in Jerusalem or operating there. Worse was to come. In 2002, at the height of the intense violence of the Second Intifada, Israeli troops stormed the PA's offices in Ramallah and other parts of Area A. They also shut down Orient House, long the center of Palestinian political activity in Jerusalem and headquarters for the teams negotiating with Israel. It remains closed to this day.[58] Israel was also able to restrict or forbid any Palestinian activities, travel, or meetings, and it used this power liberally against the PA's leaders. In effect, the PLO had entered the lion's mouth, and it did not take long for the jaws to snap shut. In September 2002, the Israeli army imposed a siege on the Muqata'a, 'Arafat's Ramallah HQ, making him a virtual prisoner for the next two years until shortly before he died.

In the quarter century since the Oslo agreements, the situation in Palestine and Israel has often been falsely described as a clash between two near-equals, between the state of Israel and the quasi-state of the Palestinian Authority. This depiction masks the unequal, unchanged colonial reality. The PA has no sovereignty, no jurisdiction, and no authority except that allowed it by Israel, which even controls a major part of its revenues in the form of customs duties and some taxes. Its primary function, to which much of its budget is devoted, is security, but not for its people: it is mandated by US and Israeli dictates to provide security for Israel's settlers and occupation forces against the resistance, violent and otherwise, of other Palestinians. Since 1967, there has been one state authority in all of the territory of Mandatory Palestine: that of Israel. The creation of the PA did nothing to change that reality, rearranging the deckchairs on the Palestinian *Titanic*, while providing Israeli colonization and occupation with an indispensable Palestinian shield. Facing the colossus that is the Israeli state is a colonized people denied equal rights and the ability to exercise their right of national self-determination, a continuous condition since the idea of self-determination took hold globally after World War I.

The intifada had brought Rabin and the Israeli security establishment to the realization that the occupation—with Israeli troops policing densely populated Palestinian centers simmering with anger—needed modification. The result of that realization, the Oslo framework, was designed to preserve those parts of the occupation that were advantageous to Israel—the privileges and prerogatives enjoyed by the state and the settlers—while offloading onerous responsibilities and simultaneously preventing genuine Palestinian self-determination, statehood, and sovereignty. Oslo I was the first such modification, with others added in subsequent years, all of them aimed at maintaining the disparity of power, irrespective of who was Israel's prime minister.

Oslo I also involved the most far-reaching modification, which was the decision to enlist the PLO as a subcontractor for the occupation—this was the actual meaning of the security deal Rabin made with 'Arafat, which my colleagues and I had announced to the American diplomats in June 1993. The key point was always security for Israel, for its occupation and settlers, while offloading the cost and liability of subjugating the Palestinian population. More bluntly, as Rabin's collaborator, Maj. Gen. Shlomo Gazit, put it publicly in 1994, "Yasser 'Arafat has a choice. He can be a Lahd or a super-Lahd."[59] Gazit's reference was to Antoine Lahd, the Lebanese commander of the Israeli-armed, Israeli-paid, and Israeli-controlled South Lebanese Army, tasked with helping to maintain Israel's occupation of south Lebanon from 1978 to 2000. With this revealing remark, Gazit confirmed the real objective of what he and his boss, Rabin, had put in place with Oslo.

The system created in Oslo and Washington was not just Israel's venture. As in 1967 and 1982, Israel was joined by its indispensable sponsor, the United States. The Oslo straitjacket could not have been imposed on the Palestinians without American connivance. From Camp David back in 1978 on, the architecture of the negotiations, with its devious and infinitely flexible interim stage and deferral of Palestinian statehood, was not enforced primarily by Israel, even if the framework was dreamed up by Begin and carried forward by his heirs in both Israeli political blocs, Likud and Labor. It was the United States that provided the muscle behind the insistence that for the Palestinians this was the only possible negotiating path, leading to only one possible outcome. The United States was not just an accessory: it was Israel's partner.

This partnership involved far more than simply acquiescence or consent on the part of every US administration from Carter until today. It has relied on American support on the political, diplomatic, military, and legal levels—the bountiful sums of money in aid, loans, and tax-free charitable donations given to support the settlements and the creeping absorption of Arab neighborhoods in Jerusalem; and the copious flow of the world's most advanced arms—to advance Israel's colonization of the entirety of Palestine. The Oslo Accords in effect constituted another internationally sanctioned American-Israeli declaration of war on the Palestinians in furtherance of the Zionist movement's century old project. But unlike 1947 and 1967, this time Palestinian leaders allowed themselves to be drawn into complicity with their adversaries.

The Sixth Declaration of War, 2000–2014

This is a unique colonialism that we've been subjected to where they have no use for us. The best Palestinian for them is either dead or gone. It's not that they want to exploit us, or that they need to keep us there in the way of Algeria or South Africa as a subclass.

—Edward Said[1]

For most Palestinians, deep disappointment with the Oslo Accords set in not long after the 1993 signing ceremony on the White House lawn. The prospect of an end to the military occupation and to the theft of land for Israeli settlements had originally been received with euphoria, and many people believed they were at the beginning of a path leading to statehood. As time went on, there was a dawning realization that despite and even because of the terms of Oslo, the colonization of Palestine was continuing apace and Israel was no closer to allowing the creation of an independent Palestinian state.

In fact, conditions grew much worse for all but a very small number of individuals whose economic or personal interests were intertwined with the Palestinian Authority and who benefited from normalized relations with Israel. For everyone else, there were consistent denials of permission to travel and move goods from one place to another as a labyrinthine system of permits, checkpoints, walls, and fences was created.

In a conscious Israeli policy of "separation," Gaza was severed from the West Bank, which was itself severed from Jerusalem; jobs within Israel did not return; the settlements and settler-only roads between them proliferated, fragmenting the West Bank to devastating effect. Between 1993 and 2004, GDP per capita declined, despite promises of a prosperity that was just around the corner.[2]

A privileged few—influential figures with the PLO or the PA—were granted VIP passes that allowed them to sail through the Israeli checkpoints. Everyone else lost the ability to move freely around Palestine. Until 1991, great numbers of Palestinians had worked in Israel without hindrance and without requiring a special permit. One could travel in a car with West Bank or Gaza license plates anywhere in Israel and in the Occupied Territories. Any expectation of having that freedom restored was quickly quashed. The majority of the population could not obtain permits to travel and was now effectively confined to the West Bank or to the Gaza Strip, to the inferior roads dotted with checkpoints intended for the indigenous population, while the settlers rode above them on a network of superb highways and overpasses that was constructed for their exclusive use.

This post-Oslo confinement was most constricting in the Gaza Strip. In the decades following 1993, the strip was cut off from the rest of the world in stages, encircled by troops on land and the Israeli navy by sea.[3] Entering and leaving required rarely issued permits and became possible only through massive fortified checkpoints resembling human cattle pens, while arbitrary Israeli closures frequently interrupted the shipment of goods in and out of the strip. The economic results of what was in effect a siege of the Gaza Strip were particularly damaging. Most Gazans depended on work in Israel or on exporting goods. With stringent restrictions on doing both, economic life underwent a slow strangulation.[4]

In Jerusalem, the largest and most important urban center in Arab Palestine, barriers placed at the entrances to the Palestinian neighborhoods of East Jerusalem prevented free movement between the city and the West Bank hinterland, on which it depended economically, culturally, and politically. Its markets, schools, businesses, cultural institutions, and professional practices had all thrived primarily on a clientele from across the Occupied Territories, as well as Palestinians from inside Israel and foreign tourists. Suddenly, Palestinians from the West Bank and Gaza were required to obtain permits, which were unattainable for most. Even if they managed to procure a permit, routine humiliation and hours of delay awaited them while passing through the Israeli checkpoints that controlled movement into the city from the West Bank. The impact of this closure of Jerusalem on the city's economy was shattering. According to a 2018 European Union report, the contribution of Arab East Jerusalem to the Palestinian GDP has shrunk from 15 percent in 1993 to 7 percent today. The EU report noted that "Due to its physical isolation and the strict Israeli permit policy, the city has largely ceased to be the economic, urban, and commercial center that it once was."[5]

These worsening conditions were barely noted in the mainstream media, and there was great surprise in international circles when the Palestinian population, still under occupation, expressed its bitter sense of betrayal via massive demonstrations in September 2000. The persistent, hazy glow of Oslo had blinded most observers, whether in Israel, the United States, or Europe, and especially within liberal Zionist circles. The myth of Oslo's beneficence continued to preclude clear-eyed analysis, even after the eruption of violence in 2000.[6]

But to the PLO's vigorous new rival, Hamas, the evidence that Oslo was not what its Palestinian advocates had made it out to be was grist for its mill. Founded at the outset of the First Intifada in December 1987, Hamas had grown quickly, capitalizing on the currents of popular discontent with the PLO that had emerged for a variety of reasons. During the intifada, Hamas had insisted on maintaining a separate identity, refusing to join the Unified National Command. It promoted itself as a more militant Islamist alternative to the PLO, denouncing the abandonment of armed struggle and turn to diplomacy that was adopted in the PNC's 1988 Declaration of Independence. Only the use of force could lead to the liberation of Palestine, Hamas argued, reasserting the claim to the entirety of Palestine, not just the areas occupied by Israel in 1967.[7]

Hamas was an outgrowth of the Palestinian branch of the Muslim Brotherhood, an organization founded in Egypt in 1928 with reformist aims, but which turned to violence in the 1940s and 1950s, only to reconcile with the Egyptian regime under Sadat in the 1970s. Hamas was begun in Gaza by militants who felt that the Brotherhood had been too accommodating toward the Israeli occupier in return for lenient treatment. Indeed, in the first two decades of the occupation, when the military authorities severely repressed all other Palestinian political, social, cultural, professional, and academic groups, they had allowed the Brotherhood to operate freely. Because of its utility to the occupation in splitting the Palestinian national movement, Israeli indulgence of the Brotherhood was extended to Hamas, notwithstanding its uncompromising and anti-Semitic program and commitment to violence.[8]

This was not the main reason for its success, however. The rise of Hamas was part of a regional trend that represented a response to what many perceived as the bankruptcy of the secular nationalist ideologies that had dominated politics in the Middle East for most of the twentieth century. In the wake of the PLO's shift away from armed struggle and toward a diplomatic path meant to lead to a Palestinian state that failed to achieve results, many Palestinians felt that the organization had lost its way—and Hamas grew in consequence, despite its extremely conservative social positions and the sketchy outline of the future it proposed.

Hamas was momentarily disconcerted by the wave of popular satisfaction when the Madrid peace conference was convened with Palestinian participation, albeit under Israeli-imposed conditions. During the Washington negotiations, Hamas nevertheless continued to criticize the very principle of negotiating with Israel and maintained its efforts to keep the intifada alive. The signing of the Oslo Accords had a similar effect in both raising Palestinian expectations and temporarily undermining Hamas. But given that the PLO's standing was linked to the results of its dealings with Israel, the widespread popular disappointment that followed the implementation of the Oslo Accords left Hamas poised to reap the benefits, and it sharpened its critique of the PLO and the newly formed PA.

Palestinians suffered another disappointment when the five-year interim period specified in the accords continued long after it should have ended. This was a further setback for 'Arafat's negotiating strategy, as was the fact that final status negotiations were never started, let alone completed, as they should have been by 1999. Another setback for the PLO was the failure in 2000 of the last-ditch Camp David summit between 'Arafat and Israel's prime minister Ehud Barak. Called by President Clinton in the final months of his second term when he was already a very lame duck, after Barak's government had lost its majority in the Knesset, and when 'Arafat's popularity was in sharp decline, the summit was poorly prepared. There had been no prior understandings between the two sides, as is normal in a summit-level meeting, and 'Arafat had to be coerced into attending, fearing being blamed for its eventual failure.

Camp David ended in disaster, with Barak avoiding substantive meetings with 'Arafat and instead putting forward a secret proposal through the Americans, while refusing any modifications. With this extraordinary procedure, the US in effect formally endorsed the Israeli position. Barak's unmodifiable proposal—which was never published, only reconstructed by participants after the event—was unacceptable to the Palestinians in several crucial respects. These included permanent Israeli control of the Jordan River Valley and of Palestine's airspace, and therefore of access to the outside world (which meant the projected Palestinian "state" would not be truly sovereign), Israel's continued control over West Bank water resources, as well as its annexation of areas that would have divided the West Bank into several isolated blocs. Not surprisingly, the greatest gulf between the two sides was over the disposition of Jerusalem. Israel demanded exclusive sovereignty, including over the entire Haram al-Sharif and most of the rest of the Old City, which was a central element in the ultimate breakdown of the talks.[9]

Clinton thereafter proceeded to blame 'Arafat for the summit's failure, although he had earlier pledged not to do so. Even before the talks ended, Barak began briefing journalists on 'Arafat's obstructionism, and was soon proclaiming that the Palestinians did not desire peace. This strategy was ultimately self-defeating: Barak looked foolish for having attended a summit that was bound to fail, if his assessment of 'Arafat and the PLO was correct. It also cast into question the entire approach of Rabin, Peres, Barak, and Israel's Labor Party. The immediate beneficiary of Barak's tactical missteps was Ariel Sharon, who now led the Likud and had the merit of consistency: he had always said no agreement was possible with the Palestinians and had ferociously opposed the Oslo Accords. On the Palestinian side, the recriminations flew after this last-ditch salvage effort confirmed that Israel was unwilling to accept anything resembling full

Palestinian sovereignty, that the Oslo process would therefore not produce a resolution that met minimal Palestinian demands, and that the miserable status quo would continue. All of this strengthened Hamas and led to unprecedented polarization in the Palestinian polity, creating a gulf within the population. At this point, Hamas constituted the most serious threat since the mid-1960s to the hegemony of Fatah within the PLO and to the monopoly of the PLO over Palestinian politics.

THE WORSENING SITUATION for Palestinians after Oslo, the fading prospect of statehood, and the intense rivalry between the PLO and Hamas combined to produce the flammable material that erupted into the Second Intifada in September 2000. It required only a match to set it off. A provocative visit by Ariel Sharon to the Haram al-Sharif, surrounded by hundreds of security personnel, provided that match. The Haram—known to Jews as the Temple Mount—had been a focus of nationalist and religious passions for both sides at least since the bloody events of 1929, when a flag-waving demonstration by rowdy Zionist Revisionist extremists at the adjacent Western Wall set off days of violence all over the country with hundreds of casualties on each side.[10] Palestinian concerns were heightened immediately after the 1967 conquest of the eastern part of the city, when the occupation authorities destroyed an entire neighborhood adjoining the Haram, Haret al-Maghariba, the Maghribi quarter, together with its mosques, shrines, homes, and shops, in order to create a vast esplanade adjoining the Western Wall. Many of the sites destroyed during the night of June 10–11 by Israeli bulldozers were *waqfs*, like the Madrassa al-Afdaliyya, established in 1190 by the Ayyubid ruler al-Malik al-Afdal, son of Saladin.[11] Another, destroyed two years later, was the ancient Zawiyya al-Fakhriyya,[12] a Sufi lodge immediately adjacent to the Haram.

With the city now closed to West Bank and Gaza Palestinians and Israeli settlers' ongoing expansion into East Jerusalem, residents feared that they were about to be supplanted. In 1999, one year earlier, Israel had opened a tunnel running beneath much of the Old City and adjoining the Haram, causing damage to properties above in the Muslim Quarter, and sparking widespread demonstrations. Sharon's visit, coming soon after the failed Camp David summit, could not have happened at a worse moment. Sharon, who was campaigning to follow Barak as prime minister, heaped fuel on the flames, declaring "the Temple Mount is in our hands and will remain in our hands."[13] Given Sharon's reckless and opportunistic record, it seems clear that he intended to exploit the volatile context to better position himself to win the upcoming elections, which he succeeded in doing a few months later.

The result of his provocation was the worst upsurge of violence in the Occupied Territories since 1967, violence which thereafter spread inside Israel via a wave of deadly suicide bombings. The increase in the level of bloodshed was striking. During the eight-plus years of the First Intifada, some 1,600 people were killed, an average of 177 per year (12 percent of them Israelis). In the calmer four years that followed, 90 people died, or about 20 per year (22 percent of them Israelis). By contrast, the eight years of the Second Intifada left 6,600 dead, an average of 825 per year—about 1,100 Israelis (just under 17 percent) and 4,916 Palestinians, who were killed by Israeli security forces and settlers (over 600 Palestinians were also killed by other Palestinians). Most of the Israelis who died in the latter period were civilians killed by Palestinian suicide bombers inside Israel, while 332, just under a third of the total, were members of the security forces. This striking increase in the number of those killed during the Second Intifada gives a sense of the sharp escalation of violence.[14]

While the rivalry between Hamas and the PLO played a role in this escalation, the Israeli forces' massive use of live ammunition against unarmed demonstrators from the outset (they fired 1.3 million bullets in "the first few days" of the uprising[15]) was a crucial factor, causing a shocking number of casualties. This mayhem eventually provoked some Palestinians—many of them from the PA's security forces—to take up arms and explosives. It seemed to perceptive observers that the Israeli military was well prepared to escalate, and may have intended to trigger just such a development.[16] Predictably, Israel turned to heavy weapons, including helicopters, tanks, and artillery, producing even higher Palestinian casualties.

Hamas and its junior partners in Islamic Jihad thereupon responded by mounting extensive assaults with suicide bombers, who mainly attacked vulnerable civilian targets—buses, cafés, and shopping centers—inside Israel. This tactic involved taking the violence, which had thus far been largely concentrated inside the Occupied Territories, to the enemy's home territory, and it was one against which Israel initially had no defense. Starting at the end of 2001, and with increasing frequency, Fatah joined in, producing a deadly competition. A murderous acceleration of suicide bombings followed, sparked in part by the rivalry between the two factions. According to one study of the first five years of the Second Intifada, almost 40 percent of the suicide bombings were carried out by Hamas, nearly 26 percent by its ally Islamic Jihad, over 26 percent by Fatah, and the rest by the latter's partners in the PLO.[17]

The PLO had renounced violence in 1988, but as large numbers of demonstrators were shot by Israeli troops and as Hamas responded with suicide attacks, the pressure on Fatah to act grew, and escalation became inevitable. Triggered by the 1994 massacre inside the Ibrahimi Mosque in Hebron of 29 Palestinians by an armed settler, between 1994 and 2000 Hamas and Islamic Jihad had pioneered the use of suicide bombers inside Israel as part of their campaign against the Oslo Accords, killing 171 Israelis in 27 bombings. By the end of that period, however, these attacks had been largely contained by the ferocious repression exercised by the PA security services. The PLO leadership pushed to stop these attacks at all costs to keep the limping Oslo process going. To that end, the PA security apparatus—largely made up of Fatah militants who had served time in Israeli jails—used torture on Hamas suspects just as freely as Israeli interrogators had used it on them. Such experiences engendered deep fratricidal hatred on both sides, which was to erupt in the open PLO-Hamas split starting in the mid-2000s.

In stark contrast to the first, the Second Intifada constituted a major setback for the Palestinian national movement. Its consequences for the Occupied Territories were severe and damaging. In 2002, with its heavy weapons causing widespread destruction, the Israeli army reoccupied the limited areas, mainly cities and towns, that had been evacuated as part of the Oslo Accords. That same year, Israeli troops imposed their siege on Yasser 'Arafat's Ramallah headquarters, where he fell mortally ill. Having avoided meeting with him after my disappointing encounter in Gaza in 1994, I was encouraged to see the ailing old man by my friend

Sari Nuseibeh, and visited him twice during the siege, finding him much diminished physically and mentally.[18] This harsh treatment of the Palestinian people's historic leader was demeaning, as Ariel Sharon intended it to be. It also confirmed the grave error the PLO had made in moving almost all of its leadership into the Occupied Territories, where they were vulnerable to such humiliations.

Coming after the collapse of the Camp David summit, Israel's reoccupation of the cities and towns of the West Bank and Gaza Strip shattered any remaining pretense that the Palestinians had or would acquire something approaching sovereignty or real authority over any part of their land. It exacerbated the political differences among Palestinians and underlined the absence of a viable alternative strategy, revealing the failure of both the PLO's diplomatic course and the armed violence of Hamas and others. These events showed that Oslo had failed, that the use of guns and suicide bombings had failed, and that for all the casualties inflicted on Israeli civilians, the biggest losers in every way were the Palestinians.

Another consequence was that the terrible violence of the Second Intifada erased the positive image of Palestinians that had evolved since 1982 and through the First Intifada and the peace negotiations. With horrifying scenes of recurrent suicide bombings transmitting globally (and with this coverage eclipsing that of the much greater violence perpetrated against the Palestinians), Israelis ceased to be seen as oppressors, reverting to the more familiar role of victims of irrational, fanatical tormentors. The potent negative impact of the Second Intifada for the Palestinians and the effect of suicide bombings on Israeli opinion and politics certainly bear out the trenchant critique of the Palestinians' employment of violence expressed by Eqbal Ahmad back in the 1980s.

Such considerations were undoubtedly far from the minds of the men (and a few women) who planned and carried out these suicide bombings. It is possible to speculate on what they sought to achieve, even while showing how flawed their aims were. Even if one accepts their own narrative which sees suicide bombings as retaliation for Israel's indiscriminate use of live ammunition against unarmed demonstrators for the first several weeks of the Second Intifada, and its attacks on Palestinian civilians and assassinations in Gaza, that begs the question of whether these bombings were meant to achieve anything more than blind revenge. It also elides the fact that Hamas and Islamic Jihad, which launched two-thirds of the suicide bombings during the intifada, had carried out over twenty such attacks in the 1990s before Sharon's visit to the Haram. It may be argued that these attacks were meant to deter Israel. This is risible, given the long-established doctrine of the Israeli military that irrespective of the cost, it must gain the upper hand in any confrontation, and establish its unchallenged capacity not only to deter its enemies, but to crush them.[19] Sharon did just that during the Second Intifada, faithfully implementing this doctrine, as had Rabin before him during the First Intifada, although in that previous case at great political cost, as Rabin himself recognized.

Equally risible is the idea that such attacks on civilians were hammer blows that might lead to a dissolution of Israeli society. This theory is based on a widespread but fatally flawed analysis of Israel as a deeply divided and "artificial" polity, which ignores the manifestly successful nation-building efforts of Zionism over more than a century, as well as the cohesiveness of Israeli society in spite of its many internal divisions. But the most important factor missing in whatever calculations were being made by those who planned the bombings was the fact that the longer the attacks continued, the more unified the Israeli public became behind Sharon's hard-line posture. In effect, suicide bombings served to unite and strengthen the adversary, while weakening and dividing the Palestinian side. By the end of the Second Intifada, according to reliable polls, most Palestinians opposed this tactic.[20] Thus, besides raising grave legal and moral issues, and depriving the Palestinians of a positive media image, on a strategic level these attacks were massively counterproductive. Whatever blame attaches to Hamas and Islamic Jihad for the suicide bombings that produced this fiasco, the PLO leadership that eventually followed suit must also share it.

YASSER 'ARAFAT DIED in November 2004 in a Paris hospital in circumstances that have remained murky. Mahmoud 'Abbas (Abu Mazin) replaced him as head of the PLO and Fatah, and was elected to the presidency of the PA for a four-year term in January 2005. No presidential election has been held since then, so 'Abbas has ruled without a democratic mandate from 2009 on. 'Arafat's death marked the passing of an era, a half century that began in the early 1950s with the first stirrings of a revived national movement and ended with Palestinian fortunes at their lowest ebb since 1948. Over the succeeding decade and a half, 'Abbas presided ineffectually over a grave deterioration in the already weakened state of the national movement, an intensification of inter-Palestinian conflict, a substantial expansion of Zionist colonization of what remained of Palestine, and a series of Israeli wars on an increasingly besieged Gaza Strip.

One of the few surviving members of the old guard of the Fatah Central Committee that had long dominated the PLO, 'Abbas was neither charismatic nor eloquent; he was not renowned for personal bravery or considered a man of the people. Overall, he was one of the least impressive of the early generation of prominent Fatah leaders. While a few of this group died of natural causes, many of them—Abu Iyad, Abu Jihad, Sa'd Sayel (Abu al-Walid), Majid Abu Sharar, Abu Yusuf Najjar, Kamal 'Adwan, Hayel 'Abd al-Hamid (Abu al-Hol), and Abu Hassan Salameh— had been killed by assassins of the Mossad or of groups backed by the Syrian, Iraqi, and Libyan regimes. With Ghassan Kanafani and Kamal Nasser, they had been among the movement's best and most effective leaders and spokespersons, and their loss left the Palestinians with a less dynamic and feebler organization. Israel's systematic liquidations under the rubric of "targeted killings," continued throughout the Second Intifada and during the 'Abbas years, as Fatah, PFLP, Hamas, and Islamic Jihad leaders were also killed. That some of these assassinations were driven by political rather than military or security considerations was made clear with the killing of Isma'il Abu Shanab, for example, who was a vocal opponent within Hamas of suicide bombings.[21]

The ongoing war on Gaza, which included major Israeli ground offensives in 2008–9, 2012, and 2014, was combined with regular Israeli military incursions into Palestinian areas of the West Bank and East Jerusalem. These involved arrests and assassinations, the demolition of homes, and the suppression of the population, all of which took place with the quiet collusion of the Fatah-run PA in Ramallah. These events confirmed that the PA was a body with no sovereignty and no real authority except that allowed it by Israel, as it collaborated in quashing protests in the West Bank while Israel pounded Gaza.

Hamas and Islamic Jihad had boycotted the presidential election of 2005, as they had earlier PA elections, in line with their rejection of the Oslo process and of the Palestinian Authority and the Palestinian Legislative Assembly that had emerged from it. Soon after, however, Hamas performed a surprising U-turn, deciding to run a slate of candidates in the parliamentary elections in January 2006. In its campaign, the organization downplayed the socially conservative Islamist message that had been its trademark, as well as its advocacy of armed resistance to Israel, instead emphasizing reform and change, which was the name of its electoral list. This was a reversal of the greatest significance. By fielding candidates for the assembly, Hamas not only accepted the PA's legitimacy but also, by extension, the legitimacy of the negotiating process that had produced it, and of the two-state solution that it was meant to lead to. Moreover, Hamas was also embracing the possibility of winning the elections, thus sharing responsibility for governing the PA together with 'Abbas.

Auja, the West Bank, in Area C: the foundations of the house of Raja Khalidi, the author's brother, bulldozed by the Israeli military

The PA's core responsibilities, as seen by its Israeli, American, and European sponsors, involved preventing violence against Israelis and security cooperation with Israel. Hamas had never conceded that this shift indeed meant what it seemed to mean, or that it contradicted the commitment to armed resistance that was its raison d'être and part of its name, of which Hamas was an acronym, the Islamic Resistance Movement.

Against all expectations, including its own, Hamas won the elections by a handsome margin. It took 74 seats to Fatah's 45 in a 132-member assembly (although with the peculiarities of the electoral system, it had won only 44 percent of the vote to Fatah's 41 percent). Exit polls after the vote showed that the result owed more to the voters' great desire for change in the Occupied Territories than to a call for Islamist governance or heightened armed resistance to Israel.[22] Even in some predominantly Christian neighborhoods, the vote went heavily for Hamas. This is evidence that many voters simply wanted to throw out the Fatah incumbents, whose strategy had failed and who were seen as corrupt and unresponsive to popular demands.

With Hamas in control of the Legislative Assembly, conflict between Fatah and Hamas escalated. As a range of Palestinian political figures recognized, a split between the two movements was potentially disastrous for the Palestine cause, a sentiment that was strongly supported by public opinion. In May 2006, the five leaders of the major groups held in Israeli prisons, including Fatah, Hamas, the PFLP, and Islamic Jihad, issued the Prisoners' Document (which deserves to be more widely known): it called for an end to the rupture between the factions on the basis of a new program whose cornerstone was a two-state solution. The document was a major event,[23] a clear statement of the wishes of the rank and file of both groups, the most respected elements of which (those who had not been assassinated) were held in Israeli prisons. The regard for prisoners in Palestinian society is very high, and over 400,000 Palestinians have been incarcerated by Israel since the occupation began.

Under this pressure from below, Hamas and Fatah repeatedly tried to form a coalition government of members of both parties. These efforts ran into fierce opposition from Israel and the United States, which rejected Hamas as part of any PA government. They insisted on explicit recognition of Israel, rather than the implicit form embodied in the Prisoners'

Document, as well as a variety of other conditions. Thus Hamas was now drawn into the same interminable dance around concessions that the PLO had been forced to endure for decades, whether the demand was that it amend its charter, agree to UN Resolution 242, renounce terrorism, or accept Israel's existence, all to gain legitimacy by those imposing the conditions. Whether the demands were made of the PLO in the 1970s or Hamas in the 2000s, they were required without the offer of any quid quo pro by the power that had expelled much of the Palestinian people, blocked their return, occupied their territory through force and collective intimidation, and prevented their self-determination.

While Israel vetoed the inclusion of Hamas in a PA coalition, the United States subjected Hamas to a boycott. Congress exercised the power of the purse to prevent US funding from going to Hamas or any PA body of which it was part. Funding sources for the Palestinians such as the Ford Foundation forced a variety of NGOs to jump through legally imposed hoops to ensure that no support went to any project even remotely connected to Hamas. Abraham Foxman, head of the fiercely pro-Israel Anti-Defamation League, was even brought in to vet the Palestinian recipients of Ford's largesse. The result was predictable: Ford effectively ceased to fund Palestinian NGOs, which precisely served Israel's goals.

Meanwhile, under the USA Patriot Act of 2001, "material support for terrorism" was so broadly defined in the Palestinian case that almost any contact with an organization associated with a group that was placed on the blacklist, as Hamas and the PFLP were, could be considered a serious criminal act involving heavy penalties. The demonization of the PLO over the decades since the 1960s was now repeated with Hamas. Yet even with the suicide bombings, with targeting civilians in violation of international law, and with the crude anti-Semitism of its charter, Hamas's record paled next to the massive toll of Palestinian civilian casualties inflicted by Israel and its elaborate structures of legal discrimination and military rule. But it was Hamas that was stuck with the terrorist label, and the weight of the US law was applied to the Palestinian side of the conflict alone.

In light of this relentless campaign, the breakdown of attempts to fashion a compromise coalition government, in spite of the popular demand for Palestinian national reconciliation, should have come as no surprise. The pressure exerted by Western and Arab funders on Fatah to shun Hamas proved too great for the old Fatah hands in the Palestinian Authority, who did not want to give up their power or the considerable material benefits they enjoyed in the gilded bubble of Ramallah. They preferred a ruinous split in the Palestinian polity to holding out against a much stronger foe and risking their privileges. What was surprising, however, was the botched attempt of the US-trained, Fatah-controlled security forces in the Gaza Strip, under their commander Muhammad Dahlan, to unseat Hamas by force. In 2007, Hamas carried out a countercoup, quickly overwhelming Dahlan's forces in the ensuing bitter fighting. The great gulf between the two sides, going back to the Fatah-dominated repression of Hamas in the mid-1990s, was now widened further by the blood that was shed copiously on both sides in the Gaza Strip. Hamas proceeded to set up its own Palestinian Authority in Gaza, while the jurisdiction of the Ramallah-based PA, such as it was, shrunk, extending to less than 20 percent of the West Bank, the area in which the Israeli military allowed it to operate. Absurdly, the Palestinians under occupation now had not one largely powerless authority, but two.

With Hamas now in control of the Gaza Strip, Israel imposed a full-blown siege. Goods entering the strip were reduced to a bare minimum; regular exports were stopped completely; fuel supplies were cut; and leaving and entering Gaza were only rarely permitted. Gaza was in effect turned into an open-air prison, where by 2018 at least 53 percent of some two million Palestinians lived in a state of poverty,[24] and unemployment stood at an astonishing 52 percent, with much higher rates for youth and women.[25] What had begun with international refusal to recognize Hamas's election victory had led to a disastrous Palestinian rupture and the blockade of Gaza. This sequence of events amounted to a new declaration of war on the Palestinians. It also provided indispensable international cover for the open warfare that was to come.

Israel was able to exploit the deep division among Palestinians and Gaza's isolation to launch three savage air and ground assaults on the strip that began in 2008 and continued in 2012 and 2014, leaving large swaths of its cities and refugee camps in rubble and struggling with rolling blackouts and contaminated water.[26] Some neighborhoods, such as

Shuja'iyya and parts of Rafah, suffered extraordinary levels of destruction. The casualty figures tell only part of the story, although they are revealing. In these three major attacks, 3,804 Palestinians were killed, of them almost one thousand minors. A total of 87 Israelis were killed, the majority of them military personnel engaged in these offensive operations. The lopsided 43:1 scale of these casualties is telling, as is the fact that the bulk of the Israelis killed were soldiers while most of the Palestinians were civilians.[27]

One might not have known this, however, from much of the mainstream US media coverage, which focused heavily on Hamas and Islamic Jihad rocket fire at Israeli civilian targets. Certainly, the use of these weapons obliged the Israeli population in the south of the country to spend long periods of time in bomb shelters. However, thanks to Israel's excellent early warning system, its state-of-the-art American-supplied anti-missile capabilities, and its network of shelters, the rockets were very rarely lethal. In 2014, the 4,000 rockets that Israel claimed were fired from the Gaza Strip killed five Israeli civilians, one of them a Bedouin in the Naqab (Negev) region, and a Thai agricultural worker, for a total of six civilian deaths.[28] This does not mitigate Hamas's violation of the rules of war by using these imprecise weapons for indiscriminate attacks

Shuja'iyya, Gaza City, July 2014. A retired American general described the Israeli bombardment as "absolutely disproportionate."

on civilian areas. But the casualty toll tells a different story than the one that emerged from the near-total media focus on Hamas rocket fire. The coverage succeeded in obscuring the extreme disproportionality of this one-sided war: one of the most powerful armies on the planet used its full might against a besieged area of one hundred and forty square miles, which is among the world's most heavily populated enclaves and whose people had no way to escape the rain of fire and steel.

Specific details of the 2014 assault underline this point: over a period of fifty-one days in July and August of 2014, Israel's air force launched more than 6,000 air attacks, while its army and navy fired about 50,000 artillery and tank shells. Together, they utilized what has been estimated as a total of 21 kilotons (21,000 tons, or 42 million pounds) of high explosives. The air assault involved weapons ranging from armed drones and American Apache helicopters firing US-made Hellfire missiles to American F-16 and F-15 fighter-bombers carrying 2,000-pound bombs. According to the commander of the Israeli air force, there were several hundred attacks by such advanced aircraft on targets in Gaza, most of them using these powerful bombs.[29] The explosion of a 2,000-pound bomb produces a crater that is roughly fifty feet wide and thirty-six feet deep and sends lethal fragments to a radius of almost a quarter mile. One or two such bombs can destroy an entire multistory building, many of which were levelled in Gaza City toward the conclusion of the Israeli air campaign at the end of August.[30] There is no public record of exactly how many of these monsters were dropped on the Gaza Strip, or whether even heavier ordnance was used.

In addition to aerial bombardment, according to a report issued by the Israeli logistical command in mid-August 2014, well before the final cease-fire took hold on August 26, 49,000 artillery and tank shells were fired into the Gaza Strip,[31] most by the US-made M109A5 155mm howitzer. Its 98-pound shells have a kill zone of about 54 yards' radius and inflict casualties within a diameter of 218 yards. Israel possesses 600 of these artillery pieces, and 175 of the longer-range American M107 175mm gun, which fires even heavier shells, weighing over 145 pounds. One instance of Israel's use of these lethal battlefield weapons suffices to show the vast disproportionality of the war on Gaza.

On July 19–20, 2014, elements of the elite Golani, Givati, and paratrooper brigades launched an assault along three axes into the Shuja'iyya district of Gaza City. The Golani brigade in particular met fierce and unexpected resistance that resulted in the death of thirteen Israeli soldiers and perhaps one hundred wounded. According to American military sources, eleven Israeli artillery battalions, employing at least 258 of these 155mm and 175mm guns, fired over 7,000 shells into this single neighborhood over a period of twenty-four hours. This included 4,800 shells during one seven-hour period. A senior Pentagon officer "with access to the daily briefings" called the scale of firepower "massive" and "deadly," noting that the US army would normally use so "huge" an amount of shellfire in support of two entire divisions comprising 40,000 troops (perhaps ten times the size of the Israeli force engaged in Shuja'iyya). Another, a former American artillery commander, estimated that the US military would employ that number of guns only in support of an army corps of several divisions. A retired American general described the Israeli bombardment—used to pound one Gaza neighborhood for over twenty-four hours, along with tank fire and attacks from the air—as "absolutely disproportionate."[32]

The artillery pieces that were used in this assault are designed for lethal area fire over a wide radius against fortifications, armored vehicles, and dug-in troops protected by body armor and helmets. While they can launch precision-guided munitions, deployed as they were against a dense neighborhood such as Shuja'iyya, they were inherently imprecise. And any air strike dropping 2,000-pound bombs in built-up areas, which Shuja'iyya, Beit Hanoun, Khan Yunis, and Rafah are, will necessarily and inevitably cause heavy civilian casualties and massive damage.[33] They cannot but do so.

This is especially true in a place as overcrowded as the Gaza Strip, where people have nowhere to flee even if they are given prior notice that their homes are about to be destroyed. Beyond the horrific injuries they inflict on human flesh, air bombardment and artillery fire on this scale cause unimaginable destruction to property: in the 2014 assault, over 16,000 buildings were rendered uninhabitable, including entire neighborhoods. A total of 277 UN and government schools, seventeen hospitals and clinics, and all six of Gaza's universities were damaged, as were over 40,000 other buildings. Perhaps 450,000 Gazans, about a quarter of the population, were forced to leave their homes, and many of them no longer had homes to go back to afterward.

These were not random occurrences, nor was this the regrettable collateral damage often lamented during a war. The weapons chosen were lethal, meant for employment on an open battlefield, not in a heavily populated urban environment. Moreover, the scale of the onslaught was entirely in keeping with Israeli military doctrine. The killing and mangling in 2014 of some 13,000 people, most of them civilians, and the destruction of the homes and property of hundreds of thousands, was intentional, the fruit of an explicit strategy adopted by the Israeli military at least since 2006, when it used such tactics in Lebanon. The Dahiya doctrine, as it is called, is named for the southern suburb of Beirut—al-Dahiya—which was destroyed by Israel's air force using 2,000-pound bombs and other ordnance. This strategy was explained in 2008 by Maj. Gen. Gadi Eizenkot, then head of Northern Command (and thereafter Israeli chief of staff):

> What happened in the Dahiya quarter . . . will happen in every village from which Israel is fired on. . . . We will apply disproportionate force on it and cause great damage and destruction there. From our standpoint, these are not civilian villages, they are military bases. . . . This is not a recommendation. This is a plan. And it has been approved.[34]

This was precisely the thinking in 2014 behind Israel's third attack on Gaza in a period of six years, according to Israeli military correspondents and security analysts.[35] Yet there was little mention of the Dahiya doctrine in statements by US politicians or in the reporting on the war by most of the mainstream American media, even though it is in fact less of a strategic approach than a blueprint for collective punishment, which entails probable war crimes.

There are a number of reasons for the silence of Washington and the media. The Arms Export Control Act of 1976 specifies that American-supplied weapons must be used "for legitimate self-defense."[36] Given this provision, the line offered by US officials from the president down—describing Israel's operations in Gaza as self-defense—may be the product of legal advice to avoid liability and potential prosecution for war crimes, alongside the Israeli officials who issued the orders and the soldiers who dropped the bombs. The media, too, rarely mentions this important legal consideration, possibly out of bias, or to protect the politicians who would otherwise be implicated, or to dodge the attacks on the media that generally follow even the mildest criticism of Israel.

There remains the issue of proportionality, which is central to determining whether certain acts of war rise to the level of war crimes. Eizenkot's own words and the actions of the forces under his command in 2006, and thereafter these attacks on Gaza, seem clearly to establish intentional disproportionality on the part of Israel. This is borne out by the nature of the battlefield weaponry used by Israel in heavily populated urban areas, and the gross disproportion in firepower between the two sides.

Were Hamas and Islamic Jihad also responsible for potential war crimes by targeting a civilian population? Leaving aside the vital distinction between force employed by an occupying army and that utilized by groups among the occupied people, all combatants are required to obey the laws of war and other provisions of international law. Deadly though the rockets fired into southern Israel could be, few of them had sophisticated guidance systems and none were precision-guided munitions. Thus their use was generally indiscriminate, and could be considered to have been aimed at civilians in a large proportion of cases.

However, none of the rockets had a warhead of the size or lethality of the over 49,000 tank and artillery shells fired by Israel in 2014. The Soviet-designed 122mm Grad or Katyusha rocket commonly used by Hamas and its allies normally carried either a 44- or 66-pound warhead (compared with the 96-pound 155mm shells), although many were fitted with smaller warheads to increase their range. Most of the home-made Qassam rockets that were used had considerably smaller warheads. Together, the 4,000 Qassam, Katyusha, Grad, and other missiles that were fired from the Gaza Strip, and that reached Israel (many were so imprecise and poorly manufactured that they fell short and landed within the strip), would have likely had less explosive power in total than a dozen 2,000-pound bombs.

While the rain of missiles launched by Hamas and its allies undoubtedly had a potent psychological effect on civilians within its range (the effect is paradoxically heightened by their inaccuracy), these weapons were not terribly powerful. Still, the death of several dozen civilians in Israel over the years from 2008 to 2014 very likely rises to the level of war crimes. What then of the killing in 2014 alone of at least two thousand civilians not engaged in combat, including some 1,300 women, children, and old people? Several years after the last of these wars on Gaza, it is clear that those responsible, protected by their American patrons, are likely to enjoy impunity for their actions.

The savage disproportionality did register in some quarters, however. While hard-core support for Israel solidified among certain groups as a result of the mainstream coverage of the 2014 bombardment—Christian Evangelicals and the older, wealthier, more conservative segments of the Jewish community—public criticism of Israel increased among younger, more progressive individuals, members of minorities, liberal Protestant denominations, and some Reform, Conservative, and unaffiliated Jews. By 2016, the numbers indicating a shift in this direction (and a parallel hardening of opinion in support of Israel among other groups) were striking.

A poll released by the Brookings Institution in December 2016 showed that 60 percent of Democrats and 46 percent of all Americans supported sanctions against Israel over its construction of illegal Jewish settlements in the West Bank. Most Democrats (55 percent) believed Israel has too much influence on US politics and policies and is a strategic burden.[37] A Pew Research Center poll taken that same year showed that the proportion of people born after 1980 and of Democrats who are sympathetic to the Palestinians is growing in relation to those who sympathize with Israel.[38] A Pew poll released in January 2018 revealed an acceleration of this trend: Democrats were almost as inclined to support the Palestinians as Israel, while twice as many liberal Democrats sympathized more with the Palestinians than with the Israelis.[39] An April 2019 Pew poll showed that the deep partisan divide over Israel and Palestine was further accentuated. When asked whether they favored the Palestinian people over the Israeli people, or vice versa, or favored both, 58 percent of Democrats favored both peoples or the Palestinians, while 76 percent of Republicans favored both peoples or the Israelis. Meanwhile, 61 percent of Republicans had a favorable view of the Israeli government, but only 26 percent of Democrats did.[40] Taken together, these figures were unprecedented.

Thus the wars on Gaza joined the 1982 war in Lebanon and the First Intifada as crucial turning points in an ongoing shift in how Palestinians and Israel are perceived by Americans. There has been no smooth upward line, but rather an ebb and flow, given the impact of suicide bombings during the Second Intifada and especially the undiminished effectiveness of Israel's ceaseless proselytizing. But the unmistakable wave of critical sentiment has in every case increased after a sequence of horrific images, and the reality they represent, has broken through the dense screen of defense carefully erected to shield Israel's behavior and to hide that reality.

DESPITE THE SLOW but steady shift in American public opinion regarding Palestine and Israel in recent years, there was little apparent change in the making of US policy, in new legislation, and in the political discourse in general. One reason for this was the Republican Party's control of the White House for all but eight years since 2000, of the Senate since 2010, of the House from 2014 until 2018, and of all branches of government between 2016 and 2018. The party's base, especially the Evangelicals—its core in many regions, older, whiter, and more likely to be conservative and male—fervently supported the most hawkish Israeli policies. Most Republican elected officials faithfully reflected the fervor of that base, as well as that of conservative donors to the party, many of whom, like Sheldon Adelson and Paul Singer (who between them donated over $100 million to Republicans during the 2016 election cycle), have been vigorously committed to an even more hawkish approach toward Israel. Additionally, the Islamophobia, xenophobia, and aggressive view of America's role in the world of much of the Republican base and party leadership matched the ethos of Israeli Prime Minister Benjamin Netanyahu and his right-wing government. Indeed, this was on ample display in the rapturous reception Netanyahu received when he spoke before two different joint sessions of a Republican-dominated Congress, in 2011 and 2015. Only Winston Churchill, who addressed Congress in 1941, 1943, and 1952, had the honor of giving more than one such speech.

The Democratic Party's case with regard to Israel and Palestine has been more complicated and contradictory. The shift in much of the party's base took place most notably among its younger, minority, and more liberal segments (representing the party's future); it was not reflected in the views of the party leadership or most of its elected officials and big donors (representing its past). The dynamic at work was both generational, race- and class-based, and also influenced by the party's big donors and powerful pressure groups such as AIPAC.

The polls show that views on Palestine and Israel often correlate closely with age: older people tend to be more conservative and conventional, and in 2019 the leaders of the Democratic Party comprised Nancy Pelosi, 78, Charles Schumer, 68, and a party machine dominated by the Clintons, both in their early seventies. All of them are rich, Pelosi exceedingly so (she is one of the wealthiest members of Congress, with a net worth, together with her husband, reportedly over $100 million). With the incessant fundraising that is the central concern of American politicians, and the rightward turn of the Democrats in the late 1980s, the party became more favorable and attractive to moneyed interests. As a result, the views of donors have been more important to the party's leaders and elected officials than those of the party's base or of its voters. And many of the biggest donors to the party, such as media mogul Haim Saban and others from the high-tech, entertainment, and financial industries, remained unfailingly committed to Israel, irrespective of its excesses.

Democrats were thus torn between the inclinations of their older leaders and many big donors to support any act of the Israeli government, and the party's rank and file, which began pushing hard for a change. This was evident in the unconventional positions on Israel and Palestine taken by presidential candidate Bernie Sanders during the 2016 Democratic primary campaign and in floor fights over the party platform at the convention that year. The split was on display as well in the party leadership struggle that followed the 2016 elections, with the front-runner, Representative Keith Ellison, subjected to smears and innuendo in part because of his outspoken position on Palestine. That the efforts to change the Democratic Party's line on Palestine had little concrete impact was seen in the bipartisan support for the annual military assistance given to Israel of over four billion dollars, and for a tide of legislation that disadvantaged the Palestinians. However, a small shift in Congress could be discerned in a bill cosponsored by thirty members of the House in November 2017, and reintroduced in April 2019 as HR 2407, that sought to ensure that US aid would not support Israeli security forces' mistreatment and imprisonment of Palestinian children, ten thousand of whom have been detained by the occupation since 2000.[41]

Although these political realities can explain much, especially where legislation and political rhetoric is concerned, they shed limited light on the making of policy. In crafting US foreign policy, the executive branch traditionally has great latitude. It is not necessarily as constrained as Congress, haunted as its members are by the election cycle and the fundraising this necessitates. American presidents indeed have repeatedly acted freely with little regard for the objections of Israel and its supporters when they considered vital, core US interests to be at stake. A false narrative would have it that the influence of Israel and its supporters on Middle East policy is always paramount, but this is true *only* when policy makers do not consider vital US strategic interests to be engaged, and when domestic political considerations are especially weighty, for example in a presidential election year.

Examples of the United States overriding strong Israeli resistance to serve Washington's perceived interest are legion: during the 1956 Suez war the US opposed aggression against Egypt as contrary to its Cold War interests; at the end of the 1968–70 War of Attrition along the Suez Canal, the United States imposed a cease-fire to Israel's strategic disadvantage to avert a US-Soviet confrontation; and between 1973 and 1975, Kissinger imposed three disengagement agreements necessitating Israeli military withdrawals, over furious Israeli objections. It is the case that most of these actions ultimately served Israel's long-range interests as well, the short-sighted objections of its leaders notwithstanding. Other examples range from the lucrative sales of advanced weapons to Saudi Arabia despite vociferous opposition by Israel and its lobby in Washington, to the Iran nuclear deal negotiated by President Barack Obama in the teeth of hostility from Netanyahu and his supporters in Congress. The point is that when vital US interests are seen to be at stake in Washington, American presidents have without hesitation acted in service of these interests, paying only limited attention to Israel's concerns.

However, when it comes to Palestine and peacemaking between Palestinians and Israelis that necessarily entails concessions from the latter, there seem to be no major US strategic or economic interests at stake, and no means to counterbalance the sustained opposition from Israel and its supporters, which is inevitably greater on this one issue than any other.[42] US presidents, from Truman to Donald Trump, have been reluctant to walk into this buzz saw of antagonism, and have thus by and large allowed Israel to dictate the pace of events and even to determine US positions on issues relating to Palestine and the Palestinians.

It could be argued that this permissive American attitude toward Israel's behavior—occasionally masked by declaratory opposition to specific measures, which rarely changed the situation on the ground—endangers US interests in the Middle East, given the widespread support for the Palestinians by the populations of the Arab world.[43] But the Middle East has for years been ruled by the largest concentration of autocratic regimes of any region in the world. Moreover, the United States has never supported the advance of democracy in the Middle East in any sustained way, preferring to deal with the dictatorships and absolute monarchies that control most countries. These undemocratic regimes have historically been subservient to the United States and valuable clients of its defense, aerospace, oil, banking, and real-estate industries. They have generally acted in defiance of their own pro-Palestinian public opinion, thus immunizing Washington from any blowback for its support of Israel's occupation and colonization of Palestine.

The key country in this regard has been Saudi Arabia, which since 1948 has publicly advocated for the Palestinian cause, often giving the PLO financial support, while doing little or nothing to pressure the United States to change its favorable policies toward Israel. The passivity of the Saudi monarchy goes back at least to August 1948, when Secretary of State George Marshall thanked King 'Abd al-'Aziz ibn Sa'ud for the Kingdom's "conciliatory manner" over Palestine. This was at the height of the 1948 war, after Israeli troops had overrun most of the country and expelled much of the Palestinian population.[44] Saudi Arabia has grown far more influential in the region since the defeat of Egypt in 1967 and the post-1973 flood of oil money into the kingdom's coffers, but otherwise little has changed in its acquiescent attitude toward Israel in the intervening decades.

This dynamic was visible during the George W. Bush administration, when both the remaining Arabists and the "peace-processors" were largely sidelined from Middle East policy-making. Bush, Cheney, and Rumsfeld instead relied on a cadre of fervently pro-Israel neoconservative hawks like Paul Wolfowitz, Richard Perle, Douglas Feith, and Lewis "Scooter" Libby, many of them retreads from the Reagan administration. They systematically excluded those knowledgeable about the region from any involvement in key decisions, whether regarding Palestine, the disastrous war they launched on Iraq, or the "War on Terror," which was waged almost entirely in the Middle East and other parts of the Muslim world. In Washington, the Sharon government shrewdly managed to sell its campaign against the violent second Palestinian intifada as an integral part of the latter war, and itself as a vital ally, while self-servingly providing much of the flimsy intellectual justification for this ideological crusade. In return, in 2004 Bush accepted the inclusion of settlement blocs—"already existing major Israeli population centers"—within Israel's frontiers in the context of a final peace settlement.[45] Bush also endorsed Sharon's sudden decision to carry out a unilateral Israeli withdrawal of troops and settlers from the Gaza Strip in 2005. Israel did this without coordination with the Palestinians, while maintaining Israel's control over entry to and exit from the strip, which remained under siege, and was soon taken over by Hamas. This set the stage for the next round of Gaza wars.

The president who occupied the White House during all three of Israel's assaults on Gaza, Barack Obama, continued the pattern of his predecessors. His election had raised the hopes of many trusting souls who believed that a US president with Hussein as his middle name, who had been photographed with Edward Said, who was my neighbor and colleague at the University of Chicago, who declared a "new beginning" for the US in the Muslim world—surely he would deal differently with Palestine. These hopes sprung from the assumption that presidents have unlimited freedom to act. But despite the considerable leeway afforded the executive branch, there remains the tenacious power of the permanent bureaucracy, of the homogenous coterie of experts circulating in and out of government, of congress, and of other structural and political factors.

There is also the potency of conventional thinking on Israel and Palestine, entrenched in the leaderships of both political parties and in the mainstream media, as well as the formidable power of the Israel lobby and the fact that there is no effective countervailing force in US politics. Any semblance of an Arab lobby has never been more than a collection of high-priced PR shops, law firms, consultants, and lobbyists paid handsomely to protect the interests of the corrupt, kleptocratic elites that misrule most of the Arab countries. Most of these dictatorial rulers are beholden to the US and are valuable clients of American defense, aerospace, oil, banking, and real estate interests, which have vast influence in Washington. These potent forces also lobby for Arab kleptocrats, but not for "the Arabs," if by that is meant the peoples of these countries.

Still, another hopeful sign was Obama's quick appointment of George Mitchell as special envoy for Middle East peace in January 2009, charged with kick-starting direct Israeli-Palestinian negotiations for a final settlement. Mitchell was a negotiator in the mold of Cyrus Vance and James Baker: an independent-minded and experienced Washington hand, who at that late stage of his career was not beholden to Israel or its lobby. He had served as governor of Maine and as Senate majority leader; as special envoy for President Bill Clinton, he had successfully negotiated the Northern Ireland Good Friday agreement in 1998, bringing the IRA in from the cold and involving them in a settlement. Unlike the peace processors of the Clinton era, Mitchell did not accept Israel's positions as the limits of US policy and strove to confront head-on the most thorny aspects of negotiations: freezing Jewish settlements, the future of Jerusalem, and the return of Palestinian refugees. Building on his success with the IRA in Ireland, he proposed involving Hamas in the negotiating process, which he saw as crucial to a comprehensive solution, but he was ultimately unsuccessful, in large measure because of Israeli opposition. But Mitchell suffered from a particular disadvantage: he was undermined from within the Obama administration. The key figure in the sabotage of Mitchell's mission was none other than the ineffable Dennis Ross.

Ross was out of government during the George W. Bush years, but he had campaigned in Florida and elsewhere for Obama in 2008, defending him against Republican accusations of insufficient support for Israel. The newly elected president was therefore beholden to him. As a sop to those unhappy with Mitchell's appointment (besides his willingness to deal with Hamas, Mitchell was partly of Lebanese ancestry, the first senior US official involved in the Middle East with that background since Philip Habib), Ross was brought in as a special advisor to Secretary of State Hillary Clinton. He was supposed to focus on the Gulf, but quickly began to involve himself in the Palestinian-Israeli negotiations, where the Israelis saw him as a preferred interlocutor. When Ross's interference with Mitchell's efforts became intolerable, as he repeatedly went behind the special envoy's back, setting up secret back channels with the Israelis, he left his post at Foggy Bottom, but he landed on his feet with a new position at the National Security Council, where he was even closer to the president. He continued to interfere with Mitchell's work, making side deals with the Netanyahu government, while the PA refused any contact with him because of his overt bias toward Israel.

It was an unequal fight: Mitchell versus the Israel lobby, Congress, and Netanyahu, with Ross all the while drawing on support from his patrons to operate behind the ex-senator's back. Instead of Israel facing a single US government representative determined to extract concessions from both sides, it was able to play the pliable and always acquiescent Ross against Mitchell. In this situation, Israel could simply stand pat, and no progress toward a settlement was possible. In the end, the coup de grâce was administered to Mitchell by his former colleagues in Congress, who decreed that involving Hamas in the negotiating process was unacceptable and violated US laws.[46] Israel had won. The status quo was preserved, the Palestinians remained divided, and Israel was not obliged to talk to Hamas or even seriously negotiate, all without having had to make much of an effort. Ross and Congress had done Israel's work for it.

Although Obama had indicated that the Palestinian issue was a priority for his administration, his response to the wars on Gaza was a truer measure of his engagement. The first of them that took place on his watch began after his election but before he was inaugurated. At no point then or subsequently did the president seek to disturb the false narrative whereby what was underway in the Gaza Strip during these ferocious onslaughts was a righteous response to terrorist rocket fire aimed at Israeli civilians. At no point did his administration interrupt the flow of American weapons that were used to kill some three thousand Palestinian civilians and maim many more. Indeed, deliveries were accelerated when Israel deemed that necessary. At no point did Obama decisively confront Israel over its siege of the Gaza Strip.

For his early intimations of a change in Washington's bias in favor of Israel, Obama was heartily loathed by its right-wing leaders and their American supporters (he fully reciprocated that sentiment), but in the end he changed nothing in Palestine. In spite of fruitless efforts to resolve the conflict by Obama's secretary of state, John Kerry, the sole mark his administration left was Security Council Resolution 2334, passed 14–1 with a US abstention, that called Israeli settlement activity in the West Bank and East Jerusalem a "flagrant violation" of international law with "no legal validity." Adopted in December 2016 when Obama was already a lame duck, the resolution provided for no sanctions and no coercive measures against Israel. Like other American declaratory posturing, the resolution was toothless, and had absolutely no effect on the situation on the ground. Obama was particularly unlucky in that just months after his inauguration, Netanyahu, with whom his relations went from frigid to awful, took office for the second time, and continued to develop his close ties with the Republican opposition to the president. For these and many other reasons, Obama left the White House in 2017 with the colonial status quo in Palestine of military occupation and expanding Jewish settlement intact, and the conditions for Palestinians even worse than when he took office eight years earlier.

The lesson is clear. Had Obama genuinely considered the issue of peace between Palestinians and Israelis to be a priority—as important as the nuclear agreement with Iran—he could have worked to push it through against congressional opposition and the efforts of AIPAC and the Israeli government, and perhaps he might have succeeded. On behalf of a matter of supreme significance, that of war and peace with Iran, Obama was able to stand up to and overcome the Israel lobby and its Israeli patrons. However, it was apparently the view of the president that breaking the stalemate in Palestine did not constitute enough of a vital strategic American interest for him to engage his prestige and power and political capital. The Mitchell initiative thus died quietly in 2011, and the efforts of Kerry in 2016, and with them the prospect of conducting negotiations between Israel and the Palestinians on an entirely new basis.

As the centenary of the war on Palestine came and went, the American metropole, the irreplaceable base for Israel's freedom of action, was as committed to the Zionist colonial project as had been Lord Balfour one hundred years earlier. The second century of the war would be marked by a new and even more destructive approach to the issue of Palestine, with the United States in close coordination with Israel and its newfound friends in the absolute monarchies of the Gulf.

A Century of War on the Palestinians

In 1917, Arthur James Balfour stated that in Palestine, the British government did not "propose even to go through the form of consulting the wishes of the present inhabitants of the country." The great powers were committed to Zionism, he continued, "and Zionism, be it right or wrong, good or bad, is rooted in age-long traditions, in present needs, in future hopes, of far profounder import than the desires and prejudices of the 700,000 Arabs who now inhabit that ancient land."[1] One hundred years later, President Donald Trump recognized Jerusalem as Israel's capital, saying, "We took Jerusalem off the table, so we don't have to talk about it anymore." Trump told Benjamin Netanyahu, "You won one point, and you'll give up some points later on in the negotiation, if it ever takes place. I don't know that it will ever take place."[2] The center of the Palestinians' history, identity, culture, and worship was thus summarily disposed of without even the pretense of consulting their wishes.

Throughout the intervening century, the great powers have repeatedly tried to act in spite of the Palestinians, ignoring them, talking for them or over their heads, or pretending that they did not exist. In the face of the heavy odds against them, however, the Palestinians have shown a stubborn capacity to resist these efforts to eliminate them politically and scatter them to the four winds. Indeed, more than 120 years after the first Zionist congress in Basel and over seventy years after the creation of Israel, the Palestinian people, represented on neither of these occasions, were no longer supposed to constitute any kind of national presence. In their place was meant to stand a Jewish state, uncontested by the indigenous society that it was meant to supplant. Yet for all its might, its nuclear weapons, and its alliance with the United States, today the Jewish state is at least as contested globally as it was at any time in the past. The Palestinians' resistance, their persistence, and their challenge to Israel's ambitions are among the most striking phenomena of the current era.

Over the decades, the United States has wavered, going back and forth between paying lip service to the existence of the Palestinians and trying to exclude them from the map of the Middle East. The provision for an Arab state in the 1947 partition resolution (albeit never implemented), Jimmy Carter's mention of a Palestinian "homeland," and nominal support for a Palestinian state from the Clinton to the Obama administrations were artifacts of that lip service. There are many more instances of American exclusion and erasure: Lyndon Johnson's backing of UNSC 242; Kissinger's years of sidelining the PLO in the 1960s and 1970s and covertly making proxy war on it; the 1978 Camp David accords; the Reagan administration's green light for the 1982 war in Lebanon; the lack of will of US presidents from Johnson to Obama to stop Israeli seizure and settlement of Palestinian land.

Regardless of its wavering, the United States, the great imperial power of the age, together with Great Britain before it, extended full backing to the Zionist movement and the state of Israel. But they have been trying to do the impossible: impose a colonial reality on Palestine in a postcolonial age. Eqbal Ahmad summed it up: "August 1947 marked the beginning of decolonization, when British rule in India ended. It was in those days of hope and fulfillment that the colonization of Palestine occurred. Thus at the dawn of decolonization, we were returned to the earliest, most intense form of colonial menace . . . exclusivist settler colonialism."[3] In other circumstances or in another era, replacing the indigenous population might have been feasible, especially in light of the long-standing and deep religious link felt by Jews to the land in question—if this were the eighteenth or nineteenth century, if the Palestinians were as few as the

Zionist settlers or as fully decimated as the native peoples of Australasia and North America. The longevity of the Palestinians' resistance to their dispossession, however, indicates that the Zionist movement, in the words of the late historian Tony Judt, "arrived too late," as it "imported a characteristically late-nineteenth-century separatist project into a world that has moved on."[4]

With the establishment of Israel, Zionism did succeed in fashioning a potent national movement and a thriving new people in Palestine. But it could not fully supplant the country's original population, which is what would have been necessary for the ultimate triumph of Zionism. Settler-colonial confrontations with indigenous peoples have only ended in one of three ways: with the elimination or full subjugation of the native population, as in North America; with the defeat and expulsion of the colonizer, as in Algeria, which is extremely rare; or with the abandonment of colonial supremacy, in the context of compromise and reconciliation, as in South Africa, Zimbabwe, and Ireland.

There is still the possibility that Israel could attempt to reprise the expulsions of 1948 and 1967 and rid itself of some or all of the Palestinians who tenaciously remain in their homeland. Forcible transfers of population on a sectarian and ethnic basis have taken place in neighboring Iraq since its invasion by the United States and in Syria following its collapse into war and chaos. The UN High Commissioner for Refugees reported in 2017 that a record sixty-eight million persons and refugees were displaced the world over. Against this horrific regional and global background, which elicits scarce concern internationally, there might seem to be little to restrain Israel from such an action. But the ferocious fight that Palestinians would wage against their removal, the intense international attention to the conflict, and the growing currency of the Palestinian narrative all mitigate against such a prospect.

Given the clarity of what is involved in ethnic cleansing in a colonial situation (rather than in circumstances of a confusing civil-cum-proxy war interlaced with extensive foreign intervention, as in Syria and Iraq), a new wave of expulsions would probably not unfold as smoothly for Israel as in the past. Even if undertaken under cover of a major regional war, such a move would have the potential to cause fatal damage to the West's support for Israel, on which it relies. Nonetheless, there are growing fears that expulsion has become more possible in the past few years than at any time since 1948, with religious nationalists and settlers dominating successive Israeli governments, explicit plans for annexations in the West Bank, and leading Israeli parliamentarians calling for the removal of some or all of the Palestinian population. Punitive Israeli policies are currently directed at forcing as many Palestinians as possible out of the country, while also evicting some within the West Bank and the Negev inside Israel from their homes and villages via home demolition, fake property sales, rezoning, and myriad other schemes. It is only a step from these tried-and-true demographic engineering tactics to a repeat of the full-blown ethnic cleansing of 1948 and 1967. Still the odds so far seem against Israeli taking such a step.

If elimination of the native population is not a likely outcome in Palestine, then what of dismantling the supremacy of the colonizer in order to make possible a true reconciliation? The advantage that Israel has enjoyed in continuing its project rests on the fact that the basically colonial nature of the encounter in Palestine has not been visible to most Americans and many Europeans. Israel appears to them to be a normal, natural nation-state like any other, faced by the irrational hostility of intransigent and often anti-Semitic Muslims (which is how Palestinians, even the Christians among them, are seen by many). The propagation of this image is one of the greatest achievements of Zionism and is vital to its survival. As Edward Said put it, Zionism triumphed in part because it "won the political battle for Palestine in the international world in which ideas, representation, rhetoric and images were at issue."[5] This is still largely true today. Dismantling this fallacy and making the true nature of the conflict evident is a necessary step if Palestinians and Israelis are to transition to a postcolonial future in which one people does not use external support to oppress and supplant the other.

RECENT POLLS HAVE revealed the shifts that have begun to take place among some segments of American public opinion. While encouraging to advocates of Palestinian freedom, they do not reflect the stance of most Americans. Nor are they necessarily based on a sound understanding of the colonial dynamic at work in the conflict. Moreover, public opinion can shift again. Events on the ground in Palestine have recently tilted the scales of sympathy slightly in favor of the Palestinians, but other events could cause them to tilt in the opposite direction, as happened during the Second Intifada. Amply funded efforts have been launched to achieve just such a reversal, in particular by smearing critics of Israel as "anti-Semites,"[6] while counterefforts to strengthen this positive trend are puny by comparison.

The experience of the past few decades shows that three approaches have been effective in expanding the way in which the reality in Palestine is understood. The first rests on the fertile comparison of the case of Palestine to other colonial-settler experiences, whether that of Native Americans or South Africans or the Irish. The second, related to the first, involves focusing on the gross imbalance of power between Israel and the Palestinians, a characteristic of all colonial encounters. The third and perhaps most important is to foreground the issue of inequality.

Establishing the colonial nature of the conflict has proven exceedingly hard given the biblical dimension of Zionism, which casts the new arrivals as indigenous and as the historic proprietors of the land they colonized. In this light, the original population of Palestine appears extraneous to the post-Holocaust resurgence of a Jewish nation-state with its roots in the kingdom of David and Solomon: they are no more than undesirable interlopers in this uplifting scenario. Challenging this epic myth is especially difficult in the United States, which is steeped in an evangelical Protestantism that makes it particularly susceptible to such an evocative Bible-based appeal and which also prides itself on its colonial past. The word "colonial" has a valence in the United States that is deeply different from its associations in the former European imperial metropoles and the countries that were once part of their empires.

Similarly, the terms "settler" and "pioneer" have positive connotations in American history, arising from the heroic tale of the conquest of the West at the expense of its indigenous population as projected in movies, literature, and television. Indeed, there are striking parallels between these portrayals of the resistance of Native Americans to their dispossession and that of the Palestinians. Both groups are cast as backward and uncivilized, a violent, murderous, and irrational obstacle to progress and modernity. While many Americans have begun to contest this strand of their national narrative, Israeli society and its supporters still celebrate—indeed, depend on—its foundational version. Moreover, comparisons between Palestine and the Native American or African American experiences are fraught because the United States has yet to fully acknowledge these dark chapters of its past or to address their toxic effects in the present. There is still a long way to go to change Americans' consciousness of their nation's history, let alone that of Palestine and Israel, in which the United States has played such a supportive role.

The second track for changing existing perceptions of the conflict—highlighting the great imbalance between the Palestinians and the powers arrayed against them—involves showing that the Zionist movement was almost always on the offensive in its effort to achieve mastery over an Arab land. Presenting this reality otherwise has been central to the discursive advantage achieved by Zionism, in which Israel is David to the Arab/Muslim Goliath. A more recent fiction casts the conflict as one of two peoples, or even two states, in an equal fight, sometimes framed as right vs. right. Even then, the accepted version is that Israel has constantly wished for peace, only to be rebuffed by the Palestinians ("there is no partner for peace," as the phrase goes, leaving Israelis, the victims, to defend themselves against unjustifiable terrorism and rocket fire). In reality, the Zionist movement and then the state of Israel always had the big battalions on their side, whether this was the British army before 1939, US and Soviet support in 1947–48, France and Britain in the 1950s and 1960s, or the situation from the 1970s until today, where besides receiving unlimited US support, Israel's armed might dwarfs that of the Palestinians, and indeed that of all the Arabs put together.

It is the issue of inequality that is most promising for expanding the understanding of the reality in Palestine. It is also the most important, since inequality was essential to the creation of a Jewish state in an overwhelmingly Arab land, and is vital to maintaining that state's dominance. Inequality is so crucial not only because it is anathema to the egalitarian, democratic societies that the Zionist project has primarily relied on for its support, but because equality of rights is key to a just, lasting resolution of the entire problem.

Within Israel, certain important rights are reserved exclusively for Jewish citizens and denied to the 20 percent of citizens who are Palestinian. Of course, the five million Palestinians living under an Israeli military regime in the Occupied Territories have no rights at all, while the half million plus Israeli colonists there enjoy full rights. This systemic ethnic discrimination was always a central facet of Zionism, which by definition aimed to create a Jewish society and polity with exclusive national rights in a land with an Arab majority. Even as Israel's 1948 Declaration of Independence proclaimed "complete equality of social and political rights to all its inhabitants irrespective of religion, race or sex,"[7] dozens of crucial laws based on inequality of rights were implemented in the ensuing years. These severely restricted or totally banned Arab access to land and to residency in all-Jewish communities, formalized the seizure of the private and collective (*waqf*) property of non-Jews, prevented most indigenous Palestinians who were made into refugees from returning to their homes while giving citizenship rights to Jewish immigrants, and limited access to many other benefits.

This core problem is even more stark today, with a total Arab population in Palestine and Israel from the Jordan River to the sea that is equal to or perhaps slightly larger than the Jewish population. That inequality is the central moral question posed by Zionism, and that it goes to the root of the legitimacy of the entire enterprise is a view that is shared by some distinguished Israelis. Imagining scholars looking back one hundred years from now, historian Zeev Sternhell asked, "When exactly did the Israelis understand that their cruelty towards the non-Jews in their grip in the Occupied Territories, their determination to break the Palestinians' hopes for independence, or their refusal to offer asylum to African refugees began to undermine the moral legitimacy of their national existence?"[8]

For decades Zionists insisted, often referring to the state's declaration of independence, that Israel could be and was both "Jewish and democratic." As the contradictions inherent in this formulation grew ever more apparent, some Israeli leaders admitted (indeed, even declared it with pride) that if they were forced to choose, the Jewish aspect would take precedence. In July 2018, the Knesset codified that choice in constitutional law, adopting the "Basic Law on the Jewish Nation-State," which institutionalized statutory inequality among Israeli citizens by arrogating the right of national self-determination exclusively to the

Jewish people, downgrading the status of Arabic, and declaring Jewish settlement a "national value" with precedence over other needs.[9] Former Justice Minister Ayelet Shaked, one of the more forthright advocates of Jewish supremacy and a sponsor of the law, had made the case bluntly a few months before the legislation came to a vote: "There are places where the character of the State of Israel as a Jewish state must be maintained and this sometimes comes at the expense of equality."[10] She added, "Israel . . . isn't a state of all its nations. That is, equal rights to all citizens but not equal national rights."

Where this ideology leads was summarized in the equally blunt words of Likud Knesset member Miki Zohar. The Palestinian, he said, "does not have the right of self-determination because he is not the proprietor of the land. I want him as a resident because of my honesty, as he was born here, he lives here, and I would never tell him to leave. I regret to say it, but they suffer from one major defect: they were not born Jews."[11] This connection between an exclusive right to land and peoplehood is central to a specific type of "blood and soil" Central European nationalism, which is the ground from which Zionism sprang. Commenting on an early draft of the Jewish Nation-State law, Sternhell, whose area of expertise is European fascism, noted that the constitutional ideas behind the legislation are consonant with those of Charles Maurras, the French anti-Semite and neo-fascist of the 1930s, or of modern-day Polish and Hungarian nationalists and the "hardest-line European chauvinists." However, he added, they are entirely at odds with the liberal ideas of the French and American revolutions.[12]

By embracing its illiberal and discriminatory essence, modern Zionism is increasingly in contradiction with the ideals, particularly that of equality, on which Western democracies are based. For the United States, Canada, Great Britain, France, and Germany, which cherish these values, even if they are often honored only in the breach, and are currently threatened by potent illiberal populist and authoritarian right-wing trends, this should be a serious matter, especially given that Israel is still dependent on the support of these Western countries.

Finally, uprooting the systemic inequality inherent in Zionism is crucial to creating a better future for both peoples, Palestinians and Israelis. Any formula advanced as a resolution of the conflict will necessarily and inevitably fail if it is not squarely based on the principle of equality. Absolute equality of human, personal, civil, political, and national rights must be enshrined in whatever future scheme is ultimately accepted by the two societies. This is a high-sounding recommendation, but nothing else will address the core of the problem, nor will it be sustainable and lasting.

This leaves the thorny issue of how to wean Israelis from their attachment to inequality, which is often coded as and justified by a need for security. This perceived need is to a large extent rooted in a real history of insecurity and persecution, but in response to this past trauma, generations have now been brought up on a reflexive dogma of aggressive nationalism whose tenacious hold will be hard to break. Thus the Jewish citizens of a regional superpower that cows its neighbors (and has bombed the capitals of seven of them with impunity[13]) suffer from a deep insecurity rooted in part in this history, and perhaps in part from an unspoken concern that the carefully constructed and justified colonial reality they live in might suddenly unravel. The syndrome that drives this imperative to dominate and discriminate can probably only be addressed by those within Israeli society (or close to it) who understand the grim direction of the country's current course, and who can challenge the distortions of history, ethics, and Judaism that this ideology constitutes. Doing so is surely the primary and the most urgent task of Israelis and their supporters who wish to change the dynamic of injustice and inequality.

Palestinians, too, need weaning from a pernicious delusion—rooted in the colonial nature of their encounter with Zionism and in its denial of Palestinian peoplehood—that Jewish Israelis are not a "real" people and that they do not have national rights. While it is true that Zionism has transmuted the Jewish religion and the historic peoplehood of the Jews into something quite different—a modern nationalism—this does not erase the fact that Israeli Jews today consider themselves a people with a sense of *national* belonging in Palestine, what they think of as the Land of Israel, no matter how this transmutation came about. Palestinians, too, today consider themselves a people with *national* links to what is indeed their ancestral homeland, for reasons that are as arbitrary and as conjunctural as those that led to Zionism, as arbitrary as any of the reasons that led to the emergence of scores of modern national movements.

Such a conclusion about the constructed nature of all national entities, enraging to apostles of nationalism, is self-evident to those who have studied its genesis in myriad different circumstances.[14]

The irony is that, like all peoples, Palestinians assume that their nationalism is pure and historically rooted while denying the same of Israeli Jews. There is of course a difference between the two: most Palestinians are descended from people who have lived in what they naturally see as their country for a very long time, for many centuries if not many millennia. Most Israeli Jews came from Europe and the Arab countries relatively recently as part of a colonial process sanctioned and brokered by the great powers. The former are indigenous, the latter settlers or descendants of settlers, although many have been there for generations now, and have a deeply felt and ancient religious connection to the country, albeit one quite different from the ancient rootedness in the country of the indigenous Palestinians. Because this is a colonial conflict, this difference matters enormously. However, no one today would deny that fully developed national entities exist in settler states like the United States, Canada, New Zealand, and Australia, despite their origins in colonial wars of extermination. Moreover, to those intoxicated by nationalism, such distinctions between settlers and indigenous peoples do not matter. As the anthropologist Ernest Gellner put it, "Nations as a natural, God-given way of classifying men, as an inherent . . . political destiny, are a myth; nationalism, which sometimes takes pre-existing cultures and turns them into nations, sometimes invents them, and often obliterates pre-existing cultures: *that* is a reality."[15]

While the fundamentally colonial nature of the Palestinian-Israel encounter must be acknowledged, there are now two peoples in Palestine, irrespective of how they came into being, and the conflict between them cannot be resolved as long as the national existence of each is denied by the other. Their mutual acceptance can only be based on complete equality of rights, including national rights, notwithstanding the crucial historical differences between the two. There is no other possible sustainable solution, barring the unthinkable notion of one people's extermination or expulsion by the other. Overcoming the resistance of those who benefit from the status quo, in order to ensure equal rights for all in this small country between the Jordan River and the sea—this is a test of the political ingenuity of all concerned. Reducing the extensive sustained external support for the discriminatory and deeply unequal status quo would certainly smooth the path ahead.

However, the war on Palestine passed the hundred-year mark with the Palestinians confronting circumstances more daunting than perhaps at any time since 1917. With his election, Donald Trump began pursuit of what he called "the deal of the century," purportedly aimed at a conclusive resolution of the conflict. Closing the deal has so far involved dispensing with decades of bedrock US policies, outsourcing strategic planning to Israel, and pouring contempt on the Palestinians. Inauspiciously, Trump's ambassador to Israel, David Friedman (his bankruptcy lawyer and a longtime financial supporter of the Jewish settler movement), spoke of an "alleged occupation" and demanded that the State Department stop using the term. In one interview, he declared that Israel has the "right" to annex "some, but unlikely all, of the West Bank."[16] Jason Greenblatt, for over two years envoy for Israel-Palestine negotiations (previously Trump's real-estate lawyer and also a donor to Israeli right-wing causes), stated that West Bank settlements "are not an obstacle to peace," rejected use of the term "occupation" in a meeting with EU envoys,[17] and endorsed Friedman's views regarding annexation.

The new administration quickly trumpeted an "outside-in" approach, in which three of the Sunni Arab Gulf monarchies—Saudi Arabia, the Emirates, and Bahrain (often falsely described as representing Sunni Arabs) were brought into a de facto alliance with Israel to stand together against Iran. The by-product of this configuration was that these and other Arab regimes allied to the US were encouraged to bully the Palestinians to accept maximalist Israeli positions that would be, and appeared intended to be, fatal to their cause. This initiative was coordinated closely with these regimes, via the mediation of presidential envoy extraordinaire Jared Kushner, Trump's son-in-law, also a real-estate mogul, and an ardent extreme Zionist whose family had also donated to Jewish settlements.

In collusion with their Gulf partners at a June 2019 conference in Bahrain and in other venues, Kushner, Greenblatt, and Friedman publicly pushed what was essentially an economic development initiative for the West Bank and Gaza Strip, meant to operate under existing conditions of virtually complete Israeli control. Kushner cast doubt on the feasibility of independent Palestinian self-rule, saying, "we'll have to see." He drew on the classic colonialist lexicon to add, "The hope is that they over time can become capable of governing." All the Palestinians deserved, in Kushner's view, was "the opportunity to live a better life . . . the opportunity to pay their mortgage."[18] With their essentially economic solution, this troika displayed remarkable ignorance of a solid expert consensus that the Palestinian economy has been strangled primarily by the systematic interference of the Israeli military occupation that their plan meant to keep in place. The Trump administration exacerbated this economic stranglehold by cutting off US aid to the PA and to UNRWA. The US also continued to support Israel's blockade of Gaza, aided by Egypt, with its disastrous effects on 1.8 million people.

The crucial political aspect of Trump's deal of the century was reportedly contained in the outlines of an American-Israeli proposal that the PA was pressured to accept. This purportedly involved creating a non-contiguous, non-sovereign entity without removal of any of the existing illegal Israeli settlements, which would be recognized, "legalized," and annexed to Israel. This entity would remain under full Israeli security control (for which the Palestinians would reportedly have to pay!) and therefore be a state in name only. It would exclude sovereignty or control over Jerusalem and be located in the Gaza Strip and the scores of disparate fragments totaling under 40 percent of the West Bank that constitute Areas A and B, with some parts of C perhaps to be included, but only subject to further negotiations.[19]

Integrally linked to such an approach was Trump's December 2017 recognition of Jerusalem as Israel's capital and the subsequent relocation of the US Embassy there. This move marked a revolutionary departure from over seventy years of US policy, going back to UNGA 181, whereby the status of the holy city was to remain undetermined pending a final resolution of the Palestine question to be mutually agreed by both sides. This affront was then followed by Trump's proclamation recognizing Israeli sovereignty over the annexed Golan Heights, another radical US policy shift.

With these two pronouncements, the administration unilaterally took issues—one of which, that of Jerusalem, Israel is treaty-bound to negotiate with the Palestinians—off the table. As well as reversing decades of American policy, the Trump ensemble spurned an entire body of international law and consensus, UN Security Council decisions, world opinion, and of course Palestinian rights. Trump accepted fully Israel's stand on the vital issue of Jerusalem and did so without any quid pro quo from Israel and without any acknowledgment of Palestinian demands for recognition of the city as the capital of Palestine. Equally important, by implication, Trump endorsed Israel's expansive definition of a "unified Jerusalem," including the extensive Arab areas in and around the city appropriated by Israel since 1967. Although the administration stated that actual borders were still to be negotiated, its proclamation meant in effect that there was nothing left to negotiate.

Through these and other actions, the White House implicitly confirmed the outlines of the American-Israeli proposal: it explicitly avoided endorsing a two-state solution; it closed the Palestinian mission in Washington, D.C., and the US consulate in East Jerusalem that had served as an informal embassy to the Palestinians; it claimed that, contrary to the status of all other refugees since World War II, the descendants of Palestinians, declared refugees in 1948, are not themselves refugees. Finally, by endorsing Israel's annexation of Jerusalem and the Golan Heights, Trump cleared the way for the annexation of whatever parts of the occupied West Bank Israel should choose to swallow up.

In exchange for these drastic derogations of Palestinian rights, the Palestinians were to be offered money, collected from the Gulf monarchies. The offer was formalized at the June 2019 conference in Bahrain that the PA refused to attend. Kushner's proposal to buy off Palestinian opposition to a plan that obviated a negotiated political settlement was in fact no more than a reheated version of similar plans for "economic peace" in lieu of rights peddled by Israeli leaders from Shimon Peres to Netanyahu. For Netanyahu and ultranationalist supporters of extremist settlers, an economic sweetener for the bitter pill the Palestinians were meant to swallow had become an essential plank in their explicitly annexationist approach.

Indeed, what was most striking about this White House's Middle

East policy was that it had been effectively outsourced to Netanyahu and his allies in Israel and the United States. Its initiatives seem to have come prepackaged from the Israeli right's storehouse of ideas: moving the US embassy to Jerusalem, recognizing the annexation of the Golan, airily dispensing with the Palestinian refugee issue, trying to liquidate UNRWA, and withdrawing from the Obama-era nuclear agreement with Iran. Only a few items remained on Netanyahu's wish list: annexation of much of the West Bank, formal American rejection of sovereign Palestinian statehood, the creation of a toothless Palestinian Quisling leadership—the entire package meant to coerce the Palestinians to accept that they are a defeated people.

None of this was entirely new, given past American practice. But Trump's people abandoned even the shabby old pretense at impartiality. With this plan, the United States ceased to be "Israel's lawyer," becoming instead the mouthpiece of the most extreme government in Israel's history, proposing to negotiate directly with the Palestinians on Israel's behalf, with the welcome assistance of its closest Arab allies. Perhaps the White House was up to something else: generating draft proposals that were so offensively pro-Israel as to be unacceptable to even the most compliant Palestinians. With this tactic, the Israeli government could paint the Palestinians as rejectionist and continue to avoid negotiations while maintaining the status quo of creeping annexation, expanding colonization, and legal discrimination. In either case, the outcome would be the same: the Palestinians were put on notice that the prospect of an independent future in their homeland was closed off and that the Israeli colonial endeavor had a free hand to shape Palestine as it wished.

This is a conclusion that most of the world rejects, and it will surely be met with resistance, both locally and globally. It is also at odds with every principle of freedom, justice, and equality that the United States is supposed to stand for. A resolution imposed strictly on harsh Israeli terms will inevitably bring more conflict and insecurity for all concerned. For the Palestinians, though, it also presents opportunities.

THE EXISTING STRATEGIES of both of the leading Palestinian political factions, Fatah and Hamas, have come to nothing, evidenced by the acceleration of Israeli control over all of Palestine. Neither dependence on US mediation in fruitless negotiations as part of the sole resort to feeble diplomacy of the 'Abbas era nor a nominal strategy of armed resistance has advanced Palestinian national aims over the past few decades. Nor is there much for the Palestinians to expect from Arab regimes like those of Egypt and Jordan, which today have no shame in signing massive gas deals with Israel, or Saudi Arabia and the UAE, which have purchased Israeli weapons and security systems through American cut-outs that only thinly disguise their origins.[20] These realizations necessitate a careful reassessment by the Palestinians of their methods, whether their national goals are defined as an end to occupation and reversing the colonization of Palestinian land; establishing a Palestinian state in the remaining 22 percent of Mandatory Palestine with Arab East Jerusalem as its capital; the return to their ancestral homeland of that half of the Palestinian people who are currently living in exile; or creating a democratic, sovereign binational state in all of Palestine with equal rights for all, or some combination or permutation of these options.

As the weaker party in the conflict, the Palestinian side cannot afford to remain divided. But before unity can be achieved, a redefinition of objectives must take place on the basis of a new national consensus. It is a searing indictment of both Fatah and Hamas that in recent decades civil society initiatives such as the Boycott, Divestment, Sanctions movement and student activism have done more to further the Palestine cause than anything either of these two main factions has undertaken. A reconciliation would at least repair some of the damage caused by their split, but reconciliation between two ideologically bankrupt political movements, important though it would be, cannot provide the dynamic new strategy needed to dislodge the Palestinian cause from its current state of stagnation and retreat.

One key change that is needed involves acknowledging that the diplomatic strategy adopted by the PLO since the 1980s was fatally flawed: the United States is not and cannot be a mediator, a broker, or a neutral party. It has long opposed Palestinian national aspirations and has formally committed itself to support the Israeli government's positions on Palestine. The Palestinian national movement must recognize the true nature of the American stance and undertake dedicated grassroots political and informational work to make its case inside the United States, as the Zionist movement has done for over a century. This task will not necessarily take generations, given the significant shifts that have already occurred in key sectors of public opinion. There is a great deal to build on.

Yet the bifurcated Palestinian leadership today appears to have no better understanding of the workings of American society and politics than its predecessors had. It does not have any idea of how to engage with American public opinion and has made no serious attempt to do so. This ignorance of the complex nature of the US political system has prevented the fashioning of a sustained program to reach potentially sympathetic elements of civil society. By contrast, in spite of the dominant position Israel and its supporters enjoy in the United States, they continue to expend lavish resources to advance their cause in the public arena. Although the effort to support Palestinian rights is poorly funded and has been comprised only of initiatives by elements of civil society, it has achieved remarkable successes in such spheres as the arts (notably cinema and theater); the legal realm, where defenders of free speech and the First Amendment have become vital allies against sustained attacks on supporters of BDS; sectors of academia, notably Middle East and American studies; some unions and churches; and key parts of the base of the Democratic Party.

Similar work needs to be directed at Europe, Russia, India, China, Brazil, and nonaligned states. Israel has made progress in recent years in cultivating the elites and public opinion in these countries, while many of them, especially China and India, are becoming more active in the Middle East.[21] Although most Arab states are controlled by undemocratic regimes subservient to the United States and desirous of Israeli approval, Arab public opinion remains acutely sensitive to the appeal of Palestine. Thus in 2016, 75 percent of respondents in twelve Arab countries considered the Palestine cause one of concern to all Arabs, and 86 percent disapproved of Arab recognition of Israel because of its policies directed against Palestine.[22] The Palestinians need to resurrect the PLO's former strategy of appealing over the heads of unresponsive regimes to sympathetic Arab public opinion.

Most important is that should entering negotiations based on a Palestinian consensus become feasible, any future diplomacy must reject the Oslo interim formula and proceed on an entirely different basis. An intensive global public relations and diplomatic campaign must be aimed at demanding international sponsorship and rejecting exclusive US control of the process (a demand that has already been feebly made by the PA). Beyond this, for the purpose of negotiations, the Palestinians ought to treat the United States as an extension of Israel. As a superpower, it would necessarily be represented at any talks, but it should be considered as an adversarial party, even seated with Israel on the opposite side of the table, which would represent its real position at least since 1967.

New negotiations would need to reopen all the crucial issues created by the 1948 war that were closed in Israel's favor in 1967 by UNSC 242: the 1947 UNGA 181 partition borders and its *corpus separatum* proposal for Jerusalem; the return and compensation of refugees; and the political, national, and civil rights of Palestinians inside Israel. Such talks should stress complete equality of treatment of both peoples, and be based on the Hague and Fourth Geneva conventions, the United Nations Charter with its stress on national self-determination, and all relevant UN Security Council and General Assembly resolutions, not just those cherry-picked by the United States to favor Israel.

The current administration in Washington and the Israeli government would of course never accept such terms, and so these would, for the moment, constitute impossible preconditions for negotiations. That is precisely the point. They are meant to move the goalposts away from formulas devised as advantageous to Israel. Continuing to negotiate on the existing deeply flawed basis can only entrench a status quo that is leading toward the final absorption of Palestine into the Greater Land of Israel. If a serious and sustained Palestinian diplomatic and public relations effort campaigned for such new terms aimed at reaching a just and equitable peace, many countries would be amenable to considering them. They might even be willing to challenge the half-century-long US monopoly on peacemaking, a monopoly that been crucial in preventing peace in Palestine.[23]

A forgotten but essential element of the Palestinian political agenda is work inside Israel, specifically convincing Israelis that there is an alternative to the ongoing oppression of the Palestinians. This is a long-term process that cannot be dismissed as a form of "normalizing" relations with Israel: neither the Algerians nor the Vietnamese shortsightedly denied themselves the opportunity to convince public opinion in the home country of their oppressor of the justice of their cause—efforts that contributed measurably to their victory. Nor should the Palestinians.

The Palestinian people, whose resistance to colonialism has involved an uphill battle, should not expect quick results. They have shown unusual patience, perseverance, and steadfastness in defending their rights, which is the main reason that their cause is still alive. It is now essential for all the elements in Palestinian society to adopt a considered, long-term strategy, which means rethinking much that has been done in the past, understanding how other liberation movements succeeded in altering an unfavorable balance of forces, and cultivating all possible allies in their struggle.

GIVEN AN ARAB world that is in a state of disarray greater than at any time since the end of World War I and a Palestinian national movement that appears to be without a compass, it might seem that this is an opportune moment for Israel and the United States to collude with their autocratic Arab partners to bury the Palestine question, dispose of the Palestinians, and declare victory. It is not likely to be quite so simple. There is the not inconsiderable matter of the Arab public, which can be fooled some of the time but not all of the time, and that emerges with Palestinian flags flying whenever democratic currents rise against autocracy, as in Cairo in 2011 and in Algiers in the spring of 2019. Israel's regional hegemony depends in very large measure on the maintenance in power of undemocratic Arab regimes that will suppress such sentiment. However distant it may seem today, real democracy in the Arab world would be a grave threat to Israel's regional dominance and freedom of action.

Just as important, there is also the popular resistance that the Palestinians can be expected to continue to mount, whatever the shabby deal to which their discredited leaders may mistakenly assent. Though Israel is the nuclear regional hegemon, its domination is not uncontested in the Middle East, nor is the legitimacy of the undemocratic Arab regimes which are increasingly becoming its clients. Finally, the United States, for all its power, has played a secondary role—sometimes no role at all—in the crises in Syria, Yemen, Libya, and elsewhere in the region. It will not necessarily maintain the near monopoly over the Palestine question, and indeed over the entire Middle East, that it has enjoyed for so long. Configurations of global power have been changing: based on their growing energy needs, China and India will have more to say about the Middle East in the twenty-first century than they did in the previous one. Being closer to the Middle East, Europe and Russia have been more affected than the United States by the instability there and can be expected to play larger roles. The United States will most likely not continue to have the free hand that Britain once did. Perhaps such changes will allow Palestinians, together with Israelis and others worldwide who wish for peace and stability with justice in Palestine, to craft a different trajectory than that of oppression of one people by another. Only such a path based on equality and justice is capable of concluding the hundred years' war on Palestine with a lasting peace, one that brings with it the liberation that the Palestinian people deserve.

NOTES

INTRODUCTION

1. Both buildings date to the late seventh century, although the Dome essentially kept its original form, while the al-Aqsa Mosque was repeatedly rebuilt and expanded.
2. The main library building, known as Turbat Baraka Khan, is described in Michael Hamilton Burgoyne, *Mamluk Jerusalem: An Architectural Study* (London: British School of Archaeology in Jerusalem and World of Islam Festival Trust, 1987), 109–16. The structure contains the tombs of Baraka Khan and his two sons. The former was a thirteenth-century military leader whose daughter was a wife of the great Mamluk sultan al-Zahir Baybars. Her son Saʿid succeeded Baybars as sultan.
3. With these funds from my great-grandmother, my grandfather renovated the building. The manuscripts and books grouped together in the library were collected by my grandfather from the holdings of various of our ancestors, including collections that had originally been put together in the eighteenth century and earlier. The library website contains basic information about it, including access to the catalogue of manuscripts: http://www.khalidilibrary.org/indexe .html.
4. Private Palestinian libraries were systematically looted by specialized teams operating in the wake of advancing Zionist forces as they occupied Arab-inhabited villages and cities, notably Jaffa, Haifa, and the Arab neighborhoods of West Jerusalem, in Spring 1948. The stolen manuscripts and books were deposited in the Hebrew University Library, now the National Library of Israel, under the heading "AP" for "abandoned property," a typically Orwellian description of a process of cultural appropriation in the wake of conquest and dispossession:

Gish Amit, "Salvage or Plunder? Israel's 'Collection' of Private Palestinian Libraries in West Jerusalem," *Journal of Palestine Studies* 40, no. 4 (2010–11): 6–25.

5. The most important source on Yusuf Diya is the section on him by Alexander Schölch, *Palestine in Transformation, 1856–1882: Studies in Social, Economic, and Political Development* (Washington, DC: Institute for Palestine Studies, 1993), 241–52. That section was reprinted in the *Jerusalem Quarterly* 24 (Summer 2005): 65–76. See also Malek Sharif, "A Portrait of Syrian Deputies in the Ottoman Parliament," in *The First Ottoman Experiment in Democracy*, ed. Christoph Herzog and Malek Sharif (Würzburg: Nomos, 2010); and R. Khalidi, *Palestinian Identity: The Construction of Modern National Consciousness*, rev. ed. (New York: Columbia University Press, 2010), 67–76.

6. His role as an upholder of constitutional rights against the absolutism of the sultan is described in R. E. Devereux, *The First Ottoman Constitutional Period: A Study of the Midhat Constitution and Parliament* (Baltimore: Johns Hopkins University Press, 1963).

7. Profiting from his service as governor in the Bitlis district of Kurdistan, in the southeast of what is today Turkey, he produced the first Arabic-Kurdish dictionary, *al-Hadiyya al-Hamidiyya fil-Lugha al-Kurdiyya*. I found copies of this book and of several of his other publications among material in the Khalidi Library. The book was published in 1310AH/1893 in Istanbul by the Ottoman Ministry of Education, and it has since been republished several times. Beyond its title, which alludes to Sultan 'Abd al-Abdul Hamid II's name, its introduction includes a fulsome dedication to the sultan, which was virtually obligatory to ensure that works passed through censorship, especially one by an author considered potentially subversive by the authorities.

8. *Der Judenstaat: Versuch einer modernen Lösung der Judenfrage* (Leipzig and Vienna: M. Breitenstein, 1896). This pamphlet is eighty-six pages long.

9. Theodor Herzl, *Complete Diaries*, ed. Raphael Patai (New York: Herzl Press, 1960), 88–89.

10. Letter from Yusuf Diya Pasha al-Khalidi, Pera, Istanbul, to Chief Rabbi Zadok Kahn, March 1, 1899, Central Zionist Archives, H1\197 [Herzl Papers]. I received a digitized copy of this document courtesy of Barnett Rubin. The letter was written from the Khedivial Hotel in the Pera district of Istanbul. All translations from the original French are my own.

11. Letter from Theodor Herzl to Yusuf Diya Pasha al-Khalidi, March 19, 1899, reprinted in Walid Khalidi, ed., *From Haven to Conquest: Readings in Zionism and the Palestine Problem* (Beirut, Institute for Palestine Studies, 1971), 91–93.

12. Ibid.

13. Herzl's attitude toward the Arabs is a contentious topic, although it should not be. Among the best and most balanced assessments are those of Walid Khalidi, "The Jewish-Ottoman Land Company: Herzl's Blueprint for the Colonization of Palestine," *Journal of Palestine Studies* 22, no. 2 (Winter 1993): 30–47; Derek Penslar, "Herzl and the Palestinian Arabs: Myth and Counter-Myth," *Journal of Israeli History* 24, no. 1 (2005), 65–77; and Muhammad Ali Khalidi, "Utopian

Zionism or Zionist Proselytism: A Reading of Herzl's *Altneuland*," *Journal of Palestine Studies*, 30, no. 4 (Summer 2001): 55–67.

14. The text of the charter can be found in Walid Khalidi, "The Jewish-Ottoman Land Company."

15. Herzl's almost utopian 1902 novel *Altneuland* ("Old New Land") described a Palestine of the future that had all these attractive characteristics. See Muhammad Ali Khalidi, "Utopian Zionism or Zionist Proselytism."

16. According to the Israeli scholar Zeev Sternhell, during the entire decade of the 1920s "the annual inflow of Jewish capital was on average 41.5 percent larger than the Jewish net domestic product (NDP). . . . its ratio to NDP did not fall below 33 percent in any of the pre-World War II years . . .": *The Founding Myths of Israel: Nationalism, Socialism, and the Making of the Jewish State* (Princeton, NJ: Princeton University Press, 1998), 217. The consequence of this remarkable inflow of capital was a growth rate of 13.2 percent annually for the Jewish economy of Palestine from 1922 to 1947: for details see R. Khalidi, *The Iron Cage: The Story of the Palestinian Struggle for Statehood* (Boston: Beacon Press, 2007), 13–14.

17. Figures on Palestinian losses during the revolt were extrapolated from statistics provided by Walid Khalidi, ed., *From Haven to Conquest*, appendix 4, 846–49; and Matthew Hughes, *Britain's Pacification of Palestine: The British Army, the Colonial State and the Arab Revolt, 1936–39* (Cambridge: Cambridge University Press, 2019), 377–84.

18. *Lord Curzon in India: Being a Selection from His Speeches as Viceroy & Governor-General of India, 1898–1905* (London: Macmillan, 1906), 589–90.

19. Ibid., 489.

20. *Der Judenstaat*, translated and excerpted in *The Zionist Idea: A Historical Analysis and Reader*, ed. Arthur Hertzberg (New York: Atheneum, 1970), 222.

21. Zangwill, in "The Return to Palestine," *New Liberal Review* (December 1901), 615, wrote that "Palestine is a country without a people; the Jews are a people without a country." For a recent example of the tendentious and never-ending reuse of this slogan, see Diana Muir, "A Land Without a People for a People Without a Land," *Middle East Quarterly* (Spring 2008), 55–62.

22. Joan Peters, *From Time Immemorial: The Origins of the Arab-Jewish Conflict over Palestine* (New York: HarperCollins, 1984). The book was mercilessly eviscerated in reviews by Norman Finkelstein, Yehoshua Porath, and numerous other scholars, who all but called it a fraud. Rabbi Arthur Hertzberg, who was briefly my colleague at Columbia University, told me that the book was produced by Peters, who had no particular Middle East expertise, at the instigation and with the resources of a right-wing Israeli institution. Essentially, he told me, they gave her their files "proving" that the Palestinians did not exist, and she wrote them up. I have no way of assessing this claim. Hertzberg died in 2006 and Peters in 2015.

23. Such works are numerous. See, e.g., Arnold Brumberg, *Zion Before Zionism, 1838–1880* (Syracuse, NY: Syracuse University Press, 1985); or in a superficially more sophisticated form, Ephraim Karsh's characteristically polemical and tendentious *Palestine Betrayed* (New Haven, CT: Yale University Press, 2011). This

book is part of a new genre of neoconservative "scholarship" funded by, among others, extreme-right-wing hedge-fund multimillionaire Roger Hertog, who receives generous thanks in the preface to Karsh's book. Another star in this neocon firmament, Michael Doran of the Hudson Institute, of which Hertog is a member of the Board of Trustees, is equally generous in his thanks to Hertog in the preface to his book *Ike's Gamble: America's Rise to Dominance in the Middle East* (New York: Simon and Schuster, 2016).

24. American public attitudes on Palestine have been shaped by the widespread disdain for Arabs and Muslims spread by Hollywood and the mass media, as is shown by Jack Shaheen in books like *Reel Bad Arabs: How Hollywood Vilifies a People* (New York: Olive Branch Press, 2001), and by similar tropes specific to Palestine and the Palestinians. Noga Kadman, *Erased from Space and Consciousness: Israel and the Depopulated Palestinian Villages of 1948* (Bloomington: Indiana University Press, 2015), shows from extensive interviewing and other sources that similar attitudes have taken deep root in the minds of many Israelis.

25. M. M. Silver, *Our Exodus: Leon Uris and the Americanization of Israel's Founding Story* (Detroit: Wayne State University Press, 2010) analyzes the impact of the book and the movie on American popular culture. Amy Kaplan argues that the novel and the movie played a central role in the Americanization of Zionism. See her article "Zionism as Anticolonialism: The Case of *Exodus*," *American Literary History* 25, no. 4 (December 1, 2013): 870–95, and most importantly, chapter 2 of her book *Our American Israel: The Story of an Entangled Alliance* (Cambridge, MA: Harvard University Press, 2018), 58–93.

26. See Zachary J. Foster, "What's a Palestinian: Uncovering Cultural Complexities," *Foreign Affairs*, March 12, 2015, http://www.foreignaffairs.com/articles/143249 /zachary-j-foster/whats-a-palestinian. Similar views are strongly held by major political donors like the billionaire casino mogul Sheldon Adelson, the largest single donor to the Republican Party for several years running, who has stated that "the Palestinians are an invented people." During every pre-presidential election "money primary," he has orchestrated the unseemly spectacle of potential Republican candidates dancing to his tune. See Jason Horowitz, "Republican Contenders Reach Out to Sheldon Adelson, Palms Up," *New York Times*, April 27, 2015, http://www.nytimes.com/2015/04/27/us/politics/republican-contenders-reach -out-to-sheldon-adelson-palms-up.html; and Jonathan Cook, "The Battle Between American-Jewish Political Donors Heats Up," *Al-Araby*, May 4, 2015, https://mail .google.com/mail/u/0/#label/Articles/14d22f412e42dbf1. One of the largest donors to Trump, Adelson got his reward when in December 2017 the United States recognized Jerusalem as Israel's capital and thereafter moved the US embassy there.

27. Vladimir (later Ze'ev) Jabotinsky, "The Iron Wall: We and the Arabs," first published in Russian under the title "O Zheleznoi Stene" in *Rassvyet*, November 4, 1923.

28. The original Hundred Years' War, between the house of Plantagenet in England and the Valois dynasty in France, actually lasted 116 years, from 1337 to 1453.

29. These include *Palestinian Identity*; *The Iron Cage*; *Under Siege: PLO Decisionmaking During the 1982 War*, rev. ed. (New York: Columbia University Press, 2014);

and *Brokers of Deceit: How the US Has Undermined Peace in the Middle East* (Boston: Beacon Press), 2013.

30. Baron, who was the Nathan L. Miller Professor of Jewish History, Literature, and Institutions at Columbia University from 1929 to 1963 and is regarded as the greatest Jewish historian of the twentieth century, taught my father, Ismail Khalidi, who was a graduate student there in the late 1940s and early 1950s. Baron told me four decades later that he remembered my father, and that he had been a good student, although given Baron's unfailing courtesy and good nature, he may simply have been trying to be kind.

31. I explored the poor choices made by leaders of the Palestinian national movement and the heavy odds they were up against in my book *The Iron Cage*.

CHAPTER 1

1. This quote is widely attributed to Arthur James Balfour, and it indeed sounds like him.

2. For details, see Roger Owen, ed., *Studies in the Economic and Social History of Palestine in the 19th and 20th Centuries* (London: Macmillan, 1982).

3. See Ben Fortna, *Imperial Classroom: Islam, the State, and Education in the Late Ottoman Empire* (Oxford: Oxford University Press, 2002); and Selçuk Somel, *The Modernization of Public Education in the Ottoman Empire, 1839–1908: Islamization, Autocracy, and Discipline* (Leiden: Brill, 2001); Thus, by 1947 nearly 45 percent of the Arab school-age population and the large majority of urban boys and girls were in school, which compared favorably with the situation in neighboring Arab countries: A. L. Tibawi, *Arab Education in Mandatory Palestine: A Study of Three Decades of British Administration* (London: Luzac, 1956), tables, 270–71. The foundation for these education advances was laid in the Ottoman era. See also R. Khalidi, *The Iron Cage*, 14–16; and Ami Ayalon, *Reading Palestine: Printing and Literacy, 1900–1948* (Austin: University of Texas Press, 2004).

4. Contrasts between the highlands and the coast are among the themes in Salim Tamari, *Mountain Against the Sea: Essays on Palestinian Society and Culture* (Oakland: University of California Press, 2008). Tamari ascribes this insight to Albert Hourani: see Hourani's 1985 lecture "Political Society in Lebanon: A Historical Introduction," http://lebanesestudies.com/wp-content/uploads/2012/04/c449fe11 .-A-political-society-in-Lebanon-Albert-Hourani-1985.pdf. See also Sherene Seikaly, *Men of Capital: Scarcity and Economy in Mandate Palestine* (Stanford, CA: Stanford University Press, 2016); Abigail Jacobson, *From Empire to Empire: Jerusalem Between Ottoman and British Rule* (Syracuse, NY: Syracuse University Press, 2011); Mahmoud Yazbak, *Haifa in the Late Ottoman Period, 1864–1914: A Muslim Town in Transition* (Leiden: Brill, 1998); and May Seikaly, *Haifa: Transformation of an Arab Society, 1918–1939* (London: I. B. Tauris, 1995).

5. These developments are explored in detail in R. Khalidi, *Palestinian Identity*. See also Muhammad Muslih, *The Origins of Palestinian Nationalism* (New York: Columbia University Press, 1988); and Ami Ayalon, *Reading Palestine*.

6. An abundance of scholarship now shows the high degree of integration of the *mizrahi* and Sephardic communities within Palestinian society, in spite of occasional friction, and anti-Semitism often spread by European Christian missionaries. See Menachem Klein, *Lives in Common: Arabs and Jews in Jerusalem, Jaffa, and Hebron* (London: Hurst, 2015); Gershon Shafir, *Land, Labor and the Origins of the Israeli-Palestinian Conflict 1882–1914* (Cambridge: Cambridge University Press, 1989); Zachary Lockman, *Comrades and Enemies: Arab and Jewish Workers in Palestine, 1906–1948* (Oakland: University of California, 1996); Abigail Jacobson, *From Empire to Empire*. See also Gabriel Piterberg, "Israeli Sociology's Young Hegelian: Gershon Shafir and the Settler-Colonial Framework," *Journal of Palestine Studies* 44, no. 3 (Spring 2015): 17–38.

7. The best brief refutation of what was once a widespread paradigm of the "decline" of Middle Eastern societies is Roger Owen, "The Middle East in the Eighteenth Century—An 'Islamic' Society in Decline? A Critique of Gibb and Bowen's *Islamic Society and the West*," *Bulletin* (British Society for Middle Eastern Studies) 3, no. 2 (1976): 110–17.

8. To cite the realm of demography alone, Justin McCarthy's *The Population of Palestine: Population Statistics of the Late Ottoman Period and the Mandate* (New York: Columbia University Press, 1990), is an example of work based mainly on Ottoman archival sources for the pre-1918 period, and which puts paid to the myths of the emptiness and barrenness of Palestine before the "miraculous" effects of Zionist colonization began to be felt.

9. Among the most important works on these transformations in Palestine are Alexander Schölch, *Palestine in Transformation, 1856–1882: Studies in Social, Economic, and Political Development*, trans. William C. Young and Michael C. Gerrity (Washington, DC: Institute for Palestine Studies, 1993); Beshara Doumani, *Rediscovering Palestine: Merchants and Peasants in Jabal Nablus, 1700–1900* (Oakland: University of California Press, 1995); and Owen, *Studies in the Economic and Social History of Palestine in the 19th and 20th Centuries*.

10. Linda Schatkowski Schilcher, "The Famine of 1915–1918 in Greater Syria," in *Problems of the Modern Middle East in Historical Perspective*, ed. John Spagnolo (Reading, UK: Ithaca Press, 1912), 234–54. For the lasting traumatic impact of the horrific suffering the population endured during the war, see Samuel Dolbee, "Seferberlik and Bare Feet: Rural Hardship, Citied Dreams, and Social Belonging in 1920s Syria," *Jerusalem Quarterly*, no. 51 (Autumn 2012), 21–35.

11. Perhaps 1.5 million Armenians perished in the genocide that started in April 1915. Even without including those victims, the 1.5 million other Ottoman wartime deaths as a proportion of total population were nearly double the next-highest tolls, those of France and Germany, at 4.4 percent and 4.3 percent of total population, respectively. Other figures put the total wartime Ottoman death toll as high as five million, or around 25 percent of the population.

12. These figures are from Edward Erikson, *Ordered to Die: A History of the Ottoman Army in World War I* (Westport, CT: Greenwood Press, 2001), 211. See also Hikmet Ozdemir, *The Ottoman Army, 1914–1918: Disease and Death on the*

Battlefield (Salt Lake City: University of Utah Press, 2008); Kristian Coates Ulrichsen, *The First World War in the Middle East* (London: Hurst, 2014); and Yigit Akin, *When the War Came Home: The Ottomans' Great War and the Devastation of an Empire* (Stanford, CA: Stanford University Press, 2018).

13. McCarthy, *The Population of Palestine*, 25–27. By way of contrast, McCarthy points out that in spite of its grave war casualties, only 1 percent of the French population was lost during the First World War, during which England and Germany "suffered no loss of total population."

14. 'Anbara Salam Khalidi, *Memoirs of an Early Arab Feminist: The Life and Activism of Anbara Salam Khalidi* (London: Pluto Press, 2013), 68–69.

15. Husayn Fakhri al-Khalidi, *Mada 'ahd al-mujamalat: Mudhakkirat Husayn Fakhri al-Khalidi* [The Era of hypocrisy (literally: niceties) has ended: The memoirs of Husayn Fakhri al-Khalidi] (Amman: Dar al-Shuruq, 2014), 1:75.

16. The impact on my aunt of the execution of her fiancé is described in *Memoirs of an Early Arab Feminist*, 63–67. 'Abd al-Ghani al-'Uraysi was coeditor of the influential Beirut newspaper *al-Mufid* and a prominent Arabist intellectual. 'Anbara Salam Khalidi's reminiscences and her memoir were among the primary sources for an article I wrote about him and his newspaper: "'Abd al-Ghani al-'Uraisi and *al-Mufid*: The Press and Arab Nationalism Before 1914," in *Intellectual Life in the Arab East, 1890–1939*, ed. Marwan Buheiri (Beirut: American University of Beirut Press, 1981), 38–61.

17. Interviews, Walid Khalidi, Cambridge, MA, October 12, 2014, and November 19, 2016. My first cousin Walid, born in 1925, heard the story of the family's wartime displacement when he was young from our grandfather. Some details are confirmed by the memoirs of our uncle, Husayn Fakhri al-Khalidi, *Mada 'ahd al-mujamalat*, 1:75.

18. Interview with Fatima al-Khalidi Salam, Beirut, March 20, 1981.

19. 'Arif Shehadeh (best known as 'Arif al-'Arif) is one of three soldiers from Palestine whose harrowing World War I memoirs are drawn on by Salim Tamari in *Year of the Locust: A Soldier's Diary and the Erasure of Palestine's Ottoman Past* (Oakland: University of California Press, 2011).

20. See Raja Shehadeh's imaginative narration of the odyssey of his great-great uncle, Najib Nassar: *A Rift in Time: Travels with my Ottoman Uncle* (New York: OR Books, 2011). See also the novel by Nassar, which recounts his adventures in semifictional and semiautobiographical form: *Riwayat Muflih al-Ghassani* [The story of Muflih al-Ghassani] (Nazareth: Dar al-Sawt, 1981).

21. See Noha Tadros Khalaf, *Les Mémoires de 'Issa al-'Issa: Journaliste et intellectuel palestinien (1878–1950)* (Paris: Karthala, 2009), 159–75.

22. For British motivations, see Jonathan Schneer, *The Balfour Declaration: The Origins of the Arab-Israeli Conflict* (London: Bloomsbury, 2010); Henry Laurens, *La question de Palestine*, vol. 1, *1799–1922: L'invention de la Terre sainte* (Paris: Fayard, 1999); and James Renton, *The Zionist Masquerade: The Birth of the Anglo-Zionist Alliance, 1914–1918* (London: Palgrave-Macmillan, 2007). See also A. L. Tibawi, *Anglo-Arab Relations and the Question of Palestine, 1914–1921* (London:

Luzac, 1977), 196–239; Leonard Stein, *The Balfour Declaration* (London: Valentine, Mitchell, 1961); and Mayir Vereté, "The Balfour Declaration and Its Makers," *Middle Eastern Studies* 6 (1970): 416–42.

23. This is a central argument of my book *British Policy Towards Syria and Palestine, 1906–1914: A Study of the Antecedents of the Husayn-McMahon Correspondence, the Sykes-Picot Agreement, and the Balfour Declaration*, St. Antony's College Middle East Monographs (Reading, UK: Ithaca Press, 1980).

24. The statement of Leon Trotsky, the Bolshevik commissar for Foreign Affairs, after he had opened up the Tsarist diplomatic archives and revealed these secret wartime Anglo-French-Russian arrangements on this occasion, is reproduced in *Soviet Documents on Foreign Policy, 1917–1924*, ed. Jane Degras, vol. 1 (Oxford: Oxford University Press, 1951).

25. Reported in Yehuda Reinharz's monumental biography, *Chaim Weizmann: The Making of a Statesman* (Oxford: Oxford University Press, 1993), 356–57.

26. Ronald Storrs, *Orientations* (London: Ivor Nicholson and Watson, 1937). The memoirs of Ronald Storrs, the first British military governor of Jerusalem, mention the strict control the British exercised over the press and over all forms of Arab political activity in Palestine: 327ff. Storrs had served as censor of the local press in his previous post, as Oriental secretary to the British high commissioner in Egypt.

27. 'Abd al-Wahhab al-Kayyali, *Watha'iq al-muqawama al-filistiniyya al-'arabiyya did al-ihtilal al-britani wal-sihyuniyya 1918–1939* [Documents of the Palestinian Arab resistance to the British occupation and to Zionism, 1918–1939] (Beirut: Institute for Palestine Studies, 1968), 1–3.

28. Special issue of *Filastin*, May 19, 1914, 1.

29. For details of these land purchases and the resulting armed clashes, see R. Khalidi, *Palestinian Identity*, 89–117. See also Shafir, *Land, Labor, and the Origins of Israeli-Palestinian Conflict*.

30. For details of this evolution, see R. Khalidi, *Palestinian Identity*, especially chapter 7, 145–76.

31. This has been strikingly shown by Margaret Macmillan, *Paris, 1919: Six Months That Changed the World* (New York: Random House, 2002).

32. See Erez Manela, *The Wilsonian Moment: Self-Determination and the International Origins of Anticolonial Nationalism* (New York: Oxford University Press, 2007). Manela rightly credits Wilson with a major role in (unintentionally) sparking the nationalist spirit of rebellion against the colonial powers in the immediate aftermath of World War I but does not sufficiently appreciate how large was the Bolshevik contribution to this process.

33. "Ghuraba' fi biladina: Ghaflatuna wa yaqthatuhum" [Strangers in our own land: Our drowsiness and their alertness], *Filastin*, March 5, 1929, 1.

34. A total of nine autobiographical memoirs and diaries have been published in Arabic by the Institute for Palestine Studies alone since 2005: Muhammad 'Abd al-Hadi Sharruf, 2017; Mahmud al-Atrash, 2016; al-Maghribi, 2015; Gabby Baramki, 2015; Hanna Naqqara, 2011; Turjuman and Fasih, 2008; Khalil Sakakini, 8 vols., 2005–2010; Rashid Hajj Ibrahim, 2005; Wasif Jawhariyya, 2005.

The institute also published the memoir of Reja-i Busailah in English in 2017. Among them, those of Sharruf, a policeman; al-Maghribi, a worker and communist organizer; and Turjuman and Fasih, enlisted men in the Ottoman army in World War I, represent non-elite points of view. See also the important memoirs of a central political figure for the Mandate period, Muhammad 'Izzat Darwaza, *Mudhakkirat, 1887–1984* (Beirut: Dar al-Gharb al-Islami, 1993).

35. One of the few works to rely on oral histories of the 1936–39 revolt is Ted Swedenburg, *Memories of Revolt: The 1936–1939 Rebellion and the Palestinian National Past* (Minneapolis: University of Minnesota Press, 1995).

36. R. Khalidi, *Palestinian Identity*, 225, n32; and Noha Khalaf, *Les Mémoires de 'Issa al-'Issa*, 58. Khalaf's book references articles by my grandfather and numerous articles and poems by al-'Isa that reflect the evolution of the Palestinian sense of identity.

37. I heard almost identical versions of this and other stories from my aunt Fatima (interview, Beirut, March 20, 1981) and from my wife's uncle, Raja al-'Isa, the son of 'Isa al-'Isa, who was also a newspaper editor (interview, Amman, July 7, 1996).

38. R. Khalidi, *Palestinian Identity*, chapter 6, 119–44, covers the treatment of Zionism in the Arabic press.

39. Storrs, *Orientations*, 341. The speech, at a dinner he hosted in honor of Weizmann and the members of the Zionist Commission, was reported by Storrs. Those in attendance included both the mayor and the mufti of Jerusalem, as well as several other leading Palestinian political and religious figures.

40. Tom Segev, *One Palestine, Complete* (New York: Metropolitan Books, 2000), 404.

41. One of the great ironies of this and many other colonial conquests is that of the five infantry regiments of the French 24th Division that defeated Arab forces at the Battle of Maysalun on July 23, 1920, and the next day occupied Damascus, only one was ethnically French: two were Senegalese, one was Algerian, and one was Moroccan. Employing colonial subjects in such a fashion was a crucial element in European imperial expansion. This divide-and-rule tactic was equally important in colonial projects in Ireland, North America, India, North and South Africa, and Palestine and the rest of the Middle East.

42. Two excellent recent articles in the *Journal of Palestine Studies* 46, no. 2 (Winter 2017) deal with this topic: Lauren Banko, "Claiming Identities in Palestine: Migration and Nationality Under the Mandate," 26–43; and Nadim Bawalsa, "Legislating Exclusion: Palestinian Migrants and Interwar Citizenship," 44–59.

43. George Antonius, in *The Arab Awakening* (London: Hamish Hamilton, 1938), was the first to reveal the details of Britain's wartime pledges to the Arabs, and to publish the documents in which they were embodied. This forced an embarrassed British government to publish the entire correspondence: Great Britain, Parliamentary Papers, Cmd. 5974, *Report of a Committee Set Up to Consider Certain Correspondence Between Sir Henry McMahon [His Majesty's High Commissioner in Egypt] and the Sharif of Mecca in 1915 and 1916* (London: His Majesty's Stationery Office, 1939).

44. Balfour's obtaining the senior position of chief secretary for Ireland, second only to the lord lieutenant, was generally ascribed to his family connection with the prime minister, Robert Cecil, Lord Salisbury, whence the popular expression, "Bob's your uncle."

45. E. L. Woodward and R. Butler, eds., *Documents on British Foreign Policy, 1919–1939,* first series, 1919–1929 (London: Her Majesty's Stationery Office, 1952), 340–48.

46. The case of George Antonius was one of many egregious instances in this regard. Trained at Cambridge, and clearly highly qualified, he was constantly passed over for high office in the mandate administration in favor of mediocre British officials: See Susan Boyle, *Betrayal of Palestine: The Story of George Antonius* (Boulder, CO: Westview, 2001); and Sahar Huneidi, *A Broken Trust: Sir Herbert Samuel, Zionism, and the Palestinians* (London: I. B. Tauris, 2001), 2.

47. Stein, *The Land Question in Palestine,* 210–11.

48. Zeev Sternhell, *The Founding Myths of Israel,* 217. According to Sternhell, the ratio of capital inflow to NDP "did not fall below 33 percent in any of the pre–World War II years."

49. Population figures can be found in W. Khalidi, ed., *From Haven to Conquest,* appendix 1, 842–43.

50. Speech to the English Zionist Federation, September 19, 1919, cited in Nur Masalha, *Expulsion of the Palestinians: The Concept of "Transfer" in Zionist Political Thought, 1882–1948* (Washington, DC: Institute for Palestine Studies, 1992), 41.

51. Edwin Black, *The Transfer Agreement: The Untold Story of the Secret Agreement Between the Third Reich and Jewish Palestine* (New York: Macmillan, 1984).

52. This is from a passage in his revealing diaries, cited in Shabtai Teveth, *Ben Gurion and the Palestine Arabs: From Peace to War* (New York: Oxford University Press, 1985), 166–68.

53. For details, see R. Khalidi, *The Iron Cage,* 54–62. The "job interview" is described on pp. 59–60.

54. How the British did this is the main subject of chapter 2 of *The Iron Cage,* 31–64.

55. This figure is based on statistics provided by W. Khalidi, *From Haven to Conquest,* appendix 4, 846–49; and Matthew Hughes, *Britain's Pacification of Palestine: The British Army, the Colonial State and the Arab Revolt, 1936–39* (Cambridge: Cambridge University Press, 2019), 377–84.

56. For details of this repression, see Matthew Hughes, "The Banality of Brutality: British Armed Forces and the Repression of the Arab Revolt in Palestine, 1936–39," *English Historical Review* 124, no. 507 (April 2009), 313–54.

57. Baruch Kimmerling and Joel S. Migdal, *The Palestinian People: A History* (Cambridge, MA: Harvard University Press, 2003), 119.

58. For a chilling account of arbitrary summary executions of Palestinians by mixed units of British soldiers and Zionist militiamen under the command of Orde Wingate see Segev, *One Palestine, Complete,* 429–32. Wingate comes off as a murderous psychopath in Segev's account; he adds that some of his men privately considered him to be mad. The Israeli Ministry of Defense later said of him: "The teaching of Orde Charles Wingate, his character and leadership were

a cornerstone for many of the Haganah's commanders, and his influence can be seen in the Israel Defense Force's combat doctrine."

59. Segev, *One Palestine, Complete*, 425–26. Many veterans of the Irish campaign, including former members of the notorious Black and Tans, were recruited into the British security forces in Palestine. See Richard Cahill, "'Going Berserk': 'Black and Tans' in Palestine," *Jerusalem Quarterly* 38 (Summer 2009), 59–68.

60. The memoirs of Ernie O'Malley, a senior IRA commander during the Irish War of Independence, *On Another Man's Wound* (Cork: Mercier Press, 2013), offers a detailed picture of the brutal means utilized by the British from 1919 to 1921 in their vain attempt to master the Irish uprising, including the burning of homes, public buildings, creameries, and other vital economic resources in retaliation for attacks on British troops, police, and armed auxiliaries.

61. H. Khalidi, *Mada 'ahd al-mujamalat*, vol. 1. The section relating to his exile in the Seychelles is 247ff.

62. Ibid., vol. 1, 247.

63. The extent of control exercised by the rebels over large parts of Palestine is assessed in an excellent article by Charles Anderson, "State Formation from Below and the Great Revolt in Palestine," *Journal of Palestine Studies* 47, no. 1 (Autumn 2017): 39–55.

64. Report by General Sir Robert Haining, August 30, 1938, cited in Anne Lesch, *Arab Politics in Palestine, 1917–1939: The Frustration of a National Movement* (Ithaca, NY: Cornell University Press, 1979), 223.

65. British National Archives, Cabinet Papers, CAB 24/282/5, Palestine, 1938, "Allegations against British Troops: Memorandum by the Secretary of State for War," January 16, 1939, 2.

66. His exile and the burning of his home are described in Khalaf, *Les Mémoires de 'Issa al-'Issa*, 227–32.

67. Ibid., 230.

68. For details on how sweeping the collaboration was between the British and the Zionists during the revolt, see Segev, *One Palestine, Complete*, 381, 426–32.

69. British National Archives, Cabinet Papers, CAB 24/283, "Committee on Palestine: Report," January 30, 1939, 24.

70. Ibid., 27.

71. This was the bitter conclusion of Dr. Husayn after the fact, as he reviewed the record of broken British promises in his memoir, *Mada 'ahd al-mujamalat*, vol. 1, 280.

72. The cabinet meeting where the British position at the St. James's Palace Conference was decided is discussed in Boyle, *Betrayal of Palestine*, 13.

73. For details of the ways in which the crucial British commitments made in the White Paper were undermined, see R. Khalidi, *The Iron Cage*, 35–36, 114–15.

74. H. Khalidi, *Mada 'ahd al-mujamalat*, vol. 1, 350–51.

75. Ibid., 300–305. In her judicious treatment of this topic, see Bayan al-Hout's masterful *al-Qiyadat wal-mu'assasat al-siyasiyya fi Filastin 1917–1948* [Political leaderships and institutions in Palestine, 1917–1948] (Beirut: Institute for Palestine Studies, 1981), 397, which comes to the same conclusion.

76. Ibid., 352–56.
77. Ibid., vol. 1, 230ff. This section of the memoir, recounting dealings with the Peel Commission, includes one among many examples Dr. Husayn gives of British bias in favor of the Zionists.
78. He also wrote a volume of memoirs in English about his Seychelles exile full of critical observations on the British titled *Exiled from Jerusalem: The Diaries of Hussein Fakhri al-Khalidi*. The book is forthcoming from Bloomsbury Press.
79. H. Khalidi, *Mada 'ahd al-mujamalat*, vol. 1, 110–14.
80. Ibid., vol. 1, 230.
81. Cited in Masalha, *Expulsion of the Palestinians*, 45.
82. "The King-Crane Commission Report, August 28, 1919," http://www.hri.org /docs/king-crane/syria-recomm.html.
83. George Orwell, "In Front of Your Nose," *Tribune*, March 22, 1946, reprinted in *The Collected Essays, Journalism, and Letters of George Orwell*, vol. 4, *In Front of Your Nose, 1945–50*, ed. Sonia Orwell and Ian Angus (New York: Harcourt Brace, 1968), 124.
84. The official was E. Mills, speaking during his secret testimony to the Peel Commission, cited in Leila Parson, "The Secret Testimony to the Peel Commission: A Preliminary Analysis," *Journal of Palestine Studies*, 49, no. 1 (Fall 2019).
85. The best study of how the League of Nations Permanent Mandates Commission oversaw the Palestine Mandate is Susan Pedersen, *The Guardians: The League of Nations and the Crisis of Empire* (New York: Oxford University Press, 2015).
86. The myth that the British were pro-Arab throughout the Mandate period, one cherished by Zionist historiography, is exploded by Segev in *One Palestine, Complete*.
87. I addressed this question in more detail in *The Iron Cage*, 118–23.

CHAPTER 2

1. https://unispal.un.org/DPA/DPR/unispal.nsf/0/07175DE9FA2DE563852568D3 006E10F3.
2. My cousin Leila, who was born in the mid-1920s, related this to me in a personal email on March 18, 2018, recalling that she had to stay up with our grandmother in order to turn on the radio for her.
3. My father later became treasurer of the institute. At one stage, Habib Katibah was also secretary: Hani Bawardi, *The Making of Arab-Americans: From Syrian Nationalism to U.S. Citizenship* (Austin: University of Texas Press, 2014), 239–95.
4. For details on the institute, see ibid.
5. An item on the conclusion of my father's tour can be found in *Filastin*, January 24, 1948, "Tasrih li-Isma'il al-Khalidi ba'd 'awdatihi li-Amirka," [Statement by Ismail al-Khalidi after his return to America].
6. My grandfather had a total of nine children: seven boys and two girls. My father, born in 1915, was the youngest.
7. I found a few letters from Dr. Husayn among my father's papers. My cousin Walid Khalidi reports, in "On Albert Hourani, the Arab Office and the Anglo-

American Committee of 1946," *Journal of Palestine Studies* 35, no. 1 (2005–6), 75, that he was also in correspondence with our uncle during his exile, and kept him supplied with books, which Dr. Husayn mentions with gratitude in the forthcoming English-language diaries of his Seychelles exile, *Exiled from Jerusalem*.

8. Mustafa Abbasi, "Palestinians Fighting Against Nazis: The Story of Palestinian Volunteers in the Second World War," *War in History* (November 2017): 1–23, https://www.researchgate.net/publication/321371251_Palestinians_fighting _against_Nazis_The_story_of_Palestinian_volunteers_in_the_Second_World _War.

9. For the text of the Biltmore declaration, see http://www.jewishvirtuallibrary.org /the-biltmore-conference-1942.

10. Denis Charbit, in *Retour à Altneuland: La traversée des utopias sionistes* (Paris: Editions de l'Eclat, 2018), 17–18, notes that the creation of a Jewish state was always prominently featured in Zionist writings, starting with the very first Zionist utopian projects in the late nineteenth century, and down to that set out by Herzl in his book *Altneuland*.

11. Amy Kaplan, *Our American Israel*, offers the most persuasive and profound examination of how and why this effort was crowned with success. See also Peter Novick's brilliant *The Holocaust in American Life* (New York: Houghton Mifflin, 1999).

12. H. Khalidi, *Mada 'ahd al-mujamalat*, vol. 1, 434–36.

13. "The Alexandria Protocol," October 7, 1944, *Department of State Bulletin*, XVI, 411, May 1947, http://avalon.law.yale.edu/20th_century/alex.asp. Saudi Arabia and Yemen joined the League in 1945.

14. W. Khalidi, "On Albert Hourani," 60–79.

15. "The Case Against a Jewish State in Palestine: Albert Hourani's Statement to the Anglo-American Committee of Enquiry of 1946," *Journal of Palestine Studies* 35, no. 1 (2005–6), 80–90.

16. Ibid., 86.

17. Ibid., 81.

18. R. Khalidi, *The Iron Cage*, 41–42, gives examples of such treatment of delegations of Palestinian leaders by Sir Herbert Samuel in 1920, and by Prime Minister Ramsay MacDonald and the colonial secretary, Lord Passfield, in 1930. Samuel told the former group: "I meet with you in a private capacity only."

19. O'Malley, *On Another Man's Wound*, illustrates amply the complexity of the centralized organization that Irish nationalists developed from 1919 to 1921 during their struggle with the British.

20. This body is also called the Arab National Treasury by Sayigh. His account from which this section was largely drawn was published in two parts: see part 1, "Desperately Nationalist, Yusif Sayigh, 1944 to 1948," as told to and edited by Rosemary Sayigh, *Jerusalem Quarterly* 28 (2006), 82; Yusuf Sayigh, *Sira ghayr muktamala* [An incomplete autobiography] (Beirut: Riyad El-Rayyes, 2009), 227–60. A full-length memoir based on these materials, but not including some of the events recounted in this two-part selection, was later edited and published

by his wife, the noted anthropologist Rosemary Sayigh: *Yusif Sayigh: Arab Economist and Palestinian Patriot: A Fractured Life Story* (Cairo: American University of Cairo Press, 2015).

21. Half of that sum was intended for land acquisition in Palestine: "100 Colonies Founded: Established in Palestine by the Jewish National Fund," *New York Times*, April 17, 1936, https://www.nytimes.com/1936/04/17/archives/100-colonies -founded-established-in-palestine-by-jewish-national.html. By the 1990s, the JNF was raising about $30 million annually in the United States. However, according to an internal investigation in 1996, only about 20 percent of that money actually went to Israel; the rest was apparently spent on administration and on US-based "Israel programming" and "Zionist Education": Cynthia Mann, "JNF: Seeds of Doubt—Report Says Only Fifth of Donations Go to Israel, but No Fraud Is Found," October 26, 1996, Jewish Telegraphic Agency, J., http://www.jweekly .com/article/full/4318/jnf-seeds-of-doubt-report-says-only-fifth-of-donations -go-to-israel-but-no-/.

22. My uncle was exiled first to the Seychelles and then to Beirut. H. al-Khalidi, *Mada 'ahd al-mujamalat*, vol. 1, 418. The British permitted al-'Alami to return to Palestine when my uncle did in 1943, but they only allowed Jamal al-Husayni, another key leader, to come back from exile in Rhodesia in 1946. Jamal al-Husayni had evaded capture by the British in Jerusalem in 1937, and eventually reached Baghdad. After the British reoccupation of Iraq in 1941, according to his daughter Serene's memoir, he and his comrades who (unlike the mufti) had "rejected the possibility of going to Germany . . . decided to give themselves up to the British," and were arrested and held in Iran, and then were moved to Rhodesia: Serene Husseini Shahid, *Jerusalem Memories* (Beirut: Naufal Group, 2000), 126–27.

23. Sayigh, "Desperately Nationalist," 69–70.

24. This is clear from his first-person account: "On Albert Hourani, the Arab Office and the Anglo-American Committee of 1946."

25. H. al-Khalidi, *Mada 'ahd al-mujamalat*, vol. 1, 432–34. Details of this trip were related to Dr. Husayn by al-'Alami himself.

26. H. al-Khalidi, *Mada 'ahd al-mujamalat*, vol. 2, 33–35. This was Col. Ernest Altounyan, a British-Syrian-Armenian surgeon, a decorated veteran of World War I, and a fellow of the Royal College of Surgeons, whose entry in *Plarr's Lives of the Fellows of the Royal College of Surgeons*, http://livesonline.rcseng.ac.uk/biogs /E004837b.htm, notes that during World War II, "His official role of medical officer was an effective cover for activities as an expert adviser on Middle Eastern affairs." He told Dr. Husayn that he was serving in military intelligence. Interestingly, both were doctors by training, and both were acting at that time in a very different capacity. Dr. Husayn mentions nothing about the colonel's background, nor in which language they spoke to one another; H. al-Khalidi, *Mada 'ahd al-mujamalat*, vol. 1, 431.

27. Sayigh, "Desperately Nationalist," 69–70.

28. Albert Hourani, "Ottoman Reform and the Politics of the Notables," in *Beginnings of Modernization in the Middle East: The Nineteenth Century*, ed. William

Polk and Richard Chambers (Chicago: University of Chicago Press, 1968), 41–68. In writing about the "notables," Hourani knew whereof he spoke, as his teaching in Beirut, his war work for Britain in Cairo, and his efforts with the Arab Office in Jerusalem brought him into close contact with many examples of this group over nearly a decade.

29. In *'Ibrat Filastin* [The lesson of Palestine] (Beirut: Dar al-Kashaf, 1949), Musa al-'Alami does suggest that implementation of the Fertile Crescent scheme would be a suitable response to the loss of Palestine, which Dr. Husayn takes as an explanation for the Iraqi government's support for al-'Alami: *Mada 'ahd al-mujamalat*, vol. 2, 30.

30. Avi Shlaim, *Collusion Across the Jordan: King Abdullah, the Zionist Movement and the Partition of Palestine* (New York: Columbia University Press, 1988), examines these negotiations in detail.

31. Walid Khalidi has recounted how he discovered this palace "back-door" on a visit to Amman in the early 1950s: personal communication with the author, January 16, 2016. Sometimes British "advice" was rendered via intermediaries, such as members of the royal family.

32. For Roosevelt's letter confirming these pledges, dated April 5, 1945, see United States Department of State, *Foreign Relations of the United States: Diplomatic Papers* [hereafter *FRUS*], *1945. The Near East and Africa*, vol. 8 (1945), http://avalon.law.yale.edu/20th_century/decad161.asp. It reaffirmed the US government's commitment regarding Palestine "that no decision be taken with respect to the basic situation in that country without full consultation with both Arabs and Jews," adding that the president "would take no action, in my capacity as Chief of the Executive Branch of this Government, which might prove hostile to the Arab people." For details, see R. Khalidi, *Brokers of Deceit: How the US Has Undermined Peace in the Middle East* (Boston: Beacon Press, 2013), 20–25.

33. Again, the basic reference is the extensive work on this topic of Walid Khalidi, notably his pioneering article "Plan Dalet: Master Plan for the Conquest of Palestine," republished in the *Journal of Palestine Studies* 18, no. 1 (Autumn 1988): 4–33. The article originally appeared in *Middle East Forum* in 1961. Other historians have since confirmed most of his basic findings, even those who disagree with him on some points like Benny Morris, *The Birth of the Palestinian Refugee Problem Revisited*, 2nd ed. (Cambridge: Cambridge University Press, 2004). See also Simha Flapan, *The Birth of Israel: Myth and Reality* (New York: Pantheon, 1987); Tom Segev, *1949: The First Israelis*, 2nd ed. (New York: Henry Holt, 1998); and Ilan Pappe, *The Ethnic Cleansing of Palestine*, 2nd ed. (London: Oneworld, 2007).

34. "Desperately Nationalist," 82. Sayigh's memoirs include a much fuller account of his experiences in this period. See Yusuf Sayigh, *Sira ghayr muktamala*, 227–60.

35. Walid Khalidi, *Dayr Yasin: al-Jum'a, 9/4/1948* [Dayr Yasin: Friday, 9/4/1948] (Beirut: Institute for Palestine Studies, 1999), table, 127.

36. Nir Hasson, "A Fight to the Death and Betrayal by the Arab World," *Haaretz*, January 5, 2018, https://www.haaretz.com/middle-east-news/palestinians

/.premium.MAGAZINE-the-most-disastrous-24-hours-in-palestinian-history
-1.5729436.

37. The best account of the Arab states' decision to enter Palestine can be found in
Walid Khalidi, "The Arab Perspective," in *The End of the Palestine Mandate*, ed. W.
R. Louis and Robert Stookey (Austin: University of Texas Press, 1986), 104–36.

38. The fate of these villages is described in detail in Walid Khalidi, ed., *All That
Remains: The Palestinian Villages Occupied and Depopulated by Israel in 1948*
(Washington, DC: Institute for Palestine Studies, 1992).

39. The ruined house is the subject of a sixty-two-page architectural paper in Hebrew that shows phases of its evolution over time and provides images of its current state. The house was not destroyed, as were most other Arab houses in the
area that became Israel in 1948, because of its revered place in Zionist history.
Before my grandfather purchased it, a group of early Zionist immigrants under
the leadership of Israel Belkind and his brother Shimshon, a group known as the
Bilu'im, rented rooms in the house for a few months in 1882 before they went
on to found Rishon LeZion, the second Zionist agricultural colony in Palestine.
The building is now called the Bilu'im House. I am grateful to Dr. Nili Belkind,
grand-niece of Israel Belkind, for this information, and for directing me to the
essay by Lihi Davidovich and Tamir Lavi, titled "Tik Ti'ud: Bet Antun Ayub-
Bet Ha-Bilu'im" [Documentation File: The Anton Ayyub House-House of the
Bilu'im], 2005/2006, which can be found on the website of the School of Architecture at Tel Aviv University: http://www.batei-beer.com/aboutus.html.

40. One of the best accounts of this transformation can be found in Tom Segev,
1949: The First Israelis (New York: The Free Press, 1986). See also Ibrahim Abu-
Lughod, *The Transformation of Palestine* (Evanston, IL: Northwestern University
Press, 1971).

41. This is the title of a chapter in Avi Shlaim, *The Politics of Partition: King Abdullah, the Zionists and Palestine, 1921–1951* (London: Oxford University Press),
18, which is an abridged paperback edition of *Collusion Across the Jordan*.

42. Mary Wilson lays out precisely how the British and 'Abdullah planned to do
this: *King Abdullah, Britain and the Making of Jordan* (Cambridge: Cambridge
University Press, 1987) 166–67ff.

43. Shlaim, *Collusion Across the Jordan*, 139. Shlaim explains in detail the elements
of this complex collusion against the Palestinians.

44. The first to explode this myth were Israeli authors, including Flapan, *The Birth of
Israel*; Tom Segev, *1949: The First Israelis*; and Avi Shlaim, *The Iron Wall: Israel and
the Arab World*, who were described as "new" or "revisionist historians" because
they challenged the encrusted received version of the founding of the Jewish state.

45. Avi Shlaim, *Collusion Across the Jordan* is indispensable for understanding how this
happened. See also Mary Wilson, *King Abdullah, Britain and the Making of Jordan*.

46. Eli Barnavi, "Jewish Immigration from Eastern Europe," in Eli Barnavi, ed., *A
Historical Atlas of the Jewish People from the Time of the Patriarchs to the Present*
(New York: Schocken Books, 1994), http://www.myjewishlearning.com/article
/jewish-immigration-from-eastern-europe/.

47. There is a voluminous literature on the topic of the Truman administration and Palestine. A quite comprehensive recent account is John Judis, *Genesis: Truman, American Jews, and the Origins of the Arab/Israeli Conflict* (New York: Farrar, Straus and Giroux, 2014). See also the authoritative biography: David McCullough, *Truman* (New York: Simon and Schuster, 1992).

48. Col. William Eddy, *FDR Meets Ibn Saud* (Washington, DC: America-Mideast Educational and Training Services, 1954; repr., Vista, CA: Selwa Press, 2005), 31.

49. Irene L. Gendzier, *Dying to Forget: Oil, Power, Palestine, and the Foundations of U.S. Power in the Middle East* (New York: Columbia University Press, 2015).

50. Secretary of State to Legation, Jedda, August 17, 1948, *FRUS 1948*, vol. 2, pt. 2, 1318.

51. For more on the Saudi-American relationship at this time, see R. Khalidi, *Brokers of Deceit*, 20–25.

52. From 1949 until 1971, total US economic and military aid to Israel topped $100 million only four times. Since 1974, it has been in the billions annually.

53. Between 1953 and 1974, the Security Council passed at least twenty-three resolutions to "condemn," "deplore," or "censure" Israeli actions in the Gaza Strip, Syria, Jordan, Lebanon, Jerusalem, and the Occupied Territories.

54. A typical and early example of criticisms of Arab performance was Constantin Zureiq's 1948 book, *The Meaning of the Catastrophe*. For details, see p. 113.

55. The poem is reproduced in Ya'qub 'Awadat, *Min a'lam al-fikr wal-adab fi Filastin* [Leading literary and intellectual figures in Palestine], 2nd ed. (Jerusalem: Dar al-Isra', 1992). The phrase "little kings," besides its general derogatory implication, is probably a reference to King 'Abdullah's short stature in particular.

56. In the words of the JNF website, "land which had been purchased for Jewish settlement belonged to the Jewish people as a whole," https://www.jnf.org/menu-3/our-history#.

57. Leena Dallasheh, "Persevering Through Colonial Transition: Nazareth's Palestinian Residents After 1948," *Journal of Palestine Studies* 45, no. 2 (Winter 2016): 8–23.

58. A memoir by one of the most senior Arab officers of the Arab Legion, Colonel Abdullah al-Tal, published in 1959, revealed details of these clandestine relations, later examined by Avi Shlaim in detail in *Collusion Across the Jordan*: 'Abdullah al-Tal, *Karithat Filastin: Mudhakkirat 'Abdullah al-Tal, qa'id ma'rakat al-Quds* [The Palestine disaster: The memoirs of 'Abdullah al-Tal, commander in the battle for Jerusalem] (Cairo: Dar al-Qalam, 1959).

59. A detailed contemporary account of the incident and its aftermath can be found in "Assassination of King Abdullah," *The Manchester Guardian*, July 21, 1951, http://www.theguardian.com/theguardian/1951/jul/21/fromthearchive.

60. Kanafani's 1962 novel has been translated by Hilary Kirkpatrick: *Men in the Sun and Other Palestinian Stories* (Boulder, CO: Lynne Rienner, 1999).

61. Gamal Abdel Nasser, *Philosophy of the Revolution* (New York: Smith, Keynes and Marshall, 1959), 28.

62. Benny Morris, *Israel's Border Wars: 1949–1956: Arab Infiltration, Israeli Retaliation, and the Countdown to the Suez War* (Oxford: Clarendon Press, 1993).

63. From 1953 to1968, when my father worked in the Political and Security Council Affairs division (now the Division of Political Affairs), Israel was condemned or censured nine times by the council for its actions.

64. This is confirmed by memoirs by military officers who served as UN observers of the armistice agreements, including E. H. Hutchinson, *Violent Truce: Arab-Israeli Conflict 1951–1955* (New York: Devin-Adair, 1956); Lieutenant General E. L. M. Burns, *Between Arab and Israeli* (London: Harrap, 1962); and Major General Carl Von Horn, *Soldiering for Peace* (New York: D. McKay, 1967).

65. On this episode, see Muhammad Khalid Az'ar, *Hukumat 'Umum Filastin fi dhikraha al-khamsin* [The All-Palestine government on its 50th anniversary] (Cairo: n.p., 1998).

66. For the condescending and almost contemptuous view that British diplomats took of the sole episode to this day of Jordanian democracy, see R. Khalidi, "Perceptions and Reality: The Arab World and the West," in *A Revolutionary Year: The Middle East in 1958*, ed. Wm. Roger Louis (London: I. B. Tauris, 2002), 197–99. When my uncle's government was dismissed by the young King Husayn in May 1957, the formidable Queen Mother, Zayn, helped the British ambassador to browbeat Jordanian politicians into accepting the formation of a "civilian" government that would serve as a cover for the military rule that Britain and the Hashemites desired, and that was ultimately established. The ambassador's description of that meeting at the royal palace is worthy of Evelyn Waugh: "The Ministers had been reluctant to assume the responsibilities of office, and had asked the King why a military Government could not be formed. . . . The Queen Mother . . . pointed out forcibly that a military Government would make any other form of Government unnecessary. Finally Her Majesty told the Minister's designate that they would not be allowed to leave the Palace until they had taken the oath of office, and it was on this not altogether encouraging basis that the new Government was eventually formed": UK Public Records Office, Ambassador Charles Johnston to Foreign Secretary Selwyn Lloyd, no. 31, May 29, 1957, F.O. 371/127880.

67. The best work on this topic is Salim Yaqub, *Containing Arab Nationalism: The Eisenhower Doctrine and the Middle East* (Chapel Hill: University of North Carolina Press, 2004).

68. This was first shown by Avi Shlaim in a pioneering article, "Conflicting Approaches to Israel's Relations with the Arabs: Ben Gurion and Sharett, 1953–1956," *Middle East Journal* 37, no. 2 (Spring 1983): 180–201.

69. These accounts can be found in Abu Iyad with Eric Rouleau, *My Home, My Land: A Narrative of the Palestinian Struggle* (New York, Times Books, 1981); and Alan Hart, *Arafat: A Political Biography* (Bloomington: Indiana University Press, 1989).

70. See the eyewitness account of the immediate aftermath of the attack by the American naval officer who was in charge of the United Nations Mixed Armistice Commission (MAC) that investigated the attack: E. H. Hutchinson, *Violent Truce*.

71. UN Security Council Resolution 101 of November 24, 1953.

72. My cousin Munzer Thabit Khalidi, who was drafted into the Jordanian army and served as an officer in a border area of the West Bank during the 1950s, related to me in 1960 that these were the orders he was given for the troops under his command. For further details on efforts by Jordan's Arab Legion to stop Palestinian infiltration in this period, see the memoir of its commander, John Bagot Glubb, *Soldier with the Arabs* (London: Hodder and Stoughton, 1957). The extent of these efforts is confirmed by the account of the chairman of the UN Mixed Armistice Commission, Commander E. H. Hutchinson, *Violent Truce*.

73. This is clear from the extracts from Sharett's diaries in Livia Rokach, *Israel's Sacred Terrorism: A Study Based on Moshe Sharett's Personal Diary and Other Documents* (Belmont, MA: Arab American University Graduates, 1985).

74. This is attested by Mordechai Bar On, who was a member of the Israeli General Staff at the time: *The Gates of Gaza: Israel's Road to Suez and Back, 1955–57* (New York: St. Martin's Press, 1994), 72–75. See also Benny Morris, *Israel's Border Wars*.

75. Avi Shlaim, "Conflicting Approaches."

76. An authoritative account of these events is the memoir of the Canadian officer Lt. Gen. Burns, who commanded the UN Truce Supervisory Organization on the Egyptian-Israeli armistice line between 1954 and 1956: *Between Arab and Israeli*. See also Shlaim, "Conflicting Approaches."

77. Matthew Connelly, *A Diplomatic Revolution: Algeria's Fight for Independence and the Origin of the Post-Cold War Era* (New York: Oxford University Press, 2002).

78. There is a vast literature on the 1956 Suez war. For a good collection of essays on the topic see *Suez 1956: The Crisis and Its Consequences*, ed. Roger Louis and Roger Owen (Oxford: Clarendon Press, 1989). See also Benny Morris, *Israel's Border Wars*.

79. "Special Report of the Director of the United Nations Relief and Works Agency for Palestine Refugees in the Near East," A/3212/Add.1 of December 15, 1956, https://unispal.un.org/DPA/DPR/unispal.nsf/0/6558F61D3DB6BD4505256593 006B06BE.

80. These massacres were the subject of a debate in the Knesset in November 1956 in which the phrase "mass murder" was used. For a detailed account by an Israeli soldier who was a witness to the slaughter, see Marek Gefen, "The Strip is Taken," *Al-Hamishmar*, April 27, 1982. These massacres are the main focus of Joe Sacco, *Footnotes in Gaza: A Graphic Novel* (New York: Metropolitan Books, 2010).

81. El-Farra later spoke about this in a United Nations oral history: http://www.unmultimedia.org/oralhistory/2013/01/el-farra-muhammad/.

82. In the second edition of his book, *The Birth of the Palestinian Refugee Problem Revisited*, Benny Morris lists twenty such massacres.

83. Jean-Pierre Filiu, *Gaza: A History* (Oxford: Oxford University Press, 2014).

CHAPTER 3

1. *Le dimanche de Bouvines: 27 juillet 1214* (Paris: Gallimard, 1973), 10. The original quote in French is: "Je tachai de voir comment un événement se fait et se défait puisque, en fin de compte, il n'existe que par ce qu'on en dit, puisqu'il est à proprement parler fabriqué par ceux qui en répandent la renommée."

2. Lyndon Johnson, *The Vantage Point: Perspectives of the Presidency* (New York: Holt, Rinehart and Winston, 1971), 293.

3. The US military and CIA estimated that Israel would handily defeat all the Arab armies combined, even if the latter attacked first. See US Department of State, *Foreign Relations, 1964–1968, Volume XIX, Arab-Israeli Crisis and War, 1967* [hereafter Foreign Relations, 1967], https://2001-2009.state.gov/r/pa/ho/frus /johnsonlb/xix/28054.htm. At a meeting with President Johnson and his top aides on May 26, 1967, the chairman of the Joint Chiefs of Staff, General Earl Wheeler, stated: "The UAR's dispositions are defensive and do not look as if they are preparatory to an invasion of Israel. . . . He concluded, however, that Israel should be able to resist or undertake [*sic*] aggression and that in the long term Israel would prevail. . . . He believed that the Israelis would win air superiority. The UAR would lose a lot of aircraft. Israel's military philosophy is to gain tactical surprise by striking airfields first" ("Memorandum for the Record," Document 72). The CIA had the same view: "Intelligence Memorandum prepared by the Central Intelligence Agency" stated: "Israel could almost certainly attain air superiority over the Sinai Peninsula in 24 hours after taking the initiative or in two or three days if the UAR struck first. . . . We estimate that armored striking forces could breach the UAR's double defense line in the Sinai within several days" (Document 76). The notions that Israel was weaker than the Arabs and was on the brink of annihilation have nevertheless become among the hardiest falsehoods about the conflict.

4. The generals—four of them major generals in 1967—were Ezer Weizman (air force commander in 1967 and later president of Israel, and a nephew of Chaim Weizmann), Chaim Herzog (chief of military intelligence until 1962 and also later president of Israel), Haim Bar Lev (deputy chief of staff in 1967 and later chief of staff), Matitiyahu Peled (a member of the General Staff in 1967), and Yeshiyahu Gavish (head of the Southern Command in 1967): Amnon Kapeliouk, "Israël était-il réellement menacé d'extermination?" *Le Monde*, June 3, 1972. See also Joseph Ryan, "The Myth of Annihilation and the Six-Day War," *Worldview*, September 1973, 38–42, which summarizes the "war of the generals" waged against this particular untruth: https://carnegiecouncil-media.storage.googleapis.com/files /v16_i009_a009.pdf.

5. It has been falsely claimed that Egypt was about to launch a surprise air attack on Israeli air bases on May 27, 1967, and was dissuaded only by the efforts of the United States and USSR: see William Quandt, *Peace Process* (Washington, DC: Brookings Institution, 1993), 512n38. The Israeli military apparently believed in this possibility, but while there was such an Egyptian contingency plan code-

named Fajr (Dawn), it was never seriously considered by Egypt's leaders, who were intensely discouraged from attacking by both the United States and USSR: see Avi Shlaim, "Israel: Poor Little Samson," in *The 1967 Arab-Israeli War*, ed. Roger Louis and Avi Shlaim (New York: Cambridge University Press, 2012), 30. A high-level Egyptian delegation was in Moscow at this time, and their Soviet interlocutors, including Soviet premier Alexei Kosygin, defense minister Andrei Grechko, and foreign minister Andrei Gromyko, all strongly advised restraint on the Egyptians: for details based on an interview with the Egyptian defense minister, Shams Badran, the accounts of several other participants, and the minutes of the meetings, see Hassan Elbahtimy, "Did the Soviet Union Deliberately Instigate the 1967 War?" Wilson Center History and Public Policy blog (his conclusion in response to the question in his title is: no), https://www.wilsoncenter .org/blog-post/did-the-soviet-union-deliberately-instigate-the-1967-war-the -middle-east.

　　For a fuller exposition of the sources and his conclusions, see Hassan Elbahtimy, "Allies at Arm's Length: Redefining Soviet Egyptian Relations in the 1967 Arab-Israeli War," *Journal of Strategic Studies* (February 2018), https://doi .org/10.1080/01402390.2018.1438893. See also Hassan Elbahtimy, "Missing the Mark: Dimona and Egypt's Slide into the 1967 Arab-Israeli War," *Nonproliferation Review* 25, nos. 5–6 (2018): 385–97, https://www.tandfonline.com/doi/full /10.1080/10736700.2018.1559482.

6. One of the first and perhaps the most influential of those who originally spread this myth was Israeli Foreign Minister Abba Eban. In one of his famous bon mots, he told the Security Council on June 8, 1967, that while many doubted Israel's "prospect of security and survival . . . The fact is that we turned out to be less cooperative than some might have hoped with the plan for our extinction." United Nations Security Council Official Records, 1351 Meeting, June 8, 1967, S/PV.1351. For more details on the rebuttal of this myth and its endurance, see Joseph Ryan, "The Myth of Annihilation and the Six-Day War," 38–42.

7. Secretary of State Mike Pompeo invoked the myth of Israel being on the brink of extermination in 1967 to justify the Trump administration's recognition of Israeli sovereignty over the Golan Heights, saying, "This is an incredible, unique situation. Israel was fighting a defensive battle to save its nation, and it cannot be the case that a U.N. resolution is a suicide pact." David Halbfinger and Isabel Kershner, "Netanyahu Says Golan Heights Move 'Proves You Can' Keep Occupied Territory," *New York Times*, March 26, 2019, https://www.nytimes.com/2019/03 /26/world/middleeast/golan-heights-israel-netanyahu.html.

8. For a summary of these issues, see Elbahtimy "Allies at Arm's Length," and Eugene Rogan and Tewfik Aclimandos, "The Yemen War and Egypt's War Preparedness," in *The 1967 Arab-Israeli War: Origins and Consequences*, ed. W. Roger Louis and Avi Shlaim (Cambridge: Cambridge University Press, 2012). See also Jesse Ferris, *Nasser's Gamble: How Intervention in Yemen Caused the Six-Day War and the Decline of Egyptian Power* (Princeton, NJ: Princeton University Press, 2012).

9. Michael Oren, *Six Days of War: June 1967 and the Making of the Modern Middle East* (Oxford: Oxford University Press, 2002), notes that the surprise air attacks were "long planned" (p. 202), and that a range of long-standing contingency plans existed for attacking and occupying the Syrian Golan Heights (p. 154), the West Bank and East Jerusalem (p. 155), and the Sinai Peninsula (p. 153).

10. Times have changed at the UN: this division is now called Political Affairs and is usually headed by an American.

11. My father can be seen briefly rising in the last row around the council table just as the resolution is passed (presumably to confirm the vote count) in a Universal Newsreel clip on the June 9 cease-fire vote, which is embedded in the Wikipedia article on the June war: http://en.wikipedia.org/wiki/Six-Day_War.

12. United Nations Security Council Official Records, 1352nd Meeting, June 9, 1967, S/PV.1352.

13. See Itamar Rabinovich, *The Road Not Taken: Early Arab-Israeli Negotiations* (New York: Oxford University Press, 1991); and Shlaim, *The Iron Wall*.

14. France had secretly provided the necessary technology for Israel's nuclear weapons, while the Israeli government systematically deceived the Americans about the nature of their nuclear program. For a 1987 Department of Defense report that was declassified by court order in 2015 touching on the technical level of Israel's nuclear weapons development, see: http://www.courthousenews.com/2015/02/12/nuc%20report.pdf. For the best description of Israel's deception of the United States regarding its nuclear program, see Avner Cohen, *Israel and the Bomb* (New York: Columbia University Press, 1999). See also Cohen's work on Israeli nuclear weapons with the Nuclear Proliferation International History Project at the Woodrow Wilson International Center for Scholars.

15. John F. Kennedy Presidential Library and Archive, http://www.jfklibrary.org/Asset-Viewer/Archives/JFKPOF-135-001.aspx. In his letter, the future president predicted nine years ahead of the event that the partition of Palestine would eventually be the outcome of the conflict.

16. Fortas's biographer, Laura Kalman, described him as a "Jew who cared more about Israel than Judaism" in *Abe Fortas: A Biography* (New Haven: Yale University Press, 1990).

17. References on Bundy et al. can be found in: https://moderate.wordpress.com/2007/06/22/lyndon-johnson-was-first-to-align-us-policy-with-israel%E2%80%99s-policies/.

18. Feinberg was president of the American Bank and Trust Company and a substantial contributor to the Democratic Party. Krim was president of United Artists and chairman of the Democratic National Party Finance Committee.

19. On Mathilde Krim see Deirdre Carmody, "Painful Political Lessons for AIDS Crusader," *New York Times*, January 30, 1991, http://www.nytimes.com/1990/01/30/nyregion/painful-political-lesson-for-aids-crusader.html; Philip Weiss, "The Not-so-Secret Life of Mathilde Krim," Mondoweiss, January 26, 2018, http://mondoweiss.net/2018/01/secret-life-mathilde; and the account of Grace Halsell, who worked in the White House as a staff writer for the president in 1967,

"How LBJ's Vietnam War Paralyzed His Mideast Policymakers," *Washington Report on Middle East Affairs*, June 1993, 20, http://www.wrmea.org/1993-june /how-lbj-s-vietnam-war-paralyzed-his-mideast-policymakers.html.

20. The official US record of the meeting is in *Foreign Relations*, 1967, Document 124, "Memorandum for the Record, June 1, 1967, Conversation between Major General Meir Amit and Secretary McNamara," https://2001-2009.state.gov/r /pa/ho/frus/johnsonlb/xix/28055.htm. For Amit's account, see Richard Parker, ed., *The Six-Day War: A Retrospective* (Gainesville: University Press of Florida, 1996), 139. The US account is vaguer than that of Amit, noting only that the general said that "he feels extreme measures are needed quickly," and that McNamara "asked Gen. Amit how many casualties he thought he would incur in an attack in the Sinai," and promised him that he would "convey Amit's views to the president." Although the official US documents and accounts of this meeting by Amit and others have long been available, the manifestly false view that the United States did not give Israel a green light to attack persists. See, e.g., Michael Oren's detailed but flawed *Six Days of War*, 146–47. Much better on this (and nearly every other) aspect of the 1967 war are Tom Segev, *1967: Israel, the War, and the Year That Transformed the Middle East* (New York: Metropolitan, 2007), 329–34; and Guy Laron, *The Six-Day War: The Breaking of the Middle East* (New Haven: Yale University Press, 2017), 278–80, 283–84.

21. Oren, *Six Days of War*, 153–55, 202.

22. I was present at this meeting, to which my father had brought me. El-Farra later spoke on the record about this American collusion with Israel in an oral history: http://www.unmultimedia.org/oralhistory/2013/01/el-farra-muhammad/.

23. United Nations Security Council Official Records, 1382nd Meeting, November 22, 1967, S/PV.1382, https://unispal.un.org/DPA/DPR/unispal.nsf/db942872b9eae4 54852560f6005a76fb/9f5f09a80bb6878b0525672300565063?OpenDocument.

24. *Sunday Times*, June 15, 1969.

25. This was during a volatile phase of the Lebanese civil war. Adam Howard, ed., *FRUS 1969–1976*, XXVI, *Arab-Israeli Dispute*, "Memorandum of Conversation," March 24, 1976 (Washington, DC: US Government Printing Office, 2012), 967.

26. According to a 2018 poll by the Arab Center for Research and Policy Studies, for every single year since 2011, over 84 percent of those polled in eleven Arab countries opposed recognition of Israel, with the main reason given for this opposition being its occupation of Palestinian lands. From 2017 to 2018, 87 percent were against recognition, with only 8 percent in favor. Three-quarters of respondents in that year considered Palestine an Arab cause, while 82 percent considered Israel the main foreign threat to the region. Negative attitudes toward US policy have gone from 49 percent in 2014 to 79 percent from 2017 to 2018: Arab Opinion Index, 2017–2018: Main Results in Brief (Washington, DC: Arab Center, 2018), file:///C:/Users/rik2101/Downloads/Arab%20Opinion%20Index-2017-2018.pdf.

27. As early as 1977, the United States made efforts to convince the PLO to accept SC 242 via the medium of indirect contacts with the organization. See Adam

Howard, ed., *FRUS*, 1977–1980, vol. VIII, Arab-Israeli Dispute, January 1977–August 1978, "Telegram from the Department of State to the Embassy in Lebanon," Washington, DC, August 17, 1977, 477, http://history.state.gov /historicaldocuments/frus1977-80v08/d93.

28. Ahmad Samih Khalidi, "Ripples of the 1967 War," *Cairo Review of Global Affairs* 20 (2017), 8.

29. The Arabic title is *al-Waqa'i' al-ghariba fi ikhtifa' Sa'id abi Nahs, al-mutasha'il.* The book was first published in Haifa in 1974, was immediately republished in Beirut, has been widely available ever since, and was later adapted for the stage as a popular one-man show by the leading Palestinian actor Muhammad Bakri, whom I saw perform it at the al-Qasaba theater in Jerusalem in the 1990s.

30. For the best treatment of Kanafani's writings, see the sections on him in Bashir Abu Manneh, *The Palestinian Novel: From 1948 to the Present* (Cambridge: Cambridge University Press, 2016), 71–95; and Barbara Harlow, *After Lives: Legacies of Revolutionary Writing* (Chicago: Haymarket, 1996). Kanafani's work has been translated into English by Barbara Harlow, Hilary Kilpatrick, and May Jayyusi, among others.

31. Notably *al-Adab al-filastini al-muqawim tahta al-ihtilal, 1948–1968* [Palestinian resistance literature under occupation, 1948–1968], 3rd ed. (Beirut: Institute for Palestine Studies, 2012).

32. The Israeli security services do not normally claim such assassinations. However, according to a seven-hundred-page book based on interviews with hundreds of senior intelligence officials and ample documentation by Ronen Bergman, *Rise and Kill First: The Secret History of Israel's Targeted Assassinations* (New York: Random House, 2018), 656fn, Kanafani was murdered by the Mossad. Crammed with details, Bergman's book is an authoritative account by someone closely connected to the intelligence milieu of Israel's liquidation of hundreds of Palestinian leaders and militants over several generations. It is severely marred by its tone of breathless admiration for those who planned and carried out these killings, and its acceptance of the unreflective, eliminationist zero-sum logic that is apparent from its title, taken from the Talmudic injunction, "If someone comes to kill you, rise up and kill him first." The title is telling: it suggests that Israel's assassinations of Palestinian leaders are justified because they would have killed Israelis were it not for these "targeted assassinations." For a critical but appreciative assessment of the book, see the review essay by Paul Aaron, "How Israel Assassinates Its 'Enemies': Ronen Bergman Counts the Ways," *Journal of Palestine Studies* 47, no. 3 (Spring 2018), 103–5.

33. The best study of MAN is Walid Kazziha, *Revolutionary Transformation in the Arab World: Habash and His Comrades from Nationalism to Marxism* (London: Charles Knight, 1975).

34. For more details, see the memoirs of Amjad Ghanma, *Jam'iyat al-'Urwa al-Wuthqa: Nash'atuha wa-nashatatuha* [The 'Urwa al-Wuthqa Society: Its origins and its activities] (Beirut: Riad El-Rayyes, 2002). He reproduces, on page 124, a photo of the "Administrative Committee" of the group in 1937–38 including my

father, with Zureiq and the AUB president, Bayard Dodge, sitting in the front row. The name of the group echoes that of the famous pan-Islamic nationalist publication produced in Paris by Jamal al-Din al-Afghani and Muhammad 'Abdu in the early 1880s, which took its name from a Quranic phrase, 2:256.

35. *Ma'na al-nakba* [The meaning of the catastrophe] (Beirut: Dar al-'Ilm lil-Milayin, 1948). This short work has been republished repeatedly, most recently in 2009 by the Institute for Palestine Studies, together with other early writings drawing on the lessons of the 1948 defeat by Musa al-'Alami ('*Ibrat Filastin* [The lesson of Palestine]), Qadri Touqan (*Ba'd al-nakba* [After the catastrophe]), and George Hanna (*Tariq al-khalas* [The path to salvation]).

36. See my article, "The 1967 War and the Demise of Arab Nationalism: Chronicle of a Death Foretold," in *The 1967 Arab-Israeli War*, ed. Louis and Shlaim, 264–84, for a discussion of how the 1967 defeat affected Arab nationalism and the reviving Palestinian national movement.

37. The standard work on the Palestinian resistance movement is Yezid Sayigh, *Armed Struggle and the Search for State: The Palestinian National Movement, 1949–1993* (Oxford: Oxford University Press, 1997). Two excellent general histories of the conflict are Charles D. Smith, *Palestine and the Arab-Israeli Conflict: A History with Documents*, 9th ed. (New York: Bedford/St. Martin's, 2016); and James Gelvin, *The Israel-Palestine Conflict: One Hundred Years of War*, 3rd ed. (Cambridge: Cambridge University Press, 2014). See also Baruch Kimmerling and Joel Migdal, *Palestinians: The Making of a People* (New York: The Free Press, 1993); and William Quandt, Fuad Jabber, and Ann Lesch, *The Politics of Palestinian Nationalism* (Oakland: University of California Press, 1973).

38. An excellent study of this topic is Paul Chamberlin, *The Global Offensive: The United States, the Palestine Liberation Organization, and the Making of the Post-Cold War Order* (Oxford, Oxford University Press, 2012).

39. For the most sophisticated analysis of how Israel managed to establish its discursive hegemony in the United States, see Kaplan, *Our American Israel*, and Novick, *The Holocaust in American Life*.

40. Bergman, *Rise and Kill First*, 162–74, gives a detailed description of this operation, in which Barak dressed as a woman.

41. Bergman, *Rise and Kill First*, 117–18, 248–61, includes many examples of such assassination attempts on 'Arafat. For an analysis of this assassination strategy and an antidote to Bergman's exculpatory approach, see Paul Aaron's review of the book, "How Israel Assassinates Its 'Enemies,'" and his two-part article, "The Idolatry of Force: How Israel Embraced Targeted Killing," and "The Idolatry of Force (Part II): Militarism in Israel's Garrison State," *Journal of Palestine Studies* 46, no. 4 (Summer 2017), 75–99, and 48, no. 2 (Winter 2019), 58–77.

42. Much of the material in this chapter and the next is based on English translations of documents from the secret appendices to the Kahan Commission of inquiry into the 1982 Sabra and Shatila massacres. In what follows, I have cited them as Kahan Papers [KP] I through VI. The documents are available on the website of the Institute for Palestine Studies: https://palestinesquare.com/2018/09/25/the

-sabra-and-shatila-massacre-new-evidence/. William Quandt, Professor Emeritus at the University of Virginia and a senior staff member of the National Security Council during the administration of President Jimmy Carter, provided IPS with scanned copies of these documents. In the course of a libel suit brought against *Time* magazine by Ariel Sharon, Quandt served as a consultant to the defense lawyers for *Time*. He received these documents as translated selections from the original Hebrew from the magazine's law firm. Experts familiar with such documents have attested that they constitute the bulk of the unpublished appendices of the Kahan report.

In KP IV, Meeting between Sharon and Bashir Gemayel, Beirut, July 8, 1982, Doc. 5, 229ff, where Gemayel asks if Israel would have any objection to his bulldozing the Palestinian refugee camps in the South of Lebanon so the refugees would not remain in the south, Sharon replied, "this is not our business: we do not want to deal with Lebanon's internal affairs." During a meeting between Sharon and Pierre and Bashir Gemayel, August 21, 1982, (KP V, 2–9), Sharon told them: "A question was raised before, what would happen to the Palestinian camps once the terrorists withdraw. . . . You've got to act . . . so that there be no terrorists, you've got to clean the camps." For more on the eliminationist logic shared by Sharon, Gemayel, and their lieutenants, see chapter 5, below.

43. Pierre Gemayel had founded the party after he visited Nazi Germany during the 1936 Olympic Games, in which he participated as the goalkeeper of the Lebanese soccer team.

44. *Jerusalem Post*, October 15, 1982. Ze'ev Schiff and Ehud Ya'ari, in *Israel's Lebanon War* (New York: Simon and Schuster, 1983), 20, indicate that Col. Binyamin Ben-Eliezer, the senior Israeli liaison officer with the LF and later Israeli minister of defense and deputy prime minister, was present at the command post where the LF directed the siege of Tal al-Za'tar in July, weeks before the camp fell. Schiff and Yaari recount the extensive collaboration between the Israeli military and intelligence services and the LF in this and subsequent periods, as does Bergman, *Rise and Kill First*.

45. KP III, minutes of meeting of Knesset Defense and Foreign Affairs Committee, September 24, 1982, 224–25.

46. Ibid., 225–26.

47. WAFA on August 13, 1976, identified the senior Syrian military intelligence officer in Lebanon, Col. Ali Madani, as being present in the LF command post in order to "supervise" the operation against the camp: see *al-Nahar* and *al-Safir*, August 13, 1976, for reports on Hassan Sabri al-Kholi's press conference on August 12, 1976. Helena Cobban, who covered the war as a reporter for the *Christian Science Monitor* and was a witness to the fall of the camp, states that Col. Madani was seen in the LF command post by other Western journalists: *The Palestinian Liberation Organization* (Cambridge: Cambridge University Press, 1984), 281n35. Other accounts identify his subordinate, Col. Muhammad Kholi, as being present as well.

48. Adam Howard, ed., *FRUS 1969–1976*, XXVI, Arab-Israeli Dispute, "Minutes of Washington Special Actions Group Meeting," Washington, DC, March 24, 1976, 963.

49. Kissinger made this statement regarding American abandonment of the Kurds of Iraq to the House Permanent Select Committee on Intelligence headed by Congressman Otis Pike in 1975.

50. KP, I, 18. This is a document apparently prepared for the Kahan Commission by the Defense Ministry in response to accusations against Sharon. Sharon is quoted on page 48 of this document as saying that "about 130 Phalange" received training in Israel, but gives the same figure for the amount of military aid.

51. Bergman, *Rise and Kill First*, 225–61.

52. Adam Howard, ed., *FRUS* 1969–1976, XXVI, Arab-Israeli Dispute, "Minutes of Washington Special Actions Group Meeting," Washington, DC, March 24, 1976, 963.

53. Ibid.

54. Henry Kissinger, *Years of Renewal* (New York: Touchstone, 1999), 351.

55. This memo was initially only available in Meron Medzini, ed., *Israel's Foreign Relations: Selected Documents, 1974–1977*, vol. 3 (Jerusalem: Ministry of Foreign Affairs, 1982), 281–90. The US government published it twenty years later in Adam Howard, ed., *FRUS*, 1969–1976, XXVI, Arab-Israeli Dispute, "Memorandum of Agreement between the Governments of Israel and the United States." A secret letter of the same date from President Ford to Israeli Prime Minister Yitzhak Rabin enshrined another crucial commitment, whereby the United States pledged that during any peace negotiations it would "make every effort to coordinate with Israel its proposals with a view to refraining from putting forward proposals that Israel would find unsatisfactory," 838–40.

56. Adam Howard, ed., *FRUS*, 1969–1976, XXVI, Arab-Israeli Dispute, "Minutes of National Security Council Meeting," Washington, DC, April 7, 1976, 1017.

57. Ibid., 831–32. See also Patrick Seale, *Asad: The Struggle for the Middle East* (Oakland: University of California Press, 1989), 278–84.

58. The description of this operation by Bergman, *Rise and Kill First*, 214–24, includes errors, such as a mention that in 1978 an Israeli undercover agent used as a cover work at an NGO "at a shelter in the Tel al-Zaatar refugee camp." The camp was destroyed two years earlier. This NGO may have been an orphanage for children who had survived the massacre at the camp, Bayt Atfal al-Sumud.

59. Bergman, *Rise and Kill First*, 242–43ff. On the "Front for the Liberation of Lebanon from Foreigners," which we now know was no more than a front group for the Israeli security services, see Remi Brulin, "The Remarkable Disappearing Act of Israel's Car-Bombing Campaign in Lebanon," Mondoweiss, May 7, 2018, https://mondoweiss.net/2018/05/remarkable-disappearing-terrorism.

60. For more on Dean's charges, see Philip Weiss, "New Book Gives Credence to US Ambassador's Claim That Israel Tried to Assassinate Him," Mondoweiss, August 23, 2018, https://mondoweiss.net/2018/08/credence-ambassadors-assassinate/.

61. The late Ambassador Dean graciously provided me with documents that cover the entire period of his ambassadorship in Beirut, from late 1978 until 1981. Those concerning the PLO are mainly from 1979. There are also at least a half dozen classified cables dealing with the contacts undertaken by Parker and Dean

with one of these intermediaries, my cousin Walid Khalidi, in Wikileaks: see, e.g., https://search.wikileaks.org/?s=1&q=khalidi&sort=0.

62. Ambassador Dean provided copies of these documents to the Institute for Palestine Studies, where they are available for consultation by researchers.

63. "Telegram from Secretary of State Vance's Delegation to Certain Diplomatic Posts," October 1, 1977, *FRUS, 1977–80, Arab-Israeli Dispute*, vol. 8, 634–36.

64. The definitive study of this topic is Seth Anziska, *Preventing Palestine: A Political History from Camp David to Oslo* (Princeton, NJ: Princeton University Press, 2018).

65. The most rigorous account of how Begin did this, based on an exhaustive study of previously unrevealed Israeli and American documents, and how he thereby laid the foundation for subsequent negotiations, including at Madrid, Washington, and Oslo in the 1990s, is Anziska, *Preventing Palestine*.

CHAPTER 4

1. http://avalon.law.yale.edu/19th_century/hague02.asp#art25.

2. Quoted in Alexander Cockburn, "A Word Not Fit to Print," *Village Voice*, September 22, 1982.

3. KP III, 196. Gur was speaking to Sharon during a meeting of the Knesset Defense and Foreign Affairs committee on June 10, 1982.

4. Chaim Herzog, *The Arab-Israeli Wars: War and Peace in the Middle East from the War of Independence Through Lebanon*, rev. ed. (New York: Random House, 1985), 344, gives the figure of eight divisions. Herzog was a retired major general, former chief of military intelligence, and later president of Israel. Other authoritative Israeli sources have suggested that as many as nine divisions were eventually involved in the invasion force.

5. This is according to the official report of the Lebanese General Security Services (*Da'irat al-Amn al-'Am*), which stated that 84 percent of the casualties in Beirut were civilians: *Washington Post*, December 2, 1982. These figures were understandably not necessarily fully accurate, given wartime circumstances.

6. The Palestine News Agency, WAFA, on August 14, 1982, reported that obituaries in the Israeli press of soldiers killed in Lebanon for the ten weeks of combat totaled 453. This discrepancy may have resulted because the Israeli military issued figures only on those killed in action, not those who died later of their wounds or were otherwise killed in a combat theater: cited in *Under Siege*, 199–200n4.

7. *The Jerusalem Post*, October 10, 1983. Sharon himself mentioned 2,500 Israeli casualties to Pierre and Bashir Gemayel on August 21, 1982: KP IV, 5. Israeli military casualties from June 1982 until the partial withdrawal of June 1985 were over 4,500. Over 500 additional Israeli soldiers were killed between 1985 and the end of the occupation of South Lebanon in May 2000, for a total of well over 800 killed from 1982 until 2000. The war and occupation of Lebanon thus produced Israel's third-highest overall military casualty toll, after the 1948 and 1973 wars, and ahead of the 1956 and 1967 wars and the 1968–70 War of Attrition along the Suez Canal.

8. Probably because of my prior role in WAFA, where I had helped Mona set up the new English service, a few journalists who were unaware of the ground rules under which I spoke to them during the war mistakenly described me as "Director of WAFA" or as "a PLO spokesman," neither of which I was (Thomas Friedman, "Palestinians Say Invaders Are Seeking to Destroy P.L.O. and Idea of a State," *New York Times*, June 9, 1982). The former appellation would have surprised WAFA's actual director, Ziyad 'Abd al-Fattah, and Ahmad 'Abd al-Rahman and Mahmud al-Labadi, who were the PLO's official spokesmen, the former for the Arabic media, and the latter for the foreign press. As head of the PLO Foreign Information section, al-Labadi was the sole person responsible for dealings with foreign journalists. All three of these officials were duty bound to put forward the position of the PLO, which I was not obliged to do. When I talked to Western journalists, it was not in any official capacity, but rather anonymously, as "an informed Palestinian source." Almost all journalists respected this convention.

9. David Shipler, "Cease-Fire in Border Fighting Declared by Israel and PLO," *New York Times*, July 25, 1981, https://www.nytimes.com/1981/07/25/world/cease -fire-border-fighting-declared-israel-plo-us-sees-hope-for-wider-peace.html.

10. I knew Habib fleetingly from when I was a teenager in Seoul accompanying my father, who from 1962 to 1965 held the top UN civilian post in South Korea, where Habib was a senior diplomat in the US embassy. He and his wife had socialized with my parents, and my mother and Mrs. Habib often played bridge together at our house. I benefited from this acquaintance when Habib agreed to be interviewed for my book on the PLO during the Lebanon War: *Under Siege: PLO Decisionmaking During the 1982 War*.

11. This was not the first time I had met Primakov, and as always I was impressed by his knowledge of Middle East politics, his intelligence, and his candor. Following the dissolution of the USSR, he became the first head of Russia's intelligence service, and then foreign minister and finally prime minister. When he was prime minister, he helped an Austrian colleague and me to reach an agreement with the Russian state archives for the publication of Soviet diplomatic documents on the Middle East from the 1940s through the 1980s. The project was aborted when Primakov was removed from office by President Boris Yeltsin in 1999. His account of the 1982 war can be found in *Russia and the Arabs: Behind the Scenes in the Middle East from the Cold War to the Present* (New York: Basic Books, 2009), 199–205.

12. In interviews in Tunis afterwards, both Abu Iyad and Abu Jihad confirmed to me that the PLO leadership had long known that war was coming, and had prepared accordingly: *Under Siege*, 198n21.

13. Arafat was apparently not surprised. In a speech in March 1982, he had predicted that the PLO and its allies would have to fight at Khaldeh: *Under Siege*, 198n20. The PLO sector commander there, Col. Abdullah Siyam, was killed in this battle on June 12, the highest-ranking PLO officer to die during the war. Two days earlier, the highest-ranking Israeli officer ever to die in combat, Maj. Gen.

Yukutiel Adam, a former deputy chief of staff and Mossad director-designate, had been killed by Palestinian fighters just down the coast in Damour, an area that had been thought pacified: *Under Siege*, 80–81.

14. This was revealed by Alexander Cockburn, "A Word Not Fit to Print," *Village Voice*, September 22, 1982.

15. Most Western journalists had decamped to the Commodore Hotel from the legendary St. George Hotel by the sea on the Corniche, which was looted and burned in 1975. The St. George had long served as the headquarters for foreign journalists, diplomats, spies, arms dealers, and other less savory types. Although more modest than the luxurious St. George, and without its spectacular sea views, the Commodore had the inestimable virtue of being relatively far from most of the battlefronts of the civil war. Said Abu Rish, *The St. George Hotel Bar* (London: Bloomsbury, 1989), chronicles some of the intrigues that took place there, noting that famous intelligence agents such as Kim Philby and Miles Copeland were habitués.

16. Ze'ev Schiff and Ehud Ya'ari, *Israel's Lebanon War* (New York: Simon and Schuster, 1983), show in some detail how extensive the Israeli espionage network in Lebanon was, as does Bergman, *Rise and Kill First*.

17. Bergman, *Rise and Kill First*, says that concerted efforts to kill the entire PLO leadership dated back at least to 1981: 244–47.

18. "123 Reported Dead, 550 Injured as Israelis Bomb PLO Targets," *New York Times*, July 18, 1981, https://www.nytimes.com/1981/07/18/world/123-reported -dead-550-injured-israelis-bomb-plo-targets-un-council-meets-beirut.html.

19. "Begin Compares Arafat to Hitler," UPI, August 5, 1982, http://www.upi.com /Archives/1982/08/05/Begin-compares-Arafat-to-Hitler/2671397368000/.

20. Bergman, *Rise and Kill First*, indicates that Israeli efforts to assassinate 'Arafat began in 1967, 117–18. On 248–61 he includes accounts of multiple attempts to kill him during the 1982 war.

21. Interview, Dr. Lamya Khalidi, Nice, June 1, 2018. There is a photo in Bergman, *Rise and Kill First*, between pages 264–65, of the commander of an Israeli assassination squad "dressed as a beggar" sitting in a street in an unidentified Arab city, probably Beirut.

22. This double agent had been infiltrated by Abu Iyad's services into the anti-PLO Abu Nidal faction based in Libya in order to undermine that group, an operation that was highly successful. He was later hired as a driver by one of Abu Iyad's top lieutenants, Abu al-Hol [Ha'il 'Abd al-Hamid]. This agent turned out to have been suborned himself (presumably by the Iraqi regime, which supported the Abu Nidal group and which was infuriated because Abu Iyad had openly opposed its invasion of Kuwait). He assassinated Abu Iyad, Abu al-Hol, and an aide on January 14, 1991, two days before the US offensive to expel Iraqi forces from Kuwait.

23. This may be the bombing described in Bergman, *Rise and Kill First*, 256: "Once they [the assassination squad] even heard 'Arafat himself on the phone and sent in a pair of fighter-bombers that razed the building, but 'Arafat had left 'not more than thirty seconds earlier,' according to Dayan [commander of the unit]." This

may be the same attack mentioned on pages 258–59 that is incorrectly dated as August 5, and incorrectly described as being directed against "the Sana'i office block, in West Beirut, where Arafat was supposed to be attending a meeting." According to Bergman, Chief of Staff Rafael Eitan personally participated in this bombing.

24. *Under Siege*, 97. *Newsweek* reporter Tony Clifton was on the scene, as was John Bulloch of the *Daily Telegraph*. Clifton offers a harrowing description of the aftermath, and says that the death toll may have been as high as 260: Tony Clifton and Catherine Leroy, *God Cried* (London: Quartet Books, 1983), 45–46. See also John Bulloch, *Final Conflict: The War in Lebanon* (London: Century, 1983), 132–33.

25. For details, see *Under Siege*, 88 and 202n39. See also Bergman, *Rise and Kill First*, 242–43, which gives details of the use of car bombs in Lebanon by the Israeli intelligence services.

26. In *Under Siege* I recounted how the PLO came to its decision to evacuate Beirut. I wrote that book on the basis of access to PLO archives that were then located in Tunis (those archives and other PLO offices were bombed by Israel on October 1, 1985, killing one of the archivists who had helped me), together with interviews with the leading American, French, and Palestinian participants in the negotiations.

27. Anziska, *Preventing Palestine*, 201.

28. Palestinians always suspected that the Abu Nidal group, which served at different times as a front for the Libyan, Iraqi, and Syrian intelligence agencies, was also penetrated by the Israeli Mossad. Bergman, *Rise and Kill First*, says that according to his Israeli sources, "British intelligence had a double agent inside the Abu Nidal cell" that carried out the attack on Argov (249). Although Bergman describes Israeli double agents as present in virtually every group considered hostile to Israel, in spite of the Abu Nidal group's spectacular attacks on Israeli and Jewish targets, his book makes no mention of its penetration by Israeli double agents, nor indeed does it have a proper index entry for the group.

29. Anziska, *Preventing Palestine*, 201–2.

30. My mother was shot and was lucky to have been only lightly wounded when she drove past another such checkpoint, this one manned by Syrian troops, in February 1977.

31. They included politicians such as Rashid Karami, Sa'eb Salam, and Salim al-Hoss, who had served as prime ministers of Lebanon under a formula that went back to the country's independence in 1943, and who were traditionally aligned with the mainly Sunni Palestinian political and military presence in Lebanon.

32. *Under Siege*, 65, 88, and 201n16. Multiple documents from the secret appendices to the Kahan Commission papers of Inquiry into the Sabra and Shatila massacres refer to massacres of Druze by the LF in the Shouf: KP I, 5; KP II, 107–8; KP III, 192; KP IV, 254, 265, 296; KP V, 56, 58; KP VI, 78. These documents can be found at: https://palestinesquare.com/2018/09/25/the-sabra-and-shatila -massacre-new-evidence/.

33. The text of the Eleven-Point Plan can be found in *Under Siege*, 183–84.

34. Beyond the massacres in the Shouf in late June and early July, documents in the secret appendices to the Kahan Commission report other atrocities: the disappearance and presumed murder of 1,200 people in Beirut at the hands of forces controlled by Elie Hobeika, chief of intelligence of the LF (KP II, 1, and KP V, 58), and a Mossad report on 500 people "liquidated" at LF roadblocks by June 23: KP II, 3, and KP VI, 56. See: https://palestinesquare.com/2018/09/25/the-sabra-and-shatila-massacre-new-evidence/.

35. *Under Siege*, 171, citing the original documents in the PLO archives.

36. The entire US-Lebanese correspondence can be found in the *Department of State Bulletin*, September 1982, vol. 82, no. 2066, 2–5.

37. Lebanese police reports cited "at least 128 killed" and over 400 wounded that day: *Under Siege*, 204n67, quoting an AP report published in the *New York Times*, August 13, 1982.

38. Diary entry for August 12, 1982, in Ronald Reagan, *The Reagan Diaries*, ed. Douglas Brinkley (New York: HarperCollins, 2007), 98.

39. For some time afterward, they were also afraid every time they heard a plane or a helicopter overhead.

40. Malcolm Kerr himself was assassinated right outside his office just sixteen months later, as were a number of my AUB colleagues.

41. Jenkins later shared a Pulitzer Prize with Thomas Friedman of the *New York Times* for reportage on the Sabra and Shatila massacre.

42. The most complete analysis of the number of victims of the massacre, based on extensive interviews and painstaking research, is by the distinguished Palestinian historian Bayan Nuwayhid al-Hout, who in *Sabra and Shatila: September 1982* (Ann Arbor: Pluto, 2004), established a minimum of close to 1,400 killed. She notes, however, that as many victims were abducted and never found, the actual number was undoubtedly larger, and is unknowable.

43. The graphic novel is by Ari Folman and David Polonsky (New York: Metropolitan Books, 2009). According to Folman's account in *Waltz with Bashir*, his unit fired the flares, creating "a brightly lit sky that helped other people kill" (107). Although the book and the film are unsparing in their depiction of the atrocity that is at the core of the entire story, their primary focus is on the subsequent psychological anguish of the Israelis who enabled the killers to do their work, rather than the suffering of the nameless victims, which is depicted at the end. In this, it has more than a passing resemblance to the well-known Israeli genre of "shooting and crying."

44. In the end, Folman's friend lets Folman off the hook with a bit of pop psychology. He tells him that it was only "in your perception," as a nineteen-year-old child of Holocaust survivors, that there was no difference between those who carried out the massacre and the Israelis in the circles surrounding them, and that "You felt guilty. . . . Against your will you were cast in the role of Nazi. . . . You fired the flares. But you didn't carry out the massacre."

45. The text of the Kahan Commission report can be found at http://www.jewishvirtuallibrary.org/jsource/History/kahan.html. A scathing critique of the

report's many flaws and omissions can be found in Noam Chomsky, *Fateful Triangle: The United States, Israel, and the Palestinians*, 2nd ed. (Cambridge, MA: South End Press, 1999), 397–410.

46. The documents released by the Israel State Archives in 2012 were made available online by the *New York Times* on the thirtieth anniversary of the Sabra and Shatila massacre, together with an op-ed on the topic by Seth Anziska, who discovered these documents in the archives: "A Preventable Massacre," *New York Times*, September 16, 2012: http://www.nytimes.com/2012/09/17/opinion/a -preventable-massacre.html?ref=opinion. The documents can be found online: "Declassified Documents Shed Light on a 1982 Massacre," *New York Times*, September 16, 2012, http://www.nytimes.com/interactive/2012/09/16/opinion /20120916_lebanondoc.html?ref=opinion.

47. As noted earlier, the English translations of the secret appendices to the report are available on the website of the Institute for Palestine Studies: https:// palestinesquare.com/2018/09/25/the-sabra-and-shatila-massacre-new -evidence/. I have cited them as Kahan Papers [KP] I through VI.

48. As early as July 19, Sharon told Habib that Israeli intelligence reports indicated that the PLO planned to leave behind "nuclei of terrorist infrastructure" and that "this is the idea concealed behind the demand that the MLF [Multilateral Force] protect the refugee camps." KP III, 163. Since this was not true, either Sharon was grossly misinformed, or he was already preparing a pretext for a planned move against the remaining Palestinian presence in Lebanon after the departure of the PLO.

49. "Declassified Documents Shed Light on a 1982 Massacre," *New York Times*, September 16, 2012.

50. KP IV, 273. Sharon also reported to this cabinet meeting that the LF had been sent into Sabra.

51. "Declassified Documents Shed Light on a 1982 Massacre." See also Anziska, *Preventing Palestine*, 217–18.

52. "Declassified Documents Shed Light on a 1982 Massacre." Speaking to the Israeli cabinet on September 16, 1982, Sharon reported on an earlier exchange with Draper, whom he accused of "extraordinary impudence" for contradicting him: KP IV, 274.

53. KP III, 222–26. As is noted in chapter 3, Sharon spoke in detail about Tal al-Za'tar at a closed meeting of the Knesset Defense and Foreign Affairs committee, September 24, 1982, and in the Knesset in October 1982. According to a Mossad report dated June 23, 1982, Bashir Gemayel stated to Mossad representatives at a meeting attended by six of his top advisors that in dealing with the Shi'a, "it is possible they will need several Deir Yassins." For Israeli knowledge about earlier LF massacres during the Israeli invasion of 1982, see notes 32 and 34 above.

54. On July 8, 1982, Bashir Gemayel asked Sharon if he would object if LF used bulldozers to remove the Palestinian camps in the south. Sharon responded, "This is not our business: we do not wish to deal with Lebanon's internal affairs," KP IV, 230. At a meeting with Maj. Gen. Saguy on July 23, 1982, Bashir Gemayel stated that there is a need to deal with the Palestinian "demographic problem,"

and if the Palestinian refugee camps in the south were destroyed most Lebanese would not care, KP VI, 244. At a meeting on August 1, 1982, Gen. Saguy stated that "The time has come for Bashir's men to prepare a plan to deal with the Palestinians," KP VI, 243. On August 21, in response to a question from Sharon about what the LF planned to do with the Palestinian refugee camps, Bashir Gemayel stated, "We are planning a real zoo," KP V, 8. A witness before the Kahan Commission, Lt. Col. Harnof, stated that LF leaders had said that "Sabra would become a zoo and Shatila Beirut's parking lot," noting that they had already carried out massacres of Palestinians in the south, KP VI, 78. The director of the Mossad (from September 1982), Nahum Admoni, told the commission that Bashir Gemayel "was preoccupied with Lebanon's demographic balance . . . When he talked in terms of demographic change it was always in terms of killing and elimination," KP VI, 80. The Mossad director until September 1982, Yitzhak Hofi, said that the LF leaders "talk about solving the Palestinian problem with a hand gesture whose meaning is physical elimination," KP VI, 81.

55. The book by two knowledgeable and respected Israeli journalists, Ze'ev Schiff and Ehud Ya'ari, *Israel's Lebanon War*, is replete with accounts of crucial instances of Israeli decisionmaking and the supportive role of American diplomacy, many of which have been borne out by newly declassified official documents from both sides. See also Schiff's article, "The Green Light," *Foreign Policy* 50 (Spring 1983), 73–85.

56. Anziska, *Preventing Palestine*, 200–201, citing Morris Draper, "Marines in Lebanon, A Ten Year Retrospective: Lessons Learned" (Quantico, VA, 1992), courtesy of Jon Randal.

57. Over a distinguished diplomatic career, Ryan Crocker served as ambassador to six countries, many of them exceedingly difficult posts like Baghdad and Kabul.

58. That was not my last brush with Syrian intelligence. An Arabic translation of *Under Siege*, which included a critical description of the Asad regime's role in the 1982 war, was halted a few years later, out of the Lebanese publisher's fear of the menacing Syrian intelligence services, which dominated Beirut in those days. I was able to publish it in Arabic in serialized form in the Kuwaiti press. The Institute for Palestine Studies finally published an Arabic translation in 2018. While it could not then be published in Arabic in Beirut, Marachot, the publishing house of the Israeli Ministry of Defense, published the book in Hebrew translation in 1988, albeit adding an occasional snide critical marginal note.

59. It took nearly eight months for AUB to obtain a residence permit for him, something that should have taken a couple of weeks: this was the Sureté Générale of the new regime installed by Sharon at work. The nature of Amin Gemayel's election can be seen in Bergman, *Rise and Kill First*, 673n262, which details how Israeli military and security personnel "escorted" Lebanese deputies to the election, and sometimes helped "persuade" them.

60. Before leaving Beirut, I visited the Lebanese senior statesman, Sa'eb Salam, who was related to us by multiple marriages, to interview him about his role during the 1982 war. He answered my questions, but asked to be left out of the book. Just before I left him, he told me about his much speculated-about visit to Bashir Gemayel

days before his assassination. This one-on-one meeting followed an acrimonious secret encounter between Gemayel and Begin at which the former refused Begin's demand to immediately sign a peace treaty with Israel. Details can be found in Schiff and Yaari, *Israel's Lebanon War*, some of which Schiff confirmed to me in an interview (Washington, DC, January 30, 1984). The now dead young president-elect had told him, "You know Sa'eb Bey [an Ottoman honorific acquired by his father], many of my top lieutenants were trained in Israel. I am not at all sure which of them are loyal to Israel, and which to me." Although his relations with Begin had soured before his death, Gemayel had many enemies. The person who planted the explosives that killed him was supposedly a Lebanese leftist working with Syrian intelligence. Transcripts of the interrogation of one of the supposed assassins, Habib al-Shartouni, can be found in the Phalangist newspaper *al-'Amal*: Part 1: https://www.lebanese-forces.com/2019/09/04/bachir-gemayel-chartouni/; Part 2: https://www.lebanese-forces.com/2019/09/02/bachir-gemayel-36/; Part 3: https://www.lebanese-forces.com/2019/09/04/bachir-gemayel-37/.

61. This is one of the conclusions that Amy Kaplan draws in her examination of US support for Israel in *Our American Israel*, 136–77, in a chapter titled "Not the Israel We Have Seen in the Past," although she concludes that in time supporters of Israel succeeded in restoring its image.

62. Interviews with Morris Draper, Robert Dillon, and Philip Habib, Washington, DC, December 14, December 6, and December 3, 1984. These were interviews for *Under Siege*, the idea for which first emerged during the war when I was reading Ibn Khaldun's account of a meeting with Timur [Tamerlane] during his siege of Damascus in 1400 and I chanced to meet with a friend, Dr. Sami Musal-lam. Like me, Sami worked part-time at the IPS, and he was also in charge of the archives of the PLO Chairman's office. I told him that after the war, while I was certainly no Ibn Khaldun, I would like access to those archives to write a docu-mentary account of what we had been witness to during the siege. Sami said that if we survived, and if he managed to get the archives out of Beirut, which he did, he would get 'Arafat's permission, which he also did.

63. I interviewed 'Arafat, Abu Iyad, Abu Jihad, Mahmud 'Abbas [Abu Mazin], Kha-lid and Hani al-Hasan, and Faruq Qaddumi [Abu Lutf] as well as other PLO officials in Tunis in March, August, and December 1984.

64. This massive World War II vessel's bombardment of Druze militias in the Shouf led some Lebanese wits to dub it the *"New Derzi,"* a play on the Arabic word for Druze.

65. Bergman, *Rise and Kill First*, 560–63, coyly intimates at great length that 'Arafat was poisoned by Israeli agents.

CHAPTER 5

1. Caius Cornelius Tacitus, *Agricola and Germania*, tr. K. B. Townsend (London: Methuen, 1893), 33.

2. Reference in this chapter is primarily to the First Intifada, the unarmed and mainly nonviolent uprising that lasted in full force from 1987 to 1993, in distinction from

the second, which started in 2000, and which eventually became an armed uprising featuring the use of suicide bombers by the Palestinians, and the employment of tanks, helicopters, and other heavy weapons by the Israeli occupation forces.

3. Francis X. Clines, "Talk with Rabin: Roots of the Conflict," *New York Times*, February 5, 1988, http://www.nytimes.com/1988/02/05/world/talk-with-rabin -roots-of-the-conflict.html.

4. For an excellent analysis of the impact of the intifada on US opinion toward Israel, see Kaplan, *Our American Israel*, chapter 4.

5. Francis X. Clines, "Talk with Rabin: Roots of the Conflict."

6. David McDowall, *Palestine and Israel: The Uprising and Beyond* (London, I. B. Tauris, 1989), 84.

7. For an acid portrait of Milson and his role, see Flora Lewis, "Foreign Affairs: How to Grow Horns," *New York Times*, April 29, 1982, http://www.nytimes.com /1982/04/29/opinion/foreign-affairs-how-to-grow-horns.html.

8. For an analysis of this particular instance of the old Orientalist phenomenon of experts studying the people they were oppressing, see Gil Eyal, *The Disenchantment of the Orient* (Stanford, CA: Stanford University Press, 2006).

9. "Colonel Says Rabin Ordered Breaking of Palestinians' Bones," Reuters, cited in the *LA Times*, June 22, 1990, http://articles.latimes.com/1990-06-22/news /mn-431_1_rabin-ordered. In his biography, *Yitzhak Rabin: Soldier, Leader, Statesman* (New Haven, CT: Yale University Press, 2017), 156–57, Itamar Rabinovitch denies the accuracy of that quote, while admitting that Rabin "clearly was the author of a policy that sought to defeat the intifada through the use of force."

10. On a trip two years later, on a Fulbright fellowship, I was denied entry into Israel. After many hours of detention, I was allowed to enter due to the intercession of the US consul-general in Tel Aviv, who had been forewarned of my arrival by the State Department.

11. These figures, collected by the Israeli human rights NGO B'tselem, include Palestinians and Israelis killed in the Occupied Territories as well as inside Israel: http://www.btselem.org/statistics/first_intifada_tables.

12. Rabinovich, *Yitzhak Rabin*, 157–58.

13. "Iron-fist Policy Splits Israelis," Jonathan Broder, *Chicago Tribune*, January 26, 1988, http://articles.chicagotribune.com/1988-01-27/news/8803270825_1 _beatings-anti-arab-anti-israeli-violence.

14. Julia Bacha's prizewinning 2017 documentary film, *Naila and the Uprising*, offers a comprehensive portrait of the central role of women in the intifada: https:// www.justvision.org/nailaandtheuprising. See also Amer Shomali's 2014 film, *The Wanted 18*: https://www.youtube.com/watch?v=ekhTuZpMw54.

15. As we have seen, in spite of the divisions it engendered, the revolt effected extensive social and political transformations before it was crushed by 100,000 British troops, backed by their Zionist auxiliaries, as well as the heavy use of air power. See the remarkable article by Charles Anderson, "State Formation from Below."

16. Bergman, *Rise and Kill First*, 311–33, says that Abu Jihad's role in the intifada was the main reason he was killed, noting (323) that some senior Israeli officials later recognized that "the assassination failed to reach its goal," of dampening the intifada, and that for these and other reasons, they came to feel that his killing had been a mistake.

17. Ibid., 316–17, reports that the planners of the operation to kill Abu Jihad deliberately decided to forgo assassinating Mahmud 'Abbas [Abu Mazin], whose home was nearby. Many Palestinians have long suspected that only those perceived by the Israeli security services as outstanding advocates of the Palestinian cause were targeted for liquidation, implying that others were not worth the effort to kill them.

18. The virulence of the rivalry between Syria and the PLO can be discerned from the claim by Bergman, ibid., 304, that undercover Israeli intelligence agents posing as dissident Palestinians covertly passed information on PLO operatives to the Syrian intelligence station in Cyprus. The Syrian security services then "got rid of about 150 PLO people," who were liquidated upon their arrival in Lebanon.

19. For details, see Richard Sale, "Israel Gave Major Aid to Hamas," UPI, February 24, 2001, and Shaul Mishal and Avraham Sela, *The Palestinian Hamas: Vision, Violence, and Coexistence* (New York: Columbia University Press, 2000). These well-connected Israeli authors make it clear that dividing Palestinian ranks was the aim of the Israeli security establishment in encouraging the rise of an Islamist rival to the PLO.

20. After the 1982 war, Shoufani joined the Syrian-backed Fatah rebels opposing 'Arafat's leadership.

21. "Statement by Yasser Arafat—14 December 1988," Israel Ministry of Foreign Affairs, Historical Documents, 1984–88, http://mfa.gov.il/MFA/ForeignPolicy /MFADocuments/Yearbook7/Pages/419%20Statement%20by%20Yasser%20 Arafat-%2014%20December%201988.aspx.

22. *FRUS*, XXVI, *Arab-Israeli Dispute, 1974–76*, Washington, DC: US Government Printing Office, 2012, 838–40, 831–32, https://history.state.gov/historicaldocuments /frus1969-76v26.

23. While as we saw in chapter 4, the Ford letter to Rabin was published by the Israeli Foreign Ministry in its *Israel's Foreign Relations: Selected Documents* series in 1982 and was thereafter available online on the Ministry website, it is never mentioned in Kissinger's voluminous memoirs, and the US government only published it in the *Foreign Relations of the United States* series in 2012, thirty years later.

24. Bergman, *Rise and Kill First*, 311.

25. I heard about this advice, embodied in a memo whose text I have been unable to find, from Ahmad himself, and from others. Some of these themes can be found in selections in Carollee Bengelsdorf, Margaret Cerullo, and Yogesh Chandrani, eds., *The Selected Writings of Eqbal Ahmad* (New York: Columbia University Press, 2006), 77–78, 296–97.

26. In a letter to a "comrade" (recipient name is blacked out) on September 17, 1982, Ahmad later gave the PLO the same advice: while he called for "armed underground resistance" to Israeli occupation forces in Lebanon, in occupied Palestine he advocated "*militant* and *creative* organization of *non-violent political struggle*" [emphasis by author]. Copy of letter in my possession, courtesy of Nubar Hovsepian. See also Ahmad's analysis along these lines in "Pioneering in the Nuclear Age: An Essay on Israel and the Palestinians," in *The Selected Writings of Eqbal Ahmad*, 298–317.

27. This was true although in 1947 Moscow had been one of the midwives of partition and of the resulting creation of Israel, whose existence it consistently supported thereafter, and had supported UNSC 242, which consecrated Israel's victories of both 1948 and 1967. The Soviets were initially suspicious of the PLO's "adventurism," and its potential for dragging its Egyptian and Syrian clients and the USSR into a conflict that they did not want.

28. For Primakov's account of his effort to avert a war (and save one of the last remaining Soviet clients from the folly of its leader), see *Missions à Bagdad: Histoire d'une négociation secrète* (Paris: Seuil, 1991). Immediately afterwards, Primakov became head of the KGB's foreign operations directorate, and after the dissolution of the USSR served as Russian foreign intelligence chief, foreign minister, and prime minister.

29. Elizabeth Thompson, *Justice Interrupted: The Struggle for Constitutional Government in the Middle East* (Cambridge, MA: Harvard University Press, 2013), 249.

30. The text of the "U.S.-Soviet Invitation to the Mideast Peace Conference in Madrid, October 18, 1991" can be found in William Quandt, *Peace Process: American Diplomacy and the Arab-Israeli Conflict Since 1967*, 3rd ed. (Washington, DC: Brookings Institution Press, 2005), appendix N, https://www.brookings.edu/wp-content/uploads/2016/07/Appendix-N.pdf. For the letter of assurances to the Palestinians, see ibid., appendix M: https://www.brookings.edu/wp-content/uploads/2016/07/Appendix-M.pdf.

31. Ibid., appendix N.

32. The letter of assurances to the Palestinians was dated October 18, 1991. See ibid., appendix M.

33. As mentioned in chapter 4 and above, this letter was only revealed by the US government when it was published in the *Foreign Relations of the United States* series in 2012. However, it had been published by Israel in its Foreign Ministry's documentary series twenty years before that in 1982, long before Madrid.

34. Aaron David Miller, "Israel's Lawyer," *Washington Post*, May 23, 2005, http://www.washingtonpost.com/wp-dyn/content/article/2005/05/22/AR2005052200883.html.

35. Aaron David Miller, *The Much Too Promised Land* (New York, Bantam, 2008), 80.

36. "'When You're Serious, Call Us,'" *Newsweek*, June 24, 1990, http://www.newsweek.com/when-youre-serious-call-us-206208.

37. John Goshko, "Baker Bars Israeli Loan Aid Unless Settlements Are Halted," *Washington Post*, February 25, 1992, https://www.washingtonpost.com/archive

/politics/1992/02/25/baker-bars-israeli-loan-aid-unless-settlements-are-halted/e7311eea-e6d3-493b-8880-a3b98e0830a1/.

38. A key text in the campaign against them was Robert Kaplan, *Arabists: Romance of an American Elite* (New York: Free Press, 1995), based on a series of scathing articles that appeared in the *Atlantic*. Another carping critic of both American diplomacy and Middle East scholarship is Martin Kramer, *Ivory Towers on Sand: The Failure of Middle Eastern Studies in America* (Washington, DC: Washington Institute for Near East Policy, 2001). A student of Bernard Lewis, Kramer is one in a long line of far-right detractors of Western policies in the Middle East as being insufficiently pro-Israel and anti-Arab, going back to the Baghdad-born British academic Elie Kedourie.

39. The former two received their PhDs in international relations (and thus were in no way Middle East experts), and Kurtzer and Miller in Middle East studies.

40. Roger Cohen, "The Making of an Iran Policy," *New York Times Magazine*, July 30, 2009, https://www.nytimes.com/2009/08/02/magazine/02Iran-t.html.

41. Peter Beinert, "Obama Betrayed Ideals on Israel," *Newsweek*, March 12, 2012, http://www.newsweek.com/peter-beinart-obama-betrayed-ideals-israel-63673.

42. Indyk was later US ambassador in Tel Aviv, where this veteran fighter for Israel's interests in Washington was vilified as too soft, as was his colleague Dan Kurtzer when he held the same position. Neither was spared continuous vulgar abuse by the Israeli hard right despite the fact that both were Jewish.

43. R. Khalidi, *Brokers of Deceit*, 56.

44. Clyde Haberman, "Shamir Is Said to Admit Plan to Stall Talks 'For 10 Years'" *New York Times*, June 27, 1992, https://www.nytimes.com/1992/06/27/world/shamir-is-said-to-admit-plan-to-stall-talks-for-10-years.html.

45. This is confirmed by Rabin's biographer and close colleague, Itamar Rabinovich, who was the lead Israeli negotiator with Syria: *Yitzhak Rabin*, 177–85, 193–99.

46. Ibid., 165.

47. Ibid., 212–14.

48. "Outline of the Palestinian Interim Self-Governing Authority (PISGA)" delivered January 14, 1992, http://www.palestine-studies.org/sites/default/files/uploads/images/PISGA%20Jan%2014%2C%201992%20%20p%201%2C2.pdf. A more detailed version of the plan was delivered to the Israeli side on March 2, 1992: "Palestinian Interim Selfgovernment Arrangements: Expanded Outline of Model of Palestinian Interim Selfgovernment Authority: Preliminary Measures and Modalities for Elections," March 2, 1993, http://www.palestine-studies.org/sites/default/files/uploads/files/Final%20outline%20PISGA%20elections%202%20Mar_%2092.pdf.

49. Rabinovich, *Yitzhak Rabin*, 183.

50. Ibid., 189–91, cites two other "alternative channels to Oslo" and to Washington that Rabin ordered opened, but does not mention this one.

51. Neither of them particularly modest, both Peres and Abu al-'Ala wrote extensively, the latter exhaustively, about their roles in Oslo: Abu al-'Ala [Ahmad Quray'], *al-Riwaya al-filistiniyya al-kamila lil-mufawadat: Min Oslo ila kharitat*

al-tariq [The complete Palestinian account of the negotiations: From Oslo to the Road Map], vols. 1–4 (Beirut: Institute for Palestine Studies, 2005–2014); Shimon Peres, *Battling for Peace: A Memoir* (New York: Random House, 1995).

52. In Rabinovich's words, *Yitzhak Rabin*, 187, "Rabin trusted former officers of the IDF," among them himself.

53. One can search in vain in the bios of these two men (and in the case of 'Ammar, who died in 2010, his obituary) for any mention of their roles in securing an Israeli-Palestinian security agreement.

54. "Draft Minutes: Meeting with the Americans," June 23, 1993, http://www.palestine-studies.org/sites/default/files/uploads/files/Minutes%20Kurtz-er%2C%20Miller%20meeting%2023%20June%2093.pdf.

55. There are many detailed analyses of the reasons for the failures of the Oslo Accords and their sequels by participants in the Palestinian-Israeli-American negotiations, including Abu al-'Ala, Shimon Peres, Yossi Beilin, Dennis Ross, Daniel Kurtzer, Aaron David Miller, Camille Mansour, Hanan 'Ashrawi, Ghassan al-Khatib, and my *Brokers of Deceit*.

56. "The Morning After," *London Review of Books* 15, no. 20, October 21, 1993, https://www.lrb.co.uk/v15/n20/edward-said/the-morning-after. This deeply skeptical article was written at a time of near-universal euphoria over the 1993 signing ceremony of the Oslo Accords on the White House lawn. Said was prescient in many respects, asking: "Does this mean, ominously, that the interim stage may be the final one?" As these lines are written, we are about to enter the twenty-seventh year of this interim stage.

57. Rabinovich, *Yitzhak Rabin*, 193.

58. Some of the documents seized there, including materials dating back to the 1930s from the historical archives of the Arab Studies Society, such as papers of Musa al-'Alami, which I examined there in the early 1990s, can now be found in the Israel National Archives, under the heading AP, for Abandoned Property. They sit alongside materials stolen from the PLO Research Center in Beirut in 1982 and books that were seized from Arab homes in an earlier organized looting spree in 1948. This continuous process of theft of Palestinian cultural and intellectual assets constitutes a form of "memoricide," an integral part of Israel's campaign of politicide against the Palestinians, again in the late Baruch Kimmerling's apt usage.

59. I was present and heard Gazit say this in response to a question from the audience during a panel discussion at Amherst College on March 4, 1994.

CHAPTER 6

1. David Barsamian, *The Pen and the Sword: Conversations with Edward Said* (Monroe, ME: Common Courage Press, 1994).

2. Palestinian GDP per capita remained at around $1,380 from 1995 to 2000. It declined by over $340 from 2000 to 2004, and even more in subsequent years.

Statistics from UNCTAD, "Report on UNCTAD's Assistance to the Palestinian People," TD/B/52/2, July 21, 2005, tables 1, 6.

3. Ben White notes that the isolation of the Gaza Strip actually began with restrictions on movement of Gaza residents into Israel via new magnetic cards in 1989, seventeen years before Hamas took over: "Gaza: Isolation and Control," Al Jazeera News, June 10, 2019, https://www.aljazeera.com/news/2019/06/gaza -isolation-control-190608081601522.html.

4. There is a plethora of scholarship on the situation in Gaza, notably the work of Sara Roy, including *The Gaza Strip: The Political Economy of De-Development* (Washington, DC: Institute for Palestine Studies, 1994); and *Hamas and Civil Society in Gaza: Engaging the Islamist Social Sector* (Princeton, NJ: Princeton University Press, 2011); as well as Jean-Pierre Filiu, *Gaza: A History* (Oxford: Oxford University Press, 2014).

5. Piotr Smolar, "Jerusalem: Les diplomates de l'EU durcissent le ton," *Le Monde*, February 2, 2018, 3, http://www.lemonde.fr/proche-orient/article/2018/01/31 /a-rebours-des-etats-unis-les-diplomates-europeens-soulignent-la-degradation -de-la-situation-a-jerusalem_5250032_3218.html.

6. Evidence of this can be found in the rapturous reception in New York of the mediocre melodrama *Oslo*, with its borderline racist caricatures of Palestinian and Israeli negotiators and hagiographic depiction of Peres, which won a Tony Award as best play in 2017, and soon was enjoying a successful run in the West End in London.

7. The literature on Hamas is extensive. It includes Tareq Baconi, *Hamas Contained: The Rise and Pacification of Palestinian Resistance* (Stanford, CA: Stanford University Press, 2018); Roy, *Hamas and Civil Society in Gaza*; Ziad Abu-Amr, *Islamic Fundamentalism in the West Bank and Gaza: Muslim Brotherhood and Islamic Jihad* (Indianapolis: Indiana University Press, 1994); Khaled Hroub, *Hamas: Political Thought and Practice* (Washington, DC: Institute for Palestine Studies, 2002); Mishal and Sela, *The Palestinian Hamas*; and Azzam Tamimi, *Hamas: A History from Within* (Northampton, MA: Olive Branch Press, 2007).

8. A good summary of how Israel supported Hamas is Mehdi Hassan, "Blowback: How Israel Went from Helping Create Hamas to Bombing It," *Intercept*, February 19, 2018, https://theintercept.com/2018/02/19/hamas-israel-palestine-conflict/. See also the sources cited in note 19 of the previous chapter.

9. There is extensive literature on the Camp David summit, much of it self-serving or meretricious, notably the work of one of its key architects, Dennis Ross, *The Missing Peace: The Inside Story of the Fight for Middle East Peace* (New York: Farrar, Straus and Giroux, 2004). The best account is by Clayton Swisher, *The Truth About Camp David: The Untold Story About the Collapse of the Middle East Peace Process* (New York: Nation Books, 2004).

10. For details, see Rana Barakat, "The Jerusalem Fellah: Popular Politics in Mandate-Era Palestine," *Journal of Palestine Studies* 46, no. 1 (Autumn 2016): 7–19; and "Criminals or Martyrs? British Colonial Legacy in Palestine and the Criminalization of Resistance," *Omran* 6, November 2013, https://omran.dohainstitute

.org/en/issue006/Pages/art03.aspx. See also Hillel Cohen, *1929: Year Zero of the Arab-Israeli Conflict* (Boston: Brandeis University Press, 2015).

11. For a list of the Muslim religious shrines and mosques destroyed as part of the creation of the Western Wall plaza, see R. Khalidi, "The Future of Arab Jerusalem," *British Journal of Middle East Studies* 19, no. 2 (Fall 1993): 139–40. The most detailed analysis of the establishment, history, and destruction of Haret al-Magariba is Vincent Lemire, "Au pied du mur: Histoire du quartier mahgrébin de Jérusalem (1187–1967)," forthcoming. Architectural and archaeological information, as well as illustrations of many of these destroyed sites, can be found in Michael Hamilton Burgoyne, *Mamluk Jerusalem: An Architectural Study* (London: World of Islam Festival Trust, 1987).

12. The Zawiya, a former sufi lodge adjacent to the Haram, had become the residence of the Abu al-Sa'ud family, who were traditionally its administrators: Yitzhak Reiter, *Islamic Endowments in Jerusalem Under British Mandate* (London: Cass, 1996), 136. This is where Yasser 'Arafat, whose mother was an Abu Sa'ud, was born in 1929, according to my cousin Raqiyya Khalidi, Um Kamil, who reported visiting her neighbors, the Abu Sa'ud family, together with her mother to congratulate them on the birth of the newborn boy: interview, Jerusalem, July 26, 1993.

13. Suzanne Goldenberg, "Rioting as Sharon Visits Islam Holy Site," *Guardian*, September 29, 2000, https://www.theguardian.com/world/2000/sep/29/israel.

14. All figures are from tables published by the indispensable B'Tselem, the Israeli Information Center for Human Rights in the Occupied Territories: https://www.btselem.org/statistics.

15. Reuven Pedatzur, "One Million Bullets," *Haaretz*, June 29, 2004, https://www.haaretz.com/1.4744778.

16. Ibid. According to Pedatzur's analysis, the Israeli high command had decided beforehand on this crushing use of force in order that the Palestinians' ultimate defeat be "burned into their consciousness."

17. Efraim Benmelech and Claude Berrebi, "Human Capital and the Productivity of Suicide Bombers," *Journal of Economic Perspectives* 21, no. 3 (Summer 2007): 223–38.

18. It was my impression that his mental decline began earlier, and may have dated back to the 1992 crash landing of a plane carrying him in the Libyan desert that killed several of those aboard and left him injured: Youssef Ibrahim, "Arafat Is Found Safe in Libyan Desert After Crash," *New York Times*, April 9, 1992, http://www.nytimes.com/1992/04/09/world/arafat-is-found-safe-in-libyan-desert-after-crash.html.

19. This doctrine is powerfully analyzed by Pedatzur, "One Million Bullets."

20. The most reliable and consistent polling over the past few decades has been done by the Jerusalem Media and Communications Centre. According to their Poll No. 52, issued in December 2004, "A majority of Palestinians opposes military operations against Israeli targets as a suitable response under the current political conditions," http://www.jmcc.org/documentsandmaps.aspx?id=448.

21. Nicholas Pelham and Max Rodenbeck, "Which Way for Hamas?" *New York Review of Books*, November 5, 2009, https://www.nybooks.com/articles/2009/11/05/which-way-for-hamas/.

22. This was clearly shown by polling done after the election by the reputable Palestine Center for Policy and Survey Research, http://www.pcpsr.org/en/node/478; and by a private firm, Near East Consulting, http://www.neareastconsulting.com/plc2006/blmain.html.

23. The final revised version, agreed to by all Palestinian factions, dated June 28, 2006, can be found here: https://web.archive.org/web/20060720162701/http://www.jmcc.org/documents/prisoners2.htm.

24. This figure is from June 2018: https://www.ochaopt.org/content/53-cent-palestinians-gaza-live-poverty-despite-humanitarian-assistance.

25. This figure is from the Israeli NGO Gisha: https://gisha.org/updates/9840. CIA World Fact Book estimates for 2016 and 2017 are lower: https://www.cia.gov/library/publications/resources/the-world-factbook/geos/gz.html.

26. Two excellent books on the Gaza wars are Norman Finkelstein, *Gaza: An Inquest into Its Martyrdom* (Oakland: University of California Press, 2018); and Noam Chomsky and Ilan Pappe, *Gaza in Crisis: Reflections on the US-Israeli War on the Palestinians* (Chicago: Haymarket Books, 2013).

27. These figures are taken from the website of B'Tselem, The Israeli Information Center for Human Rights in the Occupied Territories, https://www.btselem.org/statistics/fatalities/during-cast-lead/by-date-of-event; and https://www.btselem.org/statistics/fatalities/after-cast-lead/by-date-of-event.

28. "50 Days: More Than 500 Children: Facts and Figures on Fatalities in Gaza, Summer 2014," B'Tselem, https://www.btselem.org/2014_gaza_conflict/en/il/.

29. Barbara Opall-Rome, "Gaza War Leaned Heavily on F-16 Close-Air Support," *Defense News*, September 15, 2014, http://www.defensenews.com/article/20140915/DEFREG04/309150012/Gaza-War-Leaned-Heavily-F-16-Close-Air-Support also available via: http://www.imra.org.il/story.php3?id=64924.

30. Jodi Rudoren and Fares Akram, "Lost Homes and Dreams at Tower Israel Leveled," *New York Times*, September 15, 2014.

31. "Protective Edge, in Numbers," Ynet, August 14, 2014, http://www.ynetnews.com/articles/0,7340,L-4558916,00.html.

32. Mark Perry, "Why Israel's Bombardment of Gaza Neighborhood Left US Officers 'Stunned,'" Al Jazeera America, August 27, 2014, http://america.aljazeera.com/articles/2014/8/26/israel-bombing-stunsusofficers.html.

33. In "Why It's Hard to Believe Israel's Claim That It Did Its Best to Minimize Civilian Casualties," *The World Post*, August 21, 2014, Idan Barir, a former crew commander in the Israeli artillery corps, notes that "The truth is artillery shells cannot be aimed precisely and are not meant to hit specific targets. A standard 40-kilogram shell is nothing but a large fragmentation grenade. When it explodes, it is meant to kill anyone within a 50-meter radius and to wound anyone within a further 100 meters," and that Israel's "use of artillery fire is a deadly game of Russian roulette. The statistics, on which such firepower relies, mean that in densely

populated areas such as Gaza, civilians will inevitably be hit as well," http://www
.huffingtonpost.com/idan-barir/israel-gaza-civilian-deaths_b_5673023.html.

34. "Israel Warns Hizballah War Would Invite Destruction," *Ynetnews.com* (*Yedioth Ah-ranoth*), October 3, 2008, http://www.ynetnews.com/articles/0,7340,L-3604893,00
.html. See also Yaron London, "The Dahiya Strategy," *Ynetnews.com* (*Yedioth Ah-ranoth*), October 6, 2008, http://www.ynetnews.com/articles/0,7340,L-3605863,00
.html.

35. E.g., Amos Harel, "A Real War Is Under Way in Gaza," *Haaretz*, July 26, 2014,
http://www.haaretz.com/news/diplomacy-defense/.premium-1.607279.

36. 22 USC 2754: Purposes for which military sales or leases by the United States
are authorized; report to Congress: https://uscode.house.gov/view.xhtml?req
=(title:22%20section:2754%20edition:prelim).

37. Shibley Telhami, "American Attitudes on the Israeli-Palestinian Conflict,"
Brookings, December 2, 2016, https://www.brookings.edu/research/american
-attitudes-on-the-israeli-palestinian-conflict/.

38. "Views of Israel and Palestinians," Pew Research Center, May 5, 2016, http://
www.people-press.org/2016/05/05/5-views-of-israel-and-palestinians/.

39. "Republicans and Democrats Grow Even Further Apart in Views of Israel, Pal-estinians," Pew Research Center, January 23, 2018, http://www.people-press.org
/2018/01/23/republicans-and-democrats-grow-even-further-apart-in-views-of
-israel-palestinians/.

40. Carroll Doherty, "A New Perspective on Americans' Views of Israelis and Pal-estinians," Pew Research Center, April 24, 2019, https://www.pewresearch.org
/fact-tank/2019/04/24/a-new-perspective-on-americans-views-of-israelis-and
-palestinians/.

41. The chief sponsor of the bill was Congresswoman Betty McColum (DFL-MN):
https://mccollum.house.gov/media/press-releases/mccollum-introduces
-legislation-promote-human-rights-palestinian-children. See also https://mccollum
.house.gov/media/press-releases/mccollum-introduces-legislation-promote
-human-rights-palestinian-children.

42. These are the situations accurately described by John Mearsheimer and Steven
Walt in *The Israel Lobby and U.S. Foreign Policy* (New York: Farrar, Straus and
Giroux, 2007).

43. This emerges clearly from the previously cited poll of over 18,000 respondents
in eleven Arab countries in 2017–18 by the Arab Center for Research and Policy
Studies: https://www.dohainstitute.org/en/News/Pages/ACRPS-Releases-Arab
-Index-2017-2018.aspx.

44. Secretary of State to Legation, Jedda, August 17, 1948, *FRUS* 1948, vol. 2, pt. 2,
1318. For further details on how the Saudi regime catered to Washington over
Palestine, see R. Khalidi, *Brokers of Deceit*, xxiv–xxvii.

45. This was contained in a letter from Bush to Sharon delivered on April 14, 2004,
during a meeting in Washington: https://mfa.gov.il/mfa/foreignpolicy/peace
/mfadocuments/pages/exchange%20of%20letters%20sharon-bush%2014-apr
-2004.aspx.

46. Interviews with two senior officials directly involved with these matters who preferred to remain anonymous: February 1, 2010, and January 11, 2011.

CONCLUSION

1. "Memorandum by Mr. Balfour (Paris) respecting Syria, Palestine, and Mesopotamia," August 11, 1919, in *Documents on British Foreign Policy, 1919–1939*, ed. E. L. Woodward and Rohan Butler (London: HM Stationery Office, 1952), 340–48, http://www.yorku.ca/dwileman/2930Bal.htm.

2. "Remarks by President Trump and Prime Minister Netanyahu of Israel before Bilateral Meeting Davos, Switzerland," January 25, 2018, https://www.whitehouse.gov/briefings-statements/remarks-president-trump-prime-minister-netanyahu-israel-bilateral-meeting-davos-switzerland/.

3. C. Bengelsdorf et al., eds., *The Selected Writings of Eqbal Ahmad*, 301.

4. Judt's article, "Israel: The Alternative," *The New York Review of Books*, October 23, 2003, controversial at the time, would probably cause fewer waves today, although in the current atmosphere, his critique of Zionism might draw absurd accusations of anti-Semitism.

5. "Introduction," *Blaming the Victims: Spurious Scholarship and the Palestinian Question*, ed. Edward Said and Christopher Hitchens (New York: Verso, 1988), 1.

6. These international efforts, closely coordinated by the Israeli Ministry of Strategic Affairs, focus in particular on labeling the Boycott, Divestment and Sanctions (BDS) movement as "anti-Semitic." The *Journal of Palestine Studies* has published a series of articles on these efforts: Shir Hever, "BDS Suppression Attempts in Germany Backfire," 48, no. 3 (Spring 2019): 86–96; Barry Trachtenberg and Kyle Stanton, "Shifting Sands: Zionism and US Jewry," 48, no. 2 (Winter 2019): 79–87; Dominique Vidal, "Conflating Anti-Zionism with Anti-Semitism: France in the Crosshairs," 48, no. 1 (Autumn 2018): 119–30; Moshe Machover, "An Immoral Dilemma: The Trap of Zionist Propaganda," 47, no. 4 (Summer 2018): 69–78.

7. "The Declaration of the Establishment of the State of Israel," May 14, 1948, http://www.mfa.gov.il/mfa/foreignpolicy/peace/guide/pages/declaration%20of%20establishment%20of%20state%20of%20israel.aspx.

8. Zeev Sternhell, "En Israël pousse un racisme proche du nazisme à ses débuts," *Le Monde*, February 20, 2018, 22, my translation.

9. For a lucid analysis of the law, see Hassan Jabareen and Suhad Bishara, "The Jewish Nation-State Law: Antecedents and Constitutional Implications," *Journal of Palestine Studies*, 48, no. 2 (Winter 2019): 46–55. For its text, see pages 44–45, and for a petition to the Israeli Supreme Court on the subject of the law by Adalah, the Legal Center for Arab Minority Rights in Israel, see 56–57.

10. Revital Hovel, "Justice Minister: Israel Must Keep Jewish Majority Even at the Expense of Human Rights," *Haaretz*, February 13, 2018, https://www.haaretz.com/israel-news/justice-minister-israel-s-jewish-majority-trumps-than-human-rights-1.5811106.

11. Ibid. See also Ravit Hecht, "The Lawmaker Who Thinks Israel Is Deceiving the Palestinians: No One Is Going to Give Them a State," *Haaretz Weekend*, October 28, 2017, https://www.haaretz.com/israel-news/.premium.MAGAZINE-the-lawmaker-who-thinks-israel-is-deceiving-the-palestinians-1.5460676.

12. Sternhell, "En Israël pousse un racisme proche du nazisme à ses débuts."

13. Israeli planes have at different times bombed Tunis, Cairo, Khartoum, Amman, Beirut, Damascus, and Baghdad, several of them repeatedly, and several of them recently.

14. This is a central argument of my book, *Palestinian Identity*, in line with theses put forth by several of the most respected writers on nationalism including Benedict Anderson, Eric Hobsbawm, and Ernest Gellner.

15. Ernest Gellner, *Nations and Nationalism* (Ithaca, NY: Cornell University Press, 1983), 48–49.

16. Peter Beaumont, "Trump's Ambassador to Israel Refers to 'Alleged Occupation' of Palestinian Territories," *Guardian*, September 1, 2017, https://www.theguardian.com/us-news/2017/sep/01/trump-ambassador-israel-david-friedman-alleged-occupation-palestinian-territories; Nathan Guttman, "US Ambassador to Israel Asked State Department to Stop Using the Word 'Occupation,'" *The Forward*, December 26, 2017, https://forward.com/fast-forward/390857/us-ambassador-to-israel-asked-state-dept-to-stop-using-the-word-occupation/; David Halbfinger, "US Ambassador Says Israel Has Right to Annex Parts of West Bank," *New York Times*, June 8, 2019, https://www.nytimes.com/2019/06/08/world/middleeast/israel-west-bank-david-friedman.html.

17. Ruth Eglash, "Top Trump Adviser Says Settlements Are Not an Obstacle to Peace," *Washington Post*, November 10, 2017, https://www.washingtonpost.com/world/middle_east/top-trump-adviser-says-israeli-settlements-are-not-an-obstacle-to-peace/2016/11/10/8837b472-5c81-49a3-947c-ba6a47c4bc2f_story.html; Piotr Smolar, "Washington ouvrira son ambassade à Jerusalem en mai," *Le Monde*, February 25–26, 2018, 4.

18. Jonathan Swan, "Kushner, For First Time, Claims He Never Discussed Security Clearance with Trump," Axios, June 3, 2019, https://www.axios.com/jared-kushner-security-clearance-donald-trump-f7706db1-a978-42ec-90db-c2787f19cef3.html.

19. "Palestine Chief Negotiator Reveals Details of Trump Peace Plan," *Middle East Monitor*, January 22, 2018, https://www.middleeastmonitor.com/20180122-palestine-chief-negotiator-reveals-details-of-trump-peace-plan/.

20. Jonathan Ferziger and Peter Waldman, "How Do Israel's Tech Firms Do Business in Saudi Arabia? Very Quietly," *Bloomberg Businessweek*, February 2, 2017, https://www.bloomberg.com/news/features/2017-02-02/how-do-israel-s-tech-firms-do-business-in-saudi-arabia-very-quietly.

21. Julien Boissou, "Analyse: L'Inde s'implante au Moyen-Orient," *Le Monde*, February 27, 2018, 21.

22. "2016 Arab Opinion Index: Executive Summary," Arab Center Washington, DC, April 12, 2017, http://arabcenterdc.org/survey/arab-opinion-index-2016.

23. This is the core thesis of my book *Brokers of Deceit*.

ACKNOWLEDGMENTS

I owe a conscious or unconscious debt to all of those many people through whose experiences I have tried to tell the story of this century of war on Palestine. Reading or hearing their words is what brought me to write this book in this form. In it, I have tried to convey voices that have gone largely unheard in the confusing dissonance surrounding the question of Palestine.

In a previous book, I thanked my three aunts, 'Anbara Salam al-Khalidi, Fatima al-Khalidi Salam and Wahidi al-Khalidi, for providing me with living images drawn from their memories of the earliest decades of the twentieth century. Although as I worked on this book I deeply regretted that I was no longer able to consult any of them, or my mother, Selwa Jeha al-Khalidi, and father, Ismail Raghib al-Khalidi, about the events they lived through, I had them all constantly in mind as I wrote it. Even when I do not quote them directly, all of them are present in its pages. Each in her or his own way taught me something about the past and how it forms part of the present. Fortunately, among those I could consult and profit from were my cousin, Professor Walid Ahmad Samih Khalidi, on whose prodigious memory I called repeatedly in thinking about this topic (and on whose pioneering scholarship I relied throughout the book), my cousin Leila Husayn al-Khalidi al-Husayni, and friends, colleagues, and comrades from Beirut days too numerous to name.

I owe a debt I cannot repay to the many people with whom I have discussed the subject matter of this book, or who have inspired me to write it. My son Ismail first persuaded me that this was a worthwhile project, and helped to shape its form at the outset. This book would probably not exist but for his initial contributions. For years before I started writing it, Nawaf Salam constantly urged me to write a history of Palestine that would be accessible to uninformed readers. I hope that what follows meets his expectations.

While working on this project, I consulted many colleagues and friends who provided invaluable help, some of whom read sections of the book, and all of whom deserve my special appreciation. Among them were Bashir Abu-Manneh, Suad Amiri, Seth Anziska, Qais al-Awqati, Remi Brulin, Musa Budeiri, Leena Dallasheh, Sheila Fitzpatrick, Samer Ghaddar, Magda Ghanma, Amira Hass, Nubar Hovsepian, Rafiq Husayni, Amy Kaplan, Ahmad Khalidi, Hasan Khalidi, Raja Khalidi, Barnett Rubin, Stuart Schaar, May Seikaly, Avi Shlaim, Ramzi Tadros, Salim Tamari, Naomi Wallace, John Whitbeck, and Susan Ziadeh. I also must thank those who helped me with my research. They include Jeanette Seraphim, librarian at the Institute for Palestine Studies, Yasmeen Abdel Majeed, Dr. Nili Belkind, Linda Butler, Leshasharee Amore Carter, Andrew Victor Hinton, Sean McManus, Patricia Morel, Khadr Salameh, Malek Sharif, and Yair Svorai.

I have presented parts of this book to audiences at a variety of venues on four continents, and have benefited greatly from their comments and insights. These include the Duke University Middle East Center, the Center for Palestine Studies at the School for Oriental and African Studies, Brown University, Yale University, the Kevorkian Middle East Center at New York University, Princeton University, the Centro d'Estudios Arabes at the University of Santiago, the Issam Fares Center for Public Policy at the American University of Beirut, the Diplomatic Academy of Vienna, the Columbia Global Center in Amman, the Harvard Club of New York, and the United Nations Committee on the Unalienable Rights of the Palestinian People.

My deepest gratitude is due to those who read the entire book, first among them Tarif Khalidi, who in carefully scrutinizing the entire manuscript brought his vast expertise to bear, and thereby saved me from many errors. In helping to improve the book, Tarif did once again what he has done for many decades: provided me with invariably good advice. My old friend Jim Chandler again applied his sharp eye to improving my prose and sharpening my arguments. My harshest critic, my wife Mona, not only tolerated my many extended absences and my frequent absent-mindedness with exemplary forbearance while I was researching and writing this book, but also used her unmatched editorial skills to clarify my writing and limit my propensity for repetition. Our two daughters, Dr. Lamya Khalidi and Dima Khalidi, Esq., added their sharp critical sense to that of their mother, as did their brother Ismail, seasoned with their customary levity.

My agent, George Lucas, was invaluable in helping to provide the project with its current form at an early stage, and in introducing me to Sara Bershtel and Riva Hocherman at Metropolitan Books. Riva did far more than what a good editor normally does: as she has with so many others, she shared with me her matchless expertise, while helping to give this book the shape and form that it now has, restructuring it and improving it immensely. I owe her a great debt of gratitude.

I could not have written this book without all of this invaluable support, but it goes without saying that the responsibility for its contents is mine alone.

INDEX

Page numbers in *italics* refer to images.

Printed in the USA
CPSIA information can be obtained
at www.ICGtesting.com
LVHW040831221123
764599LV00003B/213